T0384600

# SPARTA AND THE COMMEMORATION OF WAR

The tough Spartan soldier is one of the most enduring images from antiquity. Yet Spartans, too, fell in battle – so how did ancient Sparta memorialize its wars and war dead? From the poet Tyrtaeus inspiring soldiers with rousing verse in the 7th century BCE to inscriptions celebrating the 300's last stand at Thermopylae, and from Spartan imperialists posing as liberators during the Peloponnesian War to the modern reception of the Spartan as a brave warrior defending the "West," Sparta has had an outsized role in how warfare is framed and remembered. This image has also been distorted by the Spartans themselves and their later interpreters. While debates continue to rage about the appropriateness of monuments to supposed war heroes in our civic squares, this authoritative and engaging book suggests that how the Spartans commemorated their military past, and how this shaped their military future, has perhaps never been more pertinent.

MATTHEW A. SEARS is Professor of Classics at the University of New Brunswick. He is the author of *Athens, Thrace, and the Shaping of Athenian Leadership* (Cambridge University Press, 2013) and of *Understanding Greek Warfare* (2019). He is also the coauthor (with C. Jacob Butera) of *Battles and Battlefields of Ancient Greece: A Guide to Their History, Topography, and Archaeology* (2019).

# SPARTA AND THE COMMEMORATION OF WAR

MATTHEW A. SEARS

*University of New Brunswick*

Shaftesbury Road, Cambridge CB2 8EA, United Kingdom

One Liberty Plaza, 20th Floor, New York, NY 10006, USA

477 Williamstown Road, Port Melbourne, VIC 3207, Australia

314–321, 3rd Floor, Plot 3, Splendor Forum, Jasola District Centre,
New Delhi – 110025, India

103 Penang Road, #05–06/07, Visioncrest Commercial, Singapore 238467

Cambridge University Press is part of Cambridge University Press & Assessment,
a department of the University of Cambridge.

We share the University's mission to contribute to society through the pursuit of
education, learning and research at the highest international levels of excellence.

www.cambridge.org
Information on this title: www.cambridge.org/9781316519455

DOI: 10.1017/9781009023726

First published 2024

Printed in the United Kingdom by CPI Group Ltd, Croydon CR0 4YY

*A catalogue record for this publication is available from the British Library*

*Library of Congress Cataloging-in-Publication Data*
NAMES: Sears, Matthew A., author.
TITLE: Sparta and the commemoration of war / Matthew A. Sears.
DESCRIPTION: Cambridge ; New York, NY : Cambridge University Press, 2024. |
Includes bibliographical references and index.
IDENTIFIERS: LCCN 2023027770 | ISBN 9781316519455 (hardback) | ISBN
9781009010535 (paperback) | ISBN 9781009023726 (ebook)
SUBJECTS: LCSH: War and society – Greece – Sparta (Extinct city) | War
memorials – Greece – Sparta (Extinct city) |
Memorialization – Greece – Sparta (Extinct city) | Collective
memory – Greece – Sparta (Extinct city) | Sparta (Extinct
city) – Historiography.
CLASSIFICATION: LCC DF261.S8 S676 2024 | DDC 938/.9–dc23/eng/20230729
LC record available at https://lccn.loc.gov/2023027770

ISBN 978-1-316-51945-5 Hardback

*For Cara and Kallie*

# Contents

| | | |
|---|---|---|
| *List of Figures* | | *page* viii |
| *List of Maps* | | xi |
| *Acknowledgements* | | xii |
| | Prologue: Brasidas at Amphipolis | xiv |
| 1 | Memory and Mirage | 1 |
| 2 | Warrior Poets | 33 |
| 3 | Few against Many | 64 |
| 4 | The Freedom of the Greeks | 100 |
| 5 | Remembering Sparta's Other Liberators | 142 |
| 6 | Agesilaus, First King of Greece | 171 |
| 7 | From Thermopylae to *300* | 197 |
| | Epilogue: *Dulce et Decorum Est* | 236 |
| *References* | | 250 |
| *Index* | | 267 |

# Figures

1.1 The Menelaion outside of Sparta. Author's photo. *page* 28

1.2 The "Smiling Hoplite," Archaeological Museum of Sparta. 29
Author's photo. © Hellenic Ministry of Culture and Sports /
Hellenic Organization of Cultural Resources Development.

1.3 The "Round Building" on the acropolis of Sparta. Author's 30
photo.

1.4 The "Leonidaion" or "Tomb of Leonidas" in Sparta. Author's 31
photo.

2.1 Archaic Laconian bronze votive, from the Samian Heraion, 54
Archaeological Museum of Vathy. Author's photo. ©
Hellenic Ministry of Culture and Sports / Hellenic
Organization of Cultural Resources Development.

2.2 Bronze votive, Archaeological Museum of Sparta. Author's 55
photo. © Hellenic Ministry of Culture and Sports / Hellenic
Organization of Cultural Resources Development.

2.3 Archaic Laconian ivory votive showing Perseus beheading 56
Medusa, from the Samian Heraion, Archaeological Museum
of Vathy. Author's photo. © Hellenic Ministry of Culture and
Sports / Hellenic Organization of Cultural Resources
Development.

2.4 Lead votives from the sanctuary of Artemis Orthia, 62
Archaeological Museum of Sparta. Author's photo. ©
Hellenic Ministry of Culture and Sports / Hellenic
Organization of Cultural Resources Development.

3.1 Thermopylae from the hillock of the Three Hundred's last 66
stand, looking towards Mount Kallidromos. In the
foreground is a modern monument with an inscription of the
famous Simonides epigram. Author's photo.

3.2 Fragment of an epigram supposedly honoring Marathon.    85
Athens, Agora object no. I 4256; image no. 2012.83.0052
(96–79–20). Ephorate of Antiquities of Athens City, Ancient
Agora, ASCSA: Agora Excavations. © Hellenic Ministry of
Culture and Sports / Hellenic Organization of Cultural
Resources Development (H.O.C.RE.D.).

4.1 The northern tip of Sphacteria as viewed from ancient Pylos.    113
Photo by C. Jacob Butera.

4.2 The Nike of Paionios, Archaeological Museum of Olympia.    115
Author's photo. © Hellenic Ministry of Culture and Sports /
Hellenic Organization of Cultural Resources Development.

4.3 The ossuary and gold crown from the "Tomb of Brasidas,"    132
Archaeological Museum of Amphipolis. Author's photo. ©
Hellenic Ministry of Culture and Sports / Hellenic
Organization of Cultural Resources Development.

4.4 The Treasury of the Athenians at Delphi. Author's photo.    134

5.1 The Spartan Admirals' Monument at Delphi (on the left).    159
Only the statue bases survive. The bases of the Athenian
Marathon monument (on the right) are on the other side of
the Sacred Way. Author's photo.

5.2 The Tomb of the Lacedaemonians in the Athenian    163
Kerameikos (the Acropolis can be seen in the background).
Author's photo.

5.3 Part of the surviving inscription on the Tomb of the    164
Lacedaemonians, showing the name of Thibrakos and his title
of *polemarch* in retrograde lettering. Author's photo.

6.1 Lion funerary monument at the Archaeological Museum of    191
Thebes. Author's photo. Permission courtesy of the Ephorate
of Antiquities of Boeotia. © Hellenic Ministry of Culture and
Sports /Hellenic Organization of Cultural Resources
Development (H.O.C.RE.D.).

6.2 Lion funerary monuments at the Archaeological Museum of    192
Sparta. Author's photo. © Hellenic Ministry of Culture and
Sports /Hellenic Organization of Cultural Resources
Development.

6.3 The Boeotian victory monument at Leuctra. Photo by    195
C. Jacob Butera.

7.1 Jacques-Louis David, *Leonidas at Thermopylae* (1814). Paris,    203
Louvre 3690. © RMN-Grand Palais / Art Resource, NY.

7.2 Statue of US President Harry Truman in Athens (splashed   217
with red paint after an apparent act of recent anti-American
protest). Photo by Lee Brice.

7.3 Modern Leonidas monument at Thermopylae, with the   222
inscription "*molōn labe.*" Author's photo.

7.4 The Roman theatre of Sparta beneath the acropolis, with the   230
modern town in the middle distance and Mount Taygetus in
the background. Author's photo.

7.5 Modern monument in the central square of Sparta, with   232
a paraphrase from Tyrtaeus inscribed on it. Author's photo.

7.6 Monument in Sparta to Laconian Olympic victors from 776   233
BCE to the present day. Author's photo.

E.1 The Canadian National Vimy Memorial in France, showing   239
figures representing Canada Bereft, the Spirit of Sacrifice, and
the Passing of the Torch. Author's photo.

# *Maps*

1    Greece and the Aegean, from S. Pomeroy, S. M. Burstein,    *page* xx
     W. Donlan, J. T. Roberts, D. Tandy. 2012, *Ancient Greece:*
     *A Political, Cultural, and Social History* (3rd edition), Oxford,
     inside front cover. © Oxford University Press. Reproduced
     with permission of the Licensor through PLSclear.
2    Sparta, topography and major landmarks, from Sanders 2009.    26
     Reproduced by permission of the British School at Athens.

# *Acknowledgements*

I have the pleasure of thanking many institutions, colleagues, and friends who have helped over the course of this project. The Social Sciences and Humanities Research Council of Canada generously funded this research through an Insight Grant. The University of New Brunswick (UNB) has supported the work throughout by providing research funding, sabbatical leave in 2019, and a congenial environment in which to teach and write. I have benefitted from working with many colleagues in the Departments of History and Classics and Ancient History, particularly Cindy Brown, Carolyn MacDonald, James Murray, Lisa Todd, Gary Waite, and Lee Windsor. Susan Parker and Spencer Paddock, two of UNB's stellar graduate students, helped me sort out innumerable issues pertaining to commemoration and combat motivation. The American School of Classical Studies at Athens, for which I directed the 2019 Summer Session, is the ideal academic home in Greece. The Summer Session students challenged me on a host of questions and provided keen insights in the field. In Greece, Lee Brice, Glenn Bugh, Maria Liston, Andy Stewart, and Georgia Tsouvala are always wonderful conversation partners on all things related to the country. Jack Davis, Guy Sanders, and Sharon Stocker sparked my deep interest in Sparta and the Peloponnese when they directed school trips to the region while I was a graduate student fellow.

C. Jacob Butera and Alan Sears read the entire draft manuscript carefully and conscientiously. This book would have been much poorer without their help. Many others engaged with my ideas to offer aid, correction, and unpublished or yet-to-be-published material. I thank Nathan Arrington, David Bedford, Paul Cartledge, Tim Cook, Joseph Day, John Denault, Stephen Hodkinson, Simon Oswald, Jessica Romney, Alan Sheppard, Barry Strauss, Jonathan Vance, Thom Workman, and Joanne Wright.

I am grateful to the audiences that heard and commented on parts of this research as it was developing, including the Society for Classical Studies, the Archaeological Institute of America, the Atlantic Classical Association, the Canadian Military History Colloquium, the Hellenic Society's Thermopylae 2500 Conference, Memorial University of Newfoundland, Hollins University, the University of Chicago, and the University of Winnipeg. The Classical Association of Canada hosted me as its 2022 lecturer for Ontario and Québec, which afforded a matchless opportunity to speak with fellow classicists at more than a dozen institutions as I put the finishing touches on the book.

Good editors are a boon for any writer. Adrian Lee at the *Globe and Mail* has supported me for several years, helping to render my thoughts about Sparta and Greece palatable to a wider public. At Cambridge University Press, it has been a delight to work with Michael Sharp, whose importance for the world of classical scholarship cannot be overstated. The members of the production and editorial team, including Adam Bell, Katie Idle, Bethany Johnson, and Bhavani Vijayamani, were a pleasure to work with. The anonymous readers for the press rescued me from factual errors, scholarly infelicities, and stylistic quirks. While I alone am responsible for this book's arguments, these readers have made the book far better.

My wife, Jenny, and our children, Cara and Kallie, make my home a blessed place. They also, with mostly good humor, accompanied me to Sparta and on a too long itinerary of Greek sites important for Spartan history. I could only compensate them with gyros and the occasional beach. They compensated me by making the research process far more delightful than it should have been.

# *Prologue*
## *Brasidas at Amphipolis*

Thucydides, the hard-nosed realist who wrote the history of the Peloponnesian War, was not one for fanciful tales. Other writers could dazzle their audiences with stories "reeking of myth," while Thucydides would provide all future generations with a useful, if dry, accounting of human nature and why states act the way they do. Despite this reproach aimed at his fellow historians – including, perhaps, Herodotus, the "Father of History" himself – Thucydides was not immune to the charms of real-life heroes. The most obvious hero for Thucydides was Pericles, the visionary politician and general who led Athens into war with Sparta and who delivered one of the most important and memorable speeches of the Classical Greek world, the Funeral Oration. But it was a Spartan, a soldier named Brasidas, who both beat Thucydides in the military arena and evoked for the historian the dashing figure of a warrior from Homer's *Iliad* fighting on the plains of Troy during a long-lost Heroic Age.

As befitting a hero in the Homeric mold, Brasidas died in battle. A great tactician, strategist, and diplomat, Brasidas had taken the Peloponnesian War to Athens' subject states in the north Aegean, on which Athens depended for its gigantic navy's raw materials. The jewel in the crown of Athens' northern cities was Amphipolis, defensively located on a bend in the Strymon River, a few kilometers from the sea. In 424 BCE, Brasidas marched through northern Greece in the guise of a liberator against Athenian tyranny (if, perhaps, threatening a city or two with "forced freedom" should they refuse to embrace his offer of liberation), and managed to wrest many cities from Athenian control, including Amphipolis. Tasked with defending Amphipolis was none other than Thucydides, but he was away on the island of Thasos and only managed to arrive after the city had been taken, earning himself exile from Athens and thus plenty of time to write his *History*. The loss of Amphipolis hit

Athens hard (they would try to retake the city, unsuccessfully, for much of the next several decades), and Brasidas had demonstrated himself to be Athens' most dangerous enemy. Athens sent an army in 422 to retake the city, but Brasidas, after giving a rousing speech to his men, stormed out of the city gates in a bold surprise attack against his more numerous foe. Perplexed by the sudden attack, the Athenian force was broken in two, and those who avoided being killed or wounded ran for their ships on the coast. The Athenian commander, the warmongering demagogue Cleon, was killed in the action. So, too, was Brasidas, dashing into the fray to back up his inspiring words with action.

Such bravado was typical for the renowned Spartan soldier. A few years earlier, in 425, Brasidas fainted from his wounds as he stood on the deck of a warship to urge his rowers to ram their vessel against the rocky shore of Pylos. On that shore were Athenians defending the new base they were building in Spartan territory, and Brasidas saw that he needed to take any and every measure to prevent the Athenians from succeeding. While most of the Spartans lost their nerve against the Athenians at Pylos, especially once the Athenians' superior ships entered the battle, Brasidas kept up the fight at great personal risk, if to no avail in the end. In his short military career, Brasidas stood out more than any other Spartan, being the first in the Peloponnesian War to receive official commendation at Sparta for valor in the field when on another occasion he fended off a surprise amphibious attack.

The honors Brasidas received after his death surpassed all those he had enjoyed in life. The people of Amphipolis declared Brasidas their new founder and tore down all the buildings associated with their actual founder, an Athenian named Hagnon. Even more ostentatiously, the Amphipolitans buried Brasidas in the heart of the city, right next to the agora – an extraordinary honor, since Greek burials were almost always outside of the city walls. The people of Amphipolis also instituted annual games in his honor, not unlike those games Achilles held for his slain companion, Patroclus, in the *Iliad*. Another city Brasidas had liberated near Amphipolis, Acanthus, erected a treasury building – a sort of mini temple holding dedications and other valuables – in his honor at the Panhellenic shrine of Delphi, making Brasidas the first mortal man to be named on such a building since the age of Archaic tyrants centuries earlier. Finally, in Sparta itself Brasidas was given a large cenotaph, standing out among the city's monuments even hundreds of years later, and not far from the tomb of Leonidas, the hero of Thermopylae. From one end of Greece to the other, Spartans and other Greeks could see physical monuments commemorating Brasidas' excellence, his *aretē*. And thanks to Thucydides, this Spartan's example became a Thucydidean "possession for all time."

Many readers of Thucydides have seen in Brasidas a most atypical Spartan. Where the Spartans were slow to action and stuck in their ways, Brasidas was bold and innovative. After all, he took the war to Athens' northern territories when the rest of Sparta seemed content to follow the same old strategy of invading Attica year after year; and he risked his life to dislodge the Athenians from Pylos when the rest of the Spartans were struck witless. Brasidas, however, was far more representative of Spartan military leaders than first meets the eye. Over the course of Spartan history, charismatic and ambitious warriors who sought glory and fame often led Sparta's armies. While many of these figures might have aimed at greater recognition than the Spartan authorities were prepared to give, they were doing nothing other than their Homeric exemplars had done, and Sparta, with its emphasis on and ostentatious commemoration of military prowess, implicitly encouraged them to do. How could a Spartan do anything but seek out battle and opportunities to be remembered after death? He had been raised from a young age to tolerate the harsh conditions of military life, walked regularly past the inscribed names of the Three Hundred who fought to the death at Thermopylae, and saw the cruel public humiliation of the lone Spartan who returned home alive after defeat. After 440, when Brasidas had come of age, he would have witnessed the construction of the Tomb of Leonidas, a shrine built for the repatriated remains of the dead king. In short, Sparta's emphasis on military training and the heroic dead reflected its militaristic heritage while also perpetuating it. Brasidas was merely among the most successful of Spartans doing exactly what their country expected them to do. Militarism breeds militarism.

The Spartans and other Greeks fought for many reasons, but one concern loomed over all others: to be remembered. Homer's Achilles famously chose a short but glorious life over a long but obscure one. The historian Herodotus wrote the history of the wars between Greece and Persia largely to preserve and give glory to great deeds and marvelous things done by Greeks and non-Greeks alike. Soldiers gave their lives and took the lives of others in order to be remembered by their families and communities for a long time to come. Soldiers who were remembered – in the stories of their community, in literature, inscribed on stone, or buried beneath a gleaming monument – inspired future soldiers to aim for everlasting memory too, and fight all the more eagerly and valorously on the battlefield. Brasdias' heroic life and heroic death, as commemorated by Greece's foremost historian, a cenotaph at Sparta and another on the slopes of Delphi, and a prominent tomb and annual games at Amphipolis, provided his fellow Spartans with a shining example of what was possible for those who fought and died well. Brasidas inspired other generals to strive for unsurpassed glory. He certainly also served as a model for ordinary soldiers and citizens.

This book will explore how figures like Brasidas, and their commemoration, reflected and shaped attitudes towards war in ancient Greece, especially in Sparta. As supposedly one of the most militaristic societies in world history, the Spartans relied on the glory and memory attached to warfare in order to perpetuate their way of life and achieve continued military success. Without understanding the motives of soldiers going to war, and the way society crafted and exploited those motives to keep soldiers going to war, we cannot understand Sparta and its role in Greek history. And in light of Thucydides' famous idea that "the human thing" tends to remain the same across time and space, Spartan militarism can help us understand our own world a little better, especially given the increasing popularity of Sparta and Spartan imagery in many of today's political and activist movements. Thus, understanding how Spartan militarism worked, particularly in light of how Sparta commemorated and remembered its war dead, is a topic that is not only interesting but timely and important. If war and violence are things we really seek to avoid, we best take a look at ancient Greece's most stereotypically warlike and violent society, and how it got and stayed that way.

Aside from the literary monuments to fallen Spartans, including the work of Thucydides and other historians and the poetry of Tyrtaeus and Simonides, we will explore how the physical spaces of ancient Sparta were steeped in memories of the war dead. The Roman-era travel writer Pausanias tells about the many monuments scattered around the Spartan landscape that glorified war and the war dead, including not only tombs to famous fallen leaders like Brasidas and Leonidas but also an elaborate stoa supposedly adorned with spoils from Xerxes' Persian army. Archaeologists have spent the last century trying to sort out exactly what went where in the ancient Spartan city, but there is still a lot we can learn by examining Sparta's topography and monuments, nestled under the forbidding Taygetus mountain range. Sparta's archaeological museum and other museums throughout Greece contain many funerary, honorary, and votive pieces that illuminate Spartan militarism. These pieces on their own can tell us a great deal, but they also were once set up in real physical spaces.

For instance, the famous "smiling hoplite," who many have believed to be Leonidas himself, was found by the sanctuary of Athena Chalkioikos, "of the Bronze House," on the Spartan acropolis. This was the very spot where another Spartan general of the Persian Wars, the ex-regent Pausanias, was starved to death after falling out of favor with the Spartan top brass, allegedly because he was too eager to glorify himself instead of all the Greeks for the victory at Plataea in 479, but more likely because he tried to take Spartan armies too far from Sparta and for too long. Spartans set up monuments in other places too, from the fabled pass at Thermopylae, to the sanctuary of Hera on the island of Samos, all of which can help us understand Spartan militarism more fully.

When we look at Spartan commemoration and how it changed over time, we discover some surprising things. Despite the Spartans' fearsome reputation, they fought remarkably few wars; and when they did fight, they were not nearly as invincible as their ancient and modern reputation suggests. For some time now, historians have been poking holes in the myth of Spartan invincibility. What no one has noticed until now is that Spartan militarism was kept in check by the very desire for fame and glory that animated soldiers in battle. The intuitive presumption about a society obsessed with military glory is that its members must fight at every opportunity. Late Archaic and Classical Sparta, though, seems to have fought few wars precisely because glory and fame were its only overriding concerns. Other reasons for going to war, such as defending the Greeks from foreign invaders or freeing the oppressed, reasons we might find more palatable today, were not compelling motivations for the Spartans, which kept them out of many military conflicts. Other Greeks, most notably the Athenians, embraced the rhetoric of liberation, of "Greek" versus "barbarian," and thus fought more often, further from home, and for longer periods. When the Spartans eventually embraced these reasons themselves, which their changing commemorative practices reflect, they fought, killed, and died more often, with disastrous consequences for Spartan power. Commemoration provides insight into the reasons why societies fight, and those reasons have a bearing on the likelihood of societies embracing war as a good option.

While the "monument wars" rage concerning the place of Confederate statues and other controversial pieces in contemporary America, and the purpose of commemorative sites and rituals comes into question in many other countries too, it is now time to take a new look at the Spartan commemoration of war, its literary accounts, material monuments, and topographical spaces. Sparta is not only relevant because it was seemingly more militaristic than other Greek states were. Spartan imagery and Spartan examples frequently have a central place in the activism of various pro-war and anti-immigrant groups in North America and Europe. From at least the 18th century, Sparta has served as a model for a range of movements, from the political philosophy of Rousseau to the lobbying of the National Rifle Association. Let us therefore consider military figures like Brasidas, the model they set for their fellow Spartans, and how that can inform our own ideas about how one generation of warriors passes the torch onto the next, even today.

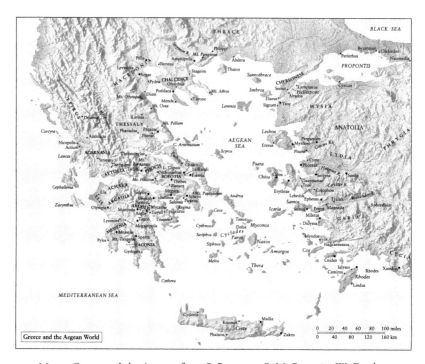

Map 1  Greece and the Aegean, from S. Pomeroy, S. M. Burstein, W. Donlan, J. T. Roberts, D. Tandy. 2012, *Ancient Greece: A Political, Cultural, and Social History* (3rd edition), Oxford, inside front cover. © Oxford University Press. Reproduced with permission of the Licensor through PLSclear.

CHAPTER I

# *Memory and Mirage*

## Introduction: Why Sparta? Why Now?

Sparta needs no introduction, let alone a justification for why it is worth studying. As ancient Romans visited Sparta centuries after its heyday and were treated to an exaggerated theme park of sorts of what Classical Sparta was really like, so, too, does much of the modern world retain a fascination for these strange Greeks – from Enlightenment political theorists, to modern Greek nationalists fighting for independence from the Ottomans, and to popular culture today. Ancient Sparta grabs our imagination because it was so *weird*, even to its fellow Greeks. Phalanxes of social equals fighting with peerless skill and bravery even in the face of certain death is bound to compel, and is an image drawn from carefully crafted propaganda, a public relations campaign initiated by the Spartans themselves. I am not prepared to go as far as Myke Cole, who, in his recent book, *The Bronze Lie*, argues that Sparta's military prowess and invincibility were entirely fabricated by the Spartans and repeated by credulous sources.[1] I do agree, however, that we need to examine this ancient society and its image with a critical eye. Even once we have done so, I believe we can still understand the Spartans as different, as outliers. Military commemoration is one subject in which this difference is starkest.

Sparta is, next to Athens, the second-most studied Classical Greek polis. It is a distant second, though, since Athens has left an overwhelming profusion of evidence by comparison – literary, architectural, artistic, archaeological, and epigraphical. Since at least the time of the Periclean Funeral Oration in Thucydides' *History of the Peloponnesian War*, Athenian commemoration has been better understood and the inspiration for more works of scholarship than any other Greek society. Brilliant recent studies, such as Nathan Arrington's *Ashes, Images, and Memories: The Presence of the War Dead in*

---

[1] Cole 2021.

I

*Fifth-Century Athens*, continue to offer new insights into and interpretations of Athenian commemoration, and the relationship between soldiers, their families, and the state for which they fought and died.[2] Scholars such as Polly Low have begun to take these scholarly approaches to parts of Greece beyond Athens, including Sparta, but a lot more work needs to be done.[3] Untangling Sparta's commemorative past is a different business than doing so for Athens, but there is some interesting evidence to work with and we can make use of some illuminating comparisons.

This is a moment in history at which memory, monuments, and commemoration have never been more important and more controversial. How we think about the past is in the news every day, from the fight to remove Confederate monuments in the United States to the ideological battles waged over the history and ethnicity behind claims to eastern Ukraine while Russia continues its assault on that country as I write these words. Modern military commemoration tends to straddle the awkward divide between celebrating heroism in order to inspire patriotic service in future generations and revealing the horrors of war in order to discourage peoples and states from taking up arms. I want to investigate how one of history's most supposedly militaristic societies commemorated war, and the links that commemoration had to whether and how often that society went to war. In the process, we will learn more about the Spartans and the ancient Greeks, but we will also have occasion to think about our own forms of commemoration and our own relationship with armed conflict. The commemoration of war, ancient and modern, both reflects and forms a society's attitudes towards war. In the case of Sparta, that particular ancient society has often been brought to bear to comment on wars today.

In what follows we will consider some ideas about commemoration, remembrance, and collective memory, and how these ideas can be used fruitfully in a study of ancient Sparta. We will next take a look at the "Spartan Mirage," namely the sources we have for Spartan society and the unique challenges those sources present. This introductory chapter will conclude with some basic principles of Sparta's commemoration of war, particularly how they relate to the ideas of their fellow Greeks. These principles will be explored in depth and complicated by the chapters that follow. We will also take a tour through Classical Sparta and pause to

---

[2] Arrington 2015. For Athens, see also Low 2010; Kucewicz 2021b; Pritchard 2022.
[3] See, for example, Low 2003; 2006; 2011; Kucewicz 2021a.

consider the topography and monuments an ancient Spartan would have encountered, and what those monuments might have meant to the observer.

## A Note on Terminology

Before moving on, I must clarify some of the most important terms I will use throughout this study, since just what the terms "Sparta" and "the Spartans" mean is more complicated than in the case of other Greek peoples. First, Sparta was a strange polis in that it was unwalled and was more an amalgamation of villages than a central urban core surrounded by rural hinterland as other poleis (the plural for "polis") were. Sparta was located in the southern Peloponnese in a region later called Laconia, separated from Messenia to the west by the formidable Taygetus mountain range. The Spartan state was technically called Lacedaemon in antiquity, and its free residents the Lacedaemonians. This term was the source of the famous lambda, or inverted "V," eventually emblazoned on Spartan hoplite shields. Sometimes, therefore, the terms Lacedaemonian and Spartan are used interchangeably in the sources, and in this book.

Classical Spartan society was stratified into three main tiers. At the top, representing a minority of the population, were the full citizens, the Spartiates, sometimes called the *homoioi*, or "similars." These were the Spartan men who trained continuously for war and who lived as if on campaign, dining together every day in common messes, even while at home and at peace. The Spartiates were eligible to serve in important offices, such as the oversight body of five annually elected ephors, and in an assembly that ratified laws and other state actions and policies. The participation of these Spartiates in government means we can understand Sparta as an oligarchy, rule by the few, even though Sparta also had two kings, so was at the same time a type of monarchy or diarchy.

The female family members of the Spartiates had more privileges and freedom than their counterparts in places like Athens, a state exceptionally restrictive to women, but, even so, women played no formal role in Spartan government or on military campaign. Spartan women and girls, however, had an important place in Sparta's military culture and its commemorative practices. Girls, for example, could exercise in public just like boys, and, as part of a compulsory public training, were expected to observe and mock the boys in order to spur Spartan males to greater martial excellence. A large percentage of the famous aphorisms, or sayings, attributed to the Spartans by Plutarch and other authors come from women, and many of these aphorisms are statements of Spartan attitudes towards war and memory. After the Spartans lost at the Battle of Leuctra in 371 BCE, Spartan women who lost husbands and sons walked around the city with joyful expressions, happy that their male family members had died gloriously rather than survived shamefully after surrendering. Spartan women, at least as portrayed by Greek male authors, were important for Spartan commemoration.[4]

Free non-citizens who lived in Spartan territory were called the *perioikoi*, or "dwellers-around." The *perioikoi* typically lived in their own villages in Laconia. They outnumbered the full Spartiates, probably by a significant margin. They were required to serve in the Spartan army and took care of many of the state's necessary economic tasks while the Spartiates trained for war. The term Lacedaemonian usually refers to both the Spartiates and the *perioikoi*. The ancient sources tend to specify when they mean only Spartiates instead of both groups together.[5]

At the bottom tier were the helots, unfree laborers who (the men, at least) mainly worked the agricultural land controlled by Sparta. We might best understand the helots as serfs, or perhaps persons enslaved by the state rather than owned as chattel by individual Spartiates and their families (as was the case with slavery in other Greek poleis, such as Athens).[6] Some helots came from Laconia, while others were from neighboring Messenia to the west, which Sparta conquered in the Archaic period. The helots were the backbone of Spartan power, providing all the produce and other essentials for the survival of the state. Many ancient sources claim that a need to control the helots, and the fear of helot rebellion, drove much of Sparta's policy and way of life.[7]

This book deals primarily with what we might call the "official" commemoration of war in Sparta – poems recited at religious festivals and remembrance ceremonies, monuments erected in public spaces,

---

[4] See Millender 2018 for a general treatment of Spartan women, with further bibliography. See also the foundational monograph on the topic by Pomeroy 2002. For a discussion on Spartan women and war, see Powell 2004.

[5] For the *perioikoi*, see Ducat 2018. For non-Spartans in the Spartan army, see the recent article by Pavlides 2020.

[6] Athens had publicly enslaved persons too. A main difference seems to be that Spartiates did not own privately enslaved persons, whereas Athens had both categories of slavery.

[7] The best resource on the helots is the edited collection of Luraghi and Alcock 2003. Luraghi 2008 discusses the Messenians in particular. For an up-to-date discussion of the state of helot scholarship, and a comparison of helotage with other slave systems in antiquity, see now Lewis 2018: 125–146. For a general overview of the political and social structure of Sparta as compared to Athens, with suggestions for further reading and sources, see Sears 2022. See also Humble 2022, in the same volume, for a closer look at Sparta.

inscriptions commissioned by "the Spartans" as a state, and so on. While I will refer to some individual monuments, dedications, and perspectives, for the majority of this study we will be considering what "the Spartans" did to remember their wars and their war dead. The sources for Sparta are lacking as it is, and it is accordingly much more difficult to assess the ideas and practices of individual Spartiates, not to mention women, *perioikoi*, or helots. These non-elites, or marginalized populations, had agency of their own (if within the confines of various systems of oppression), which would have had a bearing on commemoration. We must keep that fact in mind even as those non-Spartiate and non-"official" perspectives get lost in the shuffle. In addition to the studies pointed out in notes 4–5, I for one eagerly await further work on marginalized peoples in Lacedaemon, including in the sphere of war.

This book deals primarily with the Archaic period, dating from roughly 700 BCE (or whenever the Homeric epics were first composed, perhaps fifty or so years earlier) to 479 BCE, when Xerxes' Persian invasion was repelled from mainland Greece; and the Classical period, which runs from 479 to 323 BCE, the year Alexander the Great died. The Hellenistic period (323–30 BCE) follows the Classical, from which several of our sources derive, as they do also from the Roman period following the death of Cleopatra VII in 30 BCE. Unless otherwise stated, all dates are BCE.

Finally, a word on the terms "commemoration" and "militarism", which will feature prominently throughout the following chapters. Commemoration often conjures up images of formal monuments or ceremonies, such as the Remembrance Day observances held each November 11 in Canada (with analogues in many other countries). Marching bands, parades of veterans, and official services around the town cenotaph, a monument inscribed with the names of the war dead and the battles in which they fought are obvious examples of commemoration. I, however, take a far more expansive view. Wars and war heroes, battles and battlefields, permeate our discourse and our public and private spaces far more than formal commemorative activities would indicate. As I write these words, I have just returned from a lecture tour for which I spoke on Spartan topics at Canadian universities with names like "Waterloo," the famous battle between Napoleon and Wellington, and "Brock," a prominent general from the War of 1812. As debates rage about the nature and importance of "Western Civilization," and Canadian or British "values," wars past and present tend to feature prominently, if sometimes indirectly. Wars can be commemorated in speaking about Canada as a "peacekeeping nation" or the United States as being a great "experiment in democracy" just as much as through a recitation of the names of the war dead. I will therefore consider Spartan attitudes towards war, including, but not limited to, attitudes stemming from the reception of certain military events, as part of a broad phenomenon of commemoration.

In a similar way, I conceive of militarism as a broad subject. The eminent scholar of Sparta Stephen Hodkinson cautions against the use of the term militarism in a Spartan context, since Sparta, like other Greek states, had no clear boundary between military and civic life. Modern nation-states, with clearly demarcated militaries, on the other hand, can be properly described as more or less militaristic, depending on the prominence of those militaries in various spheres.[8] I think of militarism differently, in a way that applies to ancient Greek societies. By militarism, I mean the extent to which war and attitudes towards war inform a society's view of itself and lie behind both real policies and actions and how those policies and actions are understood and portrayed. In this sense, Sparta was more militaristic than other Greek states. The Athenians surely thought about war a lot, but for them it was less of a preoccupation and less of a crux of their identity than it was for the Spartans – whether or not there were strict divisions between the military and other spheres. A Greek state could be militaristic without military institutions or leaders having clear distinctions or any greater constitutional power. As I will argue, a greater degree of militarism did not even necessarily entail a greater degree of formal military activities.

### How Societies Remember

My city of Fredericton is replete with monuments to Max Aitken, better known as Lord Beaverbrook, a Canadian newspaper baron who had prominent positions in the British War Cabinets of both world wars. Next to the Beaverbrook Art Gallery, centrally located along the city's riverfront, is a bronze statue of Beaverbrook himself in academic regalia. One passes the Lady Beaverbrook Arena on the way to the campus of the University of New Brunswick, which boasts the Lady Beaverbrook Residence, the Aitken University Center, and the Beaverbrook Room in the main library, containing volumes from Beaverbrook's own personal collection. Beaverbrook would be most happy that he is profusely memorialized, since he understood the power of physical and spatial monuments. As Lloyd George's minister of information during the First World War,

---

[8] Hodkinson 2006.

Beaverbrook spearheaded the commissioning of war art, specifically to commemorate the achievements of Canadians on battlefields such as Ypres. He remarked that, "[i]n the years following the war Canadians will expect to be told what Canadians have done in the war. They will want the younger generation to be taught the glory of Canada."[9] Beaverbrook's sentiments are in accord with Herodotus' opening lines, in which the "Father of History" says he undertook his monumental literary project so that great and marvelous deeds might not be without their due share of glory.

The much-commemorated Beaverbrook set out to ensure that the era-defining wars of the 20th century were properly commemorated. "Commemoration," as the literal meaning of the word suggests, pertains to remembrance, to ways in which people, events, and ideas are remembered, even long afterwards. To understand what commemoration is, how it works, and what its purposes are, we need to think about memory itself, and how it operates not merely on the cognitive level of an individual but at the collective level of a society or a people. Memory is related to history but operates differently. I am partial to Jennifer Wellington's definition, which she outlines in her study of First World War memorials:

> By "memory" I mean the sensation of a proprietary, emotional connection to the past, and the community of the dead, buttressed by broadly accepted impressions of that past, as opposed to "history", which requires the recitation of facts based on verifiable evidence .... The contours of war memory may shape a population's willingness or reluctance to go to war in the future.[10]

The line between "history" and "memory" for the ancient Greeks was more nebulous than Wellington's, as suggested by, for instance, Herodotus' insistence that his work is itself a commemorative exercise. Her definition is helpful nonetheless, as is her insight that a people's memory of war affects their present attitudes to war.

Human individuals have memories of their own experiences and what has been related to them by others. It seems uncomplicated to say that a given Spartan remembered war, in the sense that the Spartan could have participated in wars or at least heard about wars from others; those memories would inform that Spartan's thinking about war. But can a people, as opposed to an individual person, have memory at all? In other words, is it accurate or useful to speak about Sparta's commemoration

---

[9] As quoted in Wellington 2017: 52.  [10] Wellington 2017: 7.

of war as if Sparta itself remembered its battles, its soldiers, and its war dead? By far the most influential theorist tackling this question is the French sociologist Maurice Halbwachs, who pioneered the concept of "collective memory." In short, while a collective does not remember like a human mind does, individuals are able to have memory at all only in a collective context. Through several case studies, Halbwachs argues that individuals can have very different memories of the past based on their participation in various collectives. The group affects and shapes the memories of the individual.[11] In a Spartan context, then, the way the community commemorated war would be vitally important for how individual Spartans remembered war and thought about current wars and their own roles in them.

There was quite a bit of pushback to Halbwachs' idea, as influential as it is. Some even denied the existence of collective memory altogether, since a collective cannot actually remember anything, memory being a neurological process. Jan Assmann has softened the idea of collective memory into what he calls "cultural memory," and in so doing has made Halbwachs' insight both more palatable and, I think, more accurate. Assmann concedes that the subject of memory must be the individual, but the individual can organize and make sense of this memory only by relying on the "frame" provided by culture.[12] Assmann elaborates on the relationship between the individual and the collective in terms of memory:

> Just as an individual forms a personal identity through memory, maintaining this despite the passage of time, so a group identity is also dependent on the reproduction of shared memories. The difference is that the group memory has no neurological basis. This is replaced by culture: a complex of identity-shaping aspects of knowledge objectified in the symbolic forms of myth, song, dance, sayings, laws, sacred texts, pictures, ornaments, paintings, processional routes, or – as in the case of the Australians – even whole landscapes.[13]

All of the factors Assmann marks as "identity-shaping" aspects of culture vis-à-vis memory were operative in ancient Sparta, and we will be looking at them throughout this book. Jay Winter, himself deeply indebted to Assmann, argues that memory and commemoration have a profound impact on a society's view of war, including whether war is a good or legitimate choice. Today, Western Europeans tend to think of war as an

---

[11] Halbwachs 1992 is a good English edition of Halbwachs' most important work and includes critical notes and interpretive material by the editor, L. A. Coser.

[12] Assmann 2011: 22.

[13] Assmann 2011: 72. See also Winter 2017: 205, who says succinctly that "how we remember affected deeply what we remember."

illegitimate abomination, which is reflected in many forms of commemoration that stress war's horrors. Eastern Europe and the United States, by contrast, cling to older forms of commemoration and therefore tend to be more militaristic and see war as a viable, even good option. We will consider the extent to which Winter's paradigm holds true for Sparta.[14]

Of particular interest in a Greek context are Assmann's observations regarding a society's treatment of the dead, which he separates into retrospective and prospective categories. The former pertains to a society continuing to live with the dead as part of the community. The latter are actions by which the living make themselves unforgettable after they die.[15] The dead were a ubiquitous presence in ancient Greece, including for the Spartans, as we will see. Anyone seeking to understand how the figurative and literal presence of the dead affects society and culture would do well to read Thomas Laqueur's beautiful book on the subject, which meditates on the power of the dead "in deep time to make communities, to do the work of culture, to announce their presence and meaning by occupying space."[16] Many Greeks, Spartans especially, were motivated by the desire to be remembered and commemorated. Homer's heroes certainly acted as if being remembered was of paramount importance, and so, too, did historical Spartans.[17]

Those who study commemoration in the modern period tend to emphasize the importance of democracy. This makes sense, since if the people doing the fighting have little or no say over wars and warfare, it is much less important to have a commemorative regime that influences popular attitudes. Even though Sparta was not a democracy, Spartiates did participate in the running of the state to a marked degree – as opposed to the subjects of early modern European monarchies. For our purposes, it is reasonable to apply the observations made about modern democratic commemoration to the Spartans, since the Spartans, especially those in the phalanx, represented a genuine community with a great deal of agency (no matter how many residents of Laconia were excluded from Spartan society). The eminent historian Eric Hobsbawm sees the rise of mass politics in modern Europe as instrumental in the invention of official traditions meant to galvanize the people for war. In post-Revolutionary France, Marianne came to embody the Republic itself for which the people fight, and local notables, from the past and present, emerged as symbols in many communities. Hobsbawm notes that French democracy led to a veritable "statuomania" in which

[14] Winter 2017, especially 202–208.  [15] Assmann 2011: 45–46.  [16] Laqueur 2016: 21–22.
[17] As Ferrario 2014: 232 points out in relation to Brasidas in the 420s. For more on Brasidas and his desire to make himself remembered, see Chapter 4.

countless public monuments were commissioned. All of this "invented tradition" was designed to get the people on board with whatever projects, including wars, the nation was undertaking.[18] In his book, *Imagined Communities*, Benedict Anderson traces the phenomenon of modern nationalism as a means to convince the people of horizontal comradeship, regardless of how inegalitarian a society really is, in order to persuade millions of people to kill and especially die for their country.[19] Official nationalism is understood by Anderson to be "an anticipatory strategy by dominant groups which are threatened with marginalization or exclusion from an emerging nationally-imagined community."[20] "Imagined communities," "invented tradition," and "cultural memory" are related ideas that help us understand why the people and those who seek to maintain influence over the people engage in commemoration, especially of war.[21]

Several scholars of classical antiquity have begun to engage with these types of analyses, and some are applying them specifically to ancient Greece. A new volume edited by Giangiulio and colleagues, *Commemorating War and War Dead*, engages with the work of Halbwachs, Assmann, and others, and provides case studies from Greek antiquity and other periods. The book is an invaluable resource for assessing the state of the field of commemoration and memory studies.[22] We will have occasion to assess Roel Konijnendijk's contribution on Sparta's use of their fearsome reputation as a weapon of war.[23] On a broader level, readers are directed to Giangiulio's own chapter, which argues that a key part of being social is the ability to draw on group experiences, even ones from very long ago that did not affect the individual directly. He adds that "the past is therefore a social construct resulting from a society's need for meaning, and from its frames of reference."[24] In the same volume, Elena Franchi, herself a scholar of Sparta, draws our attention to a study demonstrating that a Vietnamese parent's traumatic memories of the Vietnam War could be transmitted to their offspring, a sort of "vicarious memory."[25] She also reflects on commemoration as a means of preserving a military culture and promoting a state's military reputation abroad – which, I would add, the Spartans most certainly did.[26] In a related volume, Michael Jung

---

[18] Hobsbawm 2012, especially 267–272. Assmann 2011: 20 might take issue with Hobsbawm's use of "tradition," since, in his formulation, memory is a richer concept: "Dead people and memories of dead people cannot be handed down. Remembrance is a matter of emotional ties, cultural shaping, and a conscious reference to the past that over-comes the rupture between life and death. These are the elements that characterize cultural memory and take it far beyond the reaches of tradition."
[19] Anderson 2016: 7.    [20] Anderson 2016: 101.
[21] See also Evans 2019 for an illuminating discussion of public art in democratic societies.
[22] Giangiulio et al. 2019.    [23] Konijnendijk 2019.    [24] Giangiulio 2019: 26.
[25] Franchi 2019: 39.    [26] Franchi 2019: 50.

applies Pierre Nora's influential idea of *lieux de mémoire*, "places of memory," to the memory of the Persian Wars, especially Marathon and Plataea. Jung's work is important for tracing how war is remembered differently by different societies and in different eras.[27] Vincent Azoulay's work on the Tyrant-Slayers of Athens is an important resource.[28] He helps us understand how collective or cultural memory worked in ancient Greece and how it changed over time. He also explores how the commissioning of and subsequent interaction with physical monuments in addition to literary texts and other commemorative devices shaped and reflected a society's view of past and present. The way was made open for democracy in Athens when the last tyrants, Hipparchus, the son of Pisistratus, and his brother, Hippias, were, respectively, assassinated and thrown out of the city. This was a long and complicated process that entailed more than a few reversals, but most Athenians credited the assassination of Hipparchus with liberation and the subsequent democracy. Harmodius and Aristogeiton, the two men who killed Hipparchus, were revered as the Tyrannicides and honored with the first statue of mortal humans to be erected in the Agora, the heart of Athens. The original statue group was carried off in the Persian invasion of Greece in 480–479, to be replaced by a new commission, which survives only in the form of later copies (most famous in Naples) but which is a reference piece in the history of Greek art nonetheless. Azoulay traces the twists and turns in the remembrance of the Tyrannicides throughout Athenian history, and pays special attention to how the physical monument itself was received and in turn shaped Athenian ideas. Engaging with the theoretical work of Foucault, Azoulay affirms that "a monument does not simply illustrate events, but itself marks an epoch: it is an active symbol, a historical fact in its own right which, far from illustrating some reality that is independent of it, actually 'creates' and makes history."[29]

Turning from Athens, which, as I have already mentioned, received the lion's share of scholarly attention, we will think about how Sparta's monuments and other commemorative materials both reflected Spartan society and helped to create it, especially in the sphere of war. Since I think there is value to understanding this work in the context of the broader phenomenon of cultural memory, I hope we begin to think anew about how we ourselves commemorate war, how our own cultural memory operates, and whether our commemorative ideas make war more or less likely to happen.

---

[27] Jung 2006. For more on the Persian War context, see also Proietti 2021, who examines the role of memory especially before the account of Herodotus rose to prominence.

See also Nora 1997, whose monumental work explores the centrality of these "sites of memory" to French nationalism.

[28] Azoulay 2017.    [29] Azoulay 2017: 6.

## The Spartan Mirage

Athenians wrote a lot, from the history of Thucydides to the comedies and tragedies of Aristophanes and Sophocles, and from the speeches of Demosthenes to the philosophical dialogues of Plato. Literary works that have come to us through the manuscript tradition were by no means the only things Athenians wrote. They also wrote inscriptions on stone. Other Greeks inscribed laws, decrees, and the like in permanent form, but not in the sheer volume the Athenians did. Athenian inscriptions tell us about diplomatic missions, wars, and the bestowing of honors on important benefactors. Inscriptions also illuminate more mundane matters, such as how much different workers were paid while building the Erechtheum on the Acropolis, or who was responsible for taking care of the outrigging on a trireme warship. Athenians built a lot of lasting monuments, too, which both gave archaeologists more material to study and also drew archaeologists to the city in the first place, meaning that excavations have been going on in various parts of Athens for longer and more continuously than most other sites in Greece. Athenian ideas spread around the Mediterranean too, including in the material form of Attic painted pottery that was in demand across the ancient world. A majority of the most famous Athenian vases actually come from Italy, not Athens, a neat demonstration of Athens' cultural reach. Many students of Greek antiquity, and not a few scholars, often equate Athens with Greece itself, so thoroughly does that polis dominate the sources with which most are familiar. War monuments are no exception.

Spartans wrote very little, either in literary form or on stone and other permanent materials. Many other ancient Greeks wrote about Sparta but were not themselves Spartans and in many cases were either openly hostile to Sparta (usually in favor of Athens) or, as some scholars have alleged, overly enthusiastic about singing Sparta's praises. To make matters worse, our fullest accounts of Spartan society come from sources written hundreds of years later and from distant lands. During the Roman Empire, when Sparta had no meaningful power or influence to speak of beyond its borders, the once-great polis was nonetheless the stuff of legend and attracted the curiosity of those wanting to learn about the society that produced the Three Hundred who stood up to Xerxes. Several writers obliged this curiosity, and their works about Sparta were correspondingly popular. Students of ancient Sparta therefore confront a double obstacle: nonexistent or much later sources, and deliberate propagandistic distortions in the sources we do have. These distortions likely originate from the Spartans themselves, eager to trade on and supplement their reputation. In 1933 François Ollier coined the term *Le*

*Mirage spartiate*, the "Spartan Mirage," to describe the fog through which scholars approach ancient Sparta.[30] Ollier's phrasing has stuck.

Sparta's own literary output, at least that which survives in any quantity today, boils down to two 7th-century lyric poets, Alcman and Tyrtaeus. We will consider the latter of these two extensively in the chapters that follow, since he wrote poetry to exhort Spartans to fight in war, and thus touches directly on our topic. Alcman is also an invaluable source given that he tells us about various Spartan rituals and his poems were sung at several Spartan festivals. There were other Spartan writers, but their work only survives as sources referred to by later, non-Spartan authors. Herodotus wrote a lot about Sparta, but while he was from Halicarnassus on the other side of the Aegean Sea, he spent a great deal of time in Athens and produced a decidedly Atheno-centric version of events – at a time, the 430s, when Athens and Sparta were moving headlong towards war with each other. The most famous historian of that war, Thucydides, was himself an Athenian, and though he was exiled by his home polis and harbored some hard feelings towards certain elements of the Athenian democracy, he expresses his frustration at how secretive the Spartans were about themselves (Thuc. 5.68.2). The third great historian of the Classical era, Xenophon, was an Athenian like Thucydides. Also like Thucydides, at some point Xenophon was exiled from Athens. He became a close comrade with the Spartan king Agesilaus, lived on an estate in the Peloponnese, and enrolled his own sons in the Spartan education system. We will explore Xenophon's philo-Laconism, or pro-Spartan leanings, later.[31] In addition to telling the history of his area from a Spartan, or at least pro-Spartan, perspective, he wrote a flattering biography of Agesilaus and a treatise on Spartan government and society, which are crucial sources for us.

The fullest and most influential sources for Spartan society are the most problematic, primarily because they are so late. The biographer Plutarch, writing mostly in the early 2nd century CE, devotes several works to Classical Spartan leaders, including a biography of the semi-mythical lawgiver Lycurgus. He also compiled a list of Spartan sayings, which have done more than any other source to color the image of Sparta held by subsequent generations. Pausanias was a travel-writer also working in the 2nd century CE, who gives a detailed topographical description of Sparta along with lengthy excurses on Spartan history to explain what he sees. Both of these later sources had access to material now lost to us, but we must be cautious when reading them for Archaic and Classical Sparta, since many of the things they describe might be from the later Hellenistic and Roman periods.

[30] Ollier 1933–1943.    [31] See Chapter 6.

The extreme scholarly positions are represented by Nigel Kennell, who thinks the majority of Sparta's most infamous practices and quirks derive from late sources, and Paul Rahe, who argues that a fixation on the idea of the "Spartan Mirage" has become a mirage itself, causing scholars to discredit perfectly good sources.[32] Sensible middle ground is found in the work of Jean Ducat and Thomas Figueira, who argue that later distortions do affect the literary sources, but those distortions are based on genuine historical facts and ideas present in Archaic and Classical Sparta.[33]

In terms of literary sources, we will proceed with caution, especially as pertains to writers like Plutarch and Pausanias. We will pay special attention to sources that are contemporary or near contemporary with events to which they relate, including Tyrtaeus and epigrams and elegies commissioned by the Spartans to mark their wars. That said, the distortions themselves are a vital source, since how the Spartans wanted to be remembered, what they wished their reputation to be, is of course crucial to understanding their attitudes towards commemoration. Instead of focusing on what the Battle of Thermopylae was "really like," we will consider how it was remembered, and how that remembrance changed from the time immediately following the battle to the time Herodotus wrote about it, and even later as it morphed into legend.

Pausanias likely got a lot wrong in his historical digressions on Sparta. He also misidentified plenty of the monuments he saw, either because he made a mistake himself, or his local guides were drawing on distortions and a misremembered past (which is itself an interesting thing to consider). His account of the landscape and material culture of Sparta and Spartan dedications at other sites such as Olympia and Delphi is invaluable all the same. Panhellenic sanctuaries where the Spartans made their mark, alongside other Greek states vying for recognition, have been thoroughly and continuously excavated since the 19th century, yielding inscriptions, works of art, and other dedications that speak to Spartan commemoration. The site of ancient Sparta itself, where the modern town was founded in 1834 as a deliberate re-foundation of the Classical city, has also been studied by archaeologists for well over a century, and excavation and survey work continue to shed new light on the city's past.[34] Though not as famous as

---

[32] See, for example, Kennell 2018, in which he covers the reception of Sparta in the Roman period and recapitulates much of his earlier work. Rahe 2016: 1–6 provides a concise discussion of the "Spartan Mirage" (which he calls the "Spartan Enigma") and his rationale for accepting most sources.

[33] Ducat 2006a; Figueira 2016.

[34] For an overview of excavations and finds at Sparta, see Waywell 1999–2000; Sanders 2009; and Cavanaugh 2018.

Athens' Acropolis or Agora, Sparta has yielded material finds of immense importance, from monuments and burials, to inscriptions and dedications found in Sparta itself and overseas in places like Samos. We will consider the form of Spartan commemorative monuments but also their location, since most of them were meant to be seen and experienced in specific contexts. We will also include in our analysis the evidence for how and where the Spartan war dead were buried, how and where Spartans made dedications, especially of a military character, and how non-Spartans responded to the materiality of Spartan commemoration.

One element of the Spartan Mirage I should address here is the trend in recent scholarship to downplay Sparta's uniqueness. Because the sources are supposedly so distorted, the things that make Sparta so different from other Greek states, especially the various expressions of Spartan militarism, are perhaps no more than the products of later mythologizing. The leading voice in this revisionist approach to Sparta is Stephen Hodkinson, who has done a great deal to bring Sparta to the forefront of scholarly attention. In a recent chapter, for example, Hodkinson questions whether Sparta was a militaristic society at all and concludes that it was much more typical as a Greek polis than the (especially later) sources imply. For Hodkinson, not only is militarism a modern term anachronistically applied to Greek antiquity, but also reports of Spartans constantly training for war are overblown and Sparta's frequent reluctance to march out to war tells against a militaristic society.[35] Against Hodkinson, I would argue that, just because ancient Greek poleis tended not to separate civic and military life rigidly, it does not follow that one Greek society could not be more militaristic, or focused on warfare, than another. I think Xenophon's comment, written in the 4th century BCE rather than during the Roman period, concerning Spartan professionalism *as compared to other Greeks* is pretty hard to overcome: "Seeing these things [Sparta's sacrificial practices in preparation for battle], you would reckon that others were mere novices in military matters, while the Lacedaemonians alone are in fact craftsmen in the art of war" (Xen. *Lak. Pol.* 13.5).[36]

---

[35] Hodkinson 2006. See also Hodkinson 2023 for an illuminating discussion of how Plutarch downplays Sparta's military characteristics in the life of Lycurgus, only in turn to emphasize them in the section comparing Lycurgus with the unwarlike Numa. Hodkinson argues that, in the case of Lycurgus, Plutarch preferred to emphasize political reforms and civil-oriented subjects, and in so doing was reacting against earlier accounts of Sparta from authors such as Xenophon. Hodkinson's arguments here are compelling, but in no way detract from the possibility, or I think probability, that Archaic and Classical Sparta really was a militaristic society in most senses of the term.

[36] ὥστε ὁρῶν ταῦτα ἡγήσαιο ἂν τοὺς μὲν ἄλλους αὐτοσχεδιαστὰς εἶναι τῶν στρατιωτικῶν, Λακεδαιμονίους δὲ μόνους τῷ ὄντι τεχνίτας τῶν πολεμικῶν. In a more recent publication,

The sources, often focused as they are on strange or marvelous things and keen to drum up interest in Sparta and their work on Sparta, do distort and overemphasize, which has led some scholars astray in the past.[37] But one of the themes of this book is that, when it comes to commemorating war, the Spartans were at key points and in key ways different than their fellow Greeks.

## How Spartans Commemorate War: Some General Principles

In this section, we will go over some basic ideas and practices of the Spartan commemoration of war, especially the war dead. The rest of this book will explore many of these topics in much more detail, especially how commemoration changed over time through the Archaic and Classical periods. Here, however, we need to lay the foundation, recognizing that our sources for much of this material are frequently late and problematic, and that some of these commemorative practices were more prominent in some chronological periods than in others. At the outset, we must keep in mind that ancient Greek ideas of death and memory were far different from many of our ideas. In short, for the Greeks, being remembered was the paramount concern. Although he is dealing primarily with Athens, Nathan Arrington's words on this point are equally relevant for this study: "where the modern memorial may tap into notions of a blessed, peaceful afterlife or make allusions to a Christian theology of sacrifice, the ancient memorial operates in a religious context where few welcomed death. The greatest glory for the dead was not their status in the underworld, only their continued memory among the living."[38]

One of the most famous passages in all Greek literature is the Funeral Oration delivered over the collective tomb of the Athenians who died during the first year of the Peloponnesian War, as portrayed by Thucydides

---

Hodkinson 2020 allows for a degree of Spartan specialized training in comparison to other poleis, but mostly in the sphere of physical fitness rather than in technical military drills or tactics. "Professional soldiers" is therefore an anachronistic mislabeling of what the Spartans really were. I take Hodkinson's point but maintain that even their higher level of physical fitness, and their more cohesive organization, which Hodkinson also highlights, rendered the Spartan qualitatively different from their fellow Greeks on the battlefield, "professional" or otherwise.

[37] Paul Rahe's 2015, 2016, 2019, 2020 recent four volumes on Sparta are the most forceful expression of Spartan uniqueness. For an example of how new evidence can shed light on the similarities Sparta shared with other Greeks, sometimes surprisingly so, see Christesen 2018, who argues by means of a comprehensive survey of Spartan burials in the archaeological record that the Spartans shared more burial practices with their fellow Peloponnesians than had been known to previous scholars (and implied in the sources).

[38] Arrington 2015: 8.

(Thuc. 2.34–46). To set up the speech, Thucydides outlines the standard Athenian burial customs, the *patrios nomos*, or "ancestral custom." In typical cases, the remains of the Athenian war dead are brought back to the city to be buried *en masse* in the *dēmosion sēma*, or "public cemetery," located in the vicinity of the Kerameikos, which was long the site of many prominent burials.[39] Thucydides lists one important exception to mass burial in the city: Because of their exceptional valor, the Athenian dead from the Battle of Marathon in 490 were buried on the battlefield itself – their resting place is still visible today as the *soros*, or mound heaped up over their bodies.[40] This *in situ* burial, a singular honor for the Athenians, was a far more typical practice for other Greeks, including famously the Spartans.[41]

Spartan kings, as Herodotus tells us, were brought back to Sparta if they died abroad, and were afforded lavish funerary rites that would make any Greek envious (Hdt. 6.58).[42] If a king's body could not be recovered, he was honored by a cenotaph in Sparta, as were certain remarkable Spartans such as the general Brasidas. In addition to prominent tombs, Spartan kings and a select few prominent figures were given statues in their honor, sometimes several statues, which were noted by Pausanias as he walked through the city (Paus. 3.14.1–2). The most famous piece in the Archaeological Museum of Sparta, the so-called "Smiling Hoplite," might be one of these representations of a Spartan king, perhaps even Leonidas himself, though it was found buried under parts of the later theater and therefore not visible when Pausanias visited the site (Figure 1.2).[43] Typically dated to the 470s, or perhaps a bit later, this slightly larger-than-life sculpture displays the entire head and torso of a hoplite, including parts of his helmet crest (which has now been largely reconstructed) and even pieces of the legs and other body parts that are not included in the current display.[44] First identified as made out of Parian marble, Jacqueline Christien has recently demonstrated that it was carved

[39] Foundational works on this Athenian custom are Clairmont 1983; and Loraux 2006. See the more recent studies by Arrington 2015, especially 19–90 (for the Classical period); and Kucewicz 2021b, who turns the analysis back to the Archaic period and concludes that much of the *patrios nomos* was already in place in the 6th century.

[40] For the *soros* and its relation to the battle, see Krentz 2011: 111–136; Butera and Sears 2019: 3–18.

[41] The best survey of Greek customs for the burial of the war dead is still Pritchett 1985: 94–259. See more recently Bérard 2020, who stresses the remarkable parallels among Greek burial customs.

[42] Cartledge 1987: 332–337 offers a good discussion of the funerals for Spartan kings.

[43] The fullest discussion of this statue is still the original excavation report from Woodward and Hobling 1924–1925: 253–266.

[44] I am grateful to Andrew Stewart for discussing this sculpture's possible dating with me.

from stone quarried locally in Laconia.[45] The muscular and powerful soldier looks up and to his left, his head protected by a helmet of remarkable workmanship, its cheek-pieces carved to represent rams' heads. Whoever was represented by this statue – either a king like Leonidas or someone of similar stature, such as the regent Pausanias who won the Battle of Plataea, or even a mythological figure erected to honor the accomplishments of a Spartan leader – enjoyed a monument in Sparta that would hold its own among monuments erected anywhere in Greece.

When regular Spartans died abroad in war, however, they were buried on the spot, usually in a mass grave, or *polyandrion*, like the Athenian *soros* at Marathon (though not necessarily as monumental). Such *polyandria* were common in the Greek world, stretching back into the Archaic period and continuing until at least the end of the Classical period in the late 4th century.[46] We will have occasion to discuss several of these burials abroad in the chapters that follow, but here it will suffice to mention an important passage on the subject in Thucydides. In 427, when the people of Plataea pleaded with the Spartans to spare them and their city, the Plataeans adduced in their favor the fact that the tombs of the Spartan dead from the Battle of Plataea in 479 were in their territory, and that they had dutifully attended to and honored these tombs over the past half century. If the Spartans destroy Plataea, they will leave the tombs of their ancestors unattended and in hostile territory (Thuc. 3.58.4–5). The Plataeans' appeal failed – but this rhetoric might not have moved the Spartans much. The dead at Plataea were special, but plenty of Spartan war dead were buried abroad in the lands of their enemies.

Sometimes the names of the Spartan war dead might have been inscribed and displayed at Sparta itself, but it is far from clear whether or to what extent this happened. Herodotus claims to have learned the names of all the Three Hundred who died at Thermopylae, which suggests a monument of some kind, though some scholars argue that such a list of names was present only at a later period and Herodotus must have learned them by some other means.[47] No material evidence for a list of Spartan casualties has been found, a marked contrast with Athenian

---

[45] Christien 2018: 627–628.

[46] Kucewicz 2021a argues that Spartan battlefield burial developed in the Archaic period as a response to the Spartan hoplites gaining power over the aristocrats, who had initially enjoyed prominent burials in Sparta itself. The evidence for these earlier burials at Sparta, however, is flimsy. For *polyandria* and their relation to other types of burials, see Bérard 2020, who begins with a *polyandrion* from Paros dating to the 8th century, and ends with the Theban and Macedonian *polyandria* at Chaeronea from 338.

[47] For the existence or lack thereof of a *stele* commemorating the Three Hundred, see Low 2011: 3–4.

archaeology, which has uncovered a wealth of epigraphical material for the war dead.[48]

Archaeology has furnished, however, several examples of Spartan funerary monuments with the simple inscription ΕΝ ΠΟΛΕΜΩΙ, or "in war," accompanying the soldier's name. These markers of individual war dead are the only such monuments that survive for regular Spartan soldiers and *perioikoi*, and are from a variety of periods and found throughout Laconia, including in the center of Sparta.[49] This material evidence lines up nicely with a passage from Plutarch's biography of the Spartan lawgiver Lycurgus that says the only Spartans who could have their names inscribed on a tombstone were men who died in war and women who died while holding religious office (or in childbirth) (Plut. *Lyc.* 27.3).[50] The Spartans set apart the war dead for special honors because they considered all deaths in battle to be a species of the "beautiful death," the *belle mort* in the words of modern scholars.[51]

Unlike Athens, which had cemeteries such as the Kerameikos where a number of private burials were located for individuals and families who died in all manner of ways, in Sparta only kings and famous leaders received lavish tombs, while the ordinary war dead (and select women) could have their names added to simple monuments. Another difference from Athens – and most other poleis – is that the Spartans could bury their dead, including their war dead, inside the city and even close to sacred areas, whereas most Greek cemeteries were outside of the city walls to avoid any religious pollution and other taboos relating to death and burial (Plut. *Lyc.* 27). Archaeological evidence confirms the presence of burials in Sparta, usually along major roads where they could be seen regularly.[52] In a culture that privileged memory as much as the ancient Greeks did, it is all the more remarkable that the Spartans limited something as basic as a person's name on a tombstone to the war dead.

[48] For which, see Pritchard 2022.
[49] For a discussion of these monuments, including their chronological range and geographic distribution, see Low 2006.
[50] For the clause concerning women, which mentions religious office in the manuscript tradition but has been emended to mean childbirth, see Dillon 2007, who argues against this emendation. For Dillon, Sparta's exceptional piety and reverence for the gods makes special provisions for women in religious roles especially suitable. Unlike the inscriptions for the male war dead, as Dillon points out, no examples for women dying in childbirth have been found dating certainly to the Archaic or Classical periods.
[51] Used most famously and paradigmatically by Loraux 1977, 2018; and Vernant 1991.
[52] For the types and locations of Spartan burials, see Christesen 2018, who points out that there were also extra-communal (rather than "extra-mural," since Classical Sparta did not have walls) cemeteries, as recent excavations have revealed.

Whether and how the war dead in Greece were treated posthumously as heroes, that is, given cult honors as demigods or minor divinities along the lines of the heroes from myth, is a major topic in classical scholarship.[53] While shrines to heroes abounded all over the Greek world, in the Archaic and Classical periods it was unusual for the recent dead to be treated as heroes, with a few exceptions such as the founders of colonies and some famous athletes. Sparta, however, seems to have been different. Michael Flower argues that the Spartans were much more likely to recognize their dead as heroes, including those who died very recently.[54] As we considered in the prologue and will consider again in Chapter 4, the Spartan general Brasidas was the recipient of heroic honors abroad, at Amphipolis, and might have been similarly honored in Sparta. The honors he received stand out in Thucydides' *History*, but might have been expected by ambitious Spartans given their city's penchant for heroization.[55] Spartan soldiers and generals, therefore, could have been motivated in part by the posthumous rewards their city offered to the glorious dead, to a greater extent than other poleis.[56]

If the Spartans reserved special privileges for the war dead, they conversely meted out particularly grievous punishments on those who failed to do their military duty. Xenophon, in his *Constitution of the Lacedaemonians*, details the dishonor suffered by those the Spartans called *hoi tresantes*, "the tremblers." In contrast to other poleis, where the person who displayed cowardice feared only being called a coward, in Sparta he was stripped of most of his rights as a citizen, a condition known as *atimia*. He was left out of social and political activities, could not freely interact with his fellow Spartans in the common dining messes and other central social organizations, and had to bear such a degree of shame that he was forbidden from even looking cheerful. Xenophon does not wonder that so

---

[53] For an overview of heroization and hero cult, the foundational work is Habicht 1970. See also McCauley 1993; Hägg 1999; Currie 2005; Jones 2010. For the collection of "hero-reliefs" found at Sparta, an important source for the uniqueness of Spartan hero cult, see Hibler 1993.

[54] Flower 2009.

[55] For Brasidas' heroization, see Chapter 4. See also Simonton 2018; Sears 2019a.

[56] For a thorough treatment of hero cult at Sparta, see Pavlides 2011, especially 104–115, who cautions that some developments in this type of cult might be from the Hellenistic and Roman periods, and we should not confuse the great honors paid to the war dead as truly heroic honors. See also Pavlides 2010, which offers a focused discussion on the development of hero cult at Sparta in the Archaic period. Christesen 2010 provides a good argument about the intersection of heroization with political concerns at Sparta. Arrington 2015: 119 argues that, in comparison to the heroization of the Spartan war dead, and the war dead of some other poleis, such as Megara and Thasos (showing that the Spartans might not have been utterly unique), the treatment of the Athenian dead was decidedly unheroic.

many preferred to kill themselves than live in such a condition (Xen. *Lak. Pol.* 9.4–6). Several other sources talk about the fate of the "tremblers," which seems to be a uniquely Spartan disgrace.[57] On the flipside of the "in war" tombstones, in a society that holds memory of central importance, being remembered as a "trembler" would have stung especially badly.

The Spartans commissioned several major monuments to commemorate their military achievements – we will consider some of these monuments in more detail later. The most prominent of these was the so-called "Persian Stoa," located in the heart of the city, in the agora. Pausanias (3.11.3) and the Roman architectural writer Vitruvius (1.1.6) each offer a description of this structure, which was supposedly constructed with spoils taken from the Persians in 479.[58] In addition to being the "most prominent building in the agora," according to Pausanias, the stoa contained images of the Persians the Spartans had vanquished and, in the words of Vitruvius, served as a spur to future Spartans to attain the kind of manhood that provided for the defense of freedom. The Athenians similarly commemorated the Persian Wars in their own agora, particularly in the decoration of the Painted Stoa, which showed the action of the Battle of Marathon and other important engagements. Polly Low comments on the interaction of this triumphalist monument with the other commemorations of the Persian Wars in Sparta, particularly the tombs and statues of their kings and leaders, and the lists of casualties, that were near Sparta's acropolis, across from the important shrine of Athena Chalkioikos:

> If the Persian Stoa exemplified, in the most literal way possible, what Sparta had gained from the encounter, then the Persian War monuments in front of the Athena Chalkioikos sanctuary represented what Sparta had lost in that conflict – the life of one king, the reputation of another, hundreds of Spartan citizens.[59]

Triumph and loss – even if that loss was glorious – were both on display in Sparta's landscape.

The Spartans are not well known today for their literary accomplishments. The stereotype of the Spartans, especially as fleshed out by Thucydides, is as a people of few words, literally "Laconic." Yet, Sparta was a poetic and musical society, especially in the Archaic period.[60] In the following chapter, we will take a close look at Spartan poetry and the

---

[57] Ducat 2006b provides a comprehensive discussion of the "tremblers," including an analysis of all the literary sources.
[58] Duffy 2016 is an invaluable resource for the monuments commemorating the Persian Wars.
[59] Low 2011: 13.    [60] Calame 2018 evocatively calls pre-Classical Sparta a "song culture."

occasions at which this poetry was performed – overwhelmingly in a military or commemorative context. The verses of Tyrtaeus, a 7th-century poet, were used by the Spartans to inspire soldiers to courage in battle while having hope for a glorious memory afterwards. The poems of Tyrtaeus and others were performed in various religious festivals that themselves were held to remember previous victories and defeats, and the soldiers that fought in them. The Spartans were exceptionally religious, even for the Greeks, and their religion and its accompanying songs and poems had a military character, integral to Sparta's commemorative ideals.

A spectrum of individuals and groups were involved in commemoration at Sparta. Some monuments and rituals, such as the performance of martial poetry at religious festivals and monuments such as the Persian Stoa next to the agora, were done at the state level. Battlefield burials, according to some scholars, were a way for the Spartan hoplites to demonstrate their power and agency. Prior to a supposed "6th-century revolution" in Sparta, a narrow elite had dominated Sparta, and brought their war dead home to be marked with private monuments in the city.[61] If this scheme is correct, Spartan commemoration is the mirror image of that in Athens, where, instead of battlefield burials, the democratic state co-opted the treatment of the war dead from individual families by bringing the dead back to Athens for communal burial just outside the city.[62]

Private individuals, however, continued to play a role in remembering the war dead at Sparta. The "in war" tombstones were all private monuments, and they continued to be set up throughout the Classical and Hellenistic periods. After the Spartan defeat at the Battle of Leuctra in 371, the ephors commanded the women not to make a public outcry in their grief but to bear their loss in silence (Xen. *Hell.* 6.4.16). Though Spartan women are often portrayed as being among the staunchest supporters of their husbands and sons dying in battle (and even in this passage, Xenophon adds that the families of the slain carried themselves cheerfully the day after hearing the news), there is a clear implication here that they often lamented the dead openly and vigorously. This form of private mourning seems to go against stereotypical Spartan behavior, certainly at a state level, which suggests that the interplay between public and private

[61] For this argument concerning the rise of battlefield burial in Sparta, see Kucewicz 2021a. See Nafissi 1991: 253 for the argument that votive offerings reflect this rise in self-assertion of the hoplite "damos" in Sparta over and against the elites in the 6th century.

[62] For Archaic Athenian developments, see Kucewicz 2021b, who argues that state control of the war dead began in the Archaic period and was expanded, rather than initiated, by the democracy. For the Classical period in Athens, see Arrington 2015.

involved a level of nuance and complexity. Finally, prominent military leaders erected their own monuments, especially at such Panhellenic shrines as Olympia and Delphi, taking a cue from Spartan athletic victors. While we consider the Spartan commemoration of war, we must keep in mind the range of commemorative practices and commemorators alike.

These general principles are not without debate in the modern scholarship, nor are the ancient sources, literary and material, always clear about them. Nor were all of these principles equally operative in every historical period and in every circumstance. The aim of this book is to unpack these principles, to see how things changed over time and to spot where the sources might distort things and get things wrong. I also want us to think again about how Spartan commemoration has been received by subsequent generations, including our own, and what the practical effects of that reception are.

Before going further, let us be clear about the main argument of this book, which is threefold: 1. The Spartan idea of the "beautiful death" and its attendant glory even, or especially, in the context of defeat, was fully formed in the Archaic period, well before Thermopylae. 2. By the time of the Peloponnesian War, Spartan commemoration changed markedly and started to embrace the rhetoric of altruism towards and freedom for the Greeks that characterized Athenian and other non-Spartan commemoration since at least Persian Wars. 3. This change in commemorative practice and rhetoric coincided with and even encouraged an increase in the number, duration, and cost of wars in which the Spartans took part. My conclusion, perhaps counterintuitive, is that Sparta fought more wars when it changed from emphasizing the glory of war for the individual and/ or the Spartan state, often to the detriment of sound strategy and tactics, to claiming to fight for freedom and in the service of the Greeks. Though this latter form of commemoration is much more in line with our own commemorative sensibilities, and might strike us as somehow "better," it had the effect of making war more, rather than less, likely – and might still do so today.

## A Tour of Ancient Sparta

I do not find it difficult to be inspired by Sparta and its surroundings, nor, do I think, did the ancients who went there. This might surprise some readers. In the main, Thucydides was right about the reactions to Sparta and Athens of visitors to those cities in the future – that is, us. Thucydides says that Sparta's lack of imposing monuments and its nature as a collection of villages rather than a nucleated city mean that it would appear to be half as powerful as it really was, whereas Athens' monuments would trick the visitor into thinking that Athens was twice as powerful as the real historical city (Thuc. I.10.2). Going to Sparta today is certainly a much different experience than walking the bustling, tourist-filled streets of Athens beneath the gleaming white marble edifices of the Acropolis. Modern Sparta is a modest town many orders of magnitude smaller than the metropolis of Athens with its several million people. The archaeology of Sparta is similarly humble, its most impressive monument being a theater that was used in Roman times. Many travelers to the region skip Sparta altogether in favor of the nearby Byzantine city of Mistras, one of the most spectacular sites of the Peloponnese. But for those who take the time to explore and soak in the majesty of the natural surroundings, the city of Leonidas comes to life to evoke its famous past. We will return to the modern impression of Sparta in this book's final chapter.

The Spartans never built anything on the scale or of the opulence of the Parthenon. That said, Sparta's humble stature in relation to the modern Greek nation-state's capital city was not necessarily inevitable. Athens itself was a small village for centuries and was not even the first capital of the liberated modern Greece. That honor went to the town of Nafplio, nestled beneath a gigantic Venetian fortress in the northeastern Peloponnese and still a favorite destination for tourists. Athens as a capital city was the deliberate creation of Western European powers, and its population exploded over the last century to sprawl over nearly the entire Attic plain. Modern Sparta is also largely the creation of the two centuries following the Greek War of Independence, though admittedly starting from even humbler roots. To put it bluntly, there was no modern Sparta in the 19th century. Some early travelers to the area thought Mistras, nearly ten kilometers away, was the site of ancient Sparta, since nothing else presented itself as a candidate. Modern Sparta was founded, or re-founded, in an effort to revive ancient glories for the newly independent Greek state. As Paraskevas Matalas says regarding the modern town's artificiality and the incautious zeal with which it was built, "Sparta . . . is perhaps the only example of a city that was created out of nothing at a site selected because of its ancient ruins, which were subsequently partly destroyed by the construction of the modern city."[63]

---

[63] Matalas 2017: 49. Matalas's chapter is an excellent discussion of how Sparta and its landscape affected early travelers to the region. See also Macgregor Morris 2009, who remarks that Athens attracted visitors because of its ruins, whereas Sparta did because it was empty.

Sparta's ancient prominence is perhaps enough to justify modern projects at the site aimed at generating enthusiasm for the Greek nation-state. There is, however, more than just its reputation keeping Sparta's flame alight. Sparta does contain ample ancient material, despite Matalas's concern with the archaeologically irresponsible development projects of the 19th century. Excavations have laid bare several important monuments and other finds, and a visit to the acropolis, along with other sites in and around Sparta, and its fine museum reward the curious student of history. The acropolis, though but a low hill by Athenian standards, affords a good vantage over the town, from which one cannot help but be impressed with the lush green of the Eurotas valley, especially compared to rocky and arid Attica. The imposing Taygetus mountain range, among the loftiest in Greece, separating Laconia from Messenia dominates the view, providing one explanation for why ancient Sparta did not need to bother with defensive walls – the mountains, along with its warriors, were Sparta's walls. This topographical barrier also forces one to think anew about the brutal accomplishment of Sparta's centuries-long subjugation of the Messenians living on the other side, a subject to which we will return in the next chapter.

Ancient visitors to Sparta were impressed too, none more so than the second-century CE travel writer Pausanias, who provides us with a rich description of Spartan topography and monuments (Paus. 3.11–19). Julia Hell evocatively describes Pausanias' project, undertaken when Rome ruled all that was Greece, as "a lament to the cities of the conquered," and "a kind of commemorative archaeology of Greece."[64] His work is therefore an act of commemoration in and of itself, making it the ideal place to begin our study of Sparta (Map 2).

Since he was writing many centuries after the monuments he describes were supposedly built, we must approach Pausanias' account cautiously and with full consideration given to what scientific archaeological excavation has revealed. It is not enough to do what many travelers and scholars of generations past did, namely walk the town and countryside with Pausanias in hand playing a game of find-the-monument. Not only is it often difficult to square what we see on the ground with Pausanias' text, we need to remember that Pausanias himself could have been wrong with many of his identifications. Some things that he saw are no longer there, and other archaeological treasures, such as the "Smiling Hoplite," were buried by Pausanias' time. Even if we can say with confidence that such-and-such building is the very one Pausanias describes, we must weigh his

[64] Hell 2019: 91–92.

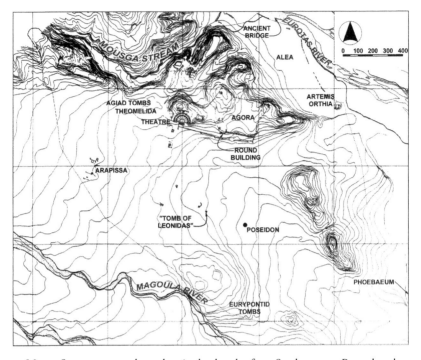

Map 2  Sparta, topography and major landmarks, from Sanders 2009. Reproduced
by permission of the British School at Athens.

description against what other evidence we have to gauge whether his
account is plausible. With these caveats in mind, let us take a walk through
Sparta and try to imagine what a Spartan of the Classical period would
have seen and experienced.[65]

In 375, our Spartan arrives in his home territory at the port of Gytheion,
forty-five kilometers south of Sparta, at the edge of the Laconian plain. It
was here that Helen absconded with Paris, leaving her husband Menelaus,
king of Sparta. The road north skirts the eastern slopes of Mount Taygetus,
rising to 2,404 meters, or 7,890 feet.[66] Mighty Olympus, far to the north

[65] What follows is inspired by Ober 2005: 17–26, who offers a similar scenario for 4th-century Athens.
Sanders 2009 provides a good critical study of Pausanias' routes through the city. Waywell 1999–
2000 offers a fulsome yet accessible overview of Sparta's topography, monuments, and excavations.
Also see Zavvou and Themis 2009 for a more recent overview of some key archaeological findings at
Sparta over the decade of excavations between 1994 and 2005.
[66] Macgregor Morris 2009: 391 remarks on the importance of this landscape to early travelers to Sparta,
calling Taygetus itself a monument.

separating Thessaly from Macedonia, is only a few hundred meters higher. On the other side of the plain rises Mount Parnon, no slouch itself at 1,935 meters, or 6,348 feet. The Spartan only grows more confident in his city's power and security, taking in the fertile Laconian plain hemmed in by mountains too high for any enemy to cross easily – not that anyone would dare enter Spartan territory. It was said that no Spartan woman, staying as she would in Sparta all her life, had ever seen the campfires of an enemy (Xen. *Hell.* 6.5.28). The Spartan knows, too, that his compatriots control the Messenian plain on the other side of Taygetus. The precipitous massif is a wall against their enemies, but no barrier to the Spartans. They had thoroughly conquered the Messenians in a series of long and brutal wars many generations ago. Two-fifths of the Peloponnese is effectively Sparta's, while much of the rest generally does Sparta's bidding. The phalanx to which our Spartan belongs makes sure of that.

Before reaching Sparta proper, the Spartan passes the village of Amyklai, part of the Lacedaemonian capital. Here the Spartans observe the ancient cult of the Hyacinthia and have a shrine to Apollo Amyklaios. The sanctuary is filled with dedications, including many spears and other weapons. Those who worship Apollo here expressed themselves as soldiers.[67] Apollo's throne, already nearly two hundred years old when our Spartan makes his way past, was one of the most elaborately decorated pieces in antiquity (Paus. 3.18–19).[68] When they wanted to be, the Archaic Lacedaemonians could be great patrons of the arts. They hired Bathycles of Magnesia to make the throne, a famous artist who fashioned on it scenes from myth, especially great battles and duels between heroes. The Spartan admires not only scenes from the mists of mythical time, but tributes to more recent triumphs too. Nearby are monumental tripods made from spoils taken long ago from the Messenians and, a mere generation before our Spartan's journey, from the Athenians at the Battle of Aegospotami. The hardy stock from which the Spartan sprang continued to produce men capable of bringing down the first Greek state, Athens, with designs on having its own empire.

From this vantage point, our Spartan can look across to the ridge running along the far side of the Eurotas River to catch a glimpse of the Menelaion, a strange ancient building constructed in several steps like a pyramid (Figure 1.1).[69] Here, at a site stretching back to the time of the Trojan War itself, the Spartans worship the hero Menelaus and his wife, Helen, who was

---

[67] For the military character of this cult, see Pavlides 2011: 58–59; and Chapter 2.
[68] For the architectural remains at the site today, and possible reconstructions, see Bilis and Magnisali 2012.
[69] For this structure, see Tomlinson 1992.

Figure 1.1 The Menelaion outside of Sparta. Author's photo.

brought back to Sparta after the fall of Troy. Our Spartan is among the many who dedicated weapons to the heroes here.[70]

As he enters the city, or what counts as a city for the Spartans, since there are no walls, he passes by numerous hero shrines, including one to the herald Talthybius from Homer's poetry. The reason the Spartans venerate this herald is because they brought about his wrath by throwing Persian heralds into a well when they had come demanding earth and water, that is, submission to the Persian Great King (Hdt. 7.133–134). The Spartans made good their sacrilege of killing the heralds, who are supposed to be inviolable, by appeasing Talthybius with a shrine and worship, and also a hereditary guild called the Talthybiadae. Our Spartan's ancestors, however, never did offer their submission to the Persians, and stood by the sentiment they expressed by murdering the king's messengers. He also sees along the roads scattered tombstones listing individual Spartans who died in war. The beautiful death was so self-evidently good that these glorious dead needed only their name and the inscription "in war" to mark themselves out as good Spartans. They alone (along with either priestesses in office or women who died in childbirth) were given the privilege of having their names written on stone. Our Spartan hopes someday to be similarly honored.

[70] For the military character of the dedications at the Menelaion, see Pavlides 2011: 45.

Figure 1.2 The "Smiling Hoplite," Archaeological Museum of Sparta. Author's photo. © Hellenic Ministry of Culture and Sports / Hellenic Organization of Cultural Resources Development.

Passing more tombs of heroes of the distant past and living memory, the Spartan comes to the agora, the center of Sparta. Here he marvels at the Stoa of the Persians, in which the Spartans lavishly display the booty they took from the Persians over a century earlier. The stoa contains images of the Spartans' enemies, including Mardonius, general of the Persians, and Artemisia, the Greek queen of Halicarnassus and an admiral in Xerxes' fleet. The Athenians also depicted real figures who fought in the Persian Wars in the Painted Stoa, or Stoa Poikile, in their Agora. The Spartans were at the forefront of Greeks using sculptural and other artistic decorations to depict themselves and their enemies in victory monuments. The pedimental sculptures showing scenes from the Trojan War from the Temple of Aphaia on Aegina are a famous example of this use of sculpture, and might have influenced the Stoa of the Persians in Sparta as well as other sculptures, such as the "Smiling Hoplite" (Figure 1.2).[71] The stoa, its origins, and its images inspire our Spartan to leave a Sparta not lesser

[71] For the date of the Aegina sculptures, which likely came before the "Smiling Hoplite," and their relationship to the Persian Wars and influence on the Classical style, see Stewart 2008a and 2008b. Dissenting from the majority of earlier opinions, Stewart convincingly argues that the Aegina pediments come after the Persian Wars and were part of that conflict's commemoration.

than the one his ancestors passed on to their descendants. Walking to the west of the agora, he continues up the slope towards Sparta's acropolis. On the way, he regards the cenotaph of Brasidas, who took the war to the Athenians by liberating cities all along the north Aegean. Brasidas led his men by example, charging against his Athenian enemy boldly (Figure 1.3). He was struck down in the fight but did not perish until he learned of his victory. His remains are in Amphipolis, where he is worshipped as a hero. He also has a treasury building dedicated to him at Delphi, an honor few Spartans before him would have dared to want.

The Spartan next passes the tombs of Leonidas, who gave his life for glory at Thermopylae and whose remains were allegedly repatriated around 440 BCE, and Pausanias, who as regent drove the Persians from Greece once and for all at Plataea (Figure 1.4). Statues of these men, in gleaming marble and shining bronze, inspire emulation. Hard by these tombs is a list of the Three Hundred, those most glorious of all Spartans, to whom every later Spartan must live up. As he makes his way to the sanctuary of Athena Chalkioikos, Athena of the "Bronze House," where the regent Pausanias had been shut in after he became too friendly with the Persians despite his earlier heroism, our Spartan examines monuments to Spartan athletic

Figure 1.3 The "Round Building" on the acropolis of Sparta. Author's photo.

Figure 1.4 The "Leonidaion" or "Tomb of Leonidas" in Sparta. Author's photo.

victors, advertising the athletes' renown alongside Sparta's military champions.[72] Among these monuments is a slender *stele* detailing the prodigious collection of victories amassed by Damonon and his son Enymakratidas throughout their matchless careers on the festival circuit.[73] Seeing Damonon's enviable distinctions, our Spartan recalls how Brasidas was honored by those he liberated as if he were a victorious athlete. Those who win glory on the racetrack and hippodrome are prone to win glory in war too.

From the acropolis, he can look down on the sanctuary of Artemis Orthia, where he dedicated small lead figurine images of hoplites, and where as a boy he partook in competitions to steal cheeses from the goddess's altar, proving his craftiness, which he would later use against his enemies on the battlefield. He can also see the flat ground where the choruses perform in the Gymnopaidiai festival in remembrance of Spartans' wars against the Argives, their archrivals in the Peloponnese.

---

[72] For the connection between military and athletic monuments at Sparta, see Low 2011: 14–15. See also Christesen 2019, who discusses the importance of athletics for Spartan society, especially since the Spartans did not often fight wars and thus turned to athletic honors as a substitute for military ones.
[73] Christesen 2019 is a full account of the Damonon Stele, which is now on display in the Archaeological Museum of Sparta, close to the "Smiling Hoplite."

He long ago committed to memory the verses of the poets giving instruc-
tion on how to fight, and why fighting is the way to win fame.[74]

Everywhere he turns, the Spartan encounters monuments to Sparta's
wars, its war leaders, and the cults that inspire military activity and receive
military dedications. He has interacted with these commemorative spaces
and participated in these commemorative rituals all his life. Sparta's
memories of war are ingrained in him, as in every other Spartan living
his whole life as if on campaign, on constant war footing. Within a few
years, in 371, the Spartan phalanx was defeated decisively by the Thebans at
Leuctra. If our Spartan survived that clash of arms, he would have lived to
see Laconia itself invaded in the winter of 370–369, the helots liberated,
and Messenia torn out of Sparta's grasp. If anything, these traumatic events
only caused the Spartans to double-down on their acts of remembrance. To
avoid the stigma of being among the "tremblers" after Leuctra, when
family members of the survivors hid themselves in shame, our Spartan
might have taken his own life. He also might have looked for the next
opportunity to throw himself recklessly against an enemy formation to die
in a premeditated act of recompense, just as one of his disgraced forebears
did when they failed to die with the rest of the Three Hundred at
Thermopylae (Hdt. 7.229–232).[75]

In the pages that follow, we will explore how the commemoration of war in
which our Spartan was steeped changed over time, differed from the practices
of other Greeks, and both reflected and shaped the Spartans' ideas about war.
The Spartans, like other ancient Greeks, believed that memory was one of the
most important elements of society and culture. How, what, and why they
remembered war is therefore fundamental to our understanding of the
Spartans, the ancient Greeks, and, I believe, ourselves.

---

[74] For more on these cults, see Chapter 2.
[75] Luraghi 2008: 209–248 discusses the forming and strengthening of national and ethnic identities
after the liberation of Messenia.

# *Warrior Poets*

## Introduction

If reliable sources for Classical Sparta are few and far between, Archaic Sparta – the polis as it was before the Persian Wars – is shrouded in even deeper mystery. Because the Spartans were so successful at promoting a carefully curated brand, part of which was the endurance and consistency of Spartan systems and values, it is difficult to detect, virtually by design, how Spartan commemoration began and how it changed. But there are some clues and some fascinating ancient texts to guide us in our study.

The verses of Tyrtaeus are the most important source for Archaic Spartan commemoration. That rarest of breeds, a Spartan poet, Tyrtaeus wrote about the importance of standing one's ground in the din of battle, the value to the community of its warriors taking up arms, and the commemorative rewards awaiting the brave, along with the shame and deprivation promised for the cowardly.[1] Foundational as Tyrtaeus is for Sparta's self-perception and self-promotion, his ideas of courage and the relationship between the warrior and the state betray important differences from later Spartan propaganda and praxis. Before we get to Tyrtaeus, however, we should first consider the attitudes of Homer's heroes to war. Homer stood as the most important guide for later Greek warriors and writers alike, including Tyrtaeus himself.

Sparta's relations with its fellow Greeks, both near and far, during the Archaic period provide other vital glimpses of Spartan ideas about war. Tyrtaeus was supposedly writing during one of a series of wars Sparta fought with its Messenian neighbors. While the wars were a close-run thing at certain points, inspiring Tyrtaeus' drive to recruit more soldiers, the result of the wars was the total subjugation of Messenia to Spartan control,

---

[1] "Rarest of breeds" only in our imagination, however. As Jessica Romney has reminded me, Sparta had two known poets from the Archaic period whose work has survived, Tyrtaeus and Alcman, while Athens had only one, Solon.

and the development of helotage. While the helots, Sparta's state-owned serfs, many of whom were Messenians, provided the agricultural backbone of Spartan society and allowed (or forced?) most Spartan citizens to train continually for war, they also posed a looming threat of revolution and kept the paranoid Spartans in arms. Classical sources attribute Sparta's traditional isolationism and militarism to a pervasive fear of a helot upris- ing. Drumming up the will to fight in the Messenian Wars and justifying a constant war footing to keep the Messenians in line had important consequences for Spartan commemoration.

Despite typically sticking close to Laconia, the Spartans had a special relationship in the Archaic period with Samos, an island on the other side of the Aegean Sea, just a few hundred meters off the coast of modern Turkey. These ties led the Spartans to engage in some foreign intervention on Samos, and also promoted a vibrant trading relationship between the two peoples. At the famed sanctuary of Hera on Samos, many works of Laconian artistry were found by excavators and are now on display in Samos' museums. Several of these votive offerings represent soldiers and other military figures, which prompts us to ask how Spartan military imagery figured in the worship of Hera across the sea. Were these pieces dedicated by Samians who developed a fascination for the Spartan warrior, or did Spartans visiting Samos give these offerings as a commemoration of their own warrior status?

Finally, we will consider the origins and purpose of a selection of Spartan cult activities. For nearly every society, religious rituals serve a vital military function, shaping how the community views and commem- orates war. The Gymnopaidiai was one of Sparta's most important festivals and one intimately linked with warfare and the ideology of the warrior. The antiquity and longevity of the Spartan Gymnopaidiai attest to its centrality in Spartan commemoration.

## Homeric Heroes

The Battle of Thermopylae in 480, in which the legendary Three Hundred made their glorious but doomed stand against Xerxes' Persian army, is without question one of the formative events of Sparta identity. Thucydides' account of the Battle of Pylos, which took place fifty-five years later, emphasizes the shock to the Greek world of nearly 300 Lacedaemonians surrendering to the Athenians. How could these captured soldiers be of the same stock as those who fought to the death against the

Persians (Thuc. 4.40)?[2] We will return to Thermopylae and its commemoration in the next chapter, but for now we must investigate how the Spartans commemorated war before that battle. The evidence, paltry as it may be, opens up the possibility that Thermopylae's influence might be overblown.

To understand the Spartan mindset as the mainland Greeks faced the might of the Persian Empire, we must start with the ultimate exemplar of the Greek warrior: Homer's heroes. The warriors at Troy fought primarily for personal honor, fame, and glory, *timē*, *kleos*, and *kudos*, respectively, with surprisingly little thought for the good of their country or their compatriots. There is more of this spirit of glory-seeking animating the Spartans at Thermopylae than later ancient sources and modern studies of this battle take into account.

The character arc of the *Iliad*'s protagonist, Achilles, is more nuanced than many readers grasp on their first encounter with the epic. He initially quits the conflict and prays for the success of the other side because the Greek coalition leader, Agamemnon, has stripped him of his war prize – the girl Briseis, captured and enslaved by the Greeks – and thus the recognition he deserves before his fellow Greeks. Achilles returns to the conflict only to avenge the death of his companion, Patroclus, at the hands of the Trojan Hector. Thus, Achilles reenters the fray because of grief for Patroclus and a desire to kill Hector, not in order (or not merely) to gain fame and recognition and the prizes that signify such things. In fact, he even spurns Agamemnon's desperate offer to return Briseis and add heaps of treasure besides, since Achilles has, it seems, transcended the standard heroic code and the hero's motivations to fight.

Yet, in the initial conflict with Agamemnon, that which sparks Achilles' wrath, the *mēnis* that stands as the very first word in Greek literature, Achilles clarifies why he came to Troy (Hom. *Il.* 1.148–171): not because the Trojans ever did him any harm but so Agamemnon and his brother Menelaus might take back their honor from the Trojans. In return, Achilles expects the prizes, *geras*, due to him as a great warrior, even if they are not quite the choice spoils Agamemnon reserves for himself as leader of the most men (even if he is not the best soldier on the battlefield). Since Achilles has been dishonored (*atimos*) by the loss of his prize, that which had assured him of a revered status, he threatens to return home instead of piling up more goods for Agamemnon without benefit to himself. Achilles then commits what we today would consider treason.

---

[2] For more on the Battle of Pylos and comparisons to Thermopylae, see Chapter 4.

He goes off sulking to his mother, the sea goddess Thetis, and asks her to implore Zeus to let the Trojans win so Agamemnon and the Greeks are made to feel the full effect of their slight. Thetis is horrified not by her son's request but by the treatment he has received, and duly complains to Zeus. Since Achilles is fated to die young, he was supposed to obtain great glory, Thetis argues to the ruler of the gods. Zeus assents and agrees to bolster the Trojans' attacks on the Greeks, guaranteeing that many Greek soldiers will die to assuage Achilles' dishonor. Even if Agamemnon acted arrogantly – which he certainly did – it is difficult for us to empathize with Achilles' response. In fact, his murderous designs against his own fellow soldiers and their cause at Troy strike many of us as monstrous, hardly the stuff of a hero to be emulated. The Greeks, though, did consider Achilles and his single-minded pursuit of recognition, even at the expense of the Greek expedition and the lives of his friends, to be a paradigm of heroism.[3]

Another character in the *Iliad*, with whom readers have less trouble, is Hector, the greatest warrior among the Trojans. Unlike Achilles, who fights or wills his friends to die for the sake of his own glory, Hector apparently fights to defend his home, people, and family. For this reason, and also because the *Iliad* concludes with Hector's funeral at Troy, it is tempting to see Hector, not Achilles, as the truly great character of the epic. We can all relate to Hector's selfless service for Troy, or at least we would like to think we can relate to it. Defending the vulnerable against an implacable foe is just about the most noble reason one could think of to go to war. Modern democracies, for example, tend to call their war ministries "defense departments," or something similar. Yes, Hector happened to be on the defensive side in the Trojan War, and he was fighting in front of his home and before the eyes of his family members (whereas the Greeks had sailed many miles from their homes and families), but his motivation for fighting was remarkably similar to Achilles'.

In the sixth book of the *Iliad*, we witness one of the most moving scenes in the whole poem, the encounter between Hector and his wife, Andromache. Andromache is with their infant son, Astyanax, who shrinks in fear from the sight of his father in his combat gear, until Hector removes his helmet. Before Hector returns to the battlefield, Andromache implores

---

[3] For the important topic of manhood and heroism in Homeric poetry, see Graziosi and Haubold 2003; and Clarke 2004. These studies complicate the picture of ideal manhood presented by the poems, suggesting that comradely solidarity was also an important part of manhood, and that heroism has to be worked out in light of human fragility and uncertainty in a world with uncaring and amoral gods. See Chapter 3 for Achilles recalled explicitly by the "New Simonides" in the context of the Spartans (at Plataea? Thermopylae?).

her husband to stay out of the fight, to prevent her and her son from losing their protector and facing the terrifying prospect of slavery. Andromache's fears lay bare the horrifying realities of ancient warfare for women and other noncombatants, and her story would be taken up by Attic tragedians to sobering effect centuries later. Hector's response to his wife is nearly as chilling as Achilles' to Agamemnon. He says that he would feel shame (*aidōs*) in front of the Trojan men and woman if he skulked away from battle. Even more than that, he is a good warrior who always fights in the front rank, among the *promachoi*, and wins fame (*kleos*) for his father, Priam, and for himself. He then says that he knows in his heart that Troy is doomed, along with his family. His defense is therefore futile, but he will fight anyway to avoid shame and win glory, even if it does nothing to ward off the "day of slavery" for Andromache and Astyanax.[4]

In Book 22, while Hector waits outside the walls of the city in order to fight a berserker Achilles who has just slain innumerable men on his way to Patroclus' killer, Hector's parents, Priam and Hecuba, beg their son to return to safety. He stands no chance against Achilles, and his death will only hasten the destruction of Troy, the shameful death of Priam, and the enslavement of Hecuba and the other women and children. Hector does not give in to the pleas of his parents, since he would feel shame (*aidōs*) in front of the Trojans for having refused earlier to lead his soldiers back into the walls in the face of Achilles' unstoppable fury. No, Hector reasons, instead of facing the taunts of lesser men, it would be better to stay and fight. Perhaps he will kill Achilles. At the very least, he will die gloriously (*eukleiōs*) in front of Troy's walls. Hector's sense of shame and desire for *kleos* outweighs the pitiable pleas of his closest family. So much for this stalwart and selfless defender.[5] Hector of course is slain by the hand of Achilles, signaling Troy's approaching doom – and the doom of Achilles too. Though killed as young men in battle, both men are famous enough to be household names today. They certainly gained personal

---

[4] Some have interpreted shame in the Homeric epics as purely defensive, or in response to a challenge, rather than an impetus to glorious deeds in its own right. Warriors, for example, are driven by shame to recover the bodies of their dead comrades, despite the danger to their personal safety. See van Wees 1996: 22–23; Kucewicz 2021b: 26, 188n56. As Hector's case shows, however, shame can indeed be an incitement to personal glory, *even if* it is both dangerous to a warrior's own safety *and* detrimental to the defense and protection of a warrior's home and family.

[5] For a discussion and further bibliography for Hector's thought process in Book 22, and how important this passage is for ideas of ancient Greece as a shame culture, see de Jong 2012: 80–84. For more on Hector and shame, including a discussion of the meeting between Hector and Andromache, see Cairns 1993: 79–83. P. A. L. Greenhalgh 1972 argued that there was a great deal of patriotism in the Homeric world, especially for one's own home, and this patriotism is indistinguishable from that demonstrated in later poets such as Tyrtaeus. As I hope to show, I think there is rather quite a bit of difference between Homer's heroes and Tyrtaeus' audience.

*kleos*. In Hector's case, although his pursuit of glory and fame did nothing to prevent his city and family coming to ruin, Troy and Priam, and Andromache and Astyanax too, were themselves made more famous by their association with Hector. No matter that Priam and Andromache would have preferred that Hector lived, even with the attendant shame in front of his fellow Trojans.

While Achilles was pursuing Hector around the walls, he repeatedly gestured with his head to prevent any other Greek from bringing down the Trojan prince with an arrow or a spear. Achilles feared that one of his comrades would win the glory, the *kudos*, by landing the decisive blow, and he himself would come in second place (Hom. *Il.* 22.205–207). If the goal was to rid the Greeks of the threat posed by Hector, a very reasonable goal given the destruction Hector had wrought throughout the Greek ranks, Achilles should have welcomed an assisting missile. Of course, the death of Hector was not the goal at all, or, at least, not the main goal. Achilles wanted to vent his rage on the Trojan for the death of Patroclus, but in that moment he wanted most to claim the glory of killing Troy's best warrior in full view of both armies.

Many of us today find the pursuit of honor, glory, and fame, and the avoidance of shame, to be unpalatable reasons for killing and dying in war. Even if we express more solidarity with fellow soldiers than Achilles did, bringing glory to our predecessors and our country is similarly frowned upon, at least as the *primary* motivation for fighting. We prefer to say that we go to war "to stop Hitler," or "to free the Afghans from theocratic oppression," or "to defend the weak from the powerful." During and after the Persian Wars, most Greek poleis phrased their stand against the Persians in similar terms. They fought to ensure that the Greeks remained free, and to defend their homes, families, and shrines from a foreign aggressor. Sparked by the Persian Wars, the dichotomy between freedom and slavery would become ever more important throughout the rest of the 5th century and in subsequent eras. Even the Roman proconsul Titus Flamininus declared at the Isthmian Games in 196 BCE that he had come to ensure the "freedom of the Greeks" from the Macedonians, carefully deploying rhetoric that could be traced back to the resistance to Xerxes' invasion. For their part, the Spartans paid little attention to this rhetorical turn, at least at first, and instead held on to the ideals espoused by Achilles and Hector. As we will see in the next chapter, whether or not the Athenians abused their position after the Persian Wars (they did), most students of history, like most other Greek poleis, are much more comfortable with the Athenian image of fighting for freedom for themselves and others than they are with the Spartan pursuit of *kleo*s.

## Tyrtaeus: Sparta's Own War Poet

Jean-Pierre Vernant drew from Homeric poetry the notion of "*la belle mort*," or "the beautiful death."[6] His student, Nicole Loraux, turned the focus to "*la belle mort Spartiate*." Her work has informed nearly all discussion of the topic since it was published in 1977. Dying in the front lines after suffering many wounds in service of the city was the ultimate source of glory for the Spartans. This, for Loraux, was the message of the 7th-century Spartan poet Tyrtaeus. Loraux rightly turns to this Archaic Spartan poet in lieu of Athenian or pro-Athenian sources like Herodotus that seem to disparage the Spartans' lack of deliberation and mindless obedience in the pursuit of the beautiful death.[7] Jessica Romney has recently discussed the important ways Tyrtaeus' poetry reflects and constructs the social identity of those living in Sparta. Tyrtaeus' martial poetry is thus a vital source for understanding Archaic Sparta, for the beautiful death, but also for a host of other important social and cultural norms.[8] If you are surprised that Sparta produced a famous poet, you are not alone. A Spartan poet is such an incongruous concept that the Athenians concocted a story that made Tyrtaeus into an Athenian poet whom the Athenians sent to Sparta. Whether they were trying to take credit for Tyrtaeus' verses themselves, or simply did not believe that a Spartan poet could write so well, the Athenians surely invented their version of events.[9]

Despite what Tyrtaeus composed in the 7th century, recent studies of the Spartan beautiful death focus on Thermopylae as an important pivot point in Spartan thinking on war. Andrew Scott has analyzed the Spartan apophthegms, or "pithy sayings," collected by Plutarch to argue that the 5th century, particularly after Thermopylae, was the period in which the Spartan ideal of dying in one's place in the line was formed.[10] Matthew Trundle argues that it was the experience of Thermopylae, and its largely invented account, that led to Spartan women saying things like "with this or on this" to their sons – that is, come back with your shield because you won, or carried on your shield because you fought to the death.[11] But, as

---

[6] Vernant 1991 focuses on the Homeric beautiful death, but also how Homer influenced later poetry, like that of the Spartan Tyrtaeus.

[7] Loraux 1977: 107. For the contrast between Spartan and Athenian courage, with a focus on the supposed centrality of deliberation of the latter, see Balot 2014, especially chapter 3.

[8] Romney 2020: 47–88. For the importance of Tyrtaeus on the formation of Spartan identity and even several institutions, see also Meier 1998, especially 229–324.

[9] For the Athenian version, see Plat. *Laws* 1.629a; Lyc. 1.106; Paus. 4.15.3. Fisher 1994: 362–364 provides a good overview of the issue, coming down firmly on the side of Athens' making the whole thing up.

[10] Scott 2015; 2017.   [11] Trundle 2018: 151.

Loraux recognized, these ideas were already fully formed in Tyrtaeus'
poetry, and as we will see, some other pieces of evidence point to
a beautiful death being a supreme Spartan ideal in the Archaic period, at
least several decades before Xerxes invaded mainland Greece.

Courageously dying for one's country and putting the good of the
community above one's own life are virtues celebrated across many cultures and eras, representing a nearly universal human value. It is worth
looking at a selection of Tyrtaeus' poems in detail to determine whether
there is anything uniquely Spartan in them. If the most famous Spartan
ideas about war, especially the beautiful death and its commemoration, can
be found in Tyrtaeus, it is important to consider next how those values
changed over time, and what the causes and consequences of those changes
were. Tracking those changes is, indeed, a central theme of this book.

Let us consider that famous aphorism named by Matthew Trundle as
the kind of sentiment enabled by Thermopylae. In Plutarch's telling,
a Spartan mother exhorted her son going off to war in typically Laconic
fashion: "Child, either this or on this," while handing him his shield.[12] The
imperative of victory or death implied by this phrase is not, however, a new
idea of the 5th century. The famous poet Archilochus, writing in the 7th
century, appears to mock this very ideal in a famous lyric: "Some Saian
delights in my shield, a faultless item, which I unwillingly left in a bush.
But I saved myself. What do I care about that shield? To hell with it. I'll get
another one just as good."[13] Archilochus, a poet living on the islands of
Paros and Thasos, and flourishing nearly two centuries before
Thermopylae, calls into question this notion of military virtue, which
tells us that holding on to your shield at all costs was a *Greek*, rather than
strictly Spartan, ideal, and one that predates the Persian Wars by a lot.[14]
Plutarch, we should note, says that the Spartans banned Archilochus from
their city because of this poem – likely an apocryphal story, but tantalizing
nonetheless (*Inst.* 34).

---

[12] Plut. *Mor.* 241f: "τέκνον" ἔφη "ἢ ταύταν ἢ ἐπὶ ταύτας."

[13] = F 5 W: ἀσπίδι μὲν Σαΐων τις ἀγάλλεται, ἣν παρὰ θάμνῳ | ἔντος ἀμώμητον κάλλιπον οὐκ ἐθέλων· | αὐτὸν δ' ἔκ μ' ἐσάωσα: τί μοι μέλει ἀσπὶς ἐκείνη; | ἐρρέτω: ἐξαῦτις κτήσομαι οὐ κακίω. Unless otherwise stated, all translations in this book are my own.

[14] For the scholarly interpretation of this poem, see Anderson 2008, who suggests, against the majority opinion, that Archilochus is not mocking heroism or proclaiming himself a coward, but instead calls to mind the vicissitudes of combat. Even if we accept Anderson's softening of Archilochus' intention – and I am not entirely convinced by his intriguing arguments – the *ideal* of keeping one's shield is still implied by the poem. Archilochus was not always so iconoclastic. Many of his other verses, such as F 3 supposedly describing the Lelantine War, contain standard treatments of war, battle, and soldiers.

Archilochus might define the Archaic Greek military ideal by its opposite, but there are important positive portrayals of it too, namely by Archilochus' 7th-century contemporaries Callinus of Ephesus and Tyrtaeus of Sparta. Callinus has only one substantial fragment to his name, and it is worth translating it here in its entirety:

> How long will you lie around? When will you bear a stout heart,
> Young men? Aren't you ashamed in front of you neighbors
> To slack off like this? Do you think it a good idea in peace
> To sit, while war grips the whole land?
>
> ... And let everyone hurl a javelin one last time as they die.
> For it is honorable and glorious for a man to fight
> For his country, his children, and his wedded wife
> Against his enemies; and death then will come whenever
> The Fates allot it. But let a man go straight ahead
> Brandishing spear and covering stout heart beneath shield
> As soon as war is mingled.
> For a man can in no way escape his fated death,
> Not even if he is born from immortal stock.
> Often escaping battle and the clang of javelins
> He comes and meets the fate of death at home;
> But the one man is not dear to nor regretted by the people,
> While small and great alike bewail the other man if he suffers anything.
> Grief for the brave-hearted man strikes the whole host
> If he dies, and if he lives he is compared to the demigods;
> For they look upon him with their eyes as if he were a tower,
> Since he alone does deeds worthy of many men.[15]

[15] = F 1:

μέχρις τεῦ κατάκεισθε; κότ' ἄλκιμον ἕξετε θυμόν,
  ὦ νέοι; οὐδ' αἰδεῖσθ' ἀμφιπερικτίονας
ὧδε λίην μεθιέντες; ἐν εἰρήνῃ δὲ δοκεῖτε
  ἦσθαι, ἀτὰρ πόλεμος γαῖαν ἅπασαν ἔχει;
... καί τις ἀποθνῄσκων ὕστατ' ἀκοντισάτω.
τιμῆέν τε γάρ ἐστι καὶ ἀγλαὸν ἀνδρὶ μάχεσθαι
  γῆς πέρι καὶ παίδων κουριδίης τ' ἀλόχου
δυσμενέσιν· θάνατος δὲ τότ' ἔσσεται, ὁππότε κεν δὴ
  Μοῖραι ἐπικλώσωσ'· ἀλλά τις ἰθὺς ἴτω
ἔγχος ἀνασχόμενος καὶ ὑπ' ἀσπίδος ἄλκιμον ἦτορ
  ἔλσας τὸ πρῶτον μειγνυμένου πολέμου·
οὐ γάρ κως θάνατόν γε φυγεῖν εἱμαρμένον ἐστὶν
  ἄνδρ', οὐδ' εἰ προγόνων ᾖ γένος ἀθανάτων.
πολλάκι δηϊοτῆτα φυγὼν καὶ δοῦπον ἀκόντων
  ἔρχεται, ἐν δ' οἴκῳ μοῖρα κίχεν θανάτου·
ἀλλ' ὁ μὲν οὐκ ἔμπης δήμῳ φίλος οὐδὲ ποθεινός,
  τὸν δ' ὀλίγος στενάχει καὶ μέγας, ἤν τι πάθῃ.

Tyrtaeus has many more fragments to his name, and we will discuss several of them here. The one that most bears comparison with the lines of Callinus is Fragment 10 W.[16] Since this poem is so important to this study and to our understanding of Greek and Spartan ideas about war in general, I will translate the whole thing:

It is a fine thing to die, falling in the front ranks,
A brave man battling for his country.
But to leave his city and its rich fields
To go begging is the most grievous of all,
Wandering with his dear mother and aged father,
With small children and wedded wife.
For he will be hateful to all he comes upon, whomever he reaches
While given over to want and loathsome poverty;
He shames his people and reproaches his shining beauty;
All evil and dishonor follows him.
So, if regard for a wandering man thus strikes no one,
Nor shame, nor respect, nor pity,
Let us fight with spirit for this land, and for our children
Let us die, not sparing our lives.
Young men, fight standing next to one another,
Do not begin shameful flight, nor be afraid,
But make the heart in your chest great and stout,
And do not cling to your life as you fight with men.
The older men, whose knees are no longer agile,
Do not leave them fallen, running away yourself;
For this is shameful, fallen among the front ranks,
That an older man dies before the younger,
With a white head and gray beard,
Breathing out his stout spirit in the dust,
Holding his bloody genitals in his own hands –
Indeed, it causes resentment to see these shameful things with the eyes –
His flesh naked. But to a young man everything is fitting,
So long as he has the shining flower of lovely youth;
He is wondrous for men to behold, and an object of desire for women,
While he lives, and noble when he falls among the front ranks.

---

λαῷ γὰρ σύμπαντι πόθος κρατερόφρονος ἀνδρὸς
θνῄσκοντος, ζώων δ᾿ ἄξιος ἡμιθέων·
ὥσπερ γὰρ πύργον μιν ἐν ὀφθαλμοῖσιν ὁρῶσιν·
ἔρδει γὰρ πολλῶν ἄξια μοῦνος ἐών.

The "W" in the fragment number stands for West 1992, whose edition of the Greek text of Tyrtaeus is the one used here.

[16] For a detailed comparison of these two poems, see Adkins 1977.

Thus let a man remain firm with legs apart, and both feet
Fixed upon the ground, biting his lip with his teeth.[17]

These are some of the best-known and most influential lines in Greek poetry, and we will consider them again in the book's epilogue.

Tyrtaeus, like Callinus, warns against the shame of avoiding war. Both poets provide the example of standing firm to which Archilochus furnishes the exception that proves the rule. In addition to offering some specific tactical advice – Callinus exhorting the dying man to hurl his weapon one more time, Tyrtaeus describing an effective battle posture – these poets speak of the benefits that accrue to the brave warrior, in life and in death. The warrior who comes through battle unscathed is admired by all, looked to as a tower in Callinus' reckoning, and sexually desired by women according to Tyrtaeus. The gloriously dead warrior is accounted as a demigod, a hero like Achilles, and judged to be *kalos*, or noble, the highest aspiration for a Greek

---

[17] = F 10 W:

τεθνάμεναι γὰρ καλὸν ἐνὶ προμάχοισι πεσόντα
　　ἄνδρ᾽ ἀγαθὸν περὶ ᾗ πατρίδι μαρνάμενον.
τὴν δ᾽ αὐτοῦ προλιπόντα πόλιν καὶ πίονας ἀγροὺς
　　πτωχεύειν πάντων ἔστ᾽ ἀνιηρότατον,
πλαζόμενον σὺν μητρὶ φίλῃ καὶ πατρὶ γέροντι
　　παισί τε σὺν μικροῖς κουριδίῃ τ᾽ ἀλόχῳ.
ἐχθρὸς μὲν γὰρ τοῖσι μετέσσεται, οὕς κεν ἵκηται
　　χρησμοσύνῃ τ᾽ εἴκων καὶ στυγερῇ πενίῃ,
αἰσχύνει τε γένος, κατὰ δ᾽ ἀγλαὸν εἶδος ἐλέγχει,
　　πᾶσα δ᾽ ἀτιμίη καὶ κακότης ἕπεται.
εἰ δέ τοι οὕτως ἀνδρὸς ἀλωμένου οὐδεμί᾽ ὤρη
　　γίγνεται οὔτ᾽ αἰδὼς οὔτ᾽ ὄπις οὔτ᾽ ἔλεος,
θυμῷ γῆς περὶ τῆσδε μαχώμεθα καὶ περὶ παίδων
　　θνήσκωμεν ψυχέων μηκέτι φειδόμενοι.
ὦ νέοι, ἀλλὰ μάχεσθε παρ᾽ ἀλλήλοισι μένοντες,
　　μηδὲ φυγῆς αἰσχρᾶς ἄρχετε μηδὲ φόβου,
ἀλλὰ μέγαν ποιεῖσθε καὶ ἄλκιμον ἐν φρεσὶ θυμόν,
　　μηδὲ φιλοψυχεῖτ᾽ ἀνδράσι μαρνάμενοι·
τοὺς δὲ παλαιοτέρους, ὧν οὐκέτι γούνατ᾽ ἐλαφρά,
　　μὴ καταλείποντες φεύγετε γηπετέας·
αἰσχρὸν γὰρ δὴ τοῦτο, μετὰ προμάχοισι πεσόντα
　　κεῖσθαι πρόσθε νέων ἄνδρα παλαιότερον,
ἤδη λευκὸν ἔχοντα κάρη πολιόν τε γένειον,
　　θυμὸν ἀποπνείοντ᾽ ἄλκιμον ἐν κονίῃ,
αἱματόεντ᾽ αἰδοῖα φίλαις ἐν χερσὶν ἔχοντα – αἰσχρὰ
　　τά γ᾽ ὀφθαλμοῖς καὶ νεμεσητὸν ἰδεῖν – καὶ
χρόα γυμνωθέντα· νέῳ δέ τε πάντ᾽ ἐπέοικεν
　　ὄφρ᾽ ἐρατῆς ἥβης ἀγλαὸν ἄνθος ἔχῃ·
ἀνδράσι μὲν θηητὸς ἰδεῖν, ἐρατὸς δὲ γυναιξίν,
　　ζωὸς ἐών, καλὸς δ᾽ ἐν προμάχοισι πεσών.
ἀλλά τις εὖ διαβὰς μενέτω ποσὶν ἀμφοτέροισιν
　　στηριχθεὶς ἐπὶ γῆς, χεῖλος ὀδοῦσι δακών.

man. Tyrtaeus adds a sterner warning about the effects of fleeing war. Callinus says that a man who dies of natural causes at home is not lamented by anyone, but Tyrtaeus paints a terrifying picture of a man wandering with his family, without country, dignity, or resources; scorned by all. Both authors point to the shame, *aischron*, that accompanies shirking from battle, while only Tyrtaeus details the practical and material consequences. Dying in battle is a good thing. Surviving through laziness or cowardice is not only a bad and shameful thing but it utterly ruins a man. Archilochus might have thought such notions were overblown. There is every reason to think that, with respect to this opinion, he was in the minority.

There is some debate whether these 7th-century poets reflect a worldview similar to Homer's, especially as found in the *Iliad*, that essential guide to Greek life and values.[18] One of the most effective discussions of this question is found in Joachim Latacz's 1977 study of Homeric warfare as reflected in the poetry of Callinus and Tyrtaeus. Where many of his predecessors argue that Homeric warriors fight solely for honor, while the 7th-century exhortations describe a great deal of selfless patriotism, Latacz points out that Homeric warriors can fight with patriotic motives too, especially if we consider the Trojan perspective.[19] Latacz goes so far as to argue that Callinus and Tyrtaeus not only convey the same values as Homer, they even do so in the context of warfare virtually identical to Homer's, even on a tactical level. This thesis goes too far, in my opinion, since I think Homer's warfare contains more of the Bronze Age than some scholars will admit, and that the 7th-century poets are speaking in and to a considerably different society than that found in the *Iliad*.[20] These later poets, however, do demonstrate that some important Homeric ideals held sway on the real battlefields of the 7th century, among the Spartans, to be sure, but in the armies of other Greeks besides.

One section of the Tyrtaeus poem especially evokes the *Iliad*. Where Tyrtaeus says that it is unseemly for an old man to die a gruesome death in battle, but that it is entirely appropriate, even beautiful, for a young man to

---

[18] For scholarly approaches to the martial exhortation elegy of the type represented by Callinus and Tyrtaeus, and its relationship to Homer and other genres, see Irwin 2005: 19–34.

[19] Latacz 1977, especially 1–20. Latacz is responding especially to Snell 1969: 21–26, who argues that, while Tyrtaeus uses Homeric diction and vocabulary, his emphasis of the warrior's patriotism represents an advance over Homer's heroes.

[20] Once upon a time, I thought it a good idea to wade into the treacherous waters of scholarship on Homeric warfare (Sears 2010). I agree with Latacz that Homeric warfare is internally consistent and contains many elements of massed combat of the sort the later poets appear to describe, but this is due to the skill of certain elite units in the *Iliad* rather than the full-scale deployment of an Archaic hoplite phalanx.

do so, he nearly quotes lines from king Priam's plea to his son, Hector, in *Iliad* 22.71–76:

> For a young man all things are fitting,
> Killed by war, sliced apart by sharp bronze,
> To lie there. Everything is fine for him, even though he is
>   dead, whatever appears.
> But when the gray head and gray beard
> And genitals of a slain old man dogs defile,
> This is the most pathetic thing for wretched mortals.[21]

Jean-Pierre Vernant, in his exploration of the beautiful death in Homer, compares this passage to Tyrtaeus' – and the latter certainly meant for the two to be compared – in order to comment on the beauty, even physical beauty, of the corpse of a young man killed while fighting nobly.[22] William Brockliss departs somewhat from Vernant's analysis by arguing that Homer seems to imply ethical beauty, rather than physical, whereas Tyrtaeus riffs with Homeric themes and language to shift the emphasis to physical beauty.[23] Even so, whether noble deeds, or beautiful bodies, or both, take precedence, both authors encourage the young to embrace a glorious death in combat, for themselves but also to spare the aged, those less fit for the battlefield. In the next chapter we will have occasion to see how some of these Homeric ideals were operative in the historical Spartan army, especially during the Persian Wars.

Tyrtaeus' next fragment (F 11 W) focuses on the proper tactical formation for Spartan warriors. Fighting shoulder-to-shoulder and keeping one's place in line is an effective way to fight, argues Tyrtaeus. Turning to flee and receiving a wound in the back is not only shameful (*aischron*) but it also leads to more of one's fellow soldiers dying. This poem is a standard reference for those wishing to reconstruct the tactics of the Archaic phalanx, but it also reinforces the glory, even delight (*harpaleon*), of standing to face and kill one's enemy, especially if they themselves are fleeing, and the shame of breaking formation in fear.[24]

---

[21] ... νέῳ δέ τε πάντ' ἐπέοικεν, | ἀρηϊκταμένῳ, δεδαϊγμένῳ ὀξέϊ χαλκῷ, | κεῖσθαι· πάντα δὲ καλὰ θανόντι περ, ὅττι φανήῃ· | ἀλλ' ὅτε δὴ πολιόν τε κάρη πολιόν τε γένειον | αἰδῶ τ' αἰσχύνωσι κύνες κταμένοιο γέροντος, | τοῦτο δὲ οἴκιστον πέλεται δειλοῖσι βροτοῖσιν.

[22] Vernant 1991: 64–66.     [23] Brockliss 2019, chapter 7.

[24] I myself have relied on this poem in my own discussion of the development of hoplite tactics (Sears 2019b: 41–43, with further bibliography). See Romney 2014 for an important discussion about the poem's surprising final few lines, in which Tyrtaeus addresses the light-armed troops and suggests that they cower behind the shields of the more heavily armed men. Romney argues that Tyrtaeus recognizes the disparity in armament and encourages the light-armed to fight despite their relative vulnerability, and thus includes them within the Spartan army.

While Tyrtaeus 10 and 11 deal with the ugly realities of war, including the possibility that one will be killed, however gloriously, fragment 12 W shifts gears to present war as an uncomplicated good. The poet gushes that war is the very definition of excellence, *aretē*, and the best and noblest prize (*aethlon ariston kalliston te*) a young man can win. War is also a common good (*xynon esthlon*) for the whole city and its people. Tyrtaeus goes further in this poem to describe the specific benefits for the brave warrior, beyond being universally lamented if he should die and sexually desired if he lives. His tomb (*tymbos*), along with his children and descendants, will be renowned among the people, and his good fame (*kleos esthlon*) and name will never perish, but he will be immortal (*athanatos*) even though he is under the earth. Tyrtaeus concludes by encouraging every man to strive in his heart for this height of excellence, and never to relax from war. Robert Luginbill correctly points out that this poem is less nuanced and more propagandistic than the other works of Tyrtaeus we possess, perhaps amounting to a recruitment advertisement for the Spartan army.[25]

From these poets we can distill the main ideals relied upon by the Archaic Greeks to inspire men to fight bravely in war. Shirking from war was a mark of shame, and also left others in the community (the elderly, children, wives) vulnerable to danger. Fighting bravely, even or especially to the death, was a mark of excellence that brought glory to the warrior while providing good things for all the people. Those who died in war were grieved and honored by the entire community, while those who survived after fighting with distinction were revered and respected, conspicuous among their fellows. Callinus and Tyrtaeus agree on these points, and even Archilochus implies that they are values shared by virtually everyone. From Tyrtaeus, either because these messages were geared to a particular Spartan context or merely because more of his poetry survives, we have more explicit assurances of the eternal glory and memory that will attend the brave warrior. In terms of commemoration, a warrior can expect a famous tomb and to imbue his descendants with fame for generations. He can also look forward to having a reputation that lasts forever, long after he is dead and buried. In conjunction with the avoidance of shame, this eternal memory is a prime motivation for entering and remaining in battle. Commemorative practices were essential for promoting a martial spirit.

The avoidance of shame and pursuit of glory and fame, with a focus on how one will be remembered and celebrated far into the future, were ideals that drove the Homeric warriors in the *Iliad* and *Odyssey*, the first literary

---

[25] Luginbill 2002.

works composed by the Greeks. Protecting one's home and loved ones was also of central concern, as the Greek Achilles shows in the grief and murderous rage he feels after the death of his companion, Patroclus, and as the Trojan Hector demonstrates as he tries to balance protecting his family and city while avoiding the shame of shirking combat. Odysseus, too, reveals a concern for reestablishing his own rule in Ithaca, but also setting things right for his home, all while he demonstrates an overwhelming need to be recognized, remembered, and showered with prestigious gifts. As Tyrtaeus follows Homer's language, sometimes verbatim, the 7th-century war-poets convey thoughts about war similar to Homer's.[26] Like Homer's warriors, those listening to Callinus and Tyrtaeus were taught to strive for excellence in battle, and to be celebrated and remembered for that excellence, ideally forever.

At this stage in Greek history, it is not so much that Spartan commemoration was drastically different from the practices of other Greeks – though, as we will see, the place of poetry might have played a larger role in remembering war at Sparta than elsewhere. Rather, other Greeks changed the way they commemorated wars and the war dead in the early 5th century, while Sparta stubbornly clung to these older ideals. Much of the remainder of this study will consider whether a conservative adherence to glory and fame above other considerations made the Spartans more or less warlike than both their fellow Greeks and Spartans of later periods.

## Sparta, Messenia, and the World of Tyrtaeus

It was not just his poetic spirit or an appreciation of the inherent goodness of martial values that drove Tyrtaeus to encourage his fellow Spartans to go to war. The ancient sources, including lines within the surviving work of Tyrtaeus, tell us that he was called upon to rally the Spartans to fight the neighboring Messenians in what modern scholars call the Second Messenian War. This conflict, seemingly formative for Sparta, is fraught with source problems, and many questions about the relationship between Sparta and Messenia, and the opposing identities of Spartans and Messenians, continue to provoke debate. The context of Tyrtaeus' poetry, namely the struggle between Sparta and Messenia, and the eventual domination of the former over the latter, are important to sort out, if we want to understand Spartan attitudes towards war and its commemoration – indeed, if we want to understand Sparta in general.

---

[26] For the centrality of Homer in Greek attitudes towards war across many eras, see Sears 2019b: 1–30, with further bibliography.

Ancient sources claim Messenia as the origin of most of Sparta's helots (though many came from Laconia, too), the state-owned serfs forced by the Spartans to provide the majority of the state's agricultural labor, serve various supporting roles in the army, and undergo ritual humiliation and other horrors to keep them subservient.[27] Not only were helots integral to the Spartan state and way of life, fear of losing helot labor and land was a frequent motivator for Spartan domestic and foreign policy. Thucydides, in the context of Brasidas' expedition to Thrace in 424 (which we will cover in detail in Chapter 4), makes a general statement about Sparta's attitude towards the helots. Sparta sent out several hundred helots with Brasidas' force, happy for the pretext (*prophasis*) to get rid of some potentially dangerous subversives. "For," according to Thucydides, "the majority of Lacedaemonian policies pertaining to the helots had always been geared towards security above all" (Thuc. 4.80.3).[28] Thucydides' use of "always" here, and the pluperfect verb, implies grammatically that Spartan official fear of helot uprisings was a long-standing motivator, in place long before Brasidas set out for Thrace. In fact, a helot uprising sometime around the 460s was largely responsible for the final break between Athens and Sparta, leading to the so-called First Peloponnesian War, and eventually the Peloponnesian War itself (Thuc. 1.101–103).

In the Roman Imperial period, Pausanias dedicates much of the fourth book of his travelogue to provide our fullest account of Sparta's conquest of Messenia, and subjugation of the helots whom Tyrtaeus describes as "worn down by great burdens, just like donkeys, bringing to their masters under grievous compulsion half of all the fruit of the soil" (F 4).[29] Because this source is so late, the historical details of the so-called Messenian Wars are often called into question. Even the formation of rigidly opposed Spartan and Messenian identities is placed in the aftermath of the Battle of Leuctra in 371, when the Thebans helped to liberate the helots and found the city of Messene as a capital for Sparta's former Messenian subjects.[30] Jack Davis and Sharon Stocker, however, the current excavators of the Bronze Age site of Pylos, suggest that key ideas of Messenian identity might stretch back to

---

[27] The most comprehensive treatments of the helots can be found in Luraghi and Alcock 2003; and Luraghi 2008. For an overview of the importance of helotage for the Spartan system, see Figueira 2018.

[28] αἰεὶ γὰρ τὰ πολλὰ Λακεδαιμονίοις πρὸς τοὺς Εἵλωτας τῆς φυλακῆς πέρι μάλιστα καθειστήκει. For more on this passage, and the horrific episode of helot mass-murder Thucydides narrates next, see Chapter 4.

[29] ὥσπερ ὄνοι μεγάλοις ἄχθεσι τειρόμενοι, | δεσποσύνοισι φέροντες ἀναγκαίης ὕπο λυγρῆς | ἥμισυ παντὸς ὅσον καρπὸν ἄρουρα φέρει.

[30] See, for example, Luraghi 2008: 68–106, 209–248; Romney 2018.

the Late Bronze Age, and that the structure of the state administered by the Palace of Nestor helped to determine the forms and methods of Sparta's conquests in Messenia.[31] Paul Rahe argues that the Spartan conquest of Messenia, particularly its reconquest in Tyrtaeus' Second Messenian War after the Messenians revolted from Spartan control, is what convinced the Spartans to form their uniquely rigid and cohesive way of life – all for the purposes of maintaining their control and holding off other Peloponnesian rivals and challengers.[32]

Rahe at times goes too far in the opposite direction from most scholars today, namely taking the sources at their word, but at least some sense of the conquest of Messenia as being formative for the Spartans was there in the Archaic and Classical periods. Thucydides' testimony is fairly clear on this point. Also, the evidence of Tyrtaeus is compelling. The poet not only names some key Messenian topics, such as Mount Ithome (F 3 W), where the 5th-century revolt against the Spartans was based, but he also vigorously recruits soldiers to the army, which, according to Luginbill, suggests that the Spartans were having a tough go of it against their neighbors to the west.[33]

The stories of the Messenian Wars remind us of something that can be easy to forget, that Sparta was not always the Sparta renowned for its military might and fearsome soldiers. There was a time when Sparta did not dominate the Peloponnese, or even its corner of the Peloponnese. In fact, the Spartans were frequently at risk of being supplanted by other Peloponnesians, and fought lengthy conflicts with Argos and the Arcadians, in addition to the Messenian Wars.[34] Tyrtaeus' Sparta was in need of military recruiting drives, which is difficult to imagine in the late Archaic and Classical Sparta of the *homoioi*, or "similars," who trained continuously for hoplite battle to win glory for themselves and their polis. Tyrtaeus' Spartan army was not even one consisting solely of hoplites, as the last few lines of F 11 demonstrate, which exhort the light-armed troops to fight among the shields of the heavy-armed and hurl their own missiles.

---

[31] Davis and Stocker 2021: 12.   [32] Rahe 2016: 104–105.

[33] Luginbill 2002. But see Romney 2020: 54–55, who argues that, in Tyrtaeus' time, the state might not have had as much power as Luginbill suggests, but rather Tyrtaeus' poetry reflects preexisting values that the state *later* used to bolster its aims. Romney also cautions against the uncritical acceptance of Tyrtaeus' role in the supposed Second Messenian War, since testimony to that effect comes only much later.

[34] For the conflicts between Sparta and Argos, see later in this chapter. For conflicts with the Arcadians, especially the Tegeans, see the account of Herodotus (1.66–68), who marks the Spartan victory over Tegea as a key stage in Sparta gaining hegemony in the Peloponnese. See Welwei 2004 for a discussion of the Archaic war with Tegea, especially the episode recorded by Herodotus of the Spartans brining the bones of the hero Orestes to Sparta in order to obtain the gods' help in achieving victory.

Jessica Romney discusses these verses and concludes that Tyrtaeus, rather than simply denigrating these fighters as cowering behind the more stalwart hoplites, means to encourage them as fully part of the Spartan army.[35] As we will see, the Spartans commemorated the Messenian Wars and the other close-run conflicts by which they gained their Peloponnesian hegemony through various religious rituals, such as the Gymnopaidiai, at which they recited poetry, including the verses of Tyrtaeus.

What we can learn from the Messenian Wars in terms of the broader scope of this study is that the Spartan commemoration of war was different during the period in which Sparta was expanding and fighting off challengers. In a recent study, Cezary Kucewicz attempts to chart this difference. He argues through a comprehensive examination of the burials of the Spartan War dead in the Archaic period that the Messenian Wars and subsequent conflicts sparked a gradual process by which regular Spartan soldiers, or the Spartan *damos*, gained power vis-à-vis the aristocrats. The aristocratic values of individual fame and conspicuous monuments in Sparta itself gave way to the common battlefield burials, or *polyandria*, of the late Archaic and Classical period – though aristocratic sentiments such as "with this or on this" continued to inspire even in these later periods.[36] I agree that important social changes took place in Archaic Sparta, likely put in motion by the Messenian Wars, which led to the society of the *homoioi* for which Sparta is famous. Kucewicz's reconstruction, however, is highly speculative, perhaps necessarily so owing to the paltry evidence. Aside from some funerary kraters (large ceramic vessels) that possibly contained military burials, and other scattered material evidence, the main source Kucewicz relies on for the original practice of burial of warriors at Sparta is Tyrtaeus' promise that the brave warrior's grave will be conspicuous (F 12 W: 29–30).[37] Yet, Tyrtaeus' line means only that the grave, along with the warrior's descendants, will be notable or visible (*arisēmos*). This does not to my mind necessitate a burial in Sparta, and thus a marked change from later practice. A famous tomb on the spot where a soldier died fighting against the neighboring Messenians could very well be famous to and even frequented by the Spartans.

A change in commemorative practices and ideological emphasis can be detected following the Messenian Wars nonetheless, though not necessarily along the lines proposed by Kucewicz. Consider Tyrtaeus' commemoration

[35] Romney 2014.    [36] Kucewicz 2021a.    [37] Kucewicz 2021a: 86–97.

of the Spartan king Theopompus, credited with winning the First Messenian War:

> To our king, Theopompus dear to the gods,
> Because of whom we took broad Messene,
> Messene good to plow and good to sow,
> For which they fought nineteen years
> Unceasingly always having a stout heart,
> The warrior fathers of our fathers.
> In the twentieth year, the enemy, leaving their rich fields,
> Fled from great Mount Ithome.[38]

Theopompus is remembered in song not just because he won a war. His victory brought valuable arable land to the Spartans, which formed the basis of their late Archaic and Classical hegemony in the Peloponnese. This could be the "common good, for the whole city and all the people" to which Tyrtaeus refers to in another of his martial exhortations (F 12 W: 15).[39]

The goods for the people, including the land that grows their food, in combination with the inclusion of the decidedly non-elite light-armed skirmishers mentioned in F 11, tell against the strictly aristocratic nature of military commemoration as argued by Kucewicz. The poetry of Tyrtaeus emphasizes glory and fame, but also a sort of patriotism and spirit of conquest for the good of all Spartans.[40] The soldiers who listened to Tyrtaeus fought wars that achieved practical things, like the defense of Sparta and Spartan families and homes, and the acquisition of territory and power. As we will see in the next chapter, in the early Classical period Spartan commemoration stood out from the commemorative practices of other Greeks, and also these earlier Spartan ones, because it lacked any overt concern for such common goods and general welfare. Where Tyrtaeus speaks of glory along with practical goods for the state and community, Spartan monuments to the Persian Wars focus on glory alone – for the state as well as the individual, to be sure, but the decidedly *impractical* concept of glory all the same.[41]

---

[38] = F 3: ἡμετέρῳ βασιλῆϊ, θεοῖσι φίλῳ Θεοπόμπῳ, | ὃν διὰ Μεσσήνην εἵλομεν εὐρύχορον, Μεσσήνην ἀγαθὴν μὲν ἀροῦν, ἀγαθὴν δὲ φυτεύειν, | ἀμφ' αὐτὴν δ' ἐμάχοντ' ἐννεακαίδεκ' ἔτη | νωλεμέως αἰεί, ταλασίφρονα θυμὸν ἔχοντες, | αἰχμηταὶ πατέρων ἡμετέρων πατέρες· | εἰκοστῷ δ' οἱ μὲν κατὰ πίονα ἔργα λιπόντες | φεῦγον Ἰθωμαίων ἐκ μεγάλων ὀρέων.

[39] ξυνὸν δ' ἐσθλὸν τοῦτο πόληΐ τε παντί τε δήμῳ.

[40] Romney 2020: 58–67 discusses the way Tyrtaeus tends to avoid naming individual Spartans, but instead focuses on the group or collective.

[41] We will return to the topic of Spartan glory in the spread of its power, particularly through the construction of military monuments in hostile territory in Chapter 5.

## Remembering Spartans on Samos

Herodotus mentions the Messenian Wars as one of the reasons for Spartan military ties with the island of Samos in the 6th century. Sparta (along with Corinth) sent out an expedition to aid a group of Samians against the tyrant Polycrates, who had expelled these Samians from their homes. The Samians claimed, according to Herodotus, that the Spartans helped because Samos sent military aid to the Spartans against the Messenians (Hdt. 3.47).[42] As Florentia Fragkopoulou outlines, there is good evidence for these ties, which extended beyond the military, in the rise of Laconian material found in Samian contexts from the late 7th to late 6th century.[43] For an infamously isolationist society like Sparta to forge a close relationship with an island on the far side of the Aegean is surprising. In fact, Sparta's close bond with Samos in the Archaic period is unique in Spartan history. The signs of this relationship stare out from behind glass cases in Samos' museums, artistic reminders of Spartan warriors and the role they played on the island.

Herodotus tells us the remarkable story of Archias and Lycopas, two Lacedaemonians who fought with especial distinction during the Spartan-led siege of Polycrates' Samos around 525. Only these two managed to enter the fortified city as they were pursuing a group of fleeing Samians, and both were killed during this daring action. Herodotus says that, if all the Lacedaemonians had fought like these two, Samos would have been taken. In an extraordinary aside, similar to his comment that he took the time to learn the names of all 300 who fell at Thermopylae, Herodotus says that in Pitana, part of the polis of Sparta, he met a certain Archias, son of Samius and grandson of the Archias who died valiantly at Samos.[44] This Archias honored the Samians above all others because they had given his grandfather the distinction of a public funeral. His father, Samius, had been in fact named after the island (the name means "the Samian").

---

[42] In their commentary on Herodotus, How and Wells 1912 note that this is the only definite reference to the Messenian Wars in Herodotus, which seems to confirm that the conflict drew in allies from around Greece for both sides, on which the much later sources are more explicit. While Herodotus' Spartan sources claim the expedition to Samos was due more to the theft of valuable dedications. The fact that the Samian sources credit the Messenian Wars, however, in the mid-5th century indicates that this conflict was seen by many as formative for Sparta (and Samos) in the Classical period, long before the liberation of the Messenians by the Thebans in the 4th century.

[43] Fragkopoulou 2012. She argues that there was in fact only one Messenian War, instead of the two mentioned by later sources, and the dates can be fixed from shortly before the time Laconian material begins showing up on Samos.

[44] See Marincola 2016 for the argument that Herodotus presents himself in a heroic mold because of the great lengths to which he went in order to honor the Three Hundred.

Two generations after the Spartan siege, one Spartan family maintained with the island special ties stemming from military heroism and conspicuous commemoration (Hdt. 3.55).

The Spartan siege of Samos was a failure, so much so that a rumor spread that Polycrates must have bribed the Spartans to leave, a tale Herodotus roundly rejects (Hdt. 3.56). The bravery of Archias and Lycopas was therefore pointless on tactical and strategic grounds, and maybe even foolhardy. Nevertheless, the Samians celebrated these Spartans, and this mere act of celebration was enough to engender generations of guest-friendship with these Spartans' descendants. This Samian episode, then, represents important themes of Spartan commemoration, namely the high value placed on the remembrance of heroic deaths in battle, even in the face of a larger defeat. The legendary status accorded the Battle of Thermopylae suggests that defeat might carry greater commemorative weight than victory, an early example of the myth of the "lost cause." If Herodotus' story is true about these two Spartans fighting to the death at Samos against impossible odds, and being rewarded with fame and glory, we would have cause to reevaluate whether the idea of the "beautiful death" was not fully formed until after Thermopylae, a battle that took place more than forty years after the siege of Samos.

One of the most important sacred precincts in the Greek world is the sanctuary of Hera on Samos. Famed for its early temple, called the "hekatompedon," or "hundred-footer," and that temple's gigantic replacement (of which only a single column stands today), the Samian Heraion is a treasure trove of archaeological and architectural material. Dedications to the goddess represent a large proportion of the material on display in the Archaeological Museum of Vathy, Samos' main collection of antiquities. Among the spectacular displays of extraordinarily rare wooden votive figurines and other material from throughout Greece and the ancient Near East are several objects of Laconian origin. These Archaic objects, dating from the 7th and 6th centuries, range from bronze warrior figurines to ornate ivory plaques that rival the artistry of the most impressive archaeological finds. That Sparta and Samos had a "special relationship" has been established by scholars based on the literary and material record.[45] We must then ask: who was making these dedications, and what message do they convey (Figure 2.1; Figure 2.2; Figure 2.3)?

---

[45] See, for example, Cartledge 1982. For Laconian pottery at the Samian Heraion, another indication of the important ties between Sparta and Samos, see Stibbe 1998.

Figure 2.1 Archaic Laconian bronze votive, from the Samian Heraion,
Archaeological Museum of Vathy. Author's photo. © Hellenic Ministry of Culture
and Sports / Hellenic Organization of Cultural Resources Development.

We should acknowledge that, in the Archaic period, Laconian art was influential, sought-after, and widely diffused, from Ionia to Thrace to Sicily. Samos was not the only foreign destination for Laconian pieces. A single statistic, however, suffices to demonstrate how important Samos was as a destination for Laconian products. Of the 155 known vases from named Laconian painters, 89 are from Samos, well over half of the total.[46] The material record confirms the Spartan–Samian "special relationship."

It is not clear who was making these dedications of Laconian objects. On the one hand, some scholars have suggested that the Samian aristocracy acquired a taste for Laconian goods, and so the material was imported to Samos but dedicated by Samians.[47] Others have left open the possibility that the dedications could have been made by Spartans visiting the island.[48] At least one object offered to Hera, a 6th-century bronze lion, was certainly dedicated by a Spartan, since it is inscribed with "Eumnastos the Spartiate,

---

[46] Prost 2018: 164.    [47] Pipili 2018; Prost 2018.    [48] Fragkopoulou 2012: 103.

Figure 2.2 Bronze votive, Archaeological Museum of Sparta. Author's photo. © Hellenic Ministry of Culture and Sports / Hellenic Organization of Cultural Resources Development.

to Hera."[49] Even if only some of the dedications were made by Spartans, who were these Spartans? I suggest that they were soldiers. The ties between Sparta and Samos were predominantly based on military assistance. Take, for example, the story of the Samians giving the Spartans military aid during the Messenian Wars. This action was mirrored by the Spartan-led campaign to dislodge the Samian tyrant Polycrates, in which the Spartans Archias and Lycopas died fighting.

I propose that at least some, if not most, of the Laconian objects dedicated on Samos – from a 6th-century bronze figurine of a hoplite to a spectacular 7th-century ivory plaque of Perseus beheading Medusa – were left by Spartan soldiers. These soldiers were on Samos as part of the military exchange between the two powers, and made these dedications not just out of piety but as a way to say, "this Spartan soldier was here." As Francis Prost

[49] IG XII,6 2:540: Εὔμναστος τᾶι Ήρᾳ, Σπαρτιάτας. See the discussion of this lion in Cartledge 1982: 255–256.

Figure 2.3 Archaic Laconian ivory votive showing Perseus beheading Medusa, from the Samian Heraion, Archaeological Museum of Vathy. Author's photo. © Hellenic Ministry of Culture and Sports / Hellenic Organization of Cultural Resources Development.

puts it, the Spartans (and other Greeks) would have seen the diffusion of their particular artistic style as "a means of expression of their identity or of their conquests." While Spartans participated in what we might call artistic colonialism in the Archaic period, by the 5th century the Spartans no longer relied on their art as a way to promote themselves abroad.[50] The material record on Samos, therefore, represents a special place and time for a type of self-representation and even commemoration for Spartan warriors.

## Remembering War through Ritual: The Gymnopaidiai

Before we turn to one of Sparta's most important festivals, we must first consider the famous Archaic battle that might have been central to that festival. As a prelude to the Battle of Thyrea, a ritualized "Battle of the

[50] Prost 2018: 173. Fragkopoulou 2012: 107 points out that commercial and political interests likely intertwined, and that the presence of Laconian pottery at a given site might indicate a Sparta desire to increase its influence there.

Champions" took place between Sparta and Argos in 546. In the context of the Lydian King Croesus appealing to the Greeks for aid against his Persian enemies, Herodotus tells the story of this conflict over a region disputed between the two Peloponnesian powers. Instead of sending out their full armies, both Sparta and Argos agreed to send 300 champions each to fight it out in a ritualized fashion. All 600 men are said to have died in the furious duel, aside from two men of Argos and one of Sparta. The two Argives returned home and claimed the victory. The lone Spartan survivor, however, one Othryadas, recovered his senses on the battlefield and despoiled the slain Argives to set up a trophy. Having kept the field, the Spartans claimed victory for their side. Since the ritualized battle failed to settle things, the entire complements of the Spartan and Argive armies clashed the next day in the Battle of Thyrea, with horrendous losses on both sides. Herodotus says that the Spartans were victorious and began to grow their hair long to remember the victory, whereas the Argives cut their hair short and kept it that way until such time as they were able to retake the lost territory. Overcome with shame at surviving when all the other Spartans died, Othryadas later killed himself (Hdt. 1.82).[51]

What does this unusual (or, for the Spartans, all too usual?) battle have to do with a religious festival? Sosibius, a Lacedaemonian who compiled an account of Spartan cultic rites and other matters at the court of Alexandria during the Hellenistic period, says that at the Gymnopaidiai festival, the Spartans commemorated the victory at Thyrea by wearing crowns of palm leaves. While wearing these crowns, groups of naked dancers – the festival name means "the naked boys" or, according to Robert Parker, "the unarmed dances" – sing songs written by Lacedaemonian poets including Thaletas, Alcman, and Dionysodotos (F 5).[52] The travel-writer Pausanias says that near the Spartan agora is a spot called the *choros*, or dancing ground, since it is the place where these dances are performed.[53] The Gymnopaidiai, according to Pausanias, is the festival the Spartans take as more important than any other,

---

[51] Pritchett 1985: 15–21 provides a comprehensive list of duels in Greek history, including this "Battle of the Champions." This kind of ritualized combat happened on several occasions. Pausanias (2.38.5–6) also gives an account of this battle and mentions the presence of mass burials at the site. See Chapter 5.

[52] For the etymology of the festival's name, see Parker 1989: 149–150.

[53] I am not convinced by Kourinou's 2000 argument that the *Choros* should be identified with the prominent "Round Building" near the Spartan agora, but it is an intriguing idea nonetheless. If this identification were correct, the Round Building would not be a building at all, but merely the terracing foundations of a round, flat space for dancing. For more on the Round Building, see Chapter 5.

indicating that remembrance of the Battle of the Champions at Thyrea was central to Spartan identity (3.11.9).[54]

Cecilia Nobili draws on the so-called "New Simonides," which many interpret to be an elegy for the dead of the Battle of Plataea in 479, to argue that Sparta had a long tradition of public songs in honor of the dead sung at festivals like the Gymnopaidiai. The famous Simonides poem, only discovered on papyrus in the late 20th century, was likely commissioned by Sparta and performed in a context similar to, or identical with, the singing and dancing described by Sosibius. The Gymnopaidiai, then, served an important function in Archaic Sparta, combining feats of athleticism and pseudo-military maneuvers, such as armed dancing, with songs of commemoration for great warriors of the past. All of these displays, and the coordination required for them, were important for inculcating the military virtues Sparta privileged, and likely accompanied the enrolling of new soldiers into the ranks. The New Simonides represents the continuation of this tradition into the early Classical period.[55] We will return to this poem in the next chapter.

Epic poetry indirectly furnishes further support for the notion that the activities associated with the Gymnopaidiai were useful for developing good soldiers. Homer's *Iliad* depicts the Myrmidons, Achilles' peerless soldiers, as engaging in athletic activities (including honing their discus, javelin, and archery skills) while they abstain from battle because of their leader's quarrel with Agamemnon (2.773–774). A *scholion* on these lines, a marginal note written in the manuscript at some point in antiquity, says that, by including this detail, "[Homer] shows that those accustomed to marching in battle engage in gymnastic activity. In fact, Lycurgus established the Gymnopaidiai so that [the Spartans] might remember such training in times of battle."[56] There are plenty of studies discussing the connection between athletics (and similarly rigorous activities) and war. Paul Christesen provides a good overview of the subject in the context of

---

[54] Since the Gymnopaidiai was supposedly founded long before the Battle of the Champions, the remembrance of that battle was obviously not original to the festival. Some have seen the Battle of Hysiai in the early 7th century between Sparta and Argos, which Sparta lost (Paus. 2.24.7), as the origin of the Gymnopaidiai, but Franchi 2018 has argued (if rather speculatively, with little ancient evidence) that an earlier battle of Thyrea marked the actual beginning of the festival, to which commemoration of the Battle of Champions was later added as various festivals and traditions merged.

[55] Nobili 2011.

[56] διδάσκει τοὺς εἰωθότας κινεῖσθαι μὴ ἀγυμναστεῖν. Λυκοῦργός τε γυμνοπαιδίας ὥρισεν, ὅπως μέμνοιντο καὶ παρὰ καιρὸν τῶν πόνων. For a discussion of this scholion and this passage's significance for the study of elite soldiers, see Sears 2010: 149.

Sparta, concluding that "to be a Spartiate was to be an athlete and a dancer."[57] The greatest warriors at Troy did not necessarily dance, but they were athletic. It is worth noting that the leader of the Myrmidons, Achilles, also played the lyre and sang poetry, just like the Spartans did at occasions like the Gymnopaidiai and likely among their fellow soldiers in the common messes and while on campaign (Hom. *Il.* 9.185–194).[58]

Natasha Bershadsky has written a fascinating, if highly speculative, chapter on the Battle of Thyrea and its role in Spartan (and Argive) ritual. She argues that a series of ritual battles held regularly between the Spartans and Argives in the territory of Thyrea throughout the Archaic period played an important role in forming civic identity and marking the coming of age. These rituals, while not strictly battles, privileged the idea of the "beautiful death" at Sparta, and provided the origin, or *aition*, of the Gymnopaidiai at which these ideas were expressed and inculcated. These ritual battles eventually came to an end when Sparta began more aggressive expansion in the Peloponnese, leading to real battles with rivals like Argos.[59]

Bershadsky's reconstruction is ingenious and worth a read in its entirety, even if it relies at some points on imaginative reconstructions in lieu of contemporary sources. I was particularly struck, however, by an offhand comment she makes in the course of laying out her case. While discussing John Dillery's study of the literary parallels between Thyrea and Thermopylae – which are immediately obvious to most readers of Herodotus – she questions Dillery's conclusion that Thermopylae provided the model for the Thyrea story as found in Herodotus and later sources. Instead, Bershadsky suggests that Thyrea could have been the model for treatments of Thermopylae, instead of the other way around.[60]

To tie this discussion back to the songs sung at the Gymnopaidiai, and how they intersect with the commemoration of war, the Palatine Anthology, a collection of epigrams from various periods in antiquity, offers the tantalizing prospect that we have a poem about Thyrea by the famous Simonides. Here is what the poem, either an epigram or an excerpt from an elegy, says:

> We three hundred here, O Sparta our fatherland, when we fought over
> Thyrea with equal numbers of the people of Inachos, we did not turn our

---

[57] Christesen 2014: 155.
[58] For the Spartans singing poetry in their groups at home and abroad on campaign, see Romney 2020: 186nn38–39.
[59] Bershadsky 2012.    [60] Bershadsky 2012: 63n75. For the more prevalent view, see Dillery 1996.

necks but gathered in the front, where our footprints were, and left our life there. A shield covered in the manly gore of Othryadas cries out: "Thyrea, Zeus, belongs to the Lacedaemonians." If anyone of the Argives fled his fate, he was descended from Adrastos. At Sparta, death is not to die, but to flee.[61]

We will return to Simonides in much more detail in the next chapter, when we discuss Persian War epigrams, but for now we should at least note that poems ascribed to him were not necessarily written by him. In fact, many poems of "Simonides" are almost certainly from centuries later, during the Hellenistic period, which is when this poem is usually dated.[62] There is no solid evidence for accepting this poem as a genuine composition of Simonides in the early 5th century, nor is there any for rejecting it as such.[63] Since Thyrea and the Gymnopaidiai are so central to Spartan identity and commemoration, we should pause for some time over this poem.

This poem is an important bit of evidence showing that Herodotus' version of the story was not the only one in antiquity. Where Othryadas committed suicide in Herodotus' account, another tradition holds that he died on the battlefield, but only after he scrawled a victory proclamation in his own gore. This is the version of events highlighted in the poem ascribed to Simonides, which so vividly tells of the shield covered in Othryadas' "manly gore," writing out a dedication to Zeus and the message that the Spartans had taken Thyrea. One reason scholars argue against the poem being a Simonidean original is that, in the Hellenistic period, the story of Othryadas dying a beautiful death on the battlefield gains more currency, as shown in several other poems of clearly Hellenistic date. Alissa Vaillancourt and Andrew G. Scott trace the development of this "historical exemplum," and they situate the "Simonides" poem in that later context.[64]

Picking up on Bershadsky's suggestion, I propose that this poem preserves the original tradition surrounding Othryadas, and that the version found in

[61] Sim. 5 G–P: Οἵδε τριηκόσιοι, Σπάρτα πατρί, τοῖς συναρίθμοις | Ἰναχίδαις Θυρέαν ἀμφὶ μαχεσσάμενοι, | αὐχένας οὐ στρέψαντες ὅπα ποδὸς ἴχνια πρᾶτον | ἁρμόσαμεν ταῦτα καὶ λίπομεν βιοτάν. | ἄρσενι δ' Ὀθρυάδαο φόνῳ κεκαλυμμένον ὅπλον | καρύσσει· "Θυρέα, Ζεῦ, Λακεδαιμονίων." | αἱ δέ τις Ἀργείων ἔφυγεν μόρον, ἧς ἀπ' Ἀδράστου· | Σπάρτα δ' οὐ τὸ θανεῖν, ἀλλὰ φυγεῖν θάνατος.
[62] For a thorough discussion of this poem and the various dates proposed for it, see Sider 2020: 401–404. For the collection of Simonidean poems circulated in the Hellenistic period, and theories concerning the various origins of the poems, including original ones written by Simonides himself, see Sider 2007.
[63] Sider (see previous note), while leaning towards a Hellenistic date, is noncommittal. Vaillancourt and Scott 2018: 153–155, 161n36 overstate the case for its Hellenistic composition, attributing to Sider a certainty in a later date that he does not in fact assert.
[64] Vaillancourt and Scott 2018.

Herodotus, based on sources the historian consulted in the 440s or 430s, was colored by the growing Thermopylae legend. If the Spartans commissioned Simonides to compose an elegy in remembrance of Plataea, they could have also done so in the case of Thyrea, perhaps even before Xerxes' invasion of Greece. The poem in question would be strange for an inscriptional epigram, but it would not be out of place as an excerpt from an elegy, like the Plataea poem in the "New Simonides." The sentiments expressed in these lines, especially the last line proclaiming Sparta's prohibition against fleeing from the enemy, is in keeping with the Tyrtaeus poems we considered above, and epigrams from the time of the Persian Wars.[65]

The nature of our sources prevents us from knowing whether this poem was sung at the Gymnopaidiai, but it would be a most appropriate set of verses for an occasion marking the victory at Thyrea. In addition to all the other ritual functions of that festival, inculcating the proper military virtues, from standing one's ground even unto death to bringing power and glory to Sparta. The coordinated singing and dancing, and the competition between various age groups in these activities, made for better soldiers in a practical, tactical sense, as the overarching commemorative program of the festival gave those soldiers a reason to fight and to die.

Other Spartan festivals celebrated and instilled martial values too.[66] For example, dedications of swords and other weapons at various shrines and sanctuaries throughout Spartan territory speak to the military nature of Spartan cult.[67] The sanctuary of Artemis Orthia, along the banks of the Eurotas River, where tens of thousands of votive lead figurines were dedicated beginning in the 7th century (many of which are hoplites and other warriors, but not all), was home to rituals designed to instill toughness and stamina in Spartan boys (Figure 2.4).[68] Today in the Archaeological Museum of Sparta are several dedications containing cutouts for the iron sickles the boys won as

---

[65] See, for example, Sim. 9 *FGE* line 3: "although they have died, they are not dead (οὐδὲ τεθνᾶσι θανόντες)"; and Sim. 73 *FGE* line 4: "an immortal monument for mortals (ἀθάνατον θνητοῖς)."

[66] For the role of religion in educating Spartans in Spartan values, especially military ones, see Kennell 1995, who argues for the late invention of many of the key ideas associated with Spartan ritual (a point that he continues to emphasize in his 2018 chapter); and Ducat 2006a: 249–279, who thinks there is a lot a genuine Archaic material in the rituals as the sources portray them. See also Flower 2018, especially 435–441, for a brief synopsis of some key Spartan festivals, including the ones covered here. Pettersson 1992 remains a standard reference for the cults of Apollo at Sparta, which had a decidedly military character. A comprehensive study of Spartan religion, with an emphasis on just how deeply religious the Spartans were, even as compared to other Greeks, is provided by Richer 2012.

[67] Pavlides 2011: 45, 58–59 discusses these dedications at the Menelaion and the Amyklaion.

[68] Pavlides 2011: 86–87 points to the emergence of cheap lead votives, replacing more expensive ones, and a growth in the preponderance of hoplite imagery as evidence for the growing power and influence of Spartan soldiers in the Archaic period.

Figure 2.4 Lead votives from the sanctuary of Artemis Orthia, Archaeological Museum of Sparta. Author's photo. © Hellenic Ministry of Culture and Sports / Hellenic Organization of Cultural Resources Development.

prizes for enduring ritual floggings and other trials the longest. These dedicators likely made excellent soldiers.[69] A late source says that the Carneia festival at Sparta was meant to replicate life in the military camp, down to the communal dining of soldiers – which was possibly part of the Archaic festival and not just a later practice retrojected into the past (Ath. 131d–f). Archaic Spartan society was, perhaps uniquely, a "song culture" in the formulation of Claude Calame.[70] These songs were often in the direct service of military exhortation, or indirectly part of festivals that also featured important elements of military remembrance and education.

## Conclusion

What we can gather from the little evidence we have from Archaic Sparta is that prior to the Persian Wars the Spartans valued the "beautiful death" on the battlefield because it brought glory and fame, but also because it won

---

[69] For these sickles, see Ducat 2006a: 210–212, all of which are from a post-Classical date save for one dedication from the 4th century. As all things Spartan, it is not clear what elements of the cult of Artemis Orthia are from the Archaic period and what are from the Hellenistic period or later. Xenophon (*Lak. Pol.* 2.9) in the 4th century describes the ritualized stealing of cheeses from the altar at the shine of Artemis Orthia, along with ritualized punishments should the thief be caught in the act. All of this was designed by Lycurgus, according to Xenophon, to instill military virtues such as endurance in the face of suffering for the reward of greater glory. Sources in the Roman period (see, for example, Plut. *Lyc.* 18.1; Paus. 3.16.10–11) describe an endurance test involving just flogging, with no mention of cheeses or theft.

[70] Calame 2018.

territory and other practical goods for Sparta. These values are commensurate with the Homeric epics, and were shared by other Greeks, as demonstrated by Callinus, a poet composing verses similar to Tyrtaeus', but from the Ionian city of Ephesus. Archilochus, another 7th-century poet, mocked these values, which serves to demonstrate that they were embraced by enough readers to be disparaged in verse by a cantankerous author challenging accepted ideas. Spartan religious festivals, especially the Gymnopaidiai, reserved a central role for the commemoration of war, including of those soldiers who died in their places on the battlefield. These festivals likely represent a uniquely Spartan phenomenon – the Spartans, in other words, seem to have sung and danced more than their fellow Greeks, largely in the service of remembering the fallen and encouraging the living. Spartan noble sacrifice won fame and remembrance abroad, too, as is shown by the Samian commemoration of two Spartans who died fighting against impossible odds. Sparta and Samos remembered their special military relationship in various ways, including by dedications at Samian sanctuaries, perhaps by Spartan soldiers.

In the next chapter we will see that, while many Greeks in addition to the Spartans shared the values espoused by Tyrtaeus and Callinus in the Archaic period, by the time of the Persian Wars new commemorative rhetoric grew in popularity. Outside of Sparta, war came to be remembered as being not just for the glory and fame for the warriors but to defend and bring aid to others, and to ensure freedom for Greece. The Spartans did not embrace this new commemorative paradigm, at least not until considerably later. Their ideas about how best to remember war did change somewhat, however. Gone was the emphasis on the practical goods wrought by war. All that remained at the time of the Persian invasion was the glory of war, the fame won by those who died the beautiful death or beat back the enemy. In fact, the Spartan stand at Thermopylae eschewed practical good sense and showed that the Spartans embraced death and glory *despite* or even *because of* a military action's impracticality.

The other Greeks moved in the direction of fighting for – or claiming to fight for – freedom. The Spartans, by contrast, continued to be driven by the pursuit of glory, more single-mindedly than they were in the period of their expansion into a leading power, when Tyrtaeus was encouraging them to fight the Messenians – or just fight in general. Even including the Persian Wars, however, the Spartan penchant for battlefield glory led the Spartans into fewer and less destructive wars than their fellow Greeks, who had taken up the rhetoric of altruism and sacrifice in the name of freedom.

CHAPTER 3

# *Few against Many*

## Introduction

In the lead-up to Xerxes' invasion of mainland Greece, the centerpiece of his *Histories*, Herodotus pauses to declare an opinion that he admits will be resented by most. Despite writing during the 430s, when Athens had become an imperial power oppressive to dozens of its fellow Greek poleis, Herodotus feels compelled to express what he believes to be the truth: that Athens was primarily responsible for saving Greece in 480. If Athens and its hundreds of warships had not led the stand against the Persian fleet at Salamis, it would only have been a matter of time before the rest of the Greek coalition fell apart and Sparta, standing alone, would have succumbed (7.139).[1] As John Marincola says in his notes to the Penguin Classics edition of Herodotus, the obvious conclusion from the Persian Wars, against which Herodotus is pushing back in this passage, is that *Sparta* saved Greece.[2] The Battle of Plataea in 479, in which the Spartans played the main part, was, indeed, the final and decisive engagement that drove the Persians from the Greek mainland for good.[3] Perhaps more famously in antiquity, and certainly today, the Spartan-led Battle of Thermopylae, which takes up much of the rest of Herodotus' seventh book, demonstrated that courageous Greeks fighting for their freedom could prove deadly foes to the sprawling army of Xerxes, even if, in the end, the pass at Thermopylae had fallen. By Herodotus' day, the Spartans were all too happy to promote their image as saviors of Greece, as were Sparta's allies who used Sparta's reputation as liberator as a tool with which to badger the Spartans into taking on a war against Athens. But in 480, as the

---

[1] Strauss 2004b certainly shares Herodotus' judgement that Salamis and the Athenian navy were the decisive factor in the defeat of Xerxes.
[2] Marincola in turn attributes this insight to Michael Flower. See the 2003 revised edition of Herodotus, *The Histories*, published by Penguin (New York), p. 669n38.
[3] For Plataea as the decisive battle, including in the estimation of many Greeks after the fact, see Cartledge 2013.

largest army perhaps anyone had ever seen was preparing to cross the Hellespont into Europe, Sparta had no interest in guaranteeing the freedom of anyone, or in any notion of a patriotic stand for something we call Greece. Such lofty and noble reasons for going to war were not the Spartan way.

As we have already seen, it is immensely difficult to get to the truth of Sparta and its society, largely because the sources we have are mostly non-Spartan and many are centuries later than the events and characters they describe. Our main source for the Persian Wars, Herodotus, was writing only a couple of generations after the events of the early 5th century, but while he was not himself Athenian the perspective he takes is very much an Athenian one and relies heavily on Athenian sources. Even the Spartans by the 430s had much different views of the war than the Spartans who had actually fought in it. Fortunately, we do have access to a body of evidence much closer to the events in question, and from a variety of points of view, namely the epigrams commemorating the Persian Wars. While many of these epigrams – short poems of only a couple of lines or so, originally inscribed on stone monuments – are preserved only in later literary sources, including Herodotus, several of them survive in their original material form. Some are even represented in both media, on stone and in literature, an invaluable source of evidence. The majority of these Persian War epigrams, from Greeks as varied as Athenians and Corinthians, Megarians and Opuntian Locrians, proclaim the struggle for the freedom of Greece and the selfless sacrifice so many Greeks made for each other. The Spartan epigrams, on the other hand, make no mention of such things. Instead, the Spartans fought for fame and glory, *kleos* and *kudos*, alone, both for themselves as individuals and their state, to the detriment of other states involved in the same conflict. This is how the Spartans remembered the Persian Wars, at least in the beginning.[4]

## The Battle of Thermopylae, 480 BCE

The Persian Great King Xerxes, picking up where his father, Darius, had left off after his forces' humiliation at Marathon in 490, invaded the Greek mainland at the head of a large land and sea force in 480. The few Greek poleis that were determined to resist the invasion first planned to meet the

---

[4] By the outbreak of the Peloponnesian War, according to Thucydides, the Corinthians chastise the Spartans for not freeing their fellow Greeks from the Athenians, especially since the Spartans enjoy the reputation of being the liberators of Greece (Thuc. 1.69.1). As we will discuss more thoroughly in Chapter 4, Sparta did eventually embrace the cause of Greek freedom, at least ostensibly.

Figure 3.1 Thermopylae from the hillock of the Three Hundred's last stand, looking
towards Mount Kallidromos. In the foreground is a modern monument with an
inscription of the famous Simonides epigram. Author's photo.

Persian threat at the Vale of Tempe, running between Mount Olympus and
Mount Ossa, the boundary between Macedonia and Thessaly. Ten thousand Greek soldiers arrived in the north to be told by the locals that there
were alternate routes into Thessaly, which rendered Tempe useless as a place
to make a stand. Plan B was to take on the Persians at Thermopylae, the
"Hot Gates," a narrow pass between the mountains and the sea in central
Greece, where a naval action could attempt to block the Persian ships off the
coast at the same time (Figure 3.1). The Battle of Thermopylae ended in
a defeat for the Greek resistance when the Persians were able to surround the
defenders by making use of a hidden path through the mountains, shown to
them by a treacherous local Greek named Ephialtes. Three hundred
Spartans, standing with their king, Leonidas, died while fighting
a desperate rear-guard action as most of the other Greeks abandoned the
pass and returned to their cities to fight another day. Xerxes then moved
unopposed into Boeotia, gaining Thebes as an ally, and sacked Athens
before being defeated at the naval Battle of Salamis later that year. The
next year, in 479, the remaining Persians under Xerxes' general Mardonius
lost the Battle of Plataea, ending the Persian invasion of Greece. Though

Thermopylae was technically a defeat, and was not one of the decisive battles that "saved Greece," the Three Hundred of Thermopylae passed into the realm of myth and legend.[5]

In the strange modern historical genre that seeks to determine and rank what the most "decisive" battles were, Thermopylae frequently comes out on top. It is on virtually all such lists.[6] Few if any ancient battles have received so much scholarly attention or generated so much public interest, so we will consider only the bare essentials here, before moving on to its commemoration, and the commemoration of the Persian Wars in general. It is important to acknowledge at the outset that Sparta's reputation and identity in the Classical period hinged on this battle, even if the battle did not change Sparta's attitudes to war as drastically as is often thought. Regardless of scholarly disagreements concerning the battle and its context, stemming from disagreements in the ancient sources themselves, its importance for Spartan commemoration by the late 5th century cannot be overstated. Nor can its role in shaping Sparta's relationship with its fellow poleis, or at least what that relationship was perceived or advertised to be.

Two major traditions about this battle have come down to us from antiquity. By far the best-known account is that given by Herodotus (7.173–239). The great historian flexes all his literary muscles for his description of this battle, and his text is required reading for all students of ancient history, society, and culture. He claims to have taken the time to learn the names of all members of the 300 Spartans who fell in the battle, a feat John Marincola argues should be seen as a sort of historiographical heroism.[7] Diodorus Siculus provides the other major version of the story

---

[5] Barry Strauss subtitled his 2004 book (Strauss 2004b) on the Battle of Salamis *The Naval Encounter that Saved Greece – and Western Civilization.* Among the vast bibliography on the Persian Wars, the best military study remains Lazenby 1993.

[6] The title of Paul Cartledge's 2007 book is representative: *Thermopylae: The Battle That Changed the World.* In the fall of 2020, I participated in a conference hosted by the Society for the Promotion of Hellenic Studies called "Thermopylae 2500," in recognition of the 2500th anniversary of the battle. The conference papers all problematized the standard accounts of the battle and its reception, and Cartledge himself commented on how much has changed in the relatively short time since he wrote his book. The most recent book-length treatment of the battle, reflecting the changing attitudes since the time of Cartledge's publication, is Carey 2019. In her recent study, Proietti 2021: 166–170 toes the line of Sparta conceiving of Thermopylae as its unique and heroically sacrificial contribution to Greek freedom. For a concise treatment of the battle, see Butera and Sears 2019: 49–66. We will return to this subject in detail in Chapter 7.

[7] Marincola 2016. Importantly, two of the 300 did not die at Thermopylae: Aristodamos, who was suffering with an eye infection and did not fight in the battle, and Pantites, who had been away on a diplomatic mission and killed himself rather than face the stigma of not falling with his comrades (Hdt. 7.229–232).

(11.4–11). Writing in the 1st century BCE, Diodorus' major source for this period was Ephorus of Cyme, a historian writing in the 4th century. Michael Flower, however, argues that the poet Simonides of Ceos, a contemporary of the battle, whom we will discuss, was a source for Diodorus for this battle.[8] The 2nd-century CE writers Plutarch (*On the Malice of Herodotus* 31–32) and Pausanias (10.20–21) also provide some details, the former giving mostly a critique and correction of Herodotus' dominant account in order to launder the reputation of the Thebans, some of whom also stayed behind to fight with Leonidas. Despite the discrepancies in the source traditions, and unlike much of the Archaic-era material we covered in the previous chapter, Thermopylae is illuminated by some contemporary or near-contemporary literature.

According to Hans van Wees, one reason for the variant traditions, even though the accounts were close in time to the battle itself, is that the stand of the Spartans against the forces of Xerxes quickly became a legend, with all the exaggerations and distortions that typically spring up around legendary material. One reason that the legend arose so early is that the Spartans were desperate to cover up the fact that the battle had been a defeat. Inconsistencies in Herodotus' version result from the historian trying to square the more far-fetched aspects of the legend with what he learned in the course of his research; at this, Herodotus was not always successful. We are left therefore with a contradictory and likely unresolvable set of accounts – though van Wees does try to clear up some major questions, such as what the Spartan tactics really were in the face of Persian archers, who are largely left out of Herodotus' version.[9] Other scholars point to anti-Spartan ideas in the surviving sources. Ellen Millender, for example, thinks that the Spartans' dogged adherence to their laws, especially refusing to yield their place in line even to the point of death, derives from Herodotus' Athenian sources, critical of what they saw as the Spartans' unthinking obedience.[10] Michael Clarke, on the other hand, suggests that some Spartans might have been critical of their state's actions at Thermopylae, calling into question notions such as the "beautiful death," which all Spartans supposedly admired.[11]

I think that some of these problems can be resolved, or at least lessened, by keeping open the possibility that the Spartans were in fact different from their fellow Greeks, at least in 480. This difference led the Spartans to do things other Greeks found strange. I also suggest modern scholars are too ready to assume that sound tactics and strategy drove the Spartans facing off

---

[8] Flower 1998.    [9] van Wees 2018.    [10] Millender 2002.    [11] Clarke 2002.

against Xerxes. These scholars suppose that "pragmatic" concerns overrode a desire to win glory and fame. If we ascribe every weird action or idea of the Spartans to post-battle Spartan propaganda or the anti-Spartan bias of Athenians (or critics in Sparta itself), we miss the fact that the Spartans actually were weird. Or, rather, that the Spartans acted in such a way at Thermopylae that they were at odds with the other Greeks, though those other Greeks would have valued similar things in previous eras. As we saw in the last chapter, during the Archaic period many Greeks were in agreement about key ideas concerning war. By the Persian invasion of Greece, and certainly in the decades that followed, the other Greeks moved on, while the Spartans stayed true to the ideas expressed by the Archaic poets.

How did those ideas influence Spartan actions in 480, when Xerxes was making his way into mainland Greece at the head of an enormous army? The military spirit reflected in Tyrtaeus' verses did not make the Spartans care about the "freedom of Greece," or even demonstrate much concern for a wider concept of "Greece" at all. The Spartans did agree to fight, however, if only to a limited extent. Those Greeks determined to resist the Persian Great King formed an alliance, and Sparta was made the head of the alliance, called "the Hellenes," not because of Sparta's good ideas or sound leadership qualities, but because the most powerful and famous Greeks get to lead. And that is the position the Spartans found themselves in as Xerxes crossed in Europe. To put that leadership in action, the Spartans took control of an infantry force sent out to block the Persian advance at Thermopylae. The narrowness of this pass meant that fewer Greeks could hope to stand against greater numbers of Persians and Persian allies. This land force worked in collaboration with a navy led by the Athenians (though, like the land force, officially under Spartan control), which hoped to block the Persian ships from sailing through the narrow waters between the mainland and the island of Euboea, not far from Thermopylae.

While the Spartans sent only a few hundred men (as many as a thousand Lacedaemonians according to the tradition in Diodorus, or only the Three Hundred Spartiates in the more influential account of Herodotus), those troops were at the head of upwards of 8,000 Greek soldiers. This decently large force, on the same order as the one originally sent to Tempe, was to work in conjunction with hundreds of Greek warships in a complex, combined-arms operation. This careful plan seems to undercut any ideas that the Spartans and their king, Leonidas, meant from the start to make a suicidal last stand. When the two sides clashed at the pass after several days of standoff, the Greeks held their own through two days of intense fighting on land, while the navy performed creditably against the larger number of ships in Xerxes' forces. In other words, a reasonably sound plan appeared to be progressing reasonably well – a far cry from soldiers in a tactically hopeless situation throwing away their lives. Had things continued to go this well, Leonidas could have entertained hopes of victory, of turning the Persians around to go back the way they had come. The commander of such a successful action would have earned a name for himself and returned home to Sparta to be feted just like Tyrtaeus' victorious warriors were.

Showing good sense, the Spartans did not risk the majority of their Spartiate soldiers in this action, but sent just enough, including one of their kings, to take command and claim the glory if the battle went well. If Leonidas and the men with him died in combat, earning for themselves one of the conspicuous monuments promised by the poets, most of the Spartan army would remain intact. The small Boeotian town of Thespiae, by contrast, lost virtually all of its soldiers, some 700 hoplites, when they joined Leonidas in the last stand – though the Thespians are often left out of the legend. We will discuss the Thespians, and their admirable if foolhardy penchant for fighting in the most dangerous circumstances, later.[12]

The image of the Spartans throwing away their lives in the pursuit of glory is not an invention of modern scholarship. An ancient source tradition from soon after the battle portrays Leonidas as knowing he was doomed before even setting out from Laconia. In this tradition, he sent away the other Greeks not to spare their lives, but to prevent them from taking any glory from him and his fellow Spartans. Herodotus says that, despite the majority opinion in the 430s that Leonidas wanted to preserve the lives of the other Greeks, Leonidas really perceived that his allies were dispirited and would be useless in the coming struggle; he wanted to remain there himself in order to win fame. Furthermore, a Delphic oracle had apparently predicted that Sparta would either lose a king or be destroyed. Thus seeing a chance at making sure a king died while Sparta survived, Leonidas selflessly opted to fight to the death (Hdt. 7.220). Diodorus' account says that Leonidas planned to die right from the beginning, before marching off to war and well before the Persians had found a way to outflank the Greek defenders. The Spartan king knew that he was taking too few men to be victorious, but just enough to win glory (Diod. 11.4).

Diodorus' version includes a story of Leonidas leading the Spartans on a daring night raid against the command tent of Xerxes, which most scholars have deemed implausible, the stuff of propaganda (Diod. 11.9–10). Such

[12] See Chapter 6.

propaganda, van Wees argues, is also behind the accounts of the final day of fighting, when the Greeks' position was doomed. The Spartans are said to have ventured out from the narrow pass to fight in the open part of the plain. Knowing they were as good as dead anyway, the Spartan hoplites threw away their tactical advantage in their fervor to kill the enemy. According to van Wees, such tactics make no sense at all, and are included in the sources for the purpose of valorizing the Spartan Three Hundred as they fought the last stage of an action that ended in defeat and loss.[13] And yet, I am not convinced that tactical good sense was much of a concern for Leonidas and his men, whatever else one makes of the source tradition.

The Spartans did send out the flower of their army, along with thousands of *perioikoi* and helots, to Plataea in 479, and achieved there a great victory under the command of the regent Pausanias. The Battle of Plataea was an unqualified success, and the Spartan phalanx was the decisive actor in that clash.[14] Even so, as we will see, Pausanias and the other Spartans were more concerned with their own fame and glory than with the fact that they had "saved Greece" or "defended freedom." And before advancing for the final charge against the Persians on the plain, Pausanias and the Spartans, as Herodotus tells the tale (9.61–62), hunkered down under a storm of Persian arrows for an outrageous amount of time, all in order to wait for the animal sacrifices to portend victory. What a remarkable example of the Spartans adhering to what seem to us the most trivial and bizarre religious scruples in lieu of good tactics or strategy, even if they did win in the end.

## Sparta Remembers the Persian Wars

Epigrams, short poems originally inscribed on material objects (though later becoming a largely literary medium rather than epigraphical), were an important part of Greek commemoration. Athletes especially favored epigrams on their monuments and dedications at sanctuaries as a way to advertise their accomplishments.[15] In the previous chapters, we remarked on the relationship between athletics and war, including in the sphere of memory, so it makes perfect sense that soldiers and athletes are

---

[13] van Wees 2018, especially 37–43.
[14] For the Battle of Plataea, and the Spartan role in it and the subsequent tradition, see Cartledge 2013.
[15] The most elaborate inscriptional commemoration of a Spartan athlete is the Damonon *stele* from the late 5th century, now in the Sparta Museum (*CEG* 378). Christesen 2019 gives a full treatment of this *stele* and what it tells us about Spartan society. The Archaic votive of the Spartan Aiglatas, with an epigram (*CEG* 374), is another important example of athletic commemoration and its context. For this inscription and its interpretation, see Nenci 2018.

commemorated in similar media, including epigrams. There is no better place to start our study of Thermopylae's legacy than the most famous Persian War epigrams of all, those recorded by Herodotus as inscribed to commemorate the dead at Thermopylae, and almost certainly representing genuine inscriptions from shortly after the battle.[16] The most renowned Greek epigram from any period speaks in the voice of the dead Spartans buried where they fell: "Stranger, go tell the Lacedaemonians that we lie here, obedient to their commands."[17] What is the stranger to tell those at home in Sparta? Only that Leonidas and the Three Hundred obediently lie dead. There is nothing here about freedom, or Greece, or any cause higher than not withdrawing before the enemy. Not even the Persians are mentioned, or any other reason for why these men fought and died. Dying rather than giving way seems to confer honor enough for the Spartans.

The other Peloponnesians who died at Thermopylae, before Leonidas dismissed all but the Spartans, Thespians, and Thebans, are remembered thus: "Once, four thousand men from the Peloponnese fought here against three million."[18] Like the epigram for the Spartans, this monument to the other Peloponnesians says nothing about why or against whom they fought, only that few stood against many.

A third epigram is also quoted by Herodotus, and while all three (and virtually all other Persian War epigrams) were later ascribed to the famous poet Simonides, only this third one is clearly labeled as such by

[16] The Greek text of most of the Persian War epigrams has been usefully collected by Kowerski 2005: 51–160. More comprehensive collections of and commentaries on Archaic and Classical Greek epigrams, both inscribed and literary, including the Persian War epigrams are provided by Page 1981; and Hansen 1983. For the epigrams surviving on stone, see also the selection of historical inscriptions edited by Meiggs and Lewis 1988. The most recent and thorough commentary and bibliography on the verse inscriptions ascribed to Simonides is found in Petrovic 2007. For the complete Simonidean corpus, including elegies in addition to epigrams, see Sider 2020. See Allgaier 2022, especially 74–82, for the use of inscriptions by Herodotus and the implications for his historiography. Tentori Montalto 2017 examines funerary epigrams for the war dead, including the ones discussed here. Inscribed epigram is an increasingly fascinating and fruitful scholarly subject. For an overview, see Baumbach, Petrovic, and Petrovic 2010; Oswald 2014; Sheppard 2016; and Henriksén 2019. See Raaflaub 2004: 59–65 for a brief survey of the rhetoric of freedom in sources from the period of the Persian Wars and immediately afterwards.
[17] = Sim. XXII(b) *FGE*: ὦ ξεῖν', ἀγγέλλειν Λακεδαιμονίοις ὅτι τῇδε | κείμεθα τοῖς κείνων ῥήμασι πειθόμενοι. An alternate version of these verses is preserved by Diodorus and others, in which "words" (ῥήμασι) is replaced by "laws" (νομίμοις). Several editors (such as Page 1981: 231–234) prefer the alternate version. I agree with those who see ῥήμασι as the *lectio difficilior* (the more difficult reading) and thus more likely to be the original reading according to the established principles of textual criticism. For the sparseness and ambiguity of these lines, open to a range of interpretations and responses, see Ziogas 2014.
[18] = Sim. XXII(a) *FGE*: μυριάσιν ποτὲ τῇδε τριηκοσίαις ἐμάχοντο | ἐκ Πελοποννάσου χιλιάδες τέτορες.

Herodotus.[19] Simonides honors his friend Megistias, a prophet from Acarnania who foresaw his own death but elected to remain with the Spartans anyway: "This is the memorial of renowned Megistias, whom once the Medes killed after they crossed the Spercheios River, a prophet who then saw clearly his approaching doom, yet could not bear to abandon the leader from Sparta."[20] According to Simonides' words, what compelled Megistias to remain at Thermopylae in the face of certain death was a conviction to stick by his Spartan commander to the end, a sentiment echoed in the Spartans' own refusal to leave their post or neglect what their leaders had said. Megistias' epigram contains four lines, instead of only two as in the case of the Spartans and Peloponnesians, allowing the poet room at least to mention that Megistias had died fighting the Medes, Greek shorthand for the army of the Persian Empire. Those who served under Leonidas and were memorialized for Herodotus (or his sources) to read on stone were not remembered as freedom fighters, or defenders of anything or anyone.

Later sources indicate that two other Greek states commemorated their dead at Thermopylae with inscribed epigrams. The geographer Strabo (9.4.2) says that the Locrians, while they joined the Persians after Thermopylae fell, nevertheless honored their fallen compatriots: "Opus, mother-city of the Locrians of fair laws, grieves these men who perished on behalf of Greece against the Medes."[21] It is difficult to sort out when this inscription was set up at Thermopylae, given that the Locrians "Medized" following the battle and thus were left off the immediate postwar monuments like the Serpent Column at Delphi, but Strabo claims to have seen five separate *stelai*, monumental slabs, at the site with this inscription being among them. (The Greeks commonly, though inaccurately, called the Persians "the Mede" after one of the principal peoples of the empire; "Medizing," therefore, meant taking the Persian side.) Page thinks that the epigram is Classical and of a quality similar to the others at the site cited earlier.[22] Unlike the Spartans and the Peloponnesians under their

---

[19] See Sider 2020: 89–90 for a discussion of the authorship of these three epigrams. Sider thinks many scholars have been too quick to dismiss Simonidean authorship, or at least the idea that Herodotus thought they were all composed by Simonides.

[20] = Sim. VI *FGE*: μνῆμα τόδε κλεινοῖο Μεγιστία, ὅν ποτε Μῆδοι | Σπερχειὸν ποταμὸν κτεῖναν ἀμειψάμενοι, | μάντιος, ὃς τότε κῆρας ἐπερχομένας σάφα εἰδώς | οὐκ ἔτλη Σπάρτης ἡγεμόνα προλιπεῖν.

[21] = Sim. XXIII *FGE*: τούσδε ποθεῖ φθιμένους ὑπὲρ Ἑλλάδος ἀντία Μήδων, | μητρόπολις Λοκρῶν εὐθυνόμων Ὀπόεις. Though Page lists this among the Simonidean epigrams, it was never attributed to him in antiquity (an unfortunately regular practice, as pointed out by Sider 2007).

[22] Page 1981: 236.

command, the Locrians give much more information about the circumstances of the soldiers' deaths, including the enemy they were fighting and
the reason they were fighting, namely on behalf of Greece. Such
Panhellenic (the idea that a broader nation of "Greece" exists and is
worth supporting) and altruistic sentiment is wholly absent from the
other epigrams at Thermopylae. Perhaps since the Locrians fought for
the Persians after this battle, they took extra care to emphasize their pro-
Greece bona fides, though, as we will see, plenty of poleis that did not
Medize deployed similar sentiments.

Stephanus of Byzantium, who compiled a geographical dictionary in the
6th century CE, quotes an epigram attributed to the otherwise unknown
Philiadas of Megara (one of only a couple of poets other than Simonides
credited with Persian War epigrams) that honored the Thespians who died:
"These men once dwelled on the brows of Helicon; broad-danced Thespiae
exults in their courage."[23] While some scholars think this poem was on one
of the five *stelai* Strabo saw at the battle site – no one deserved honor more
than the Thespians, who sacrificed the whole of their hoplite force – Page
thinks this epigram more likely to be a later literary exercise than a genuine
Classical inscription.[24] If it is genuine, it would represent another epigram in
line with the Spartan practice of not mentioning any principles like freedom
and defense, instead bringing glory to the dead and their individual polis
alone. Unlike the famous Spartan epigram, and those for the other
Peloponnesians and Megistias, the Thespians, like the Locrians, overtly
claim recognition because of the deeds of their fellow citizens.[25] There is
no mention of Megistias' home, nor of any individual Peloponnesian state.
The Lacedaemonians are highlighted as a group in their famous couplet, but
much more ambiguously than the Locrians or Thespians.[26]

Two more sets of epigrams (possibly) relate to Thermopylae, though
Page and others tend to consider them later literary exercises rather than
based on 5th-century inscriptions.[27] They survive only in the Palatine

---

[23] = Philiadas I *FGE*: ἄνδρες θ' οἵ ποτ' ἔναιον ὑπὸ κροτάφοις Ἑλικῶνος, | λήματι τῶν αὐχεῖ Θεσπιὰς
εὐρύχορος.

[24] Page 1981: 78–79.

[25] For more on Thespian commemorative practices, see the discussion of their late 5th-century
polyandrion in Chapter 6.

[26] For the ambiguity of this epigram, including even the remote possibility that a criticism of the
Spartan government is intended, see Ziogas 2014.

[27] Page 1981: 196–197, 298–299. But see Sider 2020: 90, 183–184, who considers the first of the following
epigrams to be a genuine inscription on Leonidas' lion monument at Thermopylae. He agrees, on
the other hand, that the second set of lines is unlikely to be genuine and is merely meant to be taken
by its author as an inscription on the lion monument.

Anthology (a medieval collection of ancient epigrams). The first commemorates those who died along with Leonidas: "The earth covers, Leonidas, king of broad-danced Sparta, these famous men who died here with you, after they received in battle the might of the great many arrows and swift horses of the Medes."[28] This poem mentions Sparta, affixing the common epithet "broad-danced," and also states against whom the men were fighting; but the focus is still squarely on the fame of the dead.

A set of two two-line epigrams, or just one four-line epigram as some have interpreted them, rounds out our discussion of what was or might have been inscribed at Thermopylae: "I am mightiest of the beasts, and made of stone, affixed to this grave, I guard the mightiest of men," and, "But if Leon did not have both my spirit and my name, I would not have placed my feet on this tomb."[29] Since this pair of poems are in the voice of a lion, and since a lion monument was erected to honor Leonidas (Hdt. 7.225), whose name denotes a descendant of "Leon," the Greek word for lion, they have been taken to commemorate Leonidas at Thermopylae. No mention is made of a battle, the Persians, Greece, or of Sparta (or even of Leonidas, unless indirectly) in the pair of epigrams, but the fame and might of the dead are the poems' subject.

Aside from epigrams, there is a lyric poem attributed to Simonides and quoted by Diodorus (11.11.6) that commemorates the Spartans at Thermopylae:

> The fortune of those who died at Thermopylae is glorious, their fate noble. Their tomb is an altar, and instead of mourning, they have remembrance, and their doom is praise. Neither this burial shroud, nor mold, nor all-subduing time will waste them away. This tomb of brave men has taken the renown of Greece as its enslaved attendant. To this, Leonidas, the king of Sparta, who has left behind a great ornament of excellence and eternal fame, stands as a witness.[30]

---

[28] = Sim. VII *FGE*: εὐκλέας αἶα κέκευθε, Λεωνίδα, οἳ μετὰ σεῖο | τῇδ᾽ ἔθανον, Σπάρτης εὐρυχόρου βασιλεῦ, | πλείστων δὴ τόξων τε καὶ ὠκυπόδων σθένος ἵππων | Μηδείων ἀνδρῶν δεξάμενοι πολέμωι.

[29] = Sim. LXXXIII(a–b) *FGE*: θηρῶν μὲν κάρτιστος ἐγώ, θνατῶν δ᾽ὃν ἐγὼ νῦν | φρουρῶ τῶιδε τάφωι λάινος ἐμβεβαώς. . .

> ἀλλ᾽ εἰ μὴ θυμόν γε Λέων ἐμὸν οὔνομά τ᾽ εἶχεν,
> οὐκ ἂν ἐγὼ τύμβωι τῶιδ᾽ ἐπέθηκα πόδας.

[30] = Sim. 531 *PMG*: τῶν ἐν Θερμοπύλαις θανόντων | εὐκλεὴς μὲν ἁ τύχα, καλὸς δ᾽ ὁ πότμος, | βωμὸς δ᾽ ὁ τάφος, πρὸ γόων δὲ μνᾶστις, ὁ δ᾽ οἶτος ἔπαινος. | ἐντάφιον δὲ τοιοῦτον οὔτ᾽ εὐρὼς | οὔθ᾽ ὁ πανδαμάτωρ ἀμαυρώσει χρόνος. | ἀνδρῶν ἀγαθῶν ὅδε σηκὸς οἰκέταν εὐδοξίαν | Ἑλλάδος εἵλετο. μαρτυρεῖ δὲ καὶ Λεωνίδας | ὁ Σπάρτας βασιλεύς, ἀρετᾶς μέγαν λελοιπὼς | κόσμον ἀέναόν τε κλέος. For this poem, see Steiner 1999.

Like the epigrams, these lyric lines focus on the fame and glory of the dead, even suggesting, by naming their tomb an altar, that they receive heroic honors after death. Leonidas is named directly, singled out for the signs of excellence and fame he left behind, but not for any sacrifice for a greater cause. Unlike the Thermopylae epigrams, this poem actually refers to Greece. I take the genitive in the phrase "the renown (*eudoxia*) of Greece" to be subjective, meaning the renown Greece holds for the dead, rather than renown that reflects on Greece itself. The latter would make little sense in the context of a poem celebrating the dead Spartans. Therefore, the mention of Greece in these lines serves not to highlight the Spartan sacrifice for a Panhellenic cause but rather to heighten the fame and glory enjoyed by the Spartans alone, so renowned that all of Greece recognizes their great deed.

In addition to Thermopylae, there are three other Persian War epigrams linked to Sparta. One has been tied by Bergk, with the assent of Page, to the Spartan tomb at Plataea, the other great victory of the Spartans in the war: "These men placed ceaseless fame on their fatherland, they embraced the black cloud of death; but dying they have not died, since Excellence praises them from above and leads them up from the house of Hades."[31] The Palatine Anthology declares this poem to be for the dead at Thermopylae, but Page persuasively argues that this designation must be incorrect, not least because we know of several epigrams at Thermopylae already, which do not include this one. Instead, this epigram is well suited to a battlefield *polyandrion*, and Pausanias (9.2.4) tells us that at Plataea the Spartans and Athenians had their own separate burials apart from the rest of the Greek dead, on which epitaphs composed by Simonides were inscribed.

Another epigram, paired with this one in the Palatine Anthology, is also said to have been from Thermopylae, but was likely on one of the two *polyandria* at Plataea. Page agrees with Bergk's argument that the following lines, with their Panhellenic pretensions, were likely on the Athenian grave, while the preceding poem was on the Spartan: "If the greatest part of excellence is to die well, Fortune apportioned this to us especially. For striving to invest Greece with freedom, we lie enjoying ageless praise."[32] Neither of these two poems states whom they are honoring – or states that

---

[31] = Sim. IX *FGE*: ἄσβεστον κλέος οἵδε φίληι περὶ πατρίδι θέντες | κυάνεον θανάτου ἀμφεβάλοντο νέφος· | οὐδὲ τεθνᾶσι θανόντες, ἐπεί σφ' Ἀρετὴ καθύπερθε | κυδαίνουσ' ἀνάγει δώματος ἐξ Ἀίδεω. For a discussion of this epigram and the following one, see Page 1981: 197–200.

[32] = Sim. VIII *FGE*: εἰ τὸ καλῶς θνῄσκειν ἀρετῆς μέρος ἐστὶ μέγιστον, | ἡμῖν ἐκ πάντων τοῦτ' ἀπένειμε Τύχη· | Ἑλλάδι γὰρ σπεύδοντες ἐλευθερίην περιθεῖναι | κείμεθ' ἀγηράντωι χρώμενοι εὐλογίηι. Sider 2020: 83–84 disagrees with Page and others that the mention of freedom is more appropriate for the Athenians, since more than just the Athenians, especially the Spartans who were in command, were responsible for preserving Greek freedom at Plataea. This question is precisely what is at issue in the

they are on tombs at Plataea at all – but, as we will see, the mention of freedom and fighting on behalf of Greece is out of step with Spartan commemorations, but completely in line with the practices of most other poleis, especially Athens.

The most notorious Persian War epigrams are those commissioned by Pausanias, the Spartan regent who took credit for the victory at Plataea but later fell into disgrace for his outrageous arrogance and alleged collusion with the Persians. In a famous digression, Thucydides (1.128–138) tells of Pausanias' fall from grace, which led to his ignominious death from starving after being walled in inside the temple of Athena Chalkioikos, "of the Bronze House," on the Spartan acropolis, where he had fled for refuge. The first sign of the apparently shocking self-regard Pausanias developed for himself was the epigram he had inscribed on the Serpent Column at Delphi, which was supposed to be a monument to all the Greeks who had stood against the Persians: "Commander-in-chief of the Greeks, when he destroyed the army of the Medes, Pausanias dedicated this monument to Phoebus."[33] According to Thucydides' account, the Spartans straightaway erased this inscription, which was replaced by the list of participating poleis that is still on the monument today, where it remains in the hippodrome in Istanbul, having been moved there in late antiquity by Constantine.[34] Diodorus (11.33.2) says that a new epigram was included with this list of poleis, which ran as follows: "The saviors of broad-danced Greece dedicated this, having defended the poleis from hated slavery."[35] This epigram is in line with many other non-Spartan commemorations of the Persian Wars, but it is unclear whether it was ever inscribed on the monument itself. No trace of it can be seen on the column, and no one other than Diodorus so much as mentions it.

The other epigram dedicated by Pausanias was inscribed on a gigantic bronze bowl at the entrance to the Black Sea, mentioned by Herodotus (4.81). The text of the epigram was preserved by Nymphis in the early 3rd century BCE, who is quoted by Athenaeus in the 2nd century CE: "As a monument of his excellence, to lord Poseidon on the Euxine Sea, Pausanias, ruler of broad-danced Greece, dedicated this, Lacedaemonian

---

present chapter, and it should be clear by now that I think the Spartans eschewed the mention of freedom in these commemorations.

[33] = Sim. XVII(a) *FGE*: Ἑλλάνων ἀρχαγὸς, ἐπεὶ στρατὸν ὤλεσε Μήδων, | Παυσανίας Φοίβωι μνᾶμ' ἀνέθηκε τόδε.

[34] For the surviving inscription on the Serpent Column, see ML 27.

[35] = Sim. XVII(b) *FGE*: Ἑλλάδος εὐρυχόρου σωτῆρες τόνδ' ἀνέθηκαν, | δουλοσύνης στυγερᾶς ῥυσάμενοι πόλιας.

by race, son of Cleombrotus, of the ancient lineage of Heracles."[36] As Page argues, Pausanias' claim in this epigram of being the ruler (*archon*) of Greece is even more offensive than his claim on the Serpent Column to be the Greek commander-in-chief who destroyed the Persian army. Pausanias, after all, really had been the commander at Plataea when the Persian army was decisively defeated.[37] Pausanias' two dedications seem to provide ample evidence of his unacceptable arrogance and that he was on a trajectory that would lead him to his ruin at the hands of the conservative Spartan authorities. Thucydides' account indicates that the Spartans could not countenance such self-aggrandizement and were all too ready to recall Pausanias from his leadership of the Greek coalition overseas and thereby forfeit their claim of hegemony over the Greeks – all to the advantage of imperial Athens, which stepped in to fill the power vacuum left by Sparta.

To be sure, Pausanias' mention of Greece is out of step with the other Spartan epigrams commemorating the Persian Wars, but his self-aggrandizement is not. Had he instead made claims of fighting for the freedom of Greece, he would have been far more in line with the rhetoric of other poleis, but at odds with Spartan practice in the early 5th century. By focusing on his own excellence and the memory of this excellence guaranteed by physical monuments and poetic verses, Pausanias was simply doing for himself what had been done for the Spartan dead, including Leonidas. By portraying Pausanias as offensive to Spartan sensibilities, Thucydides is fitting the Spartans into a carefully constructed literary characterization that sets them at odds with the Athenians, providing the central dichotomy of his history of the Peloponnesian War. As I have argued elsewhere, Thucydides' focus on "un-Spartan Spartans" serves to highlight stereotypical Spartan-ness, whereas, in reality, the Spartans were not as Spartan as Thucydides would like us to believe, nor were Spartan renegades so un-Spartan.[38] Fighting for personal glory, as much or more than for the glory of Sparta, is exactly what the Spartans would have been expected to do in 480–479.

In fact, the Spartans might not have been the ones to get angry with Pausanias and initiate the change to the Serpent Column dedication at all.

---

[36] = Sim. XXXIX *FGE*: μνᾶμ' ἀρετᾶς ἀνέθηκε Ποσειδάωνι ἄνακτι | Παυσανίας ἄρχων Ἑλλάδος εὐρυχόρου | πόντου ἐπ' Εὐξείνου, Λακεδαιμόνιος γένος, υἱός | Κλεομβρότου, ἀρχαίας Ἡρακλέος γενεᾶς. This is another one of those epigrams assigned to Simonides by Page, but not by any ancient source (see Sider 2007).

[37] Page 1981: 254.

[38] See Sears 2020, especially 181, for the case of Pausanias. See also Evans 1988 for the two conflicting traditions about Pausanias, one of which (the one not followed by Thucydides) is decidedly positive; and Ellis 1994 for the literary contrast between Sparta and Athens as expressed by portraits of Pausanias and Themistocles.

An alternate tradition is preserved by the 4th-century speech *Against Neaera*, delivered by an Apollodoros of Acharnae and attributed (likely erroneously) to the famous Athenian orator Demosthenes. According to this speech, it was the Plataeans who were incensed by Pausanias' epigram and brought a suit on behalf of all the allies to the Amphictyonic council, the group of poleis responsible for protecting Delphi. The result of the suit was that the original epigram was erased and replaced by the names of all contributing states, and the Lacedaemonians were fined 1,000 talents ([Dem.] 59: 97–98). Jeremy Trevett argues that there is no surefire way to adjudicate between this account and that provided by Thucydides.[39] I am inclined to agree, even favoring the tradition preserved in *Against Neaera*, considering the other epigrams that have survived and Thucydides' contrived literary program.

The Spartans did, though, put Pausanias to death, or, rather, allowed him to starve just outside of Athena's sanctuary. If his arrogance, or even his supposed Medism, did not bring him down at home, what did? I suggest that Pausanias and the Spartans really fell out when the regent started to pursue a genuinely Panhellenic policy and embroiled Sparta in commitments overseas. Immediately after Xerxes' invasion, the Spartans were eager to yield Panhellenic adventurism to the Athenians, wanting instead to revert to their tried-and-true isolationism. By this reading of history, pride did not go before Pausanias' fall, but Panhellenism did. The Spartans were so uninterested, even opposed, to fighting on behalf of others outside of Laconia and the region that they turned against the man who won at Plataea. The content of the epigram on the Black Sea, proclaiming Pausanias ruler of Greece, was far less offensive to the Spartans in the 470s than the fact that a Spartan leader was erecting monuments all the way over on the Black Sea in the first place. Being the "ruler of Greece," or "commander-in-chief" of the Greeks was fine, so long as those titles were in the service of personal glory in battles closer to home.

Before turning to the commemorative epigrams of other poleis, we must consider one other contemporaneous poetic memorial that preserves the Spartan perspective. The so-called "New Simonides," preserved on papyrus and first published only in the late 20th century, includes portions of a lengthy elegiac poem about the Persian Wars with an apparent focus on the Spartans and Plataea. While there is debate concerning who commissioned Simonides to compose the poem, and at what occasion it was originally performed, the balance of scholarly opinions comes down on the side of its being a Spartan commission performed at a Spartan

---

[39] Trevett 1990: 409–411.

ceremony, such as the dedication of the *polyandrion* at Plataea or a commemorative event at Sparta. Pausanias, who is mentioned by name in the surviving lines of the poem, might have even commissioned it himself.[40] In addition to detailing the participants in (Corinth, for example, is mentioned in the surviving text) and events of the campaign of Plataea, the elegy compares the events of 479 to the Trojan War, in particular the Greek heroes who won undying fame (*athanatos kleos*). Achilles and his death are singled out in the poem. What better model for the Spartans could there be than the hero who fought for glory and fame in the full knowledge that he would die in the process?

Lawrence M. Kowerski argues that Simonides employs Achilles as a model for all the Greeks, not just the Spartans.[41] It is my contention here, however, that only the Spartans really followed Achilles' example by fighting and dying solely for *kleos*, rather than for, say, the freedom of Greece. Herodotus' suggestion that Leonidas at Thermopylae, once the defenders' position was hopeless, sent away the other Greeks in order to maximize his own glory and that of Sparta, and to fulfill the Delphic oracle's prophecy that said a Spartan king had to die in order for Sparta to be saved, certainly fits into this mold (Hdt. 7.219–220). This account does not need to be dismissed, as it is by van Wees, as Herodotus' attempts to reckon with the legend of the battle. Neither does the tradition preserved by Diodorus and originally followed by Ephorus that Leonidas went to Thermopylae with too small a force and in full foreknowledge of his own death in order to bring the maximum amount of glory to Sparta (Diod. 11.4).[42]

---

[40] The most comprehensive treatment of the New Simonides is provided by Boedeker and Sider 2001. For a text, translation, and commentary on the poem, see Sider's chapter. For the context of the poem and connections to the Spartans, see especially the chapters by Rutherford, Aloni, Stehle, and Boedeker. Kowerski 2005, by contrast, argues that the poem is Panhellenic in nature, emphasizing the contributions of many Greek poleis. Nobili 2011 argues that the New Simonides poem fits in well with a tradition of threnodic elegy at Sparta that predated the Persian Wars. Thiel 2011 presents a compelling case for the poem's recital at the burial of the Spartan war dead after Plataea. He argues for a date prior to 477, before Pausanias was condemned for Medism. I have already pointed out above some problems with Pausanias' supposed Medism, but also the fact that he was honored with conspicuous monuments in Sparta still visible in the 2nd century CE suggests that Pausanias' fall from grace need not preclude his commemoration. A newly edited text, translation, and commentary is offered by Sider 2020: 254–293, who is noncommittal about the date and commissioning of the poem.

[41] Kowerski 2005: 96–106. But for Achilles as a Spartan exemplar, see Stehle 2001; and Boedeker 2001.

[42] van Wees 2018. I thank Joseph Day for reminding me that Ephorus' own teacher was the Athenian pamphleteer Isocrates, one of the most outspoken advocates for Panhellenism in the 4th century. Ephorus was himself a Panhellenist in terms of writing history, for which see Alonso-Núñez 2002: 35–41. Leonidas being self-interested in the pursuit of glory would not advance a Panhellenic agenda, if indeed that is what Ephorus was pursuing.

While the general theme of the poem is fairly clear, and many specific names and subjects are preserved on the papyrus, there is still a good deal of text missing. M. L. West extensively restored the text, ingeniously making use of literary parallels, to provide a more coherent and pleasing poem, but his emendations are often far from obvious and not uncontested.[43] One particularly fragmentary line (F 11.25) mentions Sparta or the Spartans, though the word's grammatical case and thus role in the sentence is not clear. West has filled out the line and the one following to indicate that the soldiers set out to ward off the "day of slavery" from Sparta and from Greece – though the mention of Greece is entirely absent from the papyrus, in this line and all the others.[44] This would be the sole instance I have found of the Spartans in an early 5th-century source being concerned with the slavery and freedom of the Greeks. The "day of slavery" (*doulion ēmar*) is a phrase with parallels in Homeric epic and probably also in Persian War epigram.[45] West restores the phrase based on the survival of the last two letters, *ar*/αρ, on the papyrus, whereas most of the line has been lost. Only Homer's *Iliad* 6.463, during the meeting of Hector and Andromache, preserves the phrase in the final position of a hexameter line, whereas all other examples are from different metrical positions. The "day of slavery," *doulion ēmar*, is by no means the only possible restoration based on the two surviving letters. Many other possibilities from epic and other sources present themselves, such as the "day of evil" (*kakon ēmar*), or "day by day" (*ēmar ep' ēmar*). What we can make out confidently in the rest of the poem – including mentions of eternal fame and Pausanias mentioned by name as leading the expedition, which includes Corinthians, Megarians, and others – is entirely in line with Pausanias' controversial epigrams and other Spartan dedications.

Epigrams, along with a short lyric poem and longer elegy ascribed to Simonides, are the strongest literary evidence that survives from the period of the Persian Wars or immediately after. In these texts, Sparta and the Spartans – along with the Peloponnesians and the Acarnanian prophet who fought beside them at Thermopylae – are concerned above all with being remembered, with gaining undying fame, or *kleos*. They also want to

---

[43] For West's text and translation, see Sider 2001: 27–29. Sider 2020: 254–293 is much more conservative in his emendations than West.

[44] F11 W, 25–26: ἀνδρῶ]ν, οἳ Σπάρτ[ηι τε καὶ Ἑλλάδι δούλιον ἦμ]αρ | ἔσχον] ἀμυνόμ[ενοι μή τιν' ἰδεῖν φανερ]ῶ[ς.

[45] Examples of the phrase: Hom. *Il.* 6.463; *Od.* 14.340, 17.323; Theog. 1.1213; Pl. *Laws* 777a2; Sim. XX(a) *FGE*, though this usage of the phrase in a 5th-century epigram is based on a reconstruction from what is thought to be a 4th-century copy; the phrase does not survive in the 5th-century version.

ensure that they are remembered as having excellence, or *aretē*, the most important of Greek virtues, from the Homeric poems and ever afterward.

To put it simply: winning fame through excellence is why the Spartans fought in 480–479; this is how they commemorated that fighting on the monuments closest in time to the events themselves. The Spartans did not seem concerned with the freedom of Greece or defending their fellow poleis from the Persians. Fighting for any kind of greater cause was not a priority. The Spartans mentioned Greece and the Greeks only to indicate their subordinate role to the Spartans in the conflict against Persia, and they named the Persian enemy only rarely. The circumstances and reasons for fighting were far less important than the fact that the Spartans fought, achieving victory or death or death in victory, and that they demonstrated excellence in doing so. In this way, the Spartans were very much like the Homeric heroes, Achilles especially, but also Hector.[46] They were very much unlike their fellow Greeks, to whom we will now turn in more detail.

## The Other Greeks Remember the Persian Wars

As we have seen, of the two epigrams that were likely inscribed on the tombs at Plataea, one is more Athenian and the other more Spartan; therefore, we can assign the verses to their respective monuments with reasonable confidence. To understand how we can make such a determination, we will first look at some of the Athenian epigrams from the Persian Wars and the adjacent periods. Then we will proceed to consider the epigrams of other Greek poleis.

The Persian Wars began earlier for the Athenians than for the Spartans and most other members of the Greek alliance. The Athenians likely experienced the Persian Wars as two separate wars.[47] Athenian conceptions of the defense of Athens and Greece developed somewhat in the

---

[46] As Joseph Day points out to me, Hector himself composed an epigram of sorts in Homer's *Iliad*. Imagining the death of a foe, Hector says that the tomb will read the following: "This is the tomb of a man who died long ago; whom, while he was showing his prowess, glorious Hector once killed (ἀνδρὸς μὲν τόδε σῆμα πάλαι κατατεθνηῶτος | ὅν ποτ᾿ ἀριστεύοντα κατέκτανε φαίδιμος Ἕκτωρ)." Hector adds that such a grave inscription will increase Hector's glory, not the dead man's (Hom. *Il.* 7.89–91). For more on this imagined inscription as an epigram, see Petrovic 2016.

[47] As suggested to me by Joseph Day. For the Athenian response to Marathon before the concept of a broader Persian War was conceived, see Proietti 2021: 12–57. Proietti stresses that Marathon was initially a source of Athenian civic pride and civic defense, rather than a grand struggle against "barbarians." As I will demonstrate, however, this civic pride likely extended to a notion of a defense of all Greece.

decade between the different phases, though Panhellenic ideas might have been there from the beginning.

The first Persian attempt to take cities in the central and southern Greek mainland, in response to Athenian and Eretrian involvement in the burning of the local Persian capital Sardis in 499, took place during the Marathon campaign of 490. Darius sent a fleet across the Aegean, first to attack and destroy Eretria on Euboea, and then to move against Athens. Darius' generals and soldiers made short work of Eretria, and then landed on the plain of Marathon, forty kilometers northeast of Athens, led by the Athenian ex-tyrant Hippias, who hoped to regain his position with Persian help. As is now the stuff of legend, ranking with Thermopylae on various lists of "decisive battles," the Athenians, just newly democratic and outnumbered by their enemies, charged the Persian army and won a great victory. The Athenian soldiers then returned to Athens on the double to meet the Persian fleet that had sailed around Cape Sounion in an attempt to take the city after the battle had turned against them. Athens and its democracy were saved, and the Persians forced back onto their ships and back across the sea. Only the Plataeans sent any help to the Athenians, providing 1,000 soldiers for the battle. Marathon was thus an essentially Athenian victory, of which the Athenians would happily remind anyone for the next century-and-a-half and then some. Those who died at Marathon were especially revered, buried under a mound of earth that is still visible on the Marathon plain. Marathon was prominent in later sources such as Herodotus, Thucydides, and the Athenian orators, when its legend had solidified. Soon after the battle, Marathon and the Marathon dead were the subject of several contemporaneous epigrams.

Callimachus, the Athenian war leader, or elected *polemarch*, officially in charge at Marathon (though Miltiades would take most of the credit), was killed in the action. An inscribed column, originally topped with a winged victory goddess, a *nikē*, is now in the Acropolis Museum in Athens. On this column is an epigram, variously interpreted by scholars. While some think that the column was originally dedicated by Callimachus before the battle in honor of an athletic victory, and more verses were added later, others think that all the lines were inscribed at the same time on Callimachus' behalf after he died.[48] It is generally agreed that Callimachus is honored on the column as the *polemarch*, and that

---

[48] The most thorough treatment of the Callimachus monument is given by Keesling 2010. See also Jacoby 1945, whose study of this monument and the following epigrams is a classic.

Marathon is mentioned explicitly.[49] Many also read "of the Greeks" in the fourth verse of the inscription, which strongly suggests that the struggle at Marathon was on behalf of all Greeks, just as is stated in other epigrams. Already in 490, then, the Athenians might have advertised their defeat of the Persians at Marathon as a Panhellenic event benefitting Greece as a whole.[50]

In his speech *Against Leocrates* (108–109) of 330 BCE, the Athenian orator Lycurgus quotes the following epigram as revealing the Athenian valor at Marathon: "Fighting on behalf of the Greeks, the Athenians at Marathon laid low the power of the gold-bearing Medes."[51] Page insists, and he has many points in his favor, that this epigram was placed beside the casualty lists of the fallen Athenians at the burial mound, or Soros, at Marathon (though not everyone agrees).[52]

This epigram's sentiment – of the Athenians performing an act for the benefit of all their fellow Greeks – is shared by another epigram that many attribute also to the Battle of Marathon. The so-called Monument of the Persian War Epigrams, based on two inscribed stones from the 5th century found in Athens and supplemented by a 4th-century copy, has occasioned much debate over the years, with some scholars arguing that at least one of the two preserved epigrams refers to Marathon, while others prefer Salamis or the Persian Wars in general.[53] Angelos Matthaiou found a third stone in the 1980s, which he used to argue persuasively that the inscriptions were part of a cenotaph commemorating Marathon and set up in Athens (Figure 3.2).[54]

---

[49] = ML 18: [Καλίμαχός μ' ἀνέθηκεν Ἀφιδναῖο[ς] τἀθεναίαι ⫶ | ἄγ[γελον ἀθ]ανάτον hοὶ Ὀ[λύμπια δόματ'] ἔχοσιν, | [. . . . 8 . . . . πολέ]μαρχο[ς] Ἀθεναίον τὸν ἀγõνα ⫶ | τὸν Μα[ραθον . . . . h]ελενονο [. . . . . 11 . . . . . . ⫶] | παισὶν Ἀθεναίον μν[. . . . . . . . . 21 . . . . . . . . . .].

[50] For the Panhellenic message of the Callimachus monument, see Keesling 2010: 128. Jung 2006: 84–95 is skeptical that such Panhellenic sentiment preexisted the battle, or even came shortly after it. I think the bulk of the evidence supports a Panhellenic reading of the Callimachus monument and other monuments and epigrams discussed here.

[51] = Sim. XXI *FGE*: Ἑλλήνων προμαχοῦντες Ἀθεναῖοι Μαραθῶνι | Χρυσοφόρων Μήδων ἐστόρεσαν δύναμιν.

[52] Page 1981: 225–231. Sider 2020: 74 argues that the lines could just as easily been applied as a label to the image of the Battle of Marathon in the Stoa Poiklie in the Agora, painted by Polygnotus in 490.

[53] ML 26; Sim. XX(a–b) *FGE*; Tentori Montalto 2017: 102–108. The following text is from *FGE*:
XX(a): ἀνδρῶν τῶνδ' ἀρετῆ[ς ἔσται κλέ]ος ἄφθι[τον] αἰεί | [. . . . . . . . . . .]ρ[] νέμωσι θεοί· | ἔσχον γὰρ πεζοί τε [καὶ] ὠκυπόρων ἐπὶ νηῶν | Ἑλλά[δα μ]ὴ πᾶσαν δούλιον ἦμαρ ἰδεῖν.
XX(b): ἦν ἄρα τοῖςζ' ἀδάμ[αντος ὑπέρβιον ἦτορ,] ὅτ' αἰχμήν | στῆσαν πρόσθε πυλῶν αν[ | ἀγχίαλον πρῆσαι ρ[c. xix litt.] | ἄστυ, βίαι Περσῶν κλινάμενο[ι προμάχους.
Page groups these epigrams under "Simonides," but no ancient source credits that author (see Sider 2007).

[54] Matthaiou 1988; 2003. See also Proietti 2011, who supports Matthaiou's identification of the monument as a cenotaph for Marathon. I thank Joe Day for the information that this stone is newly on display at the Agora Museum, as of spring 2022.

Figure 3.2 Fragment of an epigram supposedly honoring Marathon. Athens, Agora object no. I 4256; image no. 2012.83.0052 (96–79–20). Ephorate of Antiquities of Athens City, Ancient Agora, ASCSA: Agora Excavations. © Hellenic Ministry of Culture and Sports / Hellenic Organization of Cultural Resources Development (H.O.C.RE.D.).

While several of the lines have been restored in various ways by different scholars, the surviving text clearly states that the Athenians fought the Persians and demonstrated excellence, and that they fought "so that all Greece would not see the day of slavery."

A final Athenian Persian War epigram mentioning the freedom of the Greeks is found on a red-figure pyxis (a type of clay vessel) from the Acropolis, securely dated to 480 or shortly before since it was found in a Persian War destruction context. The first line of the epigram is difficult to reconstruct, but the second line mentions freedom and has been restored to say, "Greece has a beautiful crown of freedom."[55]

We should also add another epigram, for which no secure context has been proposed and which many scholars have assumed was a later literary exercise: "The sons of the Athenians destroyed the army of the Persians and warded off grievous slavery from their fatherland."[56] While this epigram

[55] = *CEG* 440: σοφροσ{σ}ύνεν ἐνὶ κλα[4–5]μιλα[ca. 14] | [hελλὰς ἐλε]υθερίας καλὸ:|ν ἔχει στέφανον. Based on several parallels, Hansen 1983: 245 considers the restoration of the second line to be reasonably secure.

[56] = Sim. XVIII *FGE*: παῖδες Ἀθηναίων Περσῶν στρατὸν ἐξολέσαντες | ἤρκεσαν ἀργαλέην πατρίδι δουλοσύνην. Page 1981: 229–230 sees no reason to discount this epigram as a genuine 5th-century composition, even an inscription, but no context is obvious. He discusses the reasons why most other scholars assigned the epigram to a later period. See also Sider 2020: 123, who sees no secure reason to credit or not to credit Simonides as the author. He does say that the lines could have been

makes no mention of Greece as a whole, it does indicate that a defense against slavery was a prime motivator for the Athenians to fight the Persians.

To be sure, while many Athenian epigrams from the Persian Wars mention the fight on behalf of all Greece and the struggle against slavery, not all do so. In the late 1990s, an exciting find was made at the villa of the Roman-era magnate Herodes Atticus at Loukou, a village in the Peloponnese. It seems that Herodes decorated this estate with a casualty list from Marathon, where Herodes was from and where he had another villa. The inscribed *stele* discovered at Loukou includes an epigram and a casualty list from the battle for the Athenian tribe of Erechtheis. It seems likely that the stone and its epigram are original to the early 5th century, despite the arguments of some that it is a later monument from the 4th century.[57] The epigram can be translated as follows: "I say: Even those ends of the earth lying beneath the dawn's light will hear of the excellence of these men, how they died fighting against the Medes and how they crowned Athens, undertaking a war against many though being only a few."[58] This epigram demonstrates that, despite the Panhellenic spirit of their other commemorations, the Athenians were also capable of focusing on the glory of the deceased and the city of Athens. The Athenians also produced several dedications from the Persian Wars that merely express thanks to various deities and mention the Persians from whom spoils were taken.[59]

Because it is Athens, we have a rich literary source from a few short years after the Persian invasion that confirms the message repeated in several Athenian epigrams, namely *The Persians* by Aeschylus. This play is the only extant tragedy from ancient Greece that refers to a real historical event, the Battle of Salamis, and was written by a veteran of the wars and performed before an audience of veterans in 472, just eight years after the battle itself.

---

part of a larger work, such as an elegy, and were not necessarily part of an epigram, which would explain the lack of any mention of the poem's context.

[57] Proietti 2013; 2015; 2019 thinks the epigram is a later composition, but this is a minority view. For the epigram as dating to the time just after Marathon, see Steinhauer 2004–2009; Keesling 2012; Oswald 2014: 114–116; and Tentori Montalto 2017: 92–102.

[58] Greek text from Tentori Montalto 2017: 92–93. Φεμί· καὶ ὁσστις ναίει ηυφ' Ἄος ἡέσσχατα γαίες, | τὸνδ' ἀνδρῶν ἀρετὲν πεύσεται, hος ἔθανον | βαρνάμενοι Μέδοισι καὶ ἐσστεφάνοσαν Ἀθένας, | παυρότεροι πολλὸν δεχσάμενοι πόλεμον. See also Oswald 2014: 114–115, who provides a slightly different reading (particularly of the first line), based on Steinhauer 2004–2009, though I think Tentori Montalto's text is to be preferred.

[59] See, for example, the Athenian thank-offering for Marathon at Olympia (ML 19), Miltiades' dedication to Pan (Sim. V *FGE*), the Athenian dedication to Artemis at Artemisium (Sim. XXIV *FGE*), and the inscription on the Athenian Stoa at Delphi (ML 25).

Like the Athenian Persian War epigrams, *The Persians* emphasizes the freedom of the Greeks. In one arresting scene, Greece and Persia are personified as women yoked to a chariot. The free Greek woman struggles violently against the yoke, while the Persian woman quietly submits. This is one of the many passages in *The Persians* that led Edith Hall, drawing on the work of the theorist Edward Said, to deem the play perhaps the first work of Orientalist literature, stereotyping the "West" as vigorously free, and the east slavish and effeminate by nature.[60] In another scene, the Greeks shout encouragement to one another as they begin the naval clash at Salamis, proclaiming that, "O sons of the Greeks, go forth! Set free your fatherland, your children, your wives, the shines of your paternal gods, and the tombs of your ancestors! Now the contest is for all!" (402–405). We do not possess comparable literature from other poleis in the early 5th century, but nothing in the Spartan epigrams suggests that they thought about the war in these terms at all.

We have already had occasion to consider the epigrams commissioned by the Locrians and Thespians at Thermopylae. Several other Greek poleis also left Persian War epigrams, especially the Corinthians, whom Herodotus sidelines and even maligns in his history. Herodotus was unfair to the Corinthians, at least according to Plutarch, who quotes many of the relevant epigrams in his essay *On the Malice of Herodotus*. The first we will consider is found in Plutarch and also survives partially on stone, and commemorates the Corinthians who died at Salamis: "Stranger, once we inhabited the well-watered city of Corinth, but now Salamis, island of Ajax, holds us. Here, we took the ships of the Phoenicians, Persians, and Medes, and rescued holy Greece."[61] The Corinthians were sure to advertise that they not only fought on behalf of "holy Greece," but that they "rescued" (*rhuomai*) Greece, a term that appears in many of these commemorations (but not the Spartan ones).[62]

[60] Hall 1989: 99.
[61] = ML 24; Sim. XI *FGE*; *CEG* 131; Tentori Montalto 2017: 110–115: ὦ ξεῖν᾽ εὔυδρόν ποκ᾽ ἐναίομες ἄστυ Κορίνθου, | Νῦν δ᾽ ἁμ᾽ Αἴαντος νᾶσος ἔχει Σαλαμίς· | ἐνθάδε Φοινίσσας νᾶας καὶ Πέρσας ἑλόντες | καὶ Μήδους ἱαρὰν Ἑλλάδα ῥυσάμεθα. Sider 2020: 99, pointing out that some have disputed whether the second pair of lines is original to the epigram (though Boegehold demonstrated that there was room on the stone), argues for genuine Simonidean authorship, based on parallels to the "New Simonides."
[62] It is worth nothing that Herodotus uses *rhuomai* primarily to denote rescuing others from slavery. See, for example, 5.49.3, 9.90.2, 9.76.2. It is a perfectly good Homeric word too. See, for example, Hom. *Il.* 7.223–224: "so that you may eagerly rescue (*rhuoisthe*) the wives and little children of the Trojans from the war-loving Achaeans (ἀλλ᾽ ἵνα μοι Τρώων ἀλόχους καὶ νήπια τέκνα | προφρονέως ῥύοισθε φιλοπτολέμων ὑπ᾽ Ἀχαιῶν)."

The next Corinthian epigram was quoted by Plutarch and is said to have been on a monument at the Isthmus of Corinth commemorating the Corinthian war dead: "All Greece, balanced on the razor's edge, we rescued with our lives, and here we lie."[63] Women from Corinth also commissioned an epigram for a dedication to Aphrodite, to whom they prayed on behalf of the Greeks: "These women, praying to Cypris on behalf of the Greeks and their close-fighting fellow compatriots, dedicated these sacred things. For divine Aphrodite was not willing to betray the Acropolis of the Greeks to the bow-wielding Medes."[64] These four lines mention the Greeks twice, once to indicate that the Corinthian women kept all Greece in their prayers, and again to indicate the salvation of the "acropolis of the Greeks," which, although Corinth itself had a spectacular acropolis, could be metaphorical here.[65] The commander of the Corinthian forces at Salamis, Adeimantos, is said to have had his own monument, on which was inscribed the following lines: "This is the tomb of Adeimantos, because of whom all Greece wears a crown of freedom."[66] That Adeimantos fought for Greek freedom contradicts Herodotus' claim that he and his forces fled before the battle, which is why Plutarch quotes this epigram.

Another Salamis epigram is worth mentioning here, even though many scholars consider that it was a literary composition or exercise rather than an actual inscription, and some question whether it is properly an epigram at all.[67] Quoted by Plutarch, this epigram honors Democritus, a man from Naxos who performed heroic deeds in the sea battle: "Democritus won third place in the battle, when the Greeks clashed with the Medes on the sea near Salamis. He took five ships, cutting them down, and a sixth ship he rescued, a Greek ship captured by a barbarian hand."[68] Democritus'

---

[63] = Sim. XII *FGE*. Only the first two lines are in Plutarch, whereas the next four were added by Aristides and are rejected by many scholars. I have provided a translation of the first two lines only. ἀκμᾶς ἑστακυῖαν ἐπὶ ξυροῦ Ἑλλάδα πᾶσαν | Ταῖς αὐτῶν ψυχαῖς κείμεθα ῥυσάμενοι | [δουλυσύνης· Πέρσαις δὲ περὶ φρεσὶ πήματα πάντα | ἥψαμεν, ἀγαλέης μνήματα ναυμαχίης. | ὀστέα δ' ἡμὶν ἔχει Σαλαμίς, πατρὶς δὲ Κόρινθος | ἀντ' εὐεργεσίης μνῆμ' ἐπέθηκε τόδε.]

[64] = Sim. XIV *FGE*: αἵδ' ὑπὲρ Ἑλλάνων τε καὶ ἀγχεμάχων πολιατᾶν | ἕστασαν εὐχόμεναι Κύπριδι δαιμόνια. | οὐ γὰρ τοξοφόροισιν ἐβούλετο δῖ' Ἀφροδίτα | Μήδοις Ἑλλάνων ἀκρόπολιν προδόμεν.

[65] As Page 1981: 211 argues. But see Sider 2020: 116, who thinks the actual Acrocorinth could be meant. Budin 2008: 339 suggests that the *stele* could have been set up on the Acrocorinth, giving this line more poignancy.

[66] = Sim. X *FGE*: οὗτος Ἀδειμάντου κείνου τάφος, ὃν διὰ πᾶσα | Ἑλλὰς ἐλευθερίας ἀμφέθετο στέφανον.

[67] See the discussion in Page 1981: 219. Sider 2020: 21 argues, on the other hand, that Simonidean authorship cannot be disproved, and nothing in the poem disqualifies it as being from the early 5th century.

[68] = Sim. XIX *FGE*: Δημόκριτος τρίτος ἦρξε μάχης, ὅτε πὰρ Σαλαμῖνα | Ἕλληνες Μήδοις σύμβαλον ἐν πελάγει· | πέντε δὲ νῆας ἕλεν δῄων, ἕκτην δ'ὑπὸ χειρός | ῥύσατο βαρβαρικῆς Δωρίδ' ἁλισκομένην.

actions are straightforwardly impressive and worth remembering, but the use of the verb "rescue" (*rhuomai*) in reference to the Greek ship he saved – and not a fellow Naxian ship, by any indication – suggests a degree of altruism and a feeling of "Greekness" absent from Spartan dedications, and more in line with the Corinthians and Athenians.

An inscription from Megara calls to mind the extensive contributions of the Megarians against Xerxes:

> Striving to strengthen the day of freedom for Greece and the Megarians, we accepted the fate of death, some near Euboea and Palion, where it is called the sanctuary of holy bow-wielding Artemis, others on the mountain of Mycale, others before Salamis ... and still others on the Boeotian plain, those who dared with their hands to attack men fighting from horseback. We citizens bore this public honor around the navel on Nisaea, in the famous agora.[69]

The Megarians strove to bring freedom to themselves but also to all Greece, thus positioning themselves as fully a part of the Panhellenic resistance to Persia.

The Palatine Anthology preserves two Persian War epigrams from Sparta's Peloponnesian neighbor, Tegea, which, according to Herodotus, featured prominently alongside Pausanias in the final clash at Plataea. The commemoration of the Tegeans who fought at Plataea is as good a context as any for these poems, but Page rejects them as later compositions, saying contemptuously, "as if there was ever an occasion in Greek history when the freedom of all Greece depended on the defense of Tegea."[70] But, as we have seen, several Greek states commemorated their own contributions as essential for Greek freedom. The introduction to the first epigram in the Anthology says it was

---

[69] = Sim. XVI *FGE*:

 Ἑλλάδι καὶ Μεγαρεῦσιν ἐλεύθερον ἆμαρ ἀέξειν
 ἱέμενοι θανάτου μοῖραν ἐδεξάμεθα,
 τοὶ μὲν ὑπ' Εὐβοίαι καὶ Παλίωι, ἔνθα καλεῖται
 ἁγνᾶς Ἀρτέμιδος τοξοφόρου τέμενος,
 τοὶ δ' ἐν ὄρει Μυκάλας, τοὶ δ' ἔμπροσθεν Σαλαμῖνος
 ⟨ ⟩
 τοὶ δὲ καὶ ἐν πεδίωι Βοιωτίωι, οἵτινες ἔτλαν
 χεῖρας ἐπ' ἀνθρώπους ἱππομάχους ἱέναι.
 ἀστοὶ δ' ἄμμι τόδε ⟨ξυνὸν⟩ γέρας ὀμφαλῶι ἀμφίς
 Νισαίων ἔπορον λαοδόκωι 'ν ἀγορᾶι.

See Sider 2020: 118–119 for a discussion of this inscription and its relationship to original verses of the early 5th century. While Simonides could indeed be the author, Sider suggests that the Megarians might have hired a local poet.

[70] Page 1981: 280.

composed by Simonides for the Greeks who ensured Tegean freedom:
"Because of the excellence of these men, the smoke of broad Tegea ablaze
will not reach the heavens, these men who are willing to leave to their children
a city flourishing in freedom, but for themselves to die among the front
ranks."[71] The second epigram encourages visitors to remember the brave
Tegeans who fell: "Let us remember the straight-fighting men, of whom
this is the tomb, who died rescuing Tegea rich in flocks, spearmen for the city,
lest Greece be stripped of freedom from its head."[72] If these verses are from the
period just after Xerxes' invasion (and the first of the two Tegean poems could
well be), it would seem that Tegea remembered its dead and advertised its role
in the war in the same spirit as the other Greek poleis, but at odds with the
dominant power in the Peloponnese, Sparta.

Plutarch tells us in his life of Aristides (19.6), one of the Athenian leaders at
Plataea, that the following epigram was inscribed on the altar of Zeus
Eleutherios ("the Liberator") at Plataea: "When the Greeks in the might of
victory, by the work of Ares and trusting in the daring might of their soul, drove
out the Persians in common for a free Greece, they set up this altar of Zeus
Eleutherios."[73] Plutarch uses this epigram to prove that all the Greeks, not just
the Spartans, Tegeans, and Athenians, who are the main Greek participants in
the actual fighting according to Herodotus' account, took part in the battle
against the Persians. In Plutarch's telling, this is a decidedly Hellenic monument, and not a Spartan one. It is only fitting that this epigram, commemorating the role of all the Greeks in common and adorning an altar to Zeus the
Liberator, should be Panhellenic in tone and mention freedom explicitly.[74]

In the past few years, an epigram from the other side at Plataea, the
Medizing polis of Thebes, has been discovered on a funerary *stele*. Nikolaos
Papazarkadas, who first published the epigram in 2014, thinks that the Battle

---

[71] = Sim. LIII *FGE*: τῶνδε δι' ἀνθρώπων ἀρετὰν οὐχ ἵκετο καπνός | αἰθέρα δαιομένας εὐρυχόρου
Τεγέας, | οἳ βούλοντο πόλιν μὲν ἐλευθερίαι τεθαλυῖαν | παισὶ λιπεῖν, αὐτοὶ δ' ἐν προμάχοισι θανεῖν.
Sider 2020: 23 sees this inscription as accompanying a *polyandrion* and thinks it could very well have
been composed by Simonides. He favors a battle between Sparta and Tegea near Tegea itself, but we
should not discount Plataea, where the Tegeans played a major role.

[72] = Sim. LIV *FGE*: εὐθυμάχων ἀνδρῶν μνησώμεθα, τῶν ὅδε τύμβος | οἳ θάνον εὔμηλον ῥυόμενοι
Τεγέαν, | αἰχμηταὶ πρὸ πόλης, ἵνα σφίσι μὴ καθέληται | Ἑλλὰς ἀποφθιμένου κρατὸς ἐλευθερίαν.
The sense of the last line and a half is very difficult to reconstruct (see Page 1981: 280), but it clearly
speaks of Greece and freedom. Sider 2020: 224–225 rejects the poem as a late literary exercise, and
a poor one.

[73] = Sim. XV *FGE*: τόνδε ποθ' Ἕλληνες Νίκης κράτει, ἔργωι Ἄρηος | [εὐτόλμωι ψυχῆς λήματι
πειθόμενοι,] | Πέρσας ἐξελάσαντες ἐλευθέραι Ἑλλάδι κοινόν | ἱδρύσαντο Διὸς βωμὸν Ἐλευθερίου.
Plutarch does not include the second line (which does appear in the Palatine Anthology), which
Sider 2020: 107–108 suggests simply did not suit Plutarch's purpose. A pentameter line like this one
would fit with the rest of the inscription.

[74] For more on Plataea as the Panhellenic victory *par excellence*, see Jung 2006: 225–297.

of Plataea is the most likely context for the inscription, but he cannot rule out an earlier date, such as the conflict with Athens in 506 or even the Battle of Tanagra in 457.[75] An interesting point about this inscription is that it was inscribed twice, in different letter forms and with different spellings. Papazarkadas proposes that the second inscription is a later reinscription on the part of the polis of Thebes, transforming the monument from a private memorial to a public one. What can be made out of the inscription can be translated as follows: "to die in war . . . for his fatherland Thebes . . . the mightiest prizes for excellence."[76] If this monument commemorated a Theban who died at Plataea (or in any battle of the Persian Wars), it makes sense that Panhellenism and freedom are absent; but the *stele* pretty clearly indicates that the person who died, after demonstrating excellence, did so in service of Thebes, and so sacrificed his life for his polis. If the Thebans wished to recall any higher ideals from their own controversial experience in the Persian Wars, this would be about the best way to do so.

Another Theban inscription, from well before the Persian Wars, might also emphasize the importance of fighting to set a city free. A small column found during the 2000–2001 excavation season in Thebes appears to commemorate events of 506, when Athens fought against the Boeotians and the Euboean city of Chalcis. The Athenians dedicated a chariot to commemorate their victory, the inscription on which survives in material and literary form.[77] The Theban inscription is more fragmentary, reading something like, "Woinoa and Phylla . . . having taken and Eleusis . . . having freed Chalcis . . . they dedicated . . . ."[78] The verb used for setting Chalcis free, *luomai*, is frequently used in the context of liberation of prisoners or slaves. For their part, the Athenians dedicated the chains of the prisoners they had used to bind those taken captive in the conflict. The Athenian and Theban monuments from their respective sides in this war certainly seem to utilize the slavery/freedom dichotomy that came into greater prominence during and after the Persian Wars.[79]

Finally, let us move considerably further to the west and look at a dedication at Delphi from the Syracusan tyrant Gelon and his brothers. According to

---

[75] Papazarkadas 2014: 223–233. See also Oswald 2014: 121–122; Tentori Montalto 2017: 126–129.

[76] Text A from Oswald 2014: 121: . . .]EPETON[..]T[.] | ‾ ˇˇ ‾ˇˇ ‾ ἐν? π]ολέμυ [θ]ανέμεν | ‾ˇˇ ‾ˇˇ ‾ˇˇ ‾]πατρίδος πέρι Θέβας | ‾ˇˇ ‾]εντο ἆθλα κράτιστ᾽ ἀρετᾶς.

[77] Fragments of two versions of this inscription have been found on the Acropolis, and the inscription's epigram is recorded by Herodotus. See ML 15.

[78] Text from Oswald 2014: 109–111: [. . .]ος ϝοινόας καὶ Φυλᾶς | [. . .] ℏελόντες κἐλευσῖνα | [. . .]αι Χαλκίδα λυσάμενοι | [. . .]μōι ἀνέθειαν.

[79] Oswald 2014: 273–274 argues that the Theban and Athenian epigrams could very well be competing against each other.

Herodotus, the mainland Greeks appealed to Gelon, who commanded vast naval and land forces, for help against the Persians, but failed to secure his alliance after they refused to give him overall command of all the Greeks – the Spartans reserved that for themselves. Gelon, however, did end up fighting a massive battle at Himera, apparently on the same day as Salamis, against the Carthaginians, and in recognition of his victory he made an impressive offering to Apollo at Delphi. Part of this dedication, including an inscription, has been identified from the excavations at Delphi, while an epigram connected to this monument has been included in the Palatine Anthology and supplemented by a quotation from the scholiast – that is, an ancient manuscript commentator – to Pindar. There are many textual and archaeological puzzles that remain unsolved regarding Gelon's dedication and what his brothers and successors might or might not have added to it. Also unclear is whether the epigram was inscribed somewhere at Delphi, and whether the first two lines or all four should be included.[80] What survives on stone simply says that Gelon, the Syracusan and son of Deinomenes, dedicated a tripod and a statue of a *nikē* to Apollo, and names those who crafted the offerings.

The epigram says the following: "I say that Gelon, Hieron, Polyzelos, Thrasyboulos, the sons of Deinomenes, dedicated these tripods after they defeated barbarian nations, and provided a great allied force for the freedom of the Greeks."[81] Several sources (Diod. 11.26.7; Ath. 6.20–21) remark on the dedications made by Gelon and his family at Delphi, indicating that the Syracusan rulers were keen to be seen as not only great men by their fellow Greeks, but also as liberators. It is tempting to accept the epigram as evidence that these tyrants wished to see their conflict against the Carthaginians as applying no less to the freedom of Greece than the fight against Xerxes did. Pindar's first *Pythian Ode* (60–80), written in 470 to celebrate the chariot victory of Hieron, son of Gelon, is in this same vein, celebrating the Sicilian tyrants for warding off slavery from the Greeks, and compares their victories to Salamis and Plataea.[82]

From this survey of the evidence of how other Greek poleis commemorated the Persian Wars during the conflict and in the years immediately following, a clear contrast between Sparta and the rest of the alliance emerges. While most Greeks speak of freedom and warding off slavery, of giving their lives to rescue their own poleis and the rest of Greece from

---

[80] See the commentary in ML 28 and Sim. XXXIV *CEG*.
[81] = Sim. XXXIV *FGE*: φημὶ Γέλων᾽, Ἱέρωνα, Πολύζηλον, Θρασύβουλον, | παῖδας Δεινομένευς, τοὺς τρίποδας θέμεναι, | βάρβαρα νικήσαντας ἔθνη, πολλὴν δὲ παρασχεῖν | σύμμαχον Ἕλλησιν χεῖρ᾽ ἐς ἐλευθερίην.
[82] See the discussion in Raaflaub 2004: 61, 79, 306n94; see also Sider 2020: 196–200.

the Persians, the Spartans are concerned only with proving their excellence, and winning the fame that their excellence entails. Eventually, Sparta would get with the program, which we will explore in the coming chapters. Even Spartan epigrams came to take on language closer to that of their fellow Greeks. On the great monument commemorating the defeat of the Athenians at Aegospotami in 405, the decisive battle of the Peloponnesian War, Lacedaemon is labelled the "Acropolis of Greece," just like Corinth was in the monuments of the early 5th century.[83] A seemingly Panhellenic sentiment, though still lacking any mention of freedom or slavery.

## Commemoration and Going to War

Let us pause here to reflect on some of the broader consequences of the Spartans' and other Greeks' understanding of war as reflected in Persian War commemorations. The evidence most contemporary with the Persian Wars reveals that the Spartans thought of war, or at least expressed their thoughts, much differently than others did. In so many ways, the Persian Wars were a watershed moment for the Greeks, a catalyst for new expressions of Greek self-definition and an understanding of the world as divided between "slave" and "free."[84] While many other Greeks, most famously the Athenians, embraced this new paradigm, and worked to shape it, the Spartans were not quick to catch on. A Spartan conservatism in maintaining that war is above all for glory and fame, instead of for freedom or "Greece" and the "Other," meant that the Spartan propensity to fight war was *less* than that of the freedom fighters like Athens – unless we count the constant war-footing the Spartans maintained in relation to the helots.[85] Commemoration and the attitudes it reflects, therefore, had real-world

---

[83] ML 95.

[84] Greek responses to the Persian Wars, especially in terms of defining "Greekness" and "freedom" versus "slavery" has been a major topic in Classical scholarship for decades. Some representative works (with, as is so often the case, a focus on Athenian material) include Hartog 1988; Hall 1989; Lissarrague 1990; Miller 1997; Cartledge 2002; Raaflaub 2004; Stewart 2008a; 2008b. Proietti 2021, especially 123-216, treats the absence of Panhellenism, or shared Greekness, in Persian War commemorations before Herodotus, emphasizing instead the claims to glory and special contributions made by each individual polis. Proietti is right to argue that genuine Panhellenic ideas came in the decades following Xerxes' invasion, but, as I have shown, even individual claims to distinction on the part of the poleis aside from Sparta refer to "Greece" and common defense.

[85] Plutarch (*Lyc.* 28.4) says that, according to Aristotle, the Spartan ephors ritually declared war upon the helots once taking office. This state of war, however, was put in place to remove any of the ritual pollution normally associated with murder from any Spartan who killed a helot. While this measure is another indication of the brutal oppression to which helots were subjected by the Spartans, it does not indicate the kinds of military activity associated with military campaigns, such as those undertaken by Athens in the 5th century.

consequences, and not in the ways we might expect. We will watch over the next chapters as Spartan views and commemorative practices changed to embrace, at least in part, this new paradigm. Before we do so, let us tie together views of war with the actual fighting of war.

In the last chapter, we considered the poetry of Tyrtaeus, and concluded that, while personal fame and glory were central to Tyrtaeus' message, so, too, was self-sacrifice for the common benefit of Sparta and the Spartans, and warriors' own families. Tyrtaeus composed his poetry in the context of Sparta's subjugation of the Messenians, a long process that included a period of brutal warfare. Homer's poetry also reflects the obligations warriors have to their cities and households, especially if those warriors, like Hector and the Trojans, are fighting to preserve their homes. In Tyrtaeus' day and in the years following, Sparta expanded its power elsewhere in the Peloponnese, becoming the dominant power in mainland Greece and finding itself in the position to be the leader of the anti-Persian alliance in 480–479. While Sparta was increasing its power and influence over its neighbors, it only makes sense that its war poetry would reflect Sparta's need for soldiers willing to fight and die for the expanding power of the polis. Robert Luginbill aptly summarized the message of one of Tyrtaeus' most famous poems as "come join the Spartan army!"[86]

In many ways, we can relate to this aspect of Tyrtaeus' verses far more than to the spirit of the Spartan Persian War epigrams, which refer solely to memory and glory, but not to any supposedly selfless reasons (if any existed) for which the soldiers fought and died. The Spartans commemorated by Persian War epigrams are far less recognizable and sympathetic to us than the other Greeks who fought against Xerxes' forces to save Greece from slavery. Unpalatable as fighting for memory and glory alone might be for us, however, framing the struggle as one for freedom and to rescue one's fellow Greeks from slavery seems to have led to far more violence and warfare in the decades after the Persian Wars. This fact ought to give us pause when we consider the best reasons for going to war and the best ways to remember war.

Prior to the 5th century, Sparta engaged in wars that sometimes lasted on-and-off for decades. We covered some of these conflicts in the previous chapter, but there are others: the First Messenian War (c. 740–720); Second Messenian War (c. 650–620); wars with Tegea (c. 590–550, Hdt. 1.65–68); a war with Argos that ended in 546 (Hdt. 1.82); an expedition with Corinth against the Samian tyrant Polycrates in 525 (Hdt. 3.44–57); an

---

[86] Luginbill 2002.

invasion of central Greece in 519 (Hdt. 6.108); and military interventions in Athens, first against the tyrant Hippias in 510, and then against Cleisthenes in 508/7 (Hdt. 5.64–75). These many wars reflect Sparta's accumulation of power in the Peloponnese and the interventionist policies of king Cleomenes I.[87] At the turn of the century, when the Greeks and Persians were on the cusp of a great conflict, Sparta's military activities slowed down considerably.

In 494, Sparta fought the Battle of Sepeia against Argos (Hdt. 6.76–82), but otherwise stayed quiet during that decade. They were far too quiet as far as Athens was concerned, since Sparta did not send soldiers to Marathon in 490, at least not in time for the battle. The Spartans did not rebuff only the Athenians at this time. Aristagoras of Miletus appealed to Sparta for help in the Ionian Revolt against the Persians in 499/8, but the Spartans sent him away empty-handed (Hdt. 5.49–51, 97.2). According to Herodotus' account, the Persian capital was simply too far away (three months from the sea!) for the Spartans to consider sending troops, and Aristagoras' offer of financial rewards too corrupting, despite the fact the Ionians' "freedom" hung in the balance. The Athenians, by contrast, sent twenty ships, and the Eretrians sent five, which is why those two poleis were the target of Darius' Marathon campaign. The Spartans famously led the Greek resistance to Xerxes' invasion, taking the lead role at Thermopylae and Plataea and being formally in command at Artemisium, Salamis, and Mycale. The Spartans, however, did not fight the Persians without controversy or resistance at home. The tiny force sent to Thermopylae, and the recurring threats to withdraw behind the isthmus to leave Athens at the mercy of the Persians imply that, before Plataea, at least, the Spartans' hearts really were not in it.[88]

Sparta's prestige and large power base in the Peloponnese in 480 guaranteed it top spot in the struggle against Persia. Yet, infamously, after the Persians were driven out of Greece, the Spartans quickly abandoned leadership of the Greeks in the Aegean, ostensibly because Pausanias was behaving too arrogantly and the Spartans feared the corruption of other leaders they might send abroad (Thuc. 1.95.7). As I have suggested above, concerns over Pausanias expanding the reasons for war beyond glory and fame, and beyond mainland Greece, were likely top of mind. Athens all too happily stepped into the vacuum left by Sparta's withdrawal, laying

---

[87] See Sears 2020: 180–181 for the extent to which Cleomenes fits the mold of other Spartan leaders.

[88] Lazenby 1993 aptly titles his eighth chapter "With Friends Like These?" to express how far the Spartans were willing to go to leave the Athenians and others on their own against the Persians after Thermopylae, and even after Salamis.

the foundations of the Athenian empire and, ultimately, the Peloponnesian War. While Thucydides portrays Sparta as all too happy to give up any overseas ambitions, Diodorus, and only Diodorus, presents a debate at Sparta in 478/7 in which the majority of Spartans wanted to take back their control over the Greeks from Athens by force, only to be persuaded against doing so by a single member of the Gerousia, the Spartan council of elders (Diod. 11.50). Many scholars doubt whether this debate happened at all, though some see it as evidence for a long-standing dispute in Sparta between isolationists and interventionists.[89] Whether or not the Spartans were torn over fighting against Athens for supremacy in the 470s, the fact remains that they did not do so, and by every measure ceded leadership of the Aegean Greeks to Athens.

The defining military event for 5th-century Sparta before the beginning of the Peloponnesian War in 431 was a major revolt of the helots in response to an earthquake in the 460s. Sparta needed several years to put down this revolt, which was a huge drain on their resources. The helot revolt caused tensions between Sparta and Athens to flare up, since Sparta first appealed to Athens for help, only to dismiss the Athenian forces once the Spartans worried that the Athenians were too industrious and represented a threat to Spartan interests in the Peloponnese. Partly as a result of this snub, an open conflict did break out between Athens and several Peloponnesian states supported by Thebes, which scholars now call the First Peloponnesian War (460–445). Sparta took part in only one major pitched battle during this conflict, the Battle of Tanagra in 457 in which the Athenians and their Argive allies were defeated. Other than Tanagra, however, Sparta's allies, especially Thebes and Corinth, undertook most of the action. The Thebans fought two more pitched battles with Athens, Oenophyta in 457 (which the Thebans lost) and Coronea in 447 (which the Thebans won). The Spartans were involved in several other campaigns, including invasions of Athenian territory, but these activities stopped short of any major battles or lasting damage to Athens or Athenian possessions on the part of Sparta. In fact, the Persians at one point attempted to bribe Sparta to attack Athens in order for Athenian pressure against Persian in Egypt to be lessened – but the Spartans refused (Thuc. 1.109).[90]

---

[89] For this scholarly debate, see Green 2006: 111n190.

[90] There are allusions in the sources to several other, apparently minor, battles and campaigns fought by Sparta – such as two battles against the Tegeans in the 470s (Hdt. 9.35), a clash at Oenoe against Argos in 459 (Diod. 11.78; see Luginbill 2014), and a "Sacred War" around Delphi (Thuc. 1.112) – but details are slim.

The period after the Persian Wars really belonged to Athens, which was involved in major military expeditions in virtually every year from 480 on, sometimes in multiple theaters at once. Athenian empire-building was made possible by the Athenian navy and marks a major change from Athenian behavior before the Persian invasion. Other than sending twenty ships to help the Ionians in the early 490s, which quickly returned home after participating in the burning of Sardis, the Athenians tended to stick close to home, fighting with enemies like Aegina, an island nearby in the Saronic Gulf. After 479, Athens spread its influence and founded colonies around the Aegean, fought the Persians in Asia Minor and Cyprus, and even sent an expedition to aid the Egyptians in revolting from the Persian Empire. The Athenian Empire is a well-documented phenomenon, as are its cultural results, such as the Periclean building program on the Acropolis and the flowering of Attic drama and other literary forms. The growth of Athenian power and influence, as opposed to a relatively stagnant Sparta resting on its laurels, is what Thucydides famously said was the truest cause of the Peloponnesian War (Thuc. 1.23).

Athens used its role in freeing the Greeks from Persian slavery – a message advertised as far back as the Athenian Persian War epigrams, including perhaps Marathon in 490, as we have seen – to justify its growing imperial power and even the subjugation of its fellow Greeks. Sparta, by contrast, used no such rhetoric in the early 5th century, and willingly gave up any imperial pretentions in the Aegean shortly after 479. In fact, according to Thucydides, the Corinthians goaded the Spartans into the Peloponnesian War by chastising them for inactivity and for ignoring Athens' growing power and tyrannical behavior towards the other Greeks. We will return to the Corinthians in the next chapter, but it is worth noting here that, like Athens, Corinth employed freedom rhetoric in its Persian War epigrams. Corinth, which competed with Athens in the early 5th century to advertise its role in freeing all of the Greeks from the Persians, was, like Athens, heavily involved in military ventures concerning alliances and influence after the Persian Wars, and did more than any other polis to ensure that a wide-ranging struggle between Sparta and Athens would take place.

Our literary sources are heavily biased in favor of covering Athenian history, and to a lesser extent Spartan history. Furthermore, we rely most on late 5th-century and even later sources, which tend to be scant on the details of Greek history prior to the Persian Wars. Nevertheless, we can observe a clear trend in the military activities of Sparta, Athens, and, to a lesser extent, Corinth. Prior to the 5th century, Sparta fought many wars to consolidate its dominant position in the Peloponnese, but fought far less in the early 5th century and after the Persian Wars, and actively refused several military expeditions outside of the Peloponnese. Athens, on the other hand, became a military superpower in the wake of Xerxes' invasion, and used its continuous military activity the 5th century to amass an empire that threatened Sparta's long-standing supremacy in Greece. Like Athens, Corinth was militarily active abroad after the Persian Wars, and came into conflict with Athens concerning who would wield influence over various overseas colonies such as Epidamnus and Potidaea. The state that fought fewer wars, Sparta, emphasized memory and glory in its military commemorations. Those that fought more, Athens and Corinth, advertised their role in freeing the Greeks and preventing slavery in the Persian Wars.

As we all know, correlation does not equal causation. I am not saying that Sparta fought less merely because it was not concerned with concepts like freedom, or that the Athenians and Corinthians fought more because they were concerned with such concepts. Several factors were surely at play, many of which we cannot hope to ascertain given the nature of our sources. And yet, we should pause before recoiling at the seeming militarism and quaint heroism implied in Sparta's Persian War epigrams – that only glory and fame matter when going to war. Much of the violence in the Aegean world of the 5th century was at the hands of those Greeks who supposedly went to war for freedom and other higher ideals.

## Conclusion

Our view of the Persian Wars stems mostly from literary sources dating to the second half of the 5th century and later; that is, at least a generation after the wars themselves. By the time Herodotus published his inquiries into "why the two peoples fought each other," the rhetoric of freedom and slavery had firmly taken hold, and even colored accounts of the Spartan participation in the resistance to Xerxes. Athens had become an imperial power, growing mighty and rich from its subjugation of fellow Greeks around the Aegean. As we will explore in the next chapter, it was in the interests of poleis such as Corinth to portray the Spartans as historic liberators, as champions against tyranny, if for no other reason than to convince Sparta to go to war with Athens and thus "free the Greeks." Sparta, or at least some leading Spartans, adopted this freedom rhetoric for themselves, both during the Peloponnesian War and during the period of Spartan supremacy after the war. From the 430s until today, Sparta, and

Thermopylae in particular, has stood as a symbol of few against many, brave freedom against craven tyranny.

It is unlikely that Spartans thought of themselves as liberators when they took the field against the Persians in 480. The small force that they sent to the pass at Thermopylae was, it turned out, not enough to stem the Persian tide. Even if the defending Greeks had not been betrayed, if the resistance at the pass had against all odds held out long enough for Xerxes to reconsider his invasion plans, that the full force of the Spartan phalanx stayed behind in the Peloponnese is nothing short of scandalous. I would be loath to ascribe cowardice to Spartan warriors (though they certainly experienced far more fear in real life than their legend lets on), but Thermopylae suggests an indifference to the plight of their fellow Greeks. When the time came to commemorate Thermopylae and the other battles of the war, the Spartans focused on the excellence of their soldiers and leaders, and the enduring fame that excellence assured. While the Athenians, Corinthians, Megarians, Locrians, Tegeans, and more celebrated their fight for the freedom of the Greeks, and their efforts to rescue Greece from slavery, the Spartans signaled their disinterest in such things by not mentioning them at all.

We should not let Sparta's lack of expressed concern for freedom trouble us too much. Those who most loudly advertised their pro-freedom and anti-tyranny credentials turned out to be more likely to intervene in the affairs of and fight wars over other Greek states in the decades after Xerxes' invasion. The Spartans remained relatively free of foreign military entanglements, certainly in contrast to the many decades of expansionist wars they fought before 500. The Spartans eventually got on the freedom bandwagon, but only after they were brow-beaten by their allies into intervening against Athens ostensibly on behalf of Greek freedom. During the Peloponnesian War, Spartan rhetoric shifts considerably, and several Spartans emerge as self-described liberators. For Sparta, as for the other Greeks, more talk of freedom in justifying and commemorating war in the end guaranteed that the Spartans would fight more wars.

# CHAPTER 4

# The Freedom of the Greeks

## Introduction

If there was a "good war" in ancient Greece, it was the struggle against Persia, in which Sparta played a lead role. While Herodotus wrote in the 430s that Athens was the one polis most responsible for the salvation of Greece, he was responding to the majority opinion that, by contrast, considered that Sparta had been Greece's liberator in 480–479. The "bad war" of Classical Greece, the Peloponnesian War, lasted twenty-seven years between the Athenian Empire and Sparta and its allies from 431–404. It began largely because the Spartans had been roused by their allies to curb Athenian power and arrogance that had grown by leaps and bounds since 479. Those allies urged Sparta to action, according to Thucydides' account, by appealing to Sparta's reputation as a liberator. The Greeks needed to be freed from Athenian tyranny, and the Spartans were best positioned, and morally obligated because of their hard-earned reputation, to free them.

As we saw in the last chapter, however, Sparta did not see their own role against Xerxes as primarily one of liberation. Instead, they remembered their battles and their fallen warriors as examples of the pursuit of glory and the demonstration of excellence – just like Homer's heroes wanted to be remembered. Even decades later, when the Peloponnesian War began in 431, the Spartans were reluctant to go to war in the name of higher principles like the freedom of the Greeks. If Thucydides is right about the Spartans eventually going to war against Athens out of a cold calculation of their national interest, the Spartans nonetheless adopted the rhetoric of liberation, a marked shift from their public attitudes towards war in the early 5th century. No one embraced this rhetoric more than Brasidas, the Spartan general who humbled Athens in the first phase of the war by freeing several Athenian subjects in the north Aegean. The people of Amphipolis rewarded Brasidas with the honors due to a city founder when he died in the cause of their freedom from Athens.

Brasidas marks a shift in the commemoration of the Spartan war dead. In terms of his energy and unconventionality, Brasidas was more or less a typical Spartan leader, despite Thucydides' portrayal of him as an un-Spartan Spartan. In the 6th and early 5th centuries, figures like Cleomenes and Pausanias had demonstrated the same penchant for intervening in the affairs of other Greeks, even while causing the Spartan authorities grief. Brasidas was different, though, in how he embraced the rhetoric of liberation to bolster his military adventurism. Pausanias, as we have seen, made no claims to have set anyone free. He only bragged about his leadership of the Greeks and defeat of the Persians. Pausanias did not need any other reason to celebrate his achievements at places like Delphi. Brasidas, on the other hand, claimed to fight for the weak and free the oppressed. Brasidas was celebrated for his supposedly noble campaigns, which brings us to the second way he changed Spartan commemoration. No Spartan – and very few Greeks at all – had ever received honors like those showered on Brasidas after his death in combat in 422, both throughout Greece and at home in Sparta. His example proved irresistible to the ambitious Spartans who followed him, like Lysander and Agesilaus, and foreshadowed the kings and generals of the Hellenistic period honored as saviors and gods. Brasidas marks a hinge point in Sparta commemoration, so we will spend considerable time with him.

The standard line in antiquity was that the Spartans were afraid of their leaders going abroad because invariably money would corrupt them. The lawgiver Lycurgus, after all, had allegedly abolished coined money at Sparta centuries back. The case of Brasidas and his successors suggests that money did not corrupt these Spartans, or at least not money alone. Excessive honors such as those received by Brasidas are what really tempted ambitious Spartans, and during the Peloponnesian War and after the pursuit of these honors drove several Spartans to fight more wars for longer periods and further afield than their predecessors had done. Whether or not we consider Brasidas and other Spartans as genuine liberators, ostensible campaigns of liberation led to more lavish honors, and also to more war. Prior to Brasidas, fighting solely for glory and fame had kept the Spartans and their war making in line. The commemoration of Brasidas changed that.

## Spurring Sparta to Action

The Spartans did not want to go to war with Athens in 431, and certainly not to set free the other Greeks. As we saw in the preceding chapter, in the years immediately following Xerxes' invasion, the Spartans did not even frame their military activities in 480–479 as acts of liberation or in the service of some larger idea of "Greece." Sparta's allies, on the other hand, did want Sparta to go to war with Athens and cajoled the Spartans into action by appealing to a mix of Sparta's reputation, deserved or not, as a liberator and Sparta's own self-interest. Because it suited their needs in the present, Sparta's allies managed to transform the commemoration of Sparta's military actions, even those generations in the past, as in the service of freeing the Greeks.

Herodotus, writing in the 430s, presents one of the most stirring vignettes of the selflessness and dedication to freedom of Spartan warriors at the time of the Persian Wars – even if, as we have seen, the real Spartans of that time likely thought differently. We saw in Chapter 1 that at Sparta there was a shrine to Talthybius, the famous herald from Homer's *Iliad*. After the Spartans threw Darius' heralds down a well, thus violating the sacrosanctity of heralds in the Greek world, Herodotus tells us that the omens at this shrine were consistently unfavorable. In order to set things right, two renowned Spartiates, Sperthias and Boulis, volunteered to be sent to Xerxes as a sacrifice to atone for the murder of the Persian heralds. As awesome as this act of self-sacrifice was, Herodotus is most impressed with these Spartans' *bon mot* once in the Persian Empire. Hydarnes, the Persian general along with Aegean coast of Asia Minor, treated the two Spartans to a feast as they journeyed to Xerxes, and asked why they did not accept the king's friendship and thus become rulers of Greece. Sperthias and Boulis replied that, while Hydarnes knew well how to be enslaved, he did not know how to be free; and if he had tasted freedom, he would use every method at his disposal to fight for it (Hdt. 7.134–135).

Few passages in the ancient sources offer such a clear contrast between enslaved Persians and free Greeks, of whom the Spartans stand out as a paradigm. If Herodotus is to be believed, even before the epochal struggles of Thermopylae and Plataea, Spartan warriors stood firm in the cause of freedom, considering it a cause worth every sacrifice. By the 430s, then, Sparta's contribution in the Persian Wars was commemorated as a principled stand for Greek freedom against Persian slavery. But, as Vito Mariggio argues, the story of Sperthias and Boulis is almost certainly later propaganda to highlight Spartan courage and patriotism, especially in comparison to the Athenian Themistocles, who eventually Medized and offered *proskynesis*, or submissive prostration, before the Persians. In fact, as Mariggio goes on to argue, the mission of Sperthias and Boulis was likely not religious in nature at all (they were never actually sacrificed and managed to return to Sparta: Hdt. 7.136–137). These two were engaged in plain old diplomacy, a fact the Spartans later tried to cover up once diplomatic ties with the Persian Empire were frowned upon.[1] The fact remains, however, that Herodotus includes this episode to commemorate – as one of the wondrous things, *thōmata*, for which he wrote his *Histories* in the first place – the daring actions and words of these men who became in later decades Spartan exemplars.

By the 430s, many Greeks also retrojected the Spartans' supposed liberation efforts to the generation before the Persian Wars. Thucydides says that the Spartans had always been free of tyrants themselves (*atyranneutos*) and principled opponents of tyranny, and had in fact ousted the tyrants from all Archaic Greece except Sicily (Thuc. 1.18.1). In 510, the Spartans, led by one of their kings, Cleomenes, liberated Athens from the tyranny of the Pisistratids, a tale told by Herodotus (5.62–65). Shortly afterwards, however, Cleomenes intervened militarily in Athens again, this time against the proto-democrat Cleisthenes in favor of the pro-Lacedaemonian Isagoras, not exactly the actions of a consistent liberator. The coalition army Cleomenes gathered against Athens is what drove Athens to seek an alliance with the Persian Empire in the first place, which had a great deal to do with the outbreak of the Persian Wars two decades later (Hdt. 5.69–76). The Spartans' reputation for opposing tyrants in the late 6th century might therefore be rather overblown.[2] The latter half of the 5th century seems to be when this reputation really took hold, and became most useful to Sparta, or at least its allies.

The several pre-war meetings among Sparta and its Peloponnesian allies, as portrayed by Thucydides, contain the clearest statements about Sparta as a historic liberator and the natural leader against the "tyrant city," Athens (as it was called by Corinth in 432: Thuc. 1.122.3, 124.3). The Corinthians were especially forceful in appealing to Sparta's better angels, since open conflicts had broken out between Corinth and Athens over the Corinthian colonies of Corcyra and Potidaea, two of the critical proximate causes of the Peloponnesian War. Thucydides would have us believe that on the eve

---

[1] Mariggio 2007. For Sperthias and Boulis, see also Boedeker 2015. The mission of Sperthias and Boulis was of especial importance in 430, and likely gained certain embellishments in the retelling, when their sons had themselves been sent as ambassadors to Persia, only to be betrayed by a Thracian king and handed over to Athens, where they were killed (Hdt. 7.137; Thuc. 2.67). Herodotus uses this later incident, the latest event he comments on in his *Histories*, as confirmation that the wrath of Talthybius still burned against the Spartans. Thucydides, on the other hand, focuses on the bad behavior of the Athenians in executing these men.

[2] For this reputation, see Hornblower 1991–2008: 1.51, 113. For the nature of Archaic tyranny, and the idea that tyrants themselves could be seen as liberators rather than oppressors, see Sears 2019a. For Cleomenes being a typical Spartan leader, rather than an outlier that can be discounted, see Sears 2020.

of the war, the vast majority of Greeks were enthusiastic about taking on Athens and rallying behind Sparta as a leader, since Athens had become tyrannical and Sparta promised to be an effective liberator (Thuc. 2.8.4).[3] The Corinthians deftly played on these feelings among the Greeks and deployed liberation rhetoric to goad the Spartans into war.

In the first debate held at Sparta in 432 about whether Athens had violated the terms of a peace treaty, the Corinthian ambassador delivered a speech that perfectly encapsulates Thucydides' characterization of the Spartans and the rhetorical techniques used to change Sparta's behavior (Thuc. 1.68–71).[4] The Corinthian speaker does not bother flattering his Spartan hosts but launches right into harsh criticism. The Spartans, alone of all the Greeks, keep quiet (*hēsuchazete*, Thuc. 1.69.4), while the Athenians are active and innovative (Thuc. 1.70.5). These characteristics have allowed the Athenians to amass an empire and oppress many of their fellow Greeks, while the Spartans simply let it happen. The Spartans' behavior is all the more blameworthy given that they enjoy the reputation of being the liberators of Greece (1.69.1) – a fine example of the Corinthians basing their arguments on Sparta's supposed history of liberating others. Thucydides reinforces the points made by his Corinthians in the first book by echoing their sentiments in his own voice in the eighth book, when he says that the slow and cautious Spartans (*bradeis, atolmoi*) are no match for the fast and bold Athenians (*oxeis, epicheirētai*). Only the Syracusans were a match for the Athenians, since the two peoples shared the most salient characteristics (Thuc. 8.96.5).[5]

Athens' response to the Corinthian speech was to justify its empire by reference to the service Athens had rendered Greece in the Persian Wars (Thuc. 1.73–78). The speech of the Athenians in Thucydides is a key piece of Athenian commemoration of the Persian Wars and reveals how differently the Greeks could frame Sparta's contributions in 480–479. While the Corinthian ambassador appealed to Sparta's reputation as liberator, the

---

[3] The Greeks might not have been quite so hostile to Athens and the Athenian Empire in the late 430s. Sainte Croix 1954 argued that Thucydides invented much of this hostility for his own purposes. Romilly 1966, on the other hand, reasserted that many poleis really were oppressed by Athens and revolted if given the chance. For more on this subject, see Low 2008: 227–231. As Raaflaub 2004: 119 succinctly states, "Athens's archē (rule, empire) represents the first extensive and long-term rule of one Greek polis over other Greek poleis," which was bound to generate hostility towards Athens and enthusiasm for a state that promised to right the situation.

[4] Jaffe 2017 offers a comprehensive study of the speeches throughout Thucydides' first book, with special emphasis on how the speeches treat national character. See also Sears 2020, especially 187–196.

[5] As Lazenby 2004: 193 points out, this characterization of the Spartans is quite unfair to Brasidas and his successor Gylippus, an observation relevant to the present chapter.

Athenian speakers trumpeted their own city's contribution to Greek freedom while arguing that the Spartans cared far less for the welfare of others in the face of Xerxes' invasion. The Athenians asserted that they ran greater risks than Sparta, suffered more, including the destruction of Athens itself, and benefitted all Greece, including Sparta, whereas Sparta looked out only for its own interests. By the Thucydidean Athenians' own reckoning (backed up by Herodotus, as we have seen), Athens, not Sparta, was the liberator of Greece, and Athens deserved the glory and material advantages due to such a great benefactor. In contrast to the Corinthian point, which tried to spur the Spartans to action by making them ashamed of their inaction in the present, the Athenians argue that Sparta had *always* been inactive, even in 480, leaving Athens to pick up the slack.

The Athenians' rhetorical commemoration during the congress at Sparta of their city's selfless struggle in the Persian Wars ties in well with the epigrammatic sources from the early 5th century, which also claim that Athens went to war to benefit the Greeks and bring freedom from the Persians. Without defending the Athenians' justification of their empire because of their war effort against Darius and Xerxes, I think that the Athenian version of early 5th-century events is more accurate than the Corinthians', and that the Spartans would not have been surprised or perturbed at the Athenians' take on things. The Corinthians, who wanted Sparta to intervene in the present conflict with Athens, had every reason to suggest that the Spartans had once been interventionist – that they enjoyed the reputation as Greece's liberator – and that their current lack of concern for the welfare of their fellow Greeks was dishonorable and out of character. Only a Sparta that had once freed Greece from tyrants could be called upon to free Greece again from the "tyrant city" Athens. Thucydides provides only one example of a city liberated from tyranny by the Spartans: Pisistratid Athens, which, as we have seen, is hardly an unambiguous case of principled anti-tyranny. That example, though, serves to support Thucydides' framing of the propaganda battle on the eve of the Peloponnesian War, as it bolsters Corinth's case.

The real Spartans of 480–479, however, did not particularly care whether they benefitted the rest of Greece or not, and, unlike Athens, made no mention of that wider benefit in their commemoration of the Persian Wars in the 470s. The Athenian ambassadors in 432 were right; Athens really had benefitted the Greeks and was unafraid to advertise that fact early and often. The Spartans had behaved differently during Xerxes' invasion and in the following decades because the Spartans conceived of war differently. War for the Spartans was solely for glory and fame, not for freedom and the benefit of others.

Important figures in Sparta continued to view war in the old way even in 432. Following the Athenians, the Spartan king Archidamus gave a speech, trying to dissuade his fellow Spartans from going to war against Athens (Thuc. 1.80–85). In enumerating the uncertainties of war and the difficulties facing anyone trying to defeat Athens, Archidamus has been compared to the "tragic warner" figures who are prominent in works like Homer's *Iliad* and Herodotus' *Histories*. Almost invariably, these warners are not heeded, just as the Spartans will decide against Archidamus' advice.[6] Beyond serving this literary function, and beyond serving as a model of sensible moderation, Archidamus restated the traditional Spartan view of war. Far from accepting the blame heaped upon them by the Corinthians, Archidamus urged the Spartans to be proud of their slowness and hesitation (*bradu, mellon*), considering these attributes rather good sense and prudence (*sōphrosunē, emphrōn*). These qualities made Sparta free and abundantly glorious (*eleutheran, eudoxotatēn*, Thuc. 1.84.1–2). Sparta has every reason to look out for its own interests, just as it always has, and should avoid being dragged into dangerous and long-term entanglements abroad.[7] This was the attitude of Sparta during and after the Persian Wars, and, according to Archidamus, it served the city well.

Archidamus' position was not universally accepted by the Spartans in 432, if, that is, it had ever been universally accepted. The Spartan king's speech was followed by a brief retort from Sthenelaidas, one of Sparta's five ephors (Thuc. 1.86). In a short but effective speech against clever speaking, which is itself a fine example of clever speaking, Sthenelaidas urges the Spartans to act based on notions of Sparta's self-interest, but more importantly in the interests of justice, namely doing what is right by their allies and punishing the Athenian wrongdoers (*adikountas*).[8] Sthenelaidas' arguments, along with those offered on behalf of Corinth, won out, and the Spartans voted for a pretext that would lead them to war, namely that the Athenians had violated a peace treaty by acting aggressively against Corinth's colonies and in other places throughout the Aegean.

At another congress at Sparta in 432, the Spartans once again canvassed opinions concerning whether to make a formal declaration of war against Athens. The only speech presented by Thucydides from this meeting is

---

[6] Pelling 1991; Hornblower 1991–2008: 1.125.

[7] As Jaffe 2017: 105 says regarding this speech, "It is not at all clear to Archidamus, however, that Corinth's troubles are really Sparta's problem."

[8] For this speech and its persuasiveness, see Allison 1984; and Bloedow 1987.

that of the Corinthians, who emphasized the need for Sparta to liberate the Greeks from Athenian tyranny, calling Athens, as we have seen, the "tyrant city" (Thuc. 1.120–124). After this speech, the majority voted in favor of war, and the Peloponnesian War began in earnest. While Sparta had self-interested reasons for checking Athenian power, liberation propaganda proved a useful tool, especially since the feelings of the Greeks, according to Thucydides, were on the side of Sparta because of its promise of liberation (Thuc. 2.8.4).[9] Most readers of Thucydides and students of Greek history have taken a cynical view of Sparta's liberation rhetoric. S. N. Jaffe, for instance, suggests that "the only Spartan who acts as if [liberation] is Sparta's true war aim is Brasidas."[10] Even Brasidas has been criticized for not being true to his word, and dressing up his own imperial-istic aims, and those of Sparta, with fancy words.[11]

In the early years of the war, one of the most ineffective appeals to Panhellenism and Sparta's liberation rhetoric is placed in the mouths of the Plataeans, pleading to the Spartans for their lives and eliciting pity from Thucydides' readers (Thuc. 3.53–59). Throughout the speech, delivered in 427 as the Spartans decided whether to spare the Plataeans and their city or side with the Thebans, the Plataeans make scattered references to expedi-ency. The rhetorical thrust of their appeal, however, consists of listing the Plataeans' Panhellenic bona fides, especially during the Persian Wars. How could Sparta destroy a city that had done such great service in the name of Greek freedom? The Plataeans also remind the Spartans that they have diligently cared for and honored the tombs of the Spartan dead from the battle of 479, and evoke the memory of those gloriously slain Spartans in an attempt to shame their descendants. If the Spartans reject the Plataeans' appeal, the Spartan dead will be left to lie in the territory of enemies (Thuc. 3.58.4–5). The Plataeans even evoke their name's inscription beneath the tripod at Delphi as a tangible sign of their service to Greece, and Sparta's obligation to them (Thuc. 3.57.2). The Spartans decided against the Plataeans, killing the remaining men and destroying their city. Perhaps

---

[9] Raaflaub 2004: 197 argues that Thucydides means to show that Sparta was only interested in their own advantage, using liberation as a mere pretext. For Spartan liberation propaganda, see also Diller 1962.

[10] Jaffe 2017: 194.

[11] See, for example, in the context of Brasidas' speech in liberation at Acanthus, Gomme et al. 1945–1981: 3.555; Wylie 1992: 80; Hornblower 1991–2008: 2.56–57; Burns 2011: 516; Dmitriev 2011: 23. See Sears 2015 for the argument that Brasidas really did mean to liberate the Greeks; and Nichols 2014: 78–106 for Sparta's mission in the north as an attempt to force Sparta to live up to its liberation propaganda.

the Thebans gave a better speech, and perhaps Spartan interest really was in
siding with the Thebans against Plataea.[12]

I argue that, whether Thucydides thinks they are good points or not,
appeals to Panhellenism and Greek liberty might not have moved many
Spartans, even in 427, four years into the war. As I argued in the previous
chapter, Pausanias' original Serpent Column inscription seems more in
line with how the Spartans wished to commemorate the Persian Wars than
the replacement inscription that included the Plataeans along with the
other allies. The Serpent Column's inclusion of the Plataeans, therefore,
might not have impressed the Spartans overmuch. Finally, the Spartans
had plenty of military tombs in hostile territory, as we have seen and as we
will see again. Spartan dead in enemy lands was rather a point of pride for
the Spartans and would hardly have persuaded them to change course.

The result of the Plataean Debate aside, in the lead-up to and during the
Peloponnesian War, some important Spartans and their allies in the
Peloponnesian League commemorated Sparta's history in a new way,
emphasizing Sparta's liberator credentials in ways that were out of keeping
with earlier forms of Spartan commemoration. Once the Peloponnesian
War was framed as a struggle for liberation led by Greece's greatest historic
liberator, new possibilities for their own reputation and commemoration
were opened up for ambitious Spartans, among whom Brasidas was the
shining example. Before we turn to Brasidas' career and commemoration as
a liberator, let us consider another way Greeks of the late 5th century
disputed the reasons for going to war and thinking about war.

## Athens, Sparta, and the Power of Shame

The Spartan concern with fame and glory, or *doxa*, so evident in the
commemoration of the Persian Wars, and the sense of shame, *aidōs* and
*aischunē*, that motivated Spartan warriors to surrender their lives in battle were
items of great concern during the Peloponnesian War and in the years
following. Two elite Athenian authors, Thucydides and Plato, both of
whom were critical of Athens' democracy, give us a glimpse of how these
terms were discussed in the late 5th century and early 4th, with relevance for

---

[12] For a discussion of this speech, and the Thebans' response in the so-called "Plataean Debate," see
MacLeod 1977; and Hornblower 1991–2008: vol. 1, 444–446. Hornblower argues that the Theban
speech was much more coherent and rhetorically sound. He also notes that it is likely significant that
this debate follows immediately after the Mytilenean Debate. The two debates had opposite
outcomes, with the Athenians deciding to spare most of the Mytileneans while the Spartans killed
the Plataeans and razed their city.

how war and the war dead were thought of and remembered. Thucydides and Plato – or at least the characters in their works – pit the traditional Spartan approach to glory and shame against the pragmatism and realism of the democratic Athenians, with the Spartans having the better of the exchange.

As we have just seen, in his speech in the first book of Thucydides' *History* (1.84.1), the Spartan king Archidamus urges the Spartans not to feel shame (*aischunē*) at the criticism of their inaction leveled against them by the Corinthians and others. The Spartans have nothing to worry about vis-à-vis their allies, since Spartan prudence has yielded a city that is both free and considered by all to be the most famous (*eudoxotatē*). If the goal is fame, Archidamus implies that Sparta's traditional policies have done the job. The purpose of shame, in Homer's epics and in plenty of later works, is to spur individuals and states to actions that add to rather than detract from fame. Hector, for example, awaits Achilles, despite Hector's almost certain death, because he fears having a bad reputation among his fellow Trojans. Shame keeps him outside of Troy's walls for the sake of his *doxa*.

Others besides Archidamus and the Spartans talk about shame being a motivator for excellence. Gregory Crane surveys the uses of shame in Thucydides, and in addition to Brasidas appealing to shame in battle on two occasions (4.126.5, 5.9.9), he includes as non-Spartan examples Pericles in the Funeral Oration (2.43.1), and a Boeotian general at the Battle of Delium in 424 (4.92.7).[13] Criticism of this use of shame is put in the mouths of the Athenian ambassadors in the Melian Dialogue, one of the most famous passages in Thucydides in which the fate of the tiny Spartan ally Melos is debated by the Athenians and Melians in 415 (5.104–111).[14] The Melians express the belief that the Spartans will come to their aid, since shame would compel the Spartans to rescue the Melians, who are kindred Dorians (5.104). The Athenians respond that the Spartans have outstanding *aretē* with respect to themselves and their own laws but follow the expedient path in relation to others (5.105). Later in the dialogue, the Athenians call into question the usefulness of shame in war. They claim that, because of shame, people often rush headlong into easily foreseen disasters, disasters all the more disgraceful because they are experienced due to the sufferers' own error rather than misfortune (5.111.3).[15]

As Crane admits, Thucydides does not necessarily subscribe to the views expressed here by the Athenian ambassadors; but Crane does argue that in

---

[13] Crane 1998: 143–144.    [14] See Crane 1998: 144–145.
[15] For Thucydides' use of various expressions of honor, shame, and disgrace in this passage, see Hornblower 2008: 247–248.

the early chapters of the *History*, which scholars call the Archaeology, Thucydides emphasizes the "hard, material forces" that drive human behavior.[16] The kind of behavior that the Athenians highlight in the Melian Dialogue, namely the Spartans' concern for themselves and reluctance to go out of their way to help others, is embraced by Archidamus as responsible for making Sparta both free and glorious. The results of this behavior seem to be a blend of material (Sparta's freedom) and ideal (its glory, which, to be sure, can yield material benefits). Thucydides thinks a great deal of Archidamus as one of the wisest rulers in the Peloponnesian War, so his sentiments in Thucydides are likely to be ones with which the historian has some sympathy.[17] This is not to say that Thucydides thinks that expediency at the expense of acting honorably in a way driven by shame is necessarily a good thing. Or, rather, acting in the way that the Athenians mock in the Melian Dialogue might be more expedient than it first appears. Whether the Melians adopted the best course by holding out against the Athenians, and thus assuring their own destruction, is up for debate, but they are certainly portrayed sympathetically by Thucydides.[18] The Athenians, on the other hand, do not come away from Melos looking like the good guys, and, as Thucydides well knew (though he died before completing that part of the *History*), the Athenians lost the war in 404 and feared that they would suffer the same sorts of violence they inflicted on others such as the Melians.[19]

In Plato's *Apology*, the great philosopher's version of the defense speech his mentor gave at his capital trial in 399, Socrates compares himself to Achilles, a rather unlikely comparison, to say the least.[20] Anticipating a possible objection to his explanation for his life of philosophy, Socrates imagines a hypothetical interlocutor who asks Socrates why he is not ashamed at living in such a way that he now runs the risk of being sentenced to death. Socrates responds by saying that anyone desiring to live well, and indeed to be a person worth anything at all, must consider nothing as more important than shame (*to aischron*), not even one's own life. This shame, according to Socrates, spurs one on to consider, and to consider only, whether one's actions are just. Socrates, like other Athenians,

---

[16] Crane 1998: 144–146.
[17] For Thucydides' views of Archidamus and the complicated way Thucydides compares and contrasts him with Brasidas, see Sears 2020: 184–186.
[18] But see Bosworth 1993, who criticizes the Melians and others for failing to take into account the full might of Athens, and for putting too much stock in Spartan propaganda.
[19] As Xenophon, who took up Thucydides' work where he left off, says explicitly (*Hell.* 2.2.3).
[20] For a nuanced discussion of this comparison, see Metcalf 2009.

applied this principle by following the orders of their generals in battle. Socrates applied it further by following the directive of Apollo that he engage in philosophy to point out his fellow citizens' ignorance. If one considers one's life more important than shame, one despises the example set by Achilles at Troy, who opted to do the right thing, namely killing Hector and avenging the slain Patroclus, despite knowing that such an action would hasten Achilles' own death (Plat. *Ap.* 28b–29a). This line of argument is consistent with Socrates' general position (according to Plato, at least) that one's wealth, status, and even physical body are nothing of importance next to living in accordance with justice. Shame is crucial to achieving the just life, even if shame can lead one into danger, as indeed it did in Socrates' own case.

What the texts of Thucydides and Plato show us is that a debate about the role and importance of shame, and the way that shame can run up against pragmatic concerns, was very much active in Athens during the Peloponnesian War and afterwards. While Plato was writing a generation after Thucydides (though his main character, Socrates, was Thucydides' contemporary), I detect a nod to Thucydides, and an indication that Plato is weighing in on the same conversation, a couple of paragraphs after Socrates' comparison with Achilles. As he continues to praise his own selfless service in the interests of the Athenians, Socrates says that his neglect of his own material well-being is contrary to human nature (*anthrōpinon*) (31b). This passage is the only one in Plato's extensive body of work in which the term *anthrōpinon*, or "human thing," is used as an abstract noun instead of as an adjective, which is predominantly used by Plato to contrast human things with divine, or *theion*, things. Socrates' use of the term in the *Apology* harks back to Thucydides' famous deployment of *to anthrōpinon* in his programmatic statement for his *History*. Because "the human thing," *to anthrōpinon*, is what it is, Thucydides assures his readers that things similar to those he narrates concerning the Peloponnesian War are bound to happen again (1.22.4).[21] Thucydides is concerned with the human thing, and Plato's Socrates claims that neglecting one's material circumstances in the pursuit of doing the right thing, as compelled by shame, is against that human thing.[22]

---

[21] This is one of the most discussed passages in all of Thucydides' work and has generated heated debate over the decades. For an overview of some of the issues, see Hornblower 1991–2008: vol. I, 59–62. For a recent treatment, with further bibliography, see Rawlings 2016.

[22] The use of *anthropinon* as an abstract concept is exceedingly rare in Classical Greek. In addition to the two passages discussed here, I can think of only Herodotus 1.86.5, where the phrase is used to denote the entire human race rather than human nature.

What are Thucydides and Plato driving at, and what does it have to do with the Spartan attitude to war and the war dead? First of all, whether or not Thucydides and Plato are presenting a caricature of democratic Athenians, both texts imply that many Athenians, even a majority, came to consider the sorts of soldierly traits admired by the Spartans to be quaintly impractical. In standing against the military might of Athens out of an adherence to principle, the Melians were simply foolish; and by flagrantly irritating the Athenians without regard for his own safety and prosperity, Socrates was a malign presence in the city and walked right into his own just deserts. The Spartans similarly were seen as burying their heads in the sand and refusing to embrace the way the world really works, and thus surrendered the leadership of Greece to Athens and sat idly by while Athens oppressed Sparta's allies and friends. Thucydides' Athenians go even further and accuse the Spartans of selectively acting on their principles only when it concerns them directly, while they leave others like the Melians to their fate based on what is practical for the Spartans – shame would not compel Sparta to come to Melos' rescue.

Thucydides and Plato imply that they disagree with this assessment of the importance of acting in accordance with shame. Plato's Socrates rejects material considerations entirely; only shame is important. On this model, the Battle of Thermopylae could well have been tactically and strategically useless, but the Spartans still did the right thing by standing firm. Thucydides is not as extreme as Plato's Socrates. The historian suggests, rather, that acting in accordance with shame, or at least giving it due consideration, can yield practical benefits. The Athenians' entirely practical considerations and rejection of the Melians' principled stand left Athens in danger of destruction at the hands of their outraged enemies a decade after Melos. According to Thucydides' scheme, the Battle of Thermopylae did yield practical benefits for Sparta, especially the fame that led to power and influence.[23]

The clearest sign that the Spartans themselves were beginning to question their adherence to shame comes from their defeat at Pylos in 425, the greatest humiliation they suffered in the war.[24] This is also the episode that reveals most obviously just how important the mystique of Thermopylae was to Sparta's reputation. After the Spartans lost a naval battle to the Athenians in the Bay of Navarino at Pylos in the southwest Peloponnese,

---

[23] For more on Thucydides and Sparta, see Cartledge and Debnar 2006. For Plato/Socrates in Sparta, see Cartledge 1999; and Lévy 2005.

[24] For this battle, see Butera and Sears 2019: 301–318.

hundreds of Spartan soldiers were stranded on an island called Sphacteria that partially closed in the bay. The Athenians eventually landed a force on the island consisting mostly of light-armed allies, who harried the Spartan hoplites with missile weapons. Unable to close with this mobile enemy, the Spartan hoplites were driven to the tip of the island and surrounded on all sides. The Spartans who had not been killed by the missiles of the light-armed skirmishers were exhausted and perplexed. They reached out to the Spartan commanders on the mainland, asking what they should do. The Spartan leadership responded that those trapped on the island should do whatever they think best, so long as they do nothing shameful (*aischron*), according to Thucydides (4.38.3). The surrounded Spartan soldiers then surrendered, to the shock of all Greeks. Some 292 troops were taken prisoner, of whom 120 were full Spartiates, while the rest were *perioikoi* (Figure 4.1).

Thucydides expresses the obvious opinion that no one would have imagined a Spartan surrender. Rather, the outcome of this battle was the most shocking thing to happen during the entire war (4.40.2). Shame and the glory it spurred soldiers towards supposedly kept the Three Hundred Spartans at their post at Thermopylae in 480, a battle Thucydides explicitly

Figure 4.1 The northern tip of Sphacteria as viewed from ancient Pylos. Photo by C. Jacob Butera.

evokes in comparison with Pylos just a few chapters earlier, "to compare small things with great" (4.36.3). How could those at Sphacteria be made of the same stuff as the Persian War generation? Were the Spartans beginning to adopt a pragmatic view of shame in line with that expressed by the Athenians at Melos later in the war? Did allowing for hundreds of soldiers to avoid death, and possibly return to fight another day, just make more sense than letting shame dictate a foolhardy sacrifice? Thucydides records an insult leveled at a Spartan prisoner by one of the troops allied to Athens to the effect that the fine and noble Spartans must have been the ones killed in the fighting. The Spartan responded that it would be quite the "spindle," his derogatory term for an arrow, that could pick out the good men from the bad, implying that the fighting style of the Spartans' enemies was ignoble.

The fact remains, however, that the Spartans did surrender; they did so after being ordered explicitly not to do anything shameful; and by so doing, they went against their reputation. John Lazenby suggests that this surrender, and the fact that none of those who gave themselves up to the Athenians seemed to have suffered lasting consequences at Sparta later, indicate the Spartans were adopting a "more civilized" attitude towards war.[25] Lazenby, I should note, plays down the consequences suffered by those captured on the island, since they were for a time stripped of their citizenship rights at Sparta, though these were later restored to them, likely out of practical necessity (Thuc. 5.34).[26] The Spartans, therefore, treated this surrender as shameful, at least to a degree.

Sparta's enemies certainly made the most of their victory at Pylos. One of the biggest draws today in the Archaeological Museum of Olympia – and, indeed, one of the reference works of Classical sculpture – is the Nike of Paionios (Figure 4.2). The colossal goddess descends from the heavens, robes flowing with her movement and clinging to reveal the body beneath. Her outstretched hand would once have held a crown of victory. As spectacular as the goddess's presence is in the museum, her original setting on a tall triangular base in front of the Temple of Zeus would have been even more impressive. The base has been reconstructed *in situ*, allowing modern visitors to envision the Nike's place in the famous sanctuary. The inscription on the base reads simply, "the Messenians and people of Naupaktos dedicated me to Olympian Zeus, a tithe taken from the

---

[25] Lazenby 1985: 149–150. He goes further to argue that any other state would have considered the stranded soldiers' performance to be a remarkable stand against impossible odds.

[26] For this punishment, and the category of the "tremblers" at Sparta, see Ducat 2006b; and Chapter 1.

Figure 4.2 The Nike of Paionios, Archaeological Museum of Olympia. Author's photo. © Hellenic Ministry of Culture and Sports / Hellenic Organization of Cultural Resources Development.

enemy," and, "Paionios from Mende made me, and making the akroteria for the temple he was victorious."[27] Pausanias clarifies that the Nike was dedicated by the Messenians and people of Naupaktos, who were Messenians settled there by Athens, in honor of their victory at Pylos in 425 (Paus. 5.26.1). Sparta's shame, and the Messenians' triumph, were on display at Olympia for all Greeks to see, and for modern visitors to ponder.[28]

## A Spartan Colony: Herakleia in Trachis

While on the subject of Thermopylae and the reputation it cemented for the Spartans, shattered at Pylos, I must mention one potential commemoration of Thermopylae the Spartans undertook just a year before Pylos and less than two before Brasidas went north on his mission of liberation.

[27] I note that Mende, Paionios' home city, was one of the sites liberated by Brasidas in the years following Pylos.
[28] See Whitley 2011 for a discussion of this piece and its place among Greek dedications and the "culture of competition."

The Spartans still had Thermopylae on their minds during the first years of the Peloponnesian War, and the Spartans themselves, not merely the other Greeks, looked to that battle as an example of Spartan courage and glory. In 426, the Spartans founded a city near where the Three Hundred stood against Xerxes. That city's location must have been significant and carefully chosen, with commemoration at least partly in the minds of the founders and everyone who visited or even heard of the city.

Cities were famously used as commemorative monuments at several points in classical antiquity. In western mainland Greece, near the promontory of Actium where Octavian defeated Antony and Cleopatra to become master of the Roman Empire, is a city Octavian (later named Augustus) founded to celebrate his victory. The city, Nikopolis, or "Victory City," thrived for centuries as a lived-in monument to Augustus' achievement. Centuries before the Battle of Actium, the Greeks saw the founding of cities to be among the most important and sacred activities, something for which the god's approval was always sought, typically from the oracle at Delphi. Those who led groups of colonists to a new foundation were among the very few mortal Greeks honored as heroes after their deaths, with full cultic celebrations. A Spartan foundation in 426, the only Spartan colony in the Classical period for which we have good evidence, stands out both as an example of Spartan expansionism – even imperialism – and as a possible act of commemoration like Augustus' Nikopolis.

Thucydides says that in 426 the Spartans founded a colony called Herakleia Trachinia in Trachis, the region containing the Thermopylae pass.[29] Thucydides mentions Thermopylae specifically, saying that it was about forty stades from Herakleia, or seven and a half kilometers. To protect the new foundation, the colonists built a wall near the Thermopylae pass itself. Thucydides gives three reasons why the Spartans were interested in the region. First of all, some groups in the area, including the Trachinians and the people of Doris, appealed to Sparta for help against their local rivals. Doris was supposed to be the ancestral homeland of the Dorians, the progenitors of the Spartans. Those making the appeal were sure to stress that point. The other two reasons were practical, that the area would be a good staging ground for attacks against Athenian interests, including the nearby island of Euboea, and that it was well located for staging expeditions north into Thrace. Duly appealing to Delphi to give the colony divine legitimacy, the Spartans sent out colonists from Sparta itself and the

---

[29] For the history and archaeology of this site, see Bouyia 2010.

surrounding area, and took along volunteers from other parts of Greece. The three Spartans who led the foundation were Leon, Alcidas, and Damagon (Thuc. 3.92–93).[30]

Scholars have suspected that Thucydides fails to give us the whole story. A. Andrewes, for instance, thinks the Spartans were far more actively imperialistic than Thucydides' characterization allows, and that the foundation of Herakleia was part of a more concerted program of expansion in the Mediterranean.[31] Simon Hornblower agrees to an extent with Andrewes's assessment, and adds that the Spartans might have seen a city in the area as a useful way to gain a vote on the Amphictyonic Council, the influential body that oversaw the sanctuary of Delphi.[32] Irad Malkin focuses on the Herakles myth, its centrality to Spartan identity, and the rationale it provided for establishing a settlement named Herakleia in a region steeped in Herakles lore.[33] Jan Rookhuijzen has recently continued this line of inquiry to propose that the Herakles myth dominated the memory of the Battle of Thermopylae and its hero, Leonidas, to the extent that key topographical landmarks mentioned by Herodotus were chosen for their Herakleian associations. The foundation of Herakleia was part of that Herakles-memory complex.[34]

Remarkably, no one has pointed out the importance of the Battle of Thermopylae for the Spartans colonizing that region a half century after the last stand of the Three Hundred. Kinship with the Dorians, associations with Herakles, strategic advantages against the Athenian Empire, even a larger expansionist plan – all of these were certainly behind the foundation of Herakleia Trachinia in 426. The continuing importance of the region to a variety of parties is amply demonstrated by Jason of Pherai destroying the city after the Battle of Leuctra in 371 to give himself breathing room as he expanded his own power in Thessaly (Xen. *Hell.* 6.4.27). Herakleia played a role in the Roman consul Glabrio's campaigns against Antiochus the Great in the region in 191 BCE (Livy 36.15–19). By 426, Herodotus' *Histories* and its heroic account of Leonidas and the Spartans at Thermopylae had been circulating for some years, and the Spartans had firmly hitched their reputation to that last stand, which the humiliation at Pylos demonstrates. To found a colony a few kilometers from Thermopylae, and to use that storied pass as part of that colony's system of defenses, surely reflected Sparta's

---

[30] Diodorus 12.59 is another account of the foundation but adds little to Thucydides' version.
[31] Andrewes 1971; 1978. See also Fragoulaki 2021, which explores the extent of Sparta's colonial presence overseas, of which Herakleia was only a small part.
[32] Hornblower 1991–2008: vol. 1, 501–508.    [33] Malkin 1994: 219–235.
[34] Rookhuijzen 2018: 148–169.

sentimental feeling for the region, even beyond fictive ties to the Dorians and strategic gains against Athens. Leon, one of the founders of this colony, shares a name, which means "lion," with Spartan kings, including the "Descendant of the Lion," Leonidas, the grandson of one of these kings. A stone lion was even erected at the pass in honor of Leonidas.[35] It beggars belief that the Spartans were not pleased with these connections, and did not see a Spartan city next to Thermopylae as a way to cement the Spartan legacy of that site.

Perhaps we should look anew at the Spartan intervention in the region on behalf of the people of Doris in the 450s too, during the so-called "First Peloponnesian War." Again, Thucydides is explicit about the Dorians hailing from the ancestral homeland of the Spartans but makes no mention of Thermopylae in this instance (Thuc. 1.107–108). It is tempting to think that memories of the battle of 480 were a factor in Sparta's decision to campaign to this part of central Greece, a campaign that resulted in a major hoplite battle against the Athenians at Tanagra and thus represents an important point in the developing rivalry between the two powers.

## Brasidas the Liberator

In her exploration of the image of the "Great Man" in Classical Greece, Sarah Ferrario makes an important point about figures like Brasidas: Much of Brasidas' behavior during his campaigns was performative, carefully calculated to make him resemble famous heroes, and thus ensure heroic recognition for himself. Some Classical Greek athletes, according to Ferrario, act in similar ways, always with an eye to their future reputation.[36] In short, if you want to be remembered like Achilles in death, you should strive to remind people of Achilles in life. Whether or not Brasidas consciously emulated mythical heroes, he certainly did achieve heroic status, literally so in the case of a posthumous cult at Amphipolis, and likely elsewhere too. After Brasidas' example, other Spartans emulated him in the hopes of similar treatment. His military career during the first phase of the Peloponnesian War was outstanding, and he combined strategic and tactical brilliance with personal charisma as

---

[35] For the significance of the name Leon, and lion imagery at Sparta, see Richer 2010: 11–13.
[36] Ferrario 2014: 230–232. See also Currie 2002 for the case of Euthymos of Locri, another figure who deliberately emulated a hero (specifically Herakles) to ensure his own heroic honors after death, but also somewhat in life. Currie 2005: 1–30 extends this line of argument. See also Rood 1998: 73, who says, "Thucydides' formulation suggests that Brasidas moulds his behaviour in awareness of the public gaze."

few others have ever managed. It is worth looking at that career at some length to consider how it set the stage for Brasidas' commemoration.

Brasidas, the son of Tellis and a full Spartiate, enters the stage during the first year of the war, and plays a decisive role in thwarting the Athenians' first offensive action against the Peloponnese. A fleet of 100 Athenian ships, joined by 50 from Corcyra and sundry other allies, sailed around the Peloponnese in 431 to wreak as much havoc as they could. This force landed at Methone, on the rugged southern tip of the westernmost of the Peloponnese's three protruding fingers. This area saw its share of action in antiquity. Agrippa, for example, the great general of Octavian, took this point of land as an important strategic asset in the lead-up to the Battle of Actium in 31 BCE. Today the site is one of the most spectacular in Greece, with a sprawling Venetian and Ottoman fortress built partially on remnants of ancient walls. In 431, the Athenians and their allies found this place unguarded and its walls in disrepair, so they counted on an easy victory. This victory was denied them, however, by Brasidas, who happened to be in the area with a detachment of 100 hoplites. When the Athenian force was scattered about the countryside, taking little heed of the enemy, Brasidas and his soldiers rushed in right through the Athenian troops, losing a few men but managing to force their way into Methone and save the settlement. Because of this act of daring (*tolmē*), Brasidas received formal praise (*epainos*) at Sparta, the first in the war to receive such a distinction (Thuc. 2.25.1–2).

Even from the very start, Brasidas signaled that he was not made of the same stuff as other Spartans.[37] As Thucydides frames the conflict, the Peloponnesian War was the paradigmatic showdown between Greece's greatest land power (Sparta) and greatest sea power (Athens). The reason the Athenians were employing naval hit-and-run tactics in the Peloponnese was because the Athenian hoplites took Pericles' direction in not venturing out from the city walls of Athens to engage the Spartan hoplites in pitched battle. At Methone, Brasidas used 100 hoplites (we do not know if they were Spartiates, *perioikoi*, or a mix of both) in an unconventional way. Thucydides describes Brasidas' force as running through (*diadromē*) the dispersed Athenian lines and, rather than engaging is pitched battle, fighting their way into the city to save it from capture and destruction.[38]

---

[37] Well, the truth is a little more complicated, as I argue in Sears 2020. Thucydides goes out of his way to portray Brasidas as an un-Spartan Spartan, but there were really many Spartans, even in earlier periods, who exhibited Brasidean boldness.

[38] Connor 1984: 128n45 remarks on the frequency of "running" words used to describe Brasidas, who is fast as opposed to the majority of Spartans, who, apparently, are slow.

Hoplites, especially Spartan hoplites, were not known for such tactics, using speed to execute a pinpoint assault rather than a dense formation against another phalanx, as at Mantinea, or an impenetrable wall of shields and spears against a lighter-armed opponent as at Thermopylae.[39] As W. R. Connor points out, Brasidas' speed and decisiveness here are very much in line with Thucydides' Athenians, and at odds with the plodding Spartans.[40] I should add that the word used for his act of daring, *tolmē*, is also used by Thucydides overwhelmingly to refer to Athenians, and never Spartans (except for those Spartans in Brasidas' footsteps, like Gylippus at Syracuse, Thuc. 7.43). I want to suggest, though, that his literal, physical speed in this episode – the Athenians did not have a monopoly on tactical speed on the battlefield in Thucydides – is reminiscent of the Homeric heroes' manner of fighting, especially swift-footed Achilles, the fastest of them all.

We next hear of Brasidas in 429/8, when he was sent along with two other Spartans to serve as advisors to the admiral Cnemus, who had just lost a naval battle to the Athenians and their commander Phormio in the Gulf of Corinth (2.85.1). Before a second naval battle, in which the Spartans hoped to make up for the previous embarrassment of the Peloponnesian fleet, which consisted mostly of Corinthian and other allied ships, Thucydides presents a paired set of speeches. On the Peloponnesian side, Brasidas, Cnemus, and the other Peloponnesian leaders spoke, while Phormio addressed his Athenian sailors in such a way that he responded to the points made by his enemies, though there is no way he could have heard their harangue.[41] Though it is impossible to tell how much of the Peloponnesian speech comes from the mind of Thucydides, Brasidas – and it is Brasidas whom Thucydides emphasizes over the other advisors sent to the gulf – tried to spur the troops on by appealing to their greater daring, their *tolmē* (Thuc. 2.87). Unfortunately for the Peloponnesians, while Brasidas might have had *tolmē* in abundance, the rest of the fleet did not. Despite early successes in the battle that followed, the Peloponnesians lost their nerve and were routed by Phormio's Athenians. The adage that it was unwise to face the Athenians at

---

[39] If we believe the story of the night raid on the Persian camp at Thermopylae, dismissed as a fabrication by most scholars, other Spartan hoplites were certainly capable of such commando operations. See Chapter 3.

[40] Connor 1984: 128n25. See also Hornblower 1991–2008: 2.41.

[41] Most scholars think these speeches were largely invented by Thucydides to emphasize his desired themes. Thucydides was fond of paired speeches, but the device is far less believable when it involves opposing forces on opposite sides of the Gulf of Corinth. The best treatment of these speeches is Romilly 2012: 80–87.

sea held up, despite the Thucydidean Brasidas' attempts to have those in the Peloponnesian fleet act contrary to their apparently cautious nature.

In 427, the Spartans once again sent Brasidas out as an advisor, this time to Alcidas who was commanding the Spartan forces at Corcyra, which was in a state of civil war between democrats supported by Athens and oligarchs supported by Sparta (Thuc. 3.69). The Peloponnesian fleet managed to score a victory at sea against the Athenians, and good military sense indicated that Alcidas should follow up this success by attacking the city at once, when his enemies were undefended and in disarray. This bold attack was the course Brasidas advised, but his opinion did not have enough weight. The Peloponnesians simply did not dare (*tolmaō*) to sail against the city, despite their advantage (Thuc. 3.79).

Brasidas is at his most dashing in 425, when, according to Thucydides, he stood out conspicuously among his fellow Spartans trying to dislodge an Athenian fortification at Pylos, deep in the Spartan-held Peloponnese. The Athenians had begun to establish a strong point right in Spartan territory, what the Greeks called an *epiteichismos*, and what we might call a forward operating base, and anyone who visits the area today can see just how rugged and defensible the spot they chose was. When Brasidas, who was in command of a trireme, saw that his fellow commanders and helm officers were reluctant to force a landing because of the roughness of the terrain, he berated his comrades, saying that it is unseemly to be worried about ships' timbers while the enemy is building a fort right under their noses. Brasidas practiced what he preached. He ordered his own helm officer to direct his trireme right against the rocks and was in the process of storming out against the Athenians when he succumbed to many wounds and fainted (Thuc. 4.11–12). While Pylos was the lowest point for the Spartans in the first phase of the war, Brasidas had been in fine form, and was singled out as such by Thucydides. Today, the rocky shore at the southern end of the strong point of ancient Pylos is called "Brasidas' Rocks," perhaps the very spot the Spartan had demonstrated his personal courage and inspiring leadership.

Thucydides devotes most of the second half of his fourth book and the first several chapters of his fifth to Brasidas' expedition to Thrace, the region on the northern shore of the Aegean Sea, where Athens had many allies and subject states (Thuc. 4.70–5.12).[42] Spanning from 424 to 423, this campaign was the most successful one for the Spartans in the first half of the war, largely making up for the embarrassing loss at Pylos in 425. The

---

[42] Badian 1999 is a good study of Brasidas and this campaign. See also the sources collected in note 81.

campaign, not only led by but also apparently the brainchild of Brasidas, represented an innovation in Sparta's war strategy by taking the conflict to Athens' northern possessions rather than merely invading Athens' home territory year after year with very little to show for it. The ultimate gain from Brasidas' expedition was the taking in 424 of the vitally important city of Amphipolis, nestled on the banks of the Strymon River, down which the timber for Athens' fleets was transported into the Aegean. Brasidas died in battle in 422 while defending Amphipolis from recapture at the hands of the Athenian general Cleon, who also died in the clash, thus bringing about the end of the Archidamian War, the Peloponnesian War's first phase, in a sort of draw for both sides. The Thracian campaign was Brasidas' crowning achievement, and a centerpiece of the whole war, at least as Thucydides saw it.

Brasidas advocated for this mission in concert with the Greeks of the Chalcidice, the three-fingered peninsula jutting into the north Aegean, and Perdiccas, the king of Macedonia. The northerners had sent messages to Sparta in secret, eager to have a Spartan army go north to offset the Athenians who dominated in the region, and Brasidas wanted to demonstrate his mettle and saw the appeal from the north as providing the perfect opportunity (Thuc. 4.79, 4.81.1). Aside from rescuing Methone in the first year of the war, Brasidas' other actions in the thick of battle and pieces of advice to his fellow Spartans, while commendable in their own right, had been in vain. The Spartans were wary of sending their best men abroad, staying true to their conservative policies, so they equipped Brasidas only with 700 helots, which he supplemented with 1,000 mercenaries gathered from elsewhere in the Peloponnese (Thuc. 4.80.5–81.1).

Thucydides implies that Brasidas and the Spartan authorities were not always on good terms, so this ragtag army was the best he could hope for (Thuc. 4.108.6–7).[43] The historian also says that, while Brasidas raised the hopes of all of Sparta's allies and potential allies, those who followed in his footsteps were not made of the same stuff, not by a longshot (Thuc. 4.81.3). In addition to their refusal to provide Brasidas with the best resources Sparta had to offer, Thucydides says the Spartan authorities saw his expedition as little other than an excuse to get rid of some helots, since they feared that the Athenian occupation of Pylos might cause a revolt of

[43] For the extent to which Brasidas and the Spartan authorities saw eye-to-eye, see Hornblower 1991–2008: vol. 2, 268–270. Lazenby 2004: 91 makes a good suggestion when he argues that Brasidas did follow official Spartan policy in the north because he had convinced the Spartans to adopt his own policy as that of the polis. For Spartan attitudes towards mercenaries and mercenary service, see Millender 2006 (who focuses more on the 4th century than the 5th).

the helot population. This statement is bolstered by a horrific episode at some unknown time in the past when the Spartan promised 2,000 exceptional helots their freedom, only to have them disappeared – likely massacred – to prevent them from challenging the Spartan social order (Thuc. 4.80).[44] Exceptional non-Spartans were not only not commemorated at Sparta but they apparently could be eliminated altogether.

There is a possibility regarding the composition of Brasidas' army that too few have explored. The Spartans perhaps gave Brasidas an army of helots and mercenaries not because they wanted to undermine Brasidas' chances out of jealousy, nor because they simply did not consider his mission to be that important, but because the use of non-Spartiate troops allowed Sparta to engage in different kinds of warfare. Though couched in the rhetoric of liberation, one could view Brasidas' goals as imperialistic in the same vein as Athens' notorious behavior – as was indeed borne out by Brasidas' successors who established Spartan garrisons and governors in states wrested from Athenian control. The Spartans tended to engage in warfare solely for glory and fame, despite what made the most strategic and tactical sense. Only reluctantly, and against the advice of one their kings, Archidamus, did the Spartans engage in open warfare against Athens in 431, and for the first several years of the war, all the Spartans did was invade Attica in a routine fashion, ravaging some crops and destroying some farmhouses. We could interpret these actions as in line with traditional notions of shame and glory, since the Spartans figured the Athenians would not overlook an enemy freely acting right in sight of Athens' walls (as expressed by Archidamus, and countered by Pericles, in Thuc. 2.11 and 13, respectively).[45] Without Spartiates bound by conservative ideas of war, Brasidas' army could fight for other reasons, without taking anything away from the Spartan drive for glory and fame. Even so, Brasidas parlayed his command of helots and mercenaries on a mission of conquest into great personal glory and commemoration as a principled liberator.[46]

While Brasidas was gathering his forces for the expedition to Thrace, bringing in allies from Corinth, Boeotia, and a few other places, he took an opportunity to intervene at Megara. The Megarians were engaged in battle

---

[44] Jordan 1990 analyses this episode as an emancipation ritual. The historicity of this atrocity is not universally accepted. See Paradiso 2004, who argues that it did not happen, while Harvey 2004 defends Thucydides' account.

[45] A central thesis of Lendon 2010 is that the Spartan and Athenian actions in the Archidamian War, especially Sparta's annual invasions of Attica and Athenian raids in the Peloponnese, are best understood as reciprocal moves taken by each side to restore their own honor vis-à-vis the enemy.

[46] On the genuineness of Brasidas' mission of liberation, see Sears 2015, with further bibliography.

with a force of Athenians trying to take the city (Thuc. 4.70–73). Showing his trademark daring, he approached the walls of the city at night, against the expectations of his Athenian enemy, and appealed to the Megarians to let him and his soldiers inside. When the Megarians hesitated, fearing that letting in Brasidas would only make a bad situation worse, Brasidas withdrew from the walls and lined his soldiers up for battle, expecting the Athenians would not engage him. In the end, this calculation proved correct; the Athenian force, though also lined up for battle, did not move from its position. When both sides withdrew without coming to blows, the Megarians figured that the Athenians had had the worst of it, being afraid to fight Brasidas' army, so they opened the gates to the Spartan general and welcomed him in. After this success, Brasidas returned to the Peloponnese to continue his preparations to march north.

With his army of 1,700 soldiers, Brasidas made his way north to those who had called for Spartan help, namely Perdiccas of Macedonia, and the Athenian subject cities in the Chalcidice. Before he could reach those new allies, however, he had to march through Thessaly, the region of broad plains in central Greece between Boeotia and Macedonia. The Thessalians tended to be friendly to Athens, which presented a problem for Brasidas. Some sympathetic Thessalians did come to escort Brasidas through their territory, but others attempted to stop his progress at the Enipeus River. Brasidas bought some time by assuring those blocking his way that he intended no hostile action against Thessaly itself. When his opposition had returned to their homes to convey his message, Brasidas rushed with all speed through the rest of Thessaly before any concerted opposition could gather, thus making it to the realm of Perdiccas (Thuc. 4.78–79.1). The verb Thucydides uses to describe Brasidas' hasty passage through Thessaly is *diedrame*, "to rush through," is the same as that used to describe his bold tactical breakthrough at Methone earlier in the war; these are the only two instances of this word in Thucydides' *History*. Daring speed once again characterizes Brasidas, and only Brasidas, as a tactician.[47]

Brasidas' first act upon arriving in the north was to annoy one of his hosts, Perdiccas. Perdiccas wanted Brasidas' help against a local Macedonian rival, Arrhabaeus, king of the Lyncestians. To Perdiccas' chagrin, Brasidas met with Arrhabaeus and was persuaded to lead his

---

[47] This verb, derived from διατρέχω, is a good Homeric word, in line with Brasidas' Homeric portrayal (see later in this chapter). It is rarely used in a tactical sense in Greek literature apart from Thucydides, and even in Homer it describes a ship cutting through the waves (*Od.* 3.177, 5.100) rather than any sort of tactical maneuver.

own army away without attacking Arrhabaeus. When Brasidas offered to arbitrate between the two enemy monarchs, Perdiccas quipped that he had not invited Brasidas north to be an arbitrator but to help him destroy his foes. In response to the slight, Perdiccas lessened the amount of money he paid Brasidas' men (Thuc. 4.83).[48] In this episode, Brasidas demonstrated fairness and integrity; he would not accept an alliance at any cost.

Many scholars think that Brasidas' supposed fairness was undercut by the very next episode, namely his mission to Acanthus, one of the Chalcidean cities subject to Athens. Marching to this city at the behest of his Chalcidean hosts, Brasidas arrived at the walls only to find the gates closed to him. Apparently not everyone in the north was eager to embrace his offer of freedom. Brasidas – an excellent speaker, for a Spartan, according to Thucydides – then delivered a speech to the Acanthians in which he proclaimed the benefits his liberation promised, and then added a threat of military force if they should still refuse to be liberated. The Acanthians relented, partly because he convinced them with his arguments, and partly because they feared the loss of their ripening crops (Thuc. 4.84–88). In a very real sense, Brasidas *forced* Acanthus to be free, which, for some, is plenty of evidence for Brasidas' duplicity and the cynical nature of his mission of liberation. On the other hand, maybe freedom, even forced freedom, really was in Acanthus' best interest, and one holdout could have threatened the freedom of all other cities in the region. In any case, Brasidas' reputation in the north did not seem to suffer after this incident.[49] In fact, the next thing Thucydides mentions is the revolt of the nearby city of Stagiros from Athens to the Spartan side (4.88). The people of Stagiros were not put off by Brasidas' threat of force at Acanthus.

Brasidas' next target was a crucial source of Athenian power, the city of Amphipolis on the Strymon River. An Athenian named Hagnon founded this city only a few years before the start of the war, after several previous attempts by Athenians and others had ended in disaster (Thuc. 4.102–108). Sitting on a high point several kilometers from the sea and surrounded on three sides by the river, Amphipolis was a formidable challenge for any military force, even one under the command of Brasidas.[50] After surprising the people inside the city by storming across a bridge on the Strymon and

---

[48] Hornblower 1991–2008: vol. 2, 274 thinks that this heated exchange genuinely took place, rather than being an invented speech of Thucydides.

[49] I talk at length about Brasidas at Acanthus in Sears 2015, and conclude that his mission of liberation was likely more genuine and principled than Brasidas' detractors suggest.

[50] For the city, its topography, and the conflict there between Brasidas and the Athenians between 424–422, see Butera and Sears 2019: 183–202.

approaching its walls with his characteristic speed, Brasidas held off attacking the city itself. Instead, once he heard that an Athenian relief force was on its way from the nearby island of Thasos, a force led by the historian Thucydides himself, Brasidas offered the people of Amphipolis total control over their own government and the Athenians in Amphipolis time to gather their belongings and leave safely. This magnanimous offer was accepted, and Brasidas entered the city without striking a blow, all before Thucydides could arrive to defend it. Thucydides had to be content with protecting the Athenian colony of Eion at the mouth of the Strymon, which Brasidas was also eyeing. The loss of Amphipolis terrified the Athenians, not only because of the resources, especially timber, it provided them, but also because they assumed more and more cities would rally to the Spartan side. The falling away of allies like dominoes did in fact happen, since the Greeks were excited by Brasidas' offer of freedom and his humane conduct, even if Athens remained a formidable force.[51] Thucydides was exiled by the Athenians for failing to protect Amphipolis, giving the great historian time to research and write his account of the war and providing him with every incentive to glorify the Spartan general who had bested him.

By showing the Spartan authorities as hesitant to send reinforcements, Thucydides hints at how the campaign clashed with Sparta's traditional war-making ethos. Brasidas, who, we will remember, demonstrated a facility with naval warfare by advising the Peloponnesians in their battle with the Athenians in the Gulf of Corinth and leading a trireme against the Athenian position at Pylos, began building his own fleet of triremes at Amphipolis – undoubtedly using the timber for which the city was famous and so prized by Athens. Since the Spartans only won the war with Athens after they built a fleet with Persian help, Brasidas' action here was strategically brilliant, if ahead of its time. When he asked the Spartans to send him another army, the Spartans refused. Thucydides says that the Spartan authorities were jealous of Brasidas and did not want to give him the ability to bolster his image even further.[52] The other reason Thucydides gives for the Spartan reluctance is that the Spartans wanted above all to get back the soldiers who had been captured on Pylos, and to end the war with Athens, goals that would not be advanced by escalating things in the north Aegean (Thuc. 4.108.7).

---

[51]  Bosworth 1993 argues that Thucydides criticizes the Greeks for underestimating Athenian military power and accepting Brasidas' propaganda at face value, even if the rest of the Spartans were unlikely to back it up.

[52]  For Brasidas and the Spartan authorities, see note 43.

Brasidas had been by far the most successful Spartan general in the Peloponnesian War up to this point, and his mission in Thrace had done far more than the annual invasions of Attica to frighten Athens and shake loose the cities of its empire. Who knows how much more Brasidas could have achieved if his government had given free rein to his innovative approach and provided the material support he wanted. But Sparta's goals were far more modest than Brasidas' and did not include open-ended liberation expeditions throughout the Greek world. Sparta's refusal to reinforce their general smacks of the underwhelming force sent to Thermopylae in 480, which was Sparta's proudest moment, despite seeming at first like a debacle.

After taking Amphipolis, Brasidas moved against the cities in the Chalcidice, taking many Athenian subjects into the Spartan alliance, including the important site of Torone. At Torone, as at other places in the north, Brasidas combined charming rhetoric with daring nighttime maneuvers and surprise assaults to defeat Athenian garrisons and win the locals over to his cause (Thuc. 4. 109–116.). In early 423, Athens and Sparta agreed to an armistice, during which neither side would take territory from the other. This, however, did not prevent Brasidas from encouraging the revolts of the Chalcidean cities of Scione and Mende, in clear violation of the armistice but to his own greater glory. The Athenians made preparations to attack these sites, while Brasidas left them in the hands of a small force as he prepared for an expedition in Macedonia (Thuc. 4.119–123).[53]

Brasidas' second foray into Macedonian affairs did not go any better than the first, and resulted in Perdiccas falling out with the Spartans and joining the Athenian alliance. The chief disagreement between Brasidas and Perdiccas was a result of the latter abandoning Brasidas' force in hostile territory, and the former appropriating Macedonian livestock and equipment he found while making his way to safety. Though the expedition was a failure, and allowed the Athenians the opportunity to retake Mende and besiege Scione, the adventure in Macedonia provided an opportunity for Brasidas once again to show his tactical acumen and inspirational leadership as he successfully extricated his force from hostile territory while surrounded by far greater numbers of Illyrian enemies. Forming his hoplites into a hollow square with his light-armed troops on the inside – a formation rarely if ever used by the Greeks at that time – Brasidas ordered his youngest soldiers to dart out from the formation against the enemy,

---

[53] Bosworth 1993: 37 says that this action of Brasidas was irresponsible and left his new acquisitions vulnerable to Athens' anger.

while he himself formed a rearguard with 300 picked troops. These tactics, along with words of inspiration to the effect that the numerous and fearsome enemy would not long attack a well-disciplined body of soldiers, carried the day, further cementing Brasidas' legend (Thuc. 4.124–128).[54] This legend was perhaps tarnished by his imposition of Spartan governors in the cities he had taken from Athens, including the hand-picked Clearidas in Amphipolis, despite Brasidas' promise to allow liberated cities their own choices in terms of internal governance (Thuc. 4.132.2–3).[55] Thucydides' fourth book, and the ninth year of the war, ends with a bold yet unsuccessful attempt on the part of Brasidas to take the city of Potidaea by night. Brasidas stealthily brought his force up to Potidaea's walls and raised a ladder just after the guard passed by, but he was discovered and had to withdraw (Thuc. 4.135).

Brasidas' crowning achievement was also the last action of his life, the defense of Amphipolis in 422 from an Athenian counterattack led by the firebrand Cleon, one of the leaders responsible for capturing the Spartan prisoners at Pylos three years earlier.[56] What more fitting end could there be for Thucydides' Achilles than an Achillean death in battle, and a victorious battle, no less? When Cleon arrived with his sizable force in the vicinity of Amphipolis, he marched up past the city on a reconnaissance mission, only to be surprised by a bold and sudden attack from Brasidas. Before leading his soldiers out of the city gates, Brasidas delivered a fine speech, ending with a promise to practice what he preached by fighting bravely himself. He then charged out with a small force and smashed into the center of the Athenian line, which was stretched out and vulnerable in the process of marching back to the coast and did not expect an engagement. Brasidas had routed the center of the Athenian line when Clearidas, Brasidas' chosen governor of Amphipolis, charged out of another city gate with the majority of the Spartan force and mopped up the rest of the Athenian stragglers. Cleon himself died in the clash, killed by one of Brasidas' allied Thracian peltasts, while Brasidas was taken from the battle mortally wounded. When he learned of his victory, he perished (Thuc. 5.6–10).

[54] As Hornblower 1991–2008: vol. 2, 400 says, "Th[ucydides] the *strategos* surely wants us to admire this achievement at the purely military level."

[55] Thucydides calls this imposition of governors "illegal" (παρανόμως). For scholarship on this event, see Hornblower 1991–2008: vol. 2, 408–410. Cartledge 1987: 92 thinks these governors were Brasidas' supporters and protégés. Despite going back on his word, Brasidas still demonstrated an eye to his future glory by making sure that the cities he captured were in the hands of his friends instead of rivals from Sparta.

[56] For this battle, see Howie 2005; and Sears and Butera 2019: 183–202.

The humiliation of Pylos had been paid back, and then some. The Athenians and Spartans then entered peace talks, ending the first phase of the war in what scholars call the Peace of Nicias, named after the Athenian who led the negotiations. Brasidas was dead, after serving the Spartans well and building up a peerless reputation in the process. In the coming years, other Spartans would follow Brasidas' lead, fighting in unconventional ways, both strategically and tactically, and pursuing even greater reputations and personal power. Brasidas had shown a new way to be a Spartan abroad, pursuing not wealth or friendship with the Persians, as Pausanias had done, but striving after fame and glory by liberating Athens' subjects. His mission of liberation had important implications for Spartan ideas about war and commemoration.

## Monuments to a Liberator

After Brasidas died heroically in battle, he was commemorated in a way that outshone even his most illustrious Spartan predecessors. At Amphipolis, the people buried him with great fanfare in the city's agora, declared him the city's founder, and honored him every year with games befitting a hero. The buildings in Amphipolis associated with Hagnon, the Athenian who had founded the city, the people tore down as they expressed their preference for Brasidas. The people of Acanthus dedicated a treasury at Delphi that they named after themselves and Brasidas, an honor for an individual not seen since the age of Archaic tyrants. At Sparta, Brasidas was commemorated with an ornate cenotaph, which may still survive on the acropolis. Brasidas' veterans, consisting primarily of freed helots and other non-Spartiate soldiers, were honored with the title "Brasideioi," and fought as a distinct unit in the Spartan army. Finally, Thucydides' *History* stands as a monument to the energy and achievements of the able Spartan who defeated Thucydides in arena of war. If Brasidas had deliberately lived in such a way as to guarantee posthumous honors, he succeeded wildly. He demonstrated to the Spartans coming after him the kinds of distinctions that were now possible, and several successors followed his example to achieve tremendous fame and devotion from others, even while they were still alive.

Brasidas' initial appearance in Thucydides' history of the Peloponnesian War, and the first we hear of him in any source, is as the recipient of a public act of praise in Sparta (*epaineō*), the very first Spartan to be so honored during the war (Thuc. 2.25.2). Brasidas received this distinction for his daring rescue of the site of Methone from an amphibious Athenian force. Thucydides' wording indicates that others received such an honor later in the conflict, and that this praise was a formal honor, rather than a mere expression of praise from the state.[57] In Thrace, Brasidas received further extraordinary honors while he was still alive. When he gained the alliance of Scione, the people there publicly bestowed on him a golden crown, on the grounds that he was the liberator of Greece. Many Scionians approached him as private individuals to garland him as if he were returning home as a victorious athlete, a semi-religious honor foreshadowing the cult he later received at Amphipolis (Thuc. 4.121.1).[58] Not only does no one else in Thucydides' history receive such honors, this particular combination of public and private adoration is rare in all of Greek history. Gold crowns did become a standard civic honor for great benefactors in Greek cities, but not to any significant extent until the 4th century (see the famous example of the crown proposed at Athens in 336 for the orator Demosthenes in his speech *On the Crown*). Brasidas was charting new ground.

Brasidas received a remarkable commemoration in a negative way, by having the Athenians proudly display the shield he had lost after fainting from his wounds at Pylos (Thuc. 4.12). Even though the Athenians likely recovered many bits of Spartan kit at Pylos, including the shields taken from those captured on the island that were eventually displayed in Athens (one of which can be seen today in the Agora Museum), Brasidas' shield was an especially impressive spoil. The Athenians used the shield to erect a trophy on the very spot where they turned back Brasidas' attack.[59] Brasidas was in a class of his own when it came to self-promotion and the honors he received at the hands of those for whom he fought. His enemies also honored him as a worthy foe.

Thucydides 5.11.1 is one of the most fascinating and important paragraphs in his *History*, and has been pored over by scholars seeking to understand everything from the political dynamics of commemoration to

---

[57] As noted by Lewis 1977: 42n102.

[58] For the singularity of these honors, and a discussion of the precise significance of the garlands, see the lengthy discussion in Hornblower 1991–2008: vol. 2, 380–385. For a recent discussion of the importance of athletics for the Spartans, including as a way to supplement or replace military honors, see Christesen 2019.

[59] For trophies, see the comprehensive study of Kinnee 2018. See also the classic study by Pritchett 1974: 246–275, which catalogues all the instances in Archaic and Classical Greek history of the erection of battlefield trophies. Hornblower 1991–2008: vol. 2, 166 sees the importance attached to Brasidas' shield as having Homeric resonances. For more on the Homeric Brasidas, see later in this chapter.

the development of hero cults for real individuals (as opposed to the mythical heroes of epic). The passage is worth quoting in full:

> After this, all the allies presenting themselves in arms buried Brasidas at public expense inside the city, in front of what is now the agora. From then on, the Amphipolitans, once they had enclosed his tomb, performed sacrifices for him as if to a hero, honored him with annual games and offerings, and transferred the colony to him as its founder. They tore down the buildings associated with Hagnon and wiped out every surviving memorial of his foundation of the colony. They did these things because they considered Brasidas to be their savior and were aiming for an alliance with the Lacedaemonians at present out of fear of the Athenians. Due to their hostility with the Athenians, Hagnon could no longer conveniently receive the same honors from them as he had.[60]

During the excavations at Amphipolis in the 1970s and 1980s, directed by Dimitris Lazaridis, a cist grave was found within the walls of the ancient city, behind the modern museum. Inside this grave was a wooden and silver ossuary containing the cremated remains of a man in his thirties or forties, and a gold wreath, both of which are on display in the museum (Figure 4.3). An adjoining chamber contained pottery, which could have been from votive offerings to the tomb's occupant. The tomb was in the courtyard of a building of the 4th century, though the earliest phases of the building date to the 5th century. While the contents of the grave itself have not been dated with any certainty (and much of the material has not been formally published), this find was heralded as the "Tomb of Brasidas."[61] One would really like to believe that this tomb, which seems to have been the object of cultic veneration and was located within the city, a distinct honor, really is that of Brasidas. Like so many other finds linked to historical individuals, however, this might be wishful thinking. Much more excavation is needed to clarify the precise layout and remains of Classical Amphipolis, since earlier work focused on outlining the ancient fortifications – which are indeed spectacular and well worth seeing. Upon walking the fields of the city's acropolis, I was struck by just how much

[60] μετὰ δὲ ταῦτα τὸν Βρασίδαν οἱ ξύμμαχοι πάντες ξὺν ὅπλοις ἐπισπόμενοι δημοσίᾳ ἔθαψαν ἐν τῇ πόλει πρὸ τῆς νῦν ἀγορᾶς οὔσης· καὶ τὸ λοιπὸν οἱ Ἀμφιπολῖται, περιείρξαντες αὐτοῦ τὸ μνημεῖον, ὡς ἥρωί τε ἐντέμνουσι καὶ τιμὰς δεδώκασιν ἀγῶνας καὶ ἐτησίους θυσίας, καὶ τὴν ἀποικίαν ὡς οἰκιστῇ προσέθεσαν, καταβαλόντες τὰ Ἀγνώνεια οἰκοδομήματα καὶ ἀφανίσαντες εἴ τι μνημόσυνόν που ἔμελλεν αὐτοῦ τῆς οἰκίσεως περιέσεσθαι, νομίσαντες τὸν μὲν Βρασίδαν σωτῆρά τε σφῶν γεγενῆσθαι καὶ ἐν τῷ παρόντι ἅμα τὴν τῶν Λακεδαιμονίων ξυμμαχίαν φόβῳ τῶν Ἀθηναίων θεραπεύοντες, τὸν δὲ Ἅγνωνα κατὰ τὸ πολέμιον τῶν Ἀθηναίων οὐκ ἂν ὁμοίως σφίσι ξυμφόρως οὐδ᾽ ἂν ἡδέως τὰς τιμὰς ἔχειν.

[61] For the excavations and the contents of the tomb, see Koukouli-Chrysanthaki 2002. Mari 2010 provides a relatively recent reappraisal of the material evidence from Amphipolis, and thinks the tomb most likely came from a century or so after the death of Brasidas.

Figure 4.3 The ossuary and gold crown from the "Tomb of Brasidas,"
Archaeological Museum of Amphipolis. Author's photo. © Hellenic Ministry of
Culture and Sports / Hellenic Organization of Cultural Resources Development.

pottery and ancient building material can be seen on the surface. Great things
there await an enterprising archaeologist.

More than his burial inside the city, the hero cult the Amphipolitans
established for Brasidas, complete with annual games and animal sacrifices,
was a tremendous honor for the Spartan general. Other city founders had
been similarly honored, such as the Athenian Miltiades who founded
a colony in the Chersonese, the modern Gallipoli Peninsula, a century
before the Peloponnesian War, but those other founders had been actual
city founders. Brasidas was not.[62] Hagnon the Athenian was Amphipolis'
real founder, and the buildings associated with him in the city indicate that
he had been the object of outstanding commemoration even while he was
still alive, which was highly unusual at this point in Greek history. Brasidas,
however, had so ingratiated himself with the people of Amphipolis that
they tore down everything that reminded them of Hagnon and decided
that they should honor Brasidas, their liberator and savior, as a founder

[62] Malkin 1987 remains the foundational text for understanding the role of religion in Greek
colonization, including the importance of city founders.

too, a distinction without parallel in the Classical Greek world. As Matthew Simonton argues, Brasidas' hero cult and its associated monuments were a key propaganda tool for those who wanted Amphipolis to be ruled by an oligarchy, as the Spartans encouraged throughout the Aegean world during the war. The cult of the tyrant-slayers in Athens was similarly a symbol for the democracy.[63] Karin Mackowiak remarks on the religious significance of the cult transfer from Hagnon to Brasidas, showing that at Amphipolis political and cultural factors intertwined in the commemoration of Brasidas.[64] Like Achilles, Brasidas had died relatively young in battle. And also like Achilles, he ensured that he would be remembered forever and even worshipped as a hero.

Not to be outdone by their neighbors, the people of Acanthus dedicated a treasury building at Delphi, which they named after themselves and their liberator. A Delphic treasury is a small temple-like structure built to house a state's dedications at the Panhellenic sanctuary (there are treasuries at Olympia, too), and to glorify the state among the community of fellow Greeks. Some of the most famous buildings at Delphi are treasuries, including the Treasury of the Athenians that, in its heavily restored splendor, dominates the Sacred Way to the Temple of Apollo, and the treasuries of the Siphnians and Sicyonians whose art adorns the Archaeological Museum of Delphi (Figure 4.4). In the Archaic period, several individuals built treasuries at Delphi, including most notably the Corinthian tyrant Cypselus, whose name was erased from his building by the Corinthians once they had driven the tyrants out. Brasidas, though, was the first individual named on such a building for two centuries or so, a remarkable commemoration. This treasury was also the first such structure erected at Delphi in forty years. It is possible that the treasury was commissioned or built while Brasidas was still alive and that he had a hand in its conception.[65] Brasidas' example impressed his successors, as shown by the Spartan admiral Lysander putting a statue of himself in the Treasury of Brasidas and the Acanthians, which Plutarch saw on a visit to the site (*Mor.* 400F, 401C; *Lys.* 1.1, 18.1).[66]

The Treasury of Brasidas and the Acanthians was a sign of things to come for ambitious Spartans and other Greeks who longed to exceed the bounds of traditional honors. The Acanthians might also have had a poignant message for the Athenians, beyond building an ostentatious monument from spoils taken from the Athenians. The people frequently embraced Archaic tyrants

---

[63] Simonton 2018.  [64] Mackowiak 2018.  [65] Currie 2005: 169–170, 191.
[66] Lysander had more elaborate monuments at Delphi too, which we will consider in the next chapter.

Figure 4.4 The Treasury of the Athenians at Delphi. Author's photo.

like Cypselus, but also Pisistratus from Athens, as liberators from aristocratic oppressors. Cypselus and Pisistratus began their respective reigns as popular champions against entrenched elites. Archaeologists' best guess for the location of the Treasury of Brasidas and the Acanthians places it in spatial and architectural competition with the Treasury of the Athenians, as first argued by Michael Scott.[67] The spatial politics of Delphi are a much remarked-on phenomenon. The Sacred Way is littered with statues and structures competing with each other, sometimes literally overshadowing their rivals. By naming the treasury after Brasidas, the Acanthians might have been signaling to the Athenians that the great Spartan was their liberator against Athens, just as Archaic tyrants had freed their own peoples. Cypselus' famous treasury seems to have been situated between that of the Athenians and the Acanthians, a prominent reminder of populist liberators of ages past. The Athenians celebrated the people's resistance to tyranny on their own treasury by depicting the mythical hero Theseus in the iconic pose of the tyrannicides, arm extended above and behind the head to deliver a fatal blow to a tyrant with a sword. Within sight of this image, the Acanthians seem to say to the Athenians that Athens is the real tyrant, and Brasidas the real liberator.[68]

[67] Scott 2010: 101–109.
[68] I talk extensively about this treasury and its message of liberation in Sears 2019a.

Though his body was at Amphipolis, Brasidas was also memorialized with a cenotaph at Sparta. Pausanias notes that he passed this monument moving westward from the agora, before he reached the theater (3.14.1). Opposite the theater, which is one of the best-known and most thoroughly excavated buildings in Sparta, were tombs of the Persian War heroes Leonidas and Pausanias, along with a *stele* listing the names of the Three Hundred. Pausanias says that each year the Spartans delivered speeches and held athletic contests next to these tombs, suggesting the formal heroization of these figures, much like in the case of Brasidas at Amphipolis. To the south of the theater, Pausanias also came across a sanctuary of Maron and Alpheius, said to be the bravest warriors at Thermopylae after Leonidas. Brasidas, then, could not be in any more illustrious company, one of only a handful of genuine Classical figures honored with a conspicuous structure in the city.

Archaeologists have not identified with certainty any of these tombs and shrines to military leaders mentioned by Pausanias. The building to the south of the theater long identified as the "Tomb of Leonidas" does not line up with Pausanias' description of the tomb as being directly opposite the theater.[69] In general, early excavations at Sparta sought to identify material remains with specific historical figures. We earlier encountered the "Smiling Hoplite," found at the sanctuary of Athena Chalkioikos on the acropolis and now residing as a centerpiece in the Archaeological Museum of Sparta. This sculpture is commonly identified as a portrait of Leonidas. Brasidas, too, has found in way into archaeological conjecture. A headless statute found in 1872 was deemed to be Brasidas, based on a location compatible with Pausanias' description.[70] The most prominent find linked to Brasidas is the "Round Building," a large circular or semi-circular edifice that today stands out on the acropolis (Figure 1.3). Several identifications have been proposed for this building, ranging from the *choros* where the festival of the Gymnopaidiai held its events, to the *skias* where various meetings were held. Scholars do not even agree about how the structure looked in classical antiquity, whether it was merely a retaining wall or was the base of a monument.[71] Some have proposed that the Round Building

---

[69] For the impact of these structures on early travelers to Sparta, and the popular identification of the Tomb of Leonidas, see Matalas 2017. Sanders 2009 argues that the Tomb of Leonidas was where Carneus was worshipped (apart from Apollo Carneus, who seems to have been honored elsewhere), also mentioned by Pausanias.

[70] Matalas 2017: 51.

[71] Kourinou 2000 argues that the Round Building was the *choros* used for the Gymnopaidiai, and was a terrace wall for an artificial rounded space. Sanders 2009: 203 restates the old argument that the Round Building was the structure that contained statues of Olympian Zeus and Aphrodite.

was the cenotaph of Brasidas.[72] The structure certainly lines up with Pausanias' account, coming as it does between the agora and the theater, though Pausanias' description has notoriously spawned endless topographical debates rendering consensus about identifying structures such as the Round Building elusive.

One of the things that makes the function of the Round Building difficult to pinpoint is that it represents several distinct building phases. Originally an Archaic structure, much of which survives in the foundation, the Round Building was renovated and repurposed in subsequent eras, so the building likely served several roles before it was seen by Pausanias. That said, the cenotaph of Brasidas was still visible in Pausanias' day, along with the other monuments that have been linked to the Round Building. One tantalizing comparison does present itself, a round structure of disputed identification in the Athenian Kerameikos, a prominent cemetery just outside of that city's walls. Next to the Tomb of the Lacedaemonians in the Kerameikos (which we will discuss in the next chapter) is a tomb of unique design, a circular structure with protruding wings on either side and topped by a marble vessel in the shape of a Panathenaic amphora. This tomb, which most date to around 400, has been prosaically dubbed "The Grave at the Third Boundary Marker," since it is located next to a Kerameikos boundary stone still *in situ* along the *dromos*, the broad road that leads to Plato's Academy.[73]

In 1977, Franz Willemsen, noting the tomb's spatial and apparent temporal relationship with the Tomb of the Lacedaemonians, suggested that it was for the Olympic victor Lakrates, mentioned by Xenophon as one of those buried in the Kerameikos along with the Spartans who died fighting for the Spartan puppet-oligarchy, the Thirty Tyrants, against the Athenian democrats in 403. Xenophon names two *polemarchs*, Spartan military commanders, along with Lakrates who were memorialized there (*Hell.* 2.4.33). Willemsen suggests that Lakrates was in fact an Athenian athlete who died fighting along with the Thirty Tyrants and the Spartans, and was thus buried next to them.[74] Most scholars reject Willemsen's arguments, especially since Xenophon's text makes it clear that Lakrates was one of the Spartans.[75] While Panos Valavanis considers the round tomb to be from the mid-4th century, Rudolf Stichel agrees with the standard date of c. 400, and its connection to

---

[72] Musti and Torelli 1991: 210–211.
[73] Willemsen 1977; Knigge 1991: 160–163; Stichel 1998; Valavanis 1999; Kienlin 2003.
[74] Willemsen 1977.
[75] Stichel 1998; Valavanis 1999. But see Kienlin 2003, who questions whether the tomb at the third boundary marker is a tomb at all, but this view is decidedly in the minority.

the Tomb of the Lacedaemonians, and suggests that the tomb belonged to Critias, the Athenian leader of the Thirty Tyrants.[76] As Stichel argues, the presence of the marble Panathenaic amphora atop the tomb, while indicating that the tomb's occupant was an athlete, indicates that the occupant was an Athenian rather than a Spartan.

I am not so sure that the Panathenaic amphora, representing the ceramic amphorae filled with oil given as prizes in the Panathenaic games, must indicate an Athenian recipient. First of all, fragments of Panathenaic amphorae have been found at the sanctuary of Athena Chalkioikos in Sparta, indicating that Spartans won prizes in those games and dedicated the symbols of their victory to the goddess once back home. That a Spartan Olympic athlete who was part of the pro-Thirty forces at Athens also took part in the Panathenaic games is not out of the question. The much more prestigious Olympic Games offered no permanent prizes beyond a wreath of olive leaves, which would not have served as well as a prominent grave marker. We cannot point to comparative evidence to make the case either way, since this marble Panathenaic amphora seems unique from the Classical period.[77] Maybe the Spartan Lakrates really did get a separate and elaborate monument at Athens. We have the first part of the inscription from the Tomb of Lacedaemonians, which lists the two *polemarchs* named by Xenophon, a remarkable confirmation of Xenophon's testimony (Figure 5.2; Figure 5.3). The inscription breaks off after these first two names, aside from the start of a letter for the next name. This letter is usually read as a *mu*, the Greek "m," which would thus not be Lakrates, whom we might expect to be listed third in order of prestige. More work needs to be done to determine whether there are any architectural or stylistic affinities between this tomb and the Round Building at Sparta (the latter is, to be sure, several times larger than the former). We might have, however, two examples of round monuments honoring dead Spartan warriors from roughly the same period – if the Round Building was indeed renovated to represent Brasidas' cenotaph. Like Brasidas' supposed tomb in Amphipolis, it is difficult to avoid the temptation to embrace a material remnant of the famous Spartan's memorialization, especially one so large and prominent on Sparta's acropolis.

Brasidas was commemorated also in the name of a unit in the Spartan army, first mentioned explicitly at the Battle of Mantinea in 418: the *Brasideioi*, or "Brasideans" (Thuc. 5.67.1). These soldiers were the helots sent along with

[76] Stichel 1998; Valavanis 1999.
[77] Tiverios 2007: 18 talks about the prestige of Panathenaic amphorae, as evidenced by their use as marble grave markers, though the only pre-Roman example he provides is this circular tomb at the third boundary marker.

Brasidas to Thrace, whom the Spartans freed in 421 in recognition of their
service (Thuc. 5.34.1). At Mantinea, this unit fought along with the
*Neodamōdeis*, another class of freed helots.[78] Simon Hornblower thinks that
the *Brasideioi* at Mantinea included not only the 700 helots who volunteered
to join Brasidas' expeditionary force as hoplites, but also 1,000 non-hoplites
hired by Brasidas for the expedition, thus making this force some 1,700 strong
(minus casualties from Thrace). Hornblower presents the possibility that the
name of this force is further evidence of Brasidas' remarkable cult of personality, but is more inclined to attribute the moniker to Thucydides' need for
a convenient way to refer to these troops.[79] This usage in Thucydides,
however, seems unique, even though other commanders during the
Peloponnesian War led distinct groups of soldiers. The light-armed troops
the Athenian Demosthenes used to defeat the Spartans on Sphacteria, for
instance, are not called the "Demostheneans." Like so many other honors
given to Brasidas, the name of this military contingent appears to be a unique
mark of distinction for the deceased general.

The final monument to Brasidas that we will discuss here is the text of
Thucydides' *History*, a work the author himself famously claimed to be "a
possession for all time." Since Brasidas was the one who wrested away
Amphipolis from under Thucydides' watch, leading to the historian's exile
from Athens, it makes sense that Thucydides would want to highlight
Brasidas' virtues. Thucydides was not beaten by a slouch. The historian
also seems to have a genuine admiration for Brasidas and uses the Spartan
general as an important part of his story, especially as a touchstone for
crafting his characterizations of the Athenians and Spartans. Whether or
not Brasidas really was an atypical Spartan – I tend to think he was more
typical than Thucydides allows – Thucydides presents him as an energetic
and innovative foil to the conservative and foot-dragging Spartans.
Brasidas is much more like Thucydides' Athenians, in fact, which serves
to highlight the contrast between the two great powers.[80] Thucydides goes
further, treating Brasidas as more than a paradigmatically skilled commander, but a virtual Homeric hero.[81] One scholar even calls Brasidas'

---

[78] For these classes in Spartan society, see Bruni 1979. See also Paradiso and Roy 2008: 27–29. We will
    discuss the Brasideioi, Neodamōdeis, and other unconventional Lacedaemonian soldiers at greater
    length in the next chapter.
[79] Hornblower 1991–2008: vol. 3, 175.
[80] For Thucydides' characterization of Brasidas, and the fact that he was more like other Spartans than
    many have recognized, see Sears 2020.
[81] Many scholars have treated Thucydides' portrayal of Brasidas. See Harley 1941; Westlake 1968: 148–
    165; Daverio Rocchi 1985; Wylie 1992; Boëldieu-Trevet 1997; Rood 1998: 69–77; Badian 1999;

career in Thucydides his *aristeia*, the word used to describe a Homeric hero's extended display of murderous excellence in the *Iliad*.[82]

Not only are Brasidas' actions Homeric, but the very words Thucydides uses have echoes in the epics. At Pylos, when Brasidas, alone among the Spartans attacking the Athenian position, urges his men forward, at great personal risk, until he is wounded, "his soul left him" (that is, he fainted, Thuc. 4.12.1).[83] As Hornblower notes, a warrior fainting from his wounds is very common in the *Iliad*, as is the word Thucydides uses here for fainting. The fact that the Athenians recovered and displayed Brasidas' shield after it slipped off his arm further reinforces the Homeric and heroic resonances of the passage.[84] Ernst Badian suggests that, in addition to having the dashing courage of an Iliadic warrior, Brasidas resembled Odysseus too in possessing and using great intelligence and shrewdness. This makes the Thucydidean Brasidas "no less courageous and more sophisticated than other Spartans of his generation."[85] Brasidas is the only character in all of Thucydides whom the historian says possess both excellence (*arete*) and intelligence (*xunesis*). Others have either one or the other of these virtues, but only Brasidas combines them in an Odyssean way.

While not a household name like Leonidas, Brasidas is nevertheless one of the most famous Spartan individuals from classical antiquity, though he appears very rarely outside of Thucydides' work (and the work of later sources derived from Thucydides). Thucydides certainly had his reasons, personal and literary, for featuring Brasidas as prominently as he does, but Brasidas might have had a hand in his own historiographical memorialization. Joseph Roisman and H. D. Westlake both argue that Brasidas, or at least someone closely connected to Brasidas, served as Thucydides' source for events to which Brasidas was connected.[86] Some of the account is just too detailed, and Brasidas' actions and attitudes too sympathetically portrayed, for Thucydides to by relying on anyone other than the Spartan general or someone close to Brasidas and on his side. As we have already seen, Brasidas seems to have lived with an eye to his reputation, even his

---

Hoffmann 2000; Howie 2005; Hornblower 1991–2008: vol. 2, 38–61; Bosworth 2009; Mari 2012; Nichols 2014: 78–106; Sears 2020.

[82] Howie 2005. While Thucydides compares Brasidas to a Homeric hero indirectly, but portraying him in such a way that the reader thinks of parallel actions in the *Iliad*, one of the characters in Plato's *Symposium* makes the comparison explicit. Brasidas, and only Brasidas, is said to be like Achilles (Plat. *Symp.* 221c).

[83] The Greek verb used is λιποψυχέω.

[84] Hornblower 1991–2008: vol. 2, 43–46, 166–167, with further bibliography. See also Badian 1999: 7–8.

[85] Badian 1999: 33–34.     [86] Westlake 1968: 148; 1980; Roisman 1987a.

posthumous reputation.[87] To have a writer with the skill and influence of Thucydides on one's side is a decided advantage in cultivating one's image. Having the writer listen to your own version of things compounds that advantage. Achilles had the divine muse to tell his story to Homer. Brasidas made due with the most widely read and revered of Greek historians.

## Conclusion

Brasidas did that one thing the Spartans apparently most feared in their leaders: He went abroad. Because he died in a battle that evened things up with the Athenians, he enjoyed a reputation closer to that of Leonidas than that of Pausanias. In practical terms, however, Brasidas resembled the alleged Medizer more than the hero of Thermopylae. Like Pausanias, Brasidas went abroad and stayed abroad for an extended period of time, taking the war to Sparta's enemies instead of hunkering down in Greece and adopting an isolationist and defensive posture. Brasidas succeeded where Pausanias failed in having many Greek states revolt from Athens to claim Sparta's protection – whereas Pausanias' arrogance had driven many Greeks into the arms of Athens, thus laying the foundations of the Athenian Empire. But like Pausanias, Brasidas' activities abroad took Sparta out of its Peloponnesian comfort zone and entailed foreign military and political commitments that went well beyond fighting hoplite battles for glory's sake alone. Also like Pausanias, Brasidas acted with an eye to his own fame and commemoration and managed to gain unprecedented honors, both while living and after death, in far-flung cities across the Aegean, at the Panhellenic sanctuary of Delphi, and at Sparta itself. Brasidas' unprecedented success in being commemorated and monumentalized guaranteed that other ambitious Spartans would follow in his footsteps and that Sparta's wars would be longer, further from home, and for reasons and pretexts beyond dying as an *anēr agathos*, a "good man," in the thick of battle.

   Many aspects of the Peloponnesian War made it a different kind of war for the Greeks and propelled Sparta into a period of prolonged military conflict abroad even well after Athens had been defeated in 404. Not least among these novel aspects was the arena that long war afforded ambitious figures on both sides of the conflict. Where Athens had for a long time encouraged the adventurism of figures like Cimon and Pericles, and had embraced the rhetoric of freedom and Panhellenism, Sparta was new to the

---

[87] Ferrario 2014: 232.

practice of commemorating their wars and warriors as forces for the liberation of others. When Sparta, best exemplified by Brasidas in the first decade of the Peloponnesian War, embraced the sorts of commemoration more familiar to us today, and generally perceived as more selfless and virtuous, the famously isolationist polis began to fight more wars for longer periods and in more places. Brasidas and his successors in outsized commemoration benefitted from this new arrangement; the cause of peace did not.

# CHAPTER 5

# Remembering Sparta's Other Liberators

## Introduction

Brasidas was honored with a treasury at Delphi, named after him and the Acanthians, whom he liberated and who built the treasury. But it was not a statue of Brasidas that adorned his treasury, despite what most ancient Greeks seemed to think. Instead, as Plutarch clarifies, the image in the treasury was that of Lysander, the Spartan leader who eventually won the war against Athens, but who has enjoyed a far more mixed reputation. Lysander took Brasidas' commemorative innovations to staggering new heights, managing to be worshipped as a virtual deity even while he was still alive. He also had far more personal power than Brasidas. Once Athens surrendered in 404, Lysander for a time ruled over much of the Aegean world, despite his self-fashioning as a liberator, and Sparta's stated goal for the Peloponnesian War to free Greece from Athenian tyranny. Lysander took things too far, even if he was just following Brasidas' lead, and he fell out of favor and out of power. Nevertheless, he left behind himself a remarkable commemorative record, including the statue mentioned by Plutarch and another, even more fabulous monument along the Sacred Way at Delphi. Lysander demonstrated what an ambitious Spartan commander could achieve by way of commemoration, and in so doing, he foreshadowed the warlords and kings of the Hellenistic Age who forged a rich monumental legacy.

Lysander's era furnishes some interesting examples of Spartan commemoration. Those Spartans who fought alongside Lysander's puppet regime in Athens in 403 were given a prominent burial next to Athens' most famous cemetery, a tomb so enduring that it can be viewed today in the Kerameikos, complete with part of its original inscription. The modern visitor can be forgiven for wondering why Athens allowed such a monument to be erected for those who fought against the Athenian democracy. Lysander himself was buried not where he fell, outside the walls of Haliartus in Boeotia, but instead in the neighboring territory of Phocis, perhaps as a reminder that he died defending the Phocians from the Boeotians (as Polly Low suggests).[1] Such ostentatious altruism in a funerary monument is out of keeping with earlier Spartan war monuments, even those outside of Spartan lands.

Before we get to Lysander, however, we must consider the career and commemoration of another Spartan liberator, Gylippus, who dealt the Athenians more damage and thus helped the Spartan cause more than nearly anyone else by leading the defeat of the Athenian expedition in Sicily in 413. Unlike Brasidas and Lysander, Gylippus left no ostentatious monuments, and while his name was well known to the Greeks and appears throughout the literary sources, he is largely overlooked and overshadowed, most notably in Thucydides' *History*. The case of Gylippus prompts us to ask why some Spartans, even controversial ones, are lavishly memorialized, while others are not, and why some are remembered as heroes, even selfless heroes, while others are paradigms of corruption and the wrong way of doing things – even if both the good and bad examples demonstrate many of the same motivations.

## Why Don't We Remember Gylippus?

In the city of Priene, a magnificently preserved Hellenistic polis in Ionia, on the west coast of Turkey, a remarkable 2nd-century BCE inscription was found in the gymnasium, a building complex tied to the education of Priene's youth. Under the heading of "ephors," the inscription lists fourteen famous Spartans (at least, those names we know are of famous Spartans; a few names are of otherwise unknown figures) (IK Priene 322, II). Along with Tyrtaeus, Cleomenes, Leonidas, and others (most of whom were not actually ephors), is listed Gylippus, sufficiently renowned to be remembered on the other side of the Aegean two and a half centuries after his death. As remarkable as this strange tribute is, the Priene inscription seems to be the only surviving physical monument honoring Gylippus in any way. His name does not so much as appear in any other inscription. And while the physical monuments of other renowned Spartans – of which we know from other sources – have disappeared since antiquity or have remained unidentified, the literary sources do not mention any monument for Gylippus anywhere. Given that Gylippus was one of the most consequential generals in Spartan history, his name even memorized by Hellenistic schoolboys in Asia Minor, this is surprising.

[1] Low 2006: 96.

For Thucydides, the Peloponnesian War turned on the hinge of the Sicilian Expedition, the disastrous Athenian military adventure from 415 to 413 that ended with the destruction of most of Athens' fleet and fighting force. Advising the Syracusans and taking charge of much of the fighting in the expedition's decisive final stages was the Spartan Gylippus (see esp. Thuc. 7.1– 6, 79–86). H. D. Westlake calls Gylippus, who fought ably and innovatively, "a worthy successor to Brasidas."[2] Paul Kern argues that Gylippus' arrival in Sicily was Thucydides' turning point for the entire campaign, which was itself a centerpiece of the historian's work.[3] Paul Cartledge and Paula Debnar, following on the advice of Simon Hornblower, worry that Gylippus' perform-ance and its treatment by modern scholars risk multiplying Brasidas-types too much, to the point at which Brasidas no longer stands out as unique.[4] As I myself have argued, Gylippus, along with several other Spartans whom we have considered in this book, reveal that Brasidas was not in fact so different from his compatriots. Rather, he merely enjoys a more spotless reputation than the others, not least because of Thucydides' heroizing treatment of him and because he died young and in the right kind of battle.[5] Gylippus *was* a worthy successor to Brasidas, and behaved pretty much in Brasidas' mold, which makes his subsequent reputation and commemoration (or, rather, lack thereof) all the more noteworthy.

The Spartans sent Gylippus to Sicily, if Thucydides is to be believed, not because of their own strategic insight, but because of the advice they received from the Athenian traitor Alcibiades. Recalled from Sicily to stand trial in Athens for an act of sacrilege, Alcibiades fled to Sparta instead, where he told the Spartans to help the Syracusans and to set up a permanent base in Athenian territory at Decelea (Thuc. 6.89–92). Both of these measures were central to Sparta's success in the war and went a long way towards Athens' undoing. The Spartans sent out Gylippus, the son of Cleandridas, to Sicily with a paltry force, but with instructions to consult with the Syracusans and Corinthians regarding how best to get reinforcements against the Athenians (Thuc. 6.93). Gylippus was to be no mere advisor, but rather the supreme commander of all the anti-Athenian forces at Syracuse.[6] Though he was not equipped with the crack soldiers that made Sparta famous, much the same as Brasidas was sent out only with helots and allies instead of Spartiate hoplites, Gylippus immediately revealed himself an adept commander, and turned the tide of the conflict

---

[2] Westlake 1968: 278.    [3] Kern 1989.
[4] Cartledge and Debnar 2006: 581; Hornblower 1991–2008: vol. 2, 59.    [5] Sears 2020.
[6] For Gylippus' role as the supreme commander in Sicily, see Gomme et al. 1945–1981: vol. 3, 380–382.

in Sicily decisively against the Athenians. He fought ably, even at night against Athens' best tactician, Demosthenes (the hero of Pylos), and inspired many to join in the fight against the Athenians, giving the Syracusan resistance a real shot in the arm. The victory against Athens in Sicily, in which Gylippus was a key player, was every bit as spectacular as Brasidas' at Amphipolis, but on a far grander scale and arguably more important for the overall course of the Peloponnesian War. The Sicilian Expedition certainly takes up much more space in Thucydides' *History*, both in terms of word count and narrative weight.

Thucydides, however, downplays Gylippus' achievements, especially in comparison to Brasidas, which students of the historian have found perplexing. A. Andrewes thinks that Gylippus' role in Sicily, and thus his treatment in the sources, declined in inverse proportion to the confidence gained by the Syracusans as the campaign progressed.[7] A decline in his importance for the resistance to the Athenians in Sicily, however, does not seem to me to explain Gylippus' treatment by Thucydides. Westlake argues that Thucydides wanted to emphasize the Syracusan leader Hermocrates instead of Gylippus, the former furnishing a more interesting comparison with the Athenians.[8] Westlake is certainly on to something. By Book 8, Thucydides has singled out the Syracusans, rather than the Spartans, as Athens' most formidable enemy, principally because the Syracusans are the Greeks most like the Athenians (8.96.5). The Syracusan Hermocrates is given more room in Thucydides' account of the Sicilian Expedition, especially in terms of direct speech, so important for Thucydides' historical method. Even Gylippus' successes are overshadowed by Thucydides' emphasis on the contributions of the Syracusans and other allies to what should properly be seen as Gylippus' victories, including the defeat of a daring Athenian night attack (Thuc. 7.43.6–7). The account of Diodorus of Sicily, by contrast, based as it is on the work of the historian Ephorus but also the Sicilians Philistus and Timaeus (the latter two interested, for obvious reasons, in southern Italian and Sicilian affairs, as was Diodorus), centers the actions and leadership of Gylippus and grants him a lengthy and persuasive speech (13.7–8, 28–32). Thucydides describes his work as a "possession for all time," a manual for understanding all human affairs and the ultimate collection of paradigmatic human motivations and actions. While Herodotus claims to record all great deeds, both of Greeks and non-Greeks, Thucydides carefully selects for his readers the things they should remember and ponder. Thucydides the historian decided that Gylippus and his military record

---

[7] Gomme et. al. 1945–1981: vol. 3, 381–382.     [8] Westlake 1968: 277–289, especially 289.

were not as worthy of memory as the careers of other war leaders, including the Syracusan Hermocrates and the Spartan Brasidas.[9]

Thucydides seems to deliver an especially pointed slight by saying that Gylippus was deprived of the "fine prize," the *kalon agnōnisma* due to a great victor, of parading the captured Athenian generals alive to Sparta. Instead, those generals, Nicias and Demosthenes, had their throats cut explicitly against the will of Gylippus (Thuc. 7.86.2). Hornblower thinks that, in his narrative of the Sicilian Expedition, Thucydides pays direct homage to the style of the poets Pindar and Bacchylides, who wrote victory odes for triumphant athletes. Thucydides thus presents the Sicilian Expedition as a great contest, or *agōn*, between the two sides – the prize for which would be the *agōnisma* desired by Gylippus to boost his own fame and glory.[10] In addition to the intertextual literary flair Thucydides applies to this passage, by directly noting that Gylippus *did not* receive his sought-after prize, the historian shines a spotlight on Gylippus' lack of recognition, his failure to be commemorated like Brasidas, whom those he liberated decked out with garlands "as a victorious Athlete."

Perhaps Gylippus was shortchanged because of his inglorious background. According to Aelian, an author writing during the 2nd and 3rd centuries CE, Gylippus was a *mōthax*, a Spartan word denoting the child of a Spartan father and a helot mother, or perhaps Spartan parents too poor for full citizenship (Ael. *VH* 12.43). Given the fame and prominence of Gylippus' father, the former option seems the more likely. His lowly status alone, though, does not explain Gylippus' lack of monuments, since Aelian also lists Lysander as a *mōthax* – along with Callicratidas, another Peloponnesian War general who met with less success than Gylippus and Lysander. Perhaps also Gylippus failed to achieve posthumous glorification because he ended his career in scandal. When Lysander sent Gylippus to Sparta laden with sacks of money, Plutarch says that Gylippus siphoned off a great deal of the money for himself (Plut. *Lys.* 16). Yet, Gylippus' combination of Spartan virtues and vices – Spartans in Plutarch tend to be corrupted when they go abroad and gain too much power – is exactly the same as that of other Spartans, including Lysander and Agesilaus, both of whom managed to obtain a commemorative legacy far outshining Gylippus.[11] No one fell further out of favor for both alleged corruption

---

[9] For more on Thucydides' relative neglect of Gylippus in favor of others, see Sears 2020, especially 189–193.

[10] Hornblower 2006: 336–342.

[11] See Lucchesi 2016 for Gylippus as a Spartan paradigm in Plutarch's works, and for Plutarch as a large reason behind the Spartans' reputation for being easily corruptible.

and fraternizing with the enemy than the Persian War general Pausanias, but even he still enjoyed a monument on the Spartan acropolis. So, Gylippus' low birth and financial indiscretions do not on their own explain his treatment at the hands of Thucydides and his lack of physical monuments and literary praise.

Maybe Gylippus' father, Cleandridas, is to blame. Cleandridas was a renowned Spartan in his own right, and went on to find fame and fortune at Thurii in southern Italy. Some archaeological evidence, including inscribed roof tiles, suggests that Cleandridas was honored as a founder at Thurii and was given his own hero shrine, just like Brasidas at Amphipolis.[12] Cleandridas' success should have provided a springboard for his son's career but for the fact that Cleandridas also had a reputation for being corrupt. During the so-called First Peloponnesian War in the 440s, the Spartan king Pleistoanax withdrew from Attica earlier than expected, and it was later suspected that he had been bribed by Pericles to do so. The Spartans exiled Pleistoanax for this crime, according to Thucydides (2.21.1). Plutarch adds the detail that the ephors assigned Cleandridas to be Pleistoanax's advisor on the expedition, and it was through Cleandridas that Pericles' bribery took place. The Spartans sentenced Cleandridas to death, but he had already gone into voluntary exile, presumably to Thurii (Plut. *Per.* 22; see also Diod. 13.106.10, who misnames Cleandridas as Clearchus). For Plutarch, Cleandridas' greed prefigured that of his son.

Plutarch's moralism aside, it is doubtful that the Spartans would have chosen Gylippus as the general to send to Sicily if his family's reputation had been damaged beyond repair (unless they wanted to get rid of him, I suppose). Furthermore, the kind of warfare ascribed to Cleandridas was sometimes celebrated as shrewd. Polyaenus, the 2nd-century CE compiler of stratagems, credits Cleandridas with sowing distrust among his enemies in Tegea by scrupulously avoiding the estates of Tegea's leaders during a ravaging campaign. This caused the Tegeans to suspect their leaders of accepting bribes from Cleandridas, and, in fear for their lives, the Tegean leaders turned into genuine traitors and betrayed the city to the Spartans (Polyaen. 2.10.3). Pericles feared that Archidamus, the respected Spartan king who invaded Attica annually during the first phase of the Peloponnesian War, might attempt a similar ruse. Pericles therefore pledged to hand over his estates to the Athenians should Archidamus

---

[12] Tantalizing as it is, this evidence is far from conclusive on Cleandridas' posthumous status. See Hornblower 1991–2008: vol. 3, 534 for a discussion of the case.

leave the estates untouched in order to sow suspicion (Plut. *Per.* 20.2). Giving and taking bribes, or least giving the appearance of bribery, were standard tools of war for the Athenians and Spartans during the 5th century. Cleandridas was not out of step with the leading generals of his day for either taking a bribe or falling under the suspicion of doing so. By the time of the Sicilian Expedition, the Spartans appear to have gotten over Cleandridas' actions three decades earlier.

Despite the moniker "First Peloponnesian War," invented by modern scholars rather than any ancient author, Sparta seemed reluctant for the conflict to get hot, especially in a direct confrontation with Athens. In the early 450s, the Spartan and Athenian hoplites had fought the Battle of Tanagra, which the Spartans handily won, but that battle was due more to the Athenians forcing a confrontation in Boeotia than to a Spartan desire for pitched battle. Lengthy and costly invasions of a powerful enemy's territory were not the Spartans' forte in the earlier 5th century, of which Archidamus warned his fellow Spartans on the eve of the Peloponnesian War. Even during that later conflict, the first phase of which consisted of Archidamus invading Attica year after year, the Spartan king had to be chided into moving his army to the heart of Athenian territory after what seemed like unnecessary procrastination on the outskirts at Oinoe, an episode Thucydides compares to Pleistoanax's shortened campaign (Thuc. 2.18–21). Some Spartans might have been angry at Pleistoanax and his advisor Cleandridas in the 440s, and Thucydides wants us to see the majority of Spartans as eager for intervention and war against Athenian interests. But, as Hornblower points out, Thucydides' presentation of Spartan attitudes in the mid-5th century is hardly the only possible interpretation, and Spartan actions appear to indicate an avoidance of war.[13] We can interpret the actions of the two future exiles, Pleistoanax and Cleandridas, as following at least one strain of Spartan foreign policy by not pressing too far into Attica.

It is important to remember that Thucydides is not the only source on Gylippus and his career, even if Thucydides' portrayal tends to dominate. Other historians, whose work has largely been lost but preserved in bits and pieces in later authors like Diodorus and Plutarch, gave Gylippus much more credit. Gylippus features prominently in Plutarch's *Life of Nicias*. Relying on earlier historians, including the Sicilians Philistus and Timaeus (with whom he sometimes openly disagrees), Plutarch contrasts Nicias, the reluctant co-commander of the Athenian expedition to Sicily, with Gylippus in a way that heavily favors the approach of the clever and active Spartan.

---

[13] Hornblower 1991–2008: vol. 1, 156–157.

Plutarch says that the entire feat of freeing Sicily and defeating the Athenians was due to Gylippus alone (Plut. *Nic.* 19.5). Plutarch claims both Thucydides and Philistus, who was an eyewitness to the events, as sources who credit Gylippus with the whole campaign. I should note that Thucydides makes no such claim, and we are without the work of Philistus except through later writers like Plutarch. Frances Tichener, who advances that argument that Gylippus is a foil for Nicias in Plutarch, thinks this judgement concerning Gylippus' indispensability must be Plutarch's own, since a Syracusan like Philistus would not have credited a Spartan instead of his own countrymen (though no evidence is brought in to back up this statement).[14]

In the same paragraph, Plutarch relates that upon the arrival of Gylippus in Sicily, and his donning of arms to combat the Athenians, some of Nicias' soldiers mocked the Spartan, who should have been resplendent in his Spartan cloak and long hair. The Athenians jeered that they had put in chains nearly 300 Lacedaemonians captured at Pylos, all of whom had been sturdier and longer-haired than Gylippus. If the Athenian soldiers really had insulted the Spartan general in this way, it would have been a poignant reversal of legendary symbols of Spartan valor and strength, and a withering use of a past military defeat to intimidate their enemies in the present. Timaeus also says that the Syracusans mocked Gylippus' long hair, but rallied around him once he demonstrated his military chops. Plutarch doubts that his source Timaeus is right about the Syracusans deriding their savior, and instead insists that the staff and cloak, symbols of Spartan glory (*axiōma*), would have inspired Gylippus' new allies to take up arms at his side (Plut. *Nic.* 19.3–4).

Diodorus gives Gylippus an honor denied him by Thucydides: a lengthy direct speech on a matter of great import. In Diodorus' account of the aftermath of the Athenian defeat in Sicily, the leaders hold a vigorous debate concerning the fate of the prisoners, namely whether to punish them to the utmost, or to offer some mercy. For this occasion, Diodorus presents two opposing speeches, in the tradition of Thucydides who depicted a similar debate at Athens concerning the fate of the rebellious city of Mytilene.[15] Diodorus sets the scene masterfully by having the debate start off with the speech of an old man named Nicolaus, whose own

---

[14] Tichener 1988: 338–339.

[15] A lot of ink has been spilled over who provided Diodorus' source material for this set of speeches. Pearson 1986: 357–358 attributes the speech of Gylippus' opponent to the Sicilian Timaeus, whereas Gylippus' speech comes from another source, probably Ephorus. Pesely 1985 thinks both speeches are from Ephorus and represent a deliberate response to Thucydides' Mytilenean Debate. Stylianou 1998: 58–61, who offers a full treatment of the debates surrounding Diodorus' use of sources, agrees with Pesely that both speeches are from Ephorus. Green (2010: 182n20), on the other hand, thinks the Sicilian Philistus, who might have been present at the speeches themselves, could be the source,

children have been killed in war. Nicolaus has to be helped up to the platform because of his infirmity, where he calls for leniency against the very soldiers who killed his family members (Diod. 13.19–27). According to Nicolaus, not only would showing mercy be the right thing to do but it would work out for the Sicilians in the long run by not engendering eternal enmity with a powerful foe.

Gylippus, presented as a firebrand Spartan, is having none of it (Diod. 13.28–32). Before launching into his arguments to rebut the aged Nicolaus, he begs his audience's indulgence in allowing him to speak bluntly in a Spartan manner.[16] While scholars squabble over Diodorus' sources for this important passage, I see no reason not to agree with Peter Green, who says,

> Though this speech, and its rebuttal by Gylippus (28–32) are no more to be taken as accurate reports of what was actually said than those of Thucydides, it is reasonable to suppose that some such public debate did take place, that Nicolaus was as real a person as Gylippus, and that the historian Philistus recorded their exchange, having almost certainly witnessed it.[17]

Instead of mercy, Gylippus argues for a harsh punishment to be meted out on the defeated Athenians, and claims he is unable to fathom how the Syracusans, who have suffered so grievously from Athenian aggression, could even think of being merciful. Gylippus' heated rhetoric carries the day, and the Athenians are shown no quarter.

In his appeal for retribution against the Athenians, Gylippus adds a striking rhetorical question: "You have voted to adorn the tombs of your dead at public expense; and what better adornment could you find than to punish their murderers?" (Diod. 13.29.2). As far as I know, Gylippus' claim that punishing the dead's enemies is a way to embellish the dead's tombs is unique in Greek literature. Of course there are many examples of the dead being more famous for having killed many enemies and having gone toe-to-toe with the greatest warriors, but the fame of the dead being enhanced by *others* killing the dead's foes after the fact is not

---

for which see later in this chapter. Given that Philistus famously modeled his historiographical method on Thucydides (for which see Levene 2010: 113n69), it seems to be sensible to ascribe a very Thucydidean set of paired speeches to Philistus. If the speeches are Ephoran, the original source might well have been Philistus in any case, given that Ephorus heaped praise upon Philistus (see Plut. *Dion*. 36.2).

[16] Since the Thucydidean Gylippus asked for leniency for the Athenian generals, whom he wanted to take to Sparta as his own personal war prize, Pesely 1985: 321n5 says that "The malicious misrepresentation of Gylippus' position is in keeping with Ephorus' anti-Spartan bias." Pearson 1986: 361n34 argues that "Gylippus's speech was certainly supposed to be typically Spartan."

[17] Green 2010: 182n20.

a regular part of Greek commemoration. The closest parallel I can think of is the mythological sacrifice of Polyxena, daughter of Priam and Hecuba, at the tomb of Achilles after the destruction of Troy, most powerfully told in Euripides' *Hecuba* performed only a decade before the Sicilian Expedition. But those sacrificing the young Trojan woman to appease the vengeful spirit of Achilles are hardly portrayed as the good guys.[18] Since Euripides was wildly popular in Sicily – Plutarch says that many Athenians captured in the Sicilian Expedition were spared by reciting the playwright's verses (Plut. *Nic.* 29.2–3) – it is tempting to think that Gylippus could have been appealing to a known Euripidean theme before his Sicilian listeners. Euripides makes much use of the word *kosmein*, to adorn, the same word used by Gylippus regarding the Sicilian tombs, in reference to the body of Polyxena slain before Achilles' monument (Eur. *Hec.* 578, 615), a body Achilles claims as his *geras*, or sign of his excellence (Eur. *Hec.* 41).

Gylippus' next line is perhaps even more astonishing: "Unless, by Zeus, you wish to leave living trophies for the departed by enrolling the captives as citizens."[19] Nowhere else in Greek literature are living enemies so explicitly deemed trophies (nor are they in Latin literature). Does the Gylippus represented in Diodorus' text imagine the captured Athenians living for the rest of their lives in Syracuse as symbols of Syracusan military power, specifically to recollect the glorious Syracusan dead?[20] Gylippus quite obviously does not expect his audience to take up his latter suggestion. Rather, he is aiming to convince them to kill the captives and thus "adorn" the tombs of their fellow citizens. Yet the mere voicing of this suggestion has strange implications for how the Greeks commemorated their dead, even if this passage is as far as we can tell unique in the ancient Mediterranean world.

Did Gylippus really utter anything like the ideas Diodorus ascribes to him (or give a speech on this occasion at all)? That Thucydides does not include a version of the speech is not necessarily reason to dismiss Diodorus' account, since, as we have seen, Thucydides emphasizes the Syracusans, especially Hermocrates, at Gylippus' expense. Likewise, it is

[18] Papastamati 2017 argues that Euripides' famous portrayal of Polyxena's death in his *Hecuba*, produced in Athens only a decade before the Sicilian Expedition, reimagines the "beautiful death" to make Polyxena's willingness to die a heroic act.

[19] κοσμεῖν ἐψηφίσασθε δημοσίᾳ τοὺς τάφους τῶν μετηλλαχότων· καὶ τίνα καλλίονα κόσμον εὑρήσετε τοῦ κολάσαι τοὺς ἐκείνων αὐτόχειρας; εἰ μὴ νὴ Δία πολιτογραφήσαντες αὐτοὺς βούλεσθε καταλιπεῖν ἔμψυχα τρόπαια τῶν μετηλλαχότων.

[20] For this passage, and the treatment of trophies in Diodorus more broadly, see Kinnee 2018: 42–44, who detects in Diodorus a shift in the conception of the trophy from battlefield monument to metaphor of power.

not an insurmountable problem that both Thucydides and Plutarch say that Gylippus argued for the Athenian generals to be spared. George Pesely describes Diodorus' account as a "malicious misrepresentation of Gylippus' position," and ascribes it to "Ephorus' anti-Spartan bias."[21] Yes, Gylippus does advocate for sparing the lives of Nicias and Demosthenes, but this is only to add to his own glory at Sparta (Thuc. 7.85–86; Plut. *Nic.* 27.5–6, 28.2). Parading the defeated Athenian generals in front of the home crowd is not out of keeping with punishing the mass of Athenian soldiers and allies (though Gylippus does criticize Nicias by name in his speech in Diodorus, 13.32.1–2). Like the speeches in Thucydides, it is unlikely that we can ever recover exactly what was said on any given occasion. But, as pointed out by Peter Green earlier, there is every reason to believe that Philistus, one of Diodorus' principal sources for Sicily, was himself present at the proceedings in 413, so Gylippus' speech rests on as firm ground as any. If we reject Philistus as the source for this passage, as Pesely, Pearson, and Stylianou do (all favoring Ephorus), we are still left with valuable information about Sparta and Spartan attitudes towards commemoration, since the speech seems designed as a stereotypical representation of Spartans and a Spartan general.

Thucydides might have neglected Gylippus, but other sources did not. For those other authors, Gylippus played the central role in Sicily while he represented the outlook of his polis, or at least an important element of that outlook. Personal glory was at the front of the mind for the Spartan leader. Commemoration, perhaps even commemoration based on the humiliation of the living and the appeasement of the dead, was also among his main concerns. Gylippus discovered, however, as Brasidas had, that he was fighting for a polis as yet uninterested in open-ended military commitments abroad. Gylippus was willing to try new things in new places to win glory and fame, but the Spartans did not back him up as much as they could. Despite a peace treaty still being in effect, war with Athens was heating back up in the proxy theater of Sicily. The Spartans, however, for the most part still preferred to win their glory closer to home, without risking a major part of their forces on distant campaigns. Gylippus might have earned a place on lists of great Spartans, but it is safe to say that he did not achieve the remembrance and glory he sought. Why were the Spartans happier to honor Brasidas, who was similarly out of step with Spartan isolationism and limited war? I am not sure that we can know the answer. Perhaps the fault lies with our privileging of some literary sources over

---

[21] Pesely 1985: 321n5.

others, and perhaps his reputation suffers because he did not have the good fortune to die in the field. There was no cenotaph of Gylippus near the Spartan acropolis, at least not one Pausanias bothered to mention.

## Commemoration in the Age of Lysander

In contrast to Gylippus, no one received more spectacular commemorative monuments than Lysander.[22] In many ways, this fame makes sense. Lysander won the Peloponnesian War, bringing Athens low after twenty-seven years of war and leaving Sparta as the only superpower in the Aegean world. Lysander accomplished this feat by drawing on his personal friendship with the Persian prince Cyrus to secure Persian money to build a Spartan navy capable of challenging Athens' mastery of the sea. After several years of naval warfare, with victories going back and forth between the two sides, Lysander destroyed the Athenian fleet at Aegospotami, in the modern Gallipoli Peninsula, in 405. The following year, in 404, he secured the surrender of Athens, which was unable to supply itself without control of the sea and therefore gave up in desperation. Under Lysander's watch, the Peloponnesians gleefully tore down the Long Walls of Athens, which had kept the city invulnerable as the Athenian navy controlled an empire. Lysander's forces destroyed Athens' fortifications to the celebratory music of flute-girls, since, as Xenophon says, everyone figured that this signaled the beginning of freedom for the Greeks (Xen. *Hell.* 2.2.23). Lysander had accomplished a marvelous victory and had every reason to expect copious fame and commemoration. He proved adept at taking advantage of the position in which he found himself after Aegospotami.

Plutarch says that Lysander not only accumulated fantastic wealth, much of which he stored ostentatiously at Delphi, and erected splendid monuments, he was the first living Greek that any polis honored as a god with altars and sacrifices. At Samos, where a temple and sanctuary of Hera had been among the wonders of the Greek world for centuries (and still commands awe from visitors today), the festival of Hera was changed from the Heraia to the Lysandreia – which goes well beyond the special

---

[22] The best book-length study of Lysander is Bommelaer 1981; see especially 7–23 for a catalogue of monuments and honors for Lysander, which is particularly germane to this study. Paul Cartledge 2022 offers an interesting discussion of another Spartan, Lichas, who was instrumental in securing Persian aid, on terms favorable to Sparta, for Sparta's plans to build a navy capable of challenging the Athenians at sea after the Sicilian Expedition. Cartledge argues that Lichas was in some ways a precursor to Lysander, even if the latter was more unscrupulous, and that, if Thucydides had completed his *History*, Lichas would have been given important direct speeches like other prominent characters from the Peloponnesian War.

relationship with Sparta the Samians seemed to have had since the Archaic period.[23] The Samians also dedicated a statue of Lysander at Olympia, for which Pausanias quotes two inscribed epigrams (6.3.14) proclaiming that Lysander has won immortal glory for his country and father, and the fame of excellence.[24] With such honors, Plutarch says that Lysander was more powerful than any Greek had ever been, and that his pride and pretension outmatched even his great power (Plut. *Lys.* 18).

How did Lysander reach these heights? Was he a new type of Spartan, or merely a continuation of trends and attitudes that could be seen among Sparta and Sparta's leaders by anyone who cared to look? Hunter Rawlings argued that Thucydides wrote his account of Brasidas in the north with Lysander in mind. While the historian died before completing the final books of his *History*, Rawlings imagines the unwritten latter sections of Thucydides' work as demonstrating how Lysander contrasted with his predecessor, and how Sparta had changed during the course of the war.[25] W. R. Connor sees Lysander as the embodiment of many of the themes of Thucydides' *History*, such as the priority of advantage over justice and the distortion of language to suit the aims of the speaker.[26] Beyond Lysander appearing as the logical endpoint of the inexorable change in Spartan (and Greek) character brought about by decades of war, he has also been seen as a precursor to the strongman tyrants of the 4th century in places like Sicily and Thessaly.[27] As I will argue, Lysander does not merely represent a shift to a more imperialistic Sparta brought on by the horrors of war, nor does he revel in a new degree of honors and commemoration unseen in Sparta and the rest of Greece before his time. Rather, Lysander and his policies are what we should expect to result from a state shifting to embrace the commemorative rhetoric of altruism and liberation.

One way to approach Lysander and his storied career, about which much has been written, is to consider who he was not. While we have already had occasion to mention how he was not Brasidas or Gylippus, even if he was a further step along the same evolutionary path, Xenophon provides us with a clear foil for Lysander, namely the admiral Callicratidas (Xen. *Hell.* 1.6). Lysander's first term of office as naval commander, or *navarch*, ended on a reasonably high note. The wily Spartan had built

---

[23] For this relationship, see Chapter 2.

[24] = FGE CXVb: ἀθάνατον πάτραι καὶ Ἀριστοκρίτωι κλέος ἔργων, | Λύσανδρ᾽, ἐκτελέσας δόξαν ἔχεις ἀρετᾶς.

[25] Rawlings 1981: 236–243.     [26] Connor 1984: 139n80.

[27] See Berve 1967: 213, who also sees Brasidas and Gylippus in this line, though to a lesser extent than Lysander.

a close personal relationship with the Persian prince Cyrus and thereby secured steady funding for the Spartan fleet. Lysander had used that fleet to win a naval victory against the Athenians at the Battle of Notium in 406, which bolstered Spartan confidence and led to the exile of the Athenian leader Alcibiades, one of the most dangerous enemies the Spartans had. But the Spartans adhered to strict term limits and sent out Callicratidas to take over from Lysander the war effort in Ionia. Whether or not it makes good sense to change up commanders in the middle of a campaign, Lysander certainly did not enjoy the prospect of his path to personal power being derailed by the success of another commander, so he resolved to make Callicratidas' life difficult.

Xenophon says that the two commanders immediately taunted each other. Lysander declared that he was handing over the fleet as master of the sea, a haughty boast that was not justified by the victory at Notium, which still left the Athenians in possession of a large fleet. Callicratidas responded in kind by daring his predecessor to sail past the Athenians openly, a move beyond all good sense and a challenge Lysander could not possibly have accepted. The dispute went beyond barbs and bravado. Lysander ensured that his allies from among the Ionians would stir up trouble for Callicratidas within the Peloponnesian fleet, and he returned the money for paying the sailors to Cyrus instead of handing it over to the new commander, leaving Callicratidas with a huge force he could not afford to pay or provision. Lysander's machinations left the Peloponnesian force in a tough spot in the middle of a raging war. Personal ambition clearly outweighed the good of Sparta in Lysander's calculations.

Callicratidas went to Cyrus to ask for the money he needed and which the Persian prince had previously given to Lysander. Xenophon's account implies that Cyrus, too, was out to discredit Callicratidas to Lysander's advantage. Cyrus refused to meet with the new Spartan commander, telling Callicratidas to wait for two days. The Spartan responded with indignation and stormed off, remarking on the sorry state of the Greeks reduced to begging the Persians for money, and promising to work to reconcile Athens and Sparta if he ever returned home. This Panhellenist statement – which Callicratidas never put into practice, but rather kept prosecuting the war against Athens to the best of his ability – has occasioned lots of scholarly comment. Many students of Xenophon have seen in this passage clear sympathy on the part of the historian for Callicratidas, who expresses a sentiment close to Xenophon's own Panhellenist ideals. Callicratidas, the champion of traditional Spartan values, stands in stark contrast to the unscrupulous Lysander. Others think that, since Callicratidas never followed through with his vow, he demonstrated a naïve idealism and inexperience that ill served the Spartan war effort, in contrast to the pragmatic Lysander, who had realized how ineffective a dogmatic adherence to traditional values is. Still others argue that Xenophon's portrait of Callicratidas is nuanced and ambiguous, neither in favor nor against, but simply demonstrating the successes and failures of a real historical commander in difficult circumstances.[28]

Sources other than Xenophon are much more explicit in their praise of Callicratidas, especially in contrast to Lysander. Diodorus, introducing the new commander, calls him, among other flattering things, the most just man of all the Spartans. He was also, like all good Spartans, of simple and straightforward disposition, especially since he had yet no experience with foreign peoples (supposedly the greatest danger for Spartans) (Diod. 13.76). Until recent decades, modern scholars of antiquity have been prone to adopting the views of Diodorus and other effusive ancient sources on the point of Callicratidas' virtues. George Grote, the eminent 19th-century British historian of Greece, laments that the fates were so unkind to Callicratidas, since the Spartan leader was "one of the noblest characters of his age," a plain dealer, an exemplar of "Pan-hellenic patriotism."[29] The idealistic Spartan was everything Lysander was not, and his reputation in the sources, where he is commemorated as an ideal, if tragic, type, is commensurably brilliant.

The ancient sources portray Callicratidas as fighting in the service of personal glory even in the face of certain death, and despite good tactical and strategic sense – not unlike Leonidas, the ultimate Spartan. Prior to the naval Battle of Arginusae, which the Peloponnesian fleet would lose, Xenophon says that the pilot of Callicratidas' own ship advised the Spartan commander to sail away, since the Athenians outnumbered them. Callicratidas responded that Sparta would be no worse for the wear, or no more poorly inhabited (according to the strange phrase in Xenophon's text), if he himself should die, whereas flight would bring shame (Xen. *Hell.* 1.6.32). Plutarch relates that Callicratidas was faced with prophecies predicting his own death if he were to fight in the battle, to which he responded that Sparta is not dependent on one man. Plutarch

---

[28] For an overview of scholarly opinions regarding Xenophon and Callicratidas, see Moles 1994, especially 70n4. For Panhellenism in Xenophon, see Laforse 1998. Roisman 1987b argues that Callicratidas was a Panhellenist only when it was useful for his opposition to Athens. Bearzot 2005 argues that in Plutarch the contrast between the two generals is based not on Panhellenism, but on *philotimia*, the ambition that can either drive personal interests or service to the state.

[29] Grote 1851: 218.

finds fault with Callicratidas' reasoning, since a general is far more important than one ordinary man (Plut. *Pelop.* 2.1–2). The biographer's larger
point about the importance of command, however, does not imply that he
finds fault with the Spartan's desire to fight even if he was guaranteed to
die. In his biography of Lysander, Plutarch is clear that he thinks
Callicratidas was a great moral exemplar, embodying the best of the
Spartans and able to vie with the greatest of the Greeks in terms of justice,
greatness of soul, and courage (Plut. *Lys.* 6–7.1).

Despite Callicratidas' personal courage – or perhaps because of it – the
Peloponnesians lost the Battle of Arginusae in 406. Callicratidas himself
was killed in action, and the Spartans sent a delegation to Athens to ask for
peace, an overture the Athenians rejected. After the battle, Athens experienced a particularly turbulent moment even though the city had been
victorious. The generals from the battle were put on trial at Athens *en
masse*, against Athenian law, because they had failed to rescue survivors and
collect the dead due to a change in the weather. The trial and condemna-
tion of these generals, who had *won* the battle, is often seen as the ultimate
sign of Athenian democracy's decadence and dangerous populism, of
which the framers of the United States Constitution took note and
opted for a republic over a democracy. To the delight of Sparta's allies
across the Aegean, Lysander was back in charge of the fleet, and he reversed
the Peloponnesians' fortunes. In the following year, 405, he led the fleet,
backed once again by Cyrus and the Persians, to final victory over the
Athenians at Aegospotami. Lysander was then at the height of his power.
Callicratidas' supposedly stereotypical Spartan behavior, namely putting
personal glory (or the avoidance of shame) ahead of sound military sense,
had very nearly cost Sparta the war. Only Lysander's seemingly un-Spartan
character, helped by Athenian rashness, rescued victory from the wrecks of
Arginusae. Even though he did not like Lysander, Xenophon knew well
that the controversial Spartan had won the war, and that Callicratidas'
obstinacy had done little or nothing to advance the Peloponnesian cause.
Some scholars, therefore, detect in Xenophon's account a veiled criticism
of Callicratidas, though the Athenian historian might have admired his
old-fashioned Spartan attributes.

The only wrinkle in this scheme is that one of Callicratidas' supposed
Spartan virtues is nothing of the sort. Agesilaus, the 4th-century Spartan
king and patron of Xenophon, to whom we will return in the next chapter,
might indeed have been a committed Panhellenist, but as such he was an
outlier. We have explored in detail how the Spartan commemoration of the
Persian Wars indicates that Spartans did not fight and die for Greece, or

even to help others, but to win glory for themselves and their city. Leonidas and the Three Hundred did so at Thermopylae despite the tactical and even strategic situation. During the period between the Persian and Peloponnesian Wars, Sparta continued to stay out of things beyond the Peloponnese, and only entered the war against Athens after much cajoling on the part of the Corinthians and other allies. Nothing in Callicratidas' rhetoric of uniting the two warring Greek sides against the Persians is traditionally Spartan. Regardless of their personal style and affect, both Callicratidas and Lysander expressed concern for their own personal glory, even at the expense of their state and their official duties as commanders, which was well in line with "traditional" Spartans. Where they diverged from Spartan attitudes of old was in pursuing this glory in the sphere of international relations and "liberation" campaigns abroad. Callicratidas' supposed Panhellenism was firmly in this trend *away from* how the Spartans once thought about and remembered war. He was rewarded for this distinctly un-Spartan attitude by being commemorated fulsomely in the ancient literary sources, even if he lacked the copious physical monuments dedicated by and for Lysander.

As one makes one's way along the Sacred Way at Delphi, one of the very first monuments one encounters is the thank offering for Aegospotami, sometimes called the Spartan Admirals' Monument, lying provocatively in front of the Athenian monument to Marathon (Figure 5.1).[30] The Aegospotami offering might be the most elaborate contestant in the Delphic "battle of the bronzes" through which states and sometimes individuals compete along the path to the Temple of Apollo. Miltiades and the Athenian heroes and deities who fought for freedom at Marathon nearly a century before Aegospotami are figuratively and literally overshadowed by Lysander's achievement, which was also vying for recognition as a feat of liberation. After the Aegospotami dedication, the Arcadians in turn dedicated the spoils they had taken from the Spartans in 369, demonstrating that the commemorative battle continued to rage. Pausanias gives us a full description of the Aegospotami monument, a collection of images that was flamboyant, to say the least (10.9.7–11). In the front row, next to images of Olympian gods, stood Lysander, his helmsman, and his seer, who predicted the battle's outcome. The latter, named Agias, also received a statue on the Spartan acropolis (Paus. 3.11.5). In the second row were images of other Spartan admirals and the admirals of Sparta's allies. Parts of

---

[30] For this monument, see Keesling 2017: 104–108.

Figure 5.1 The Spartan Admirals' Monument at Delphi (on the left). Only the statue bases survive. The bases of the Athenian Marathon monument (on the right) are on the other side of the Sacred Way. Author's photo.

this monument have been recovered by the excavators at Delphi, and we can still read portions of its dedicatory inscriptions.[31]

Nothing about imagery or placement of the Delphi dedication is out of step with previous eras of Spartan commemoration. Lysander might have had more money and power than previous Spartans, but not for lack of those Spartans trying. We have already seen that after Plataea, the regent Pausanias commemorated himself at Delphi on the Serpent Column, and, although the original inscription was replaced, he managed to have other elaborate dedications set up elsewhere. The Acanthians honored Brasidas by name on a Delphic treasury, an honor that no individual had received since the Archaic tyrants of the 6th century, and no one, certainly not at Sparta, seemed to be upset by Brasidas' honors at the sanctuary, or the extraordinary ones proper to heroes and city founders he received at Amphipolis. The Athenian Marathon dedication, to which the Aegospotami monument was responding, featured Miltiades, a mortal Athenian, amidst the eponymous heroes of the Athenian tribes and the

---

[31] For the inscriptions, see ML 95

Olympian gods Athena and Apollo, suggesting that not even Lysander's spatial affiliation with actual gods was beyond bounds (Paus. 10.10.1–2). The inscribed epigrams, on the other hand, are a different story.

There is some debate concerning when the epigrams for the monument were composed. Some think that they were part of the original monument, set up shortly after the victory in 405. Others, however, argue that the epigrams are later additions of the 4th century, inscribed to instruct visitors concerning the purpose of the monument and the identity of its figures, a view held by the majority today. The question will likely never be settled, but the sentiments of the epigrams are not out of keeping with Spartan Panhellenic liberation propaganda adopted during and after the Peloponnesian War, at least from the time of Brasidas (though Spartan support for Gylippus in Sicily had been lukewarm). In the previous chapter, we saw that Sparta's allies had to coax the superpower into adopting an interventionist policy, which was a considerable shift for a society that had been bent largely on its own fame and glory without a thought for the affairs of Greece as a whole. While considering the Persian Wars, we discovered that in the 470s Sparta was an outlier among the other members of the Hellenic League in terms of the epigrams they commissioned to honor achievements against Darius and Xerxes. The Aegospotami epigrams are different. Epigram B, once supposed to be for the nominal Spartan admiral Arakos to whom Lysander was technically subordinate, is now generally taken to represent Polydeuces, one of the mythical Dioscuri and more commonly known to us as Pollux. On this stone, Polydeuces is hailed as being prior to the Spartan admiral, and first among the generals of Greece, a clear Panhellenic claim for the leadership of Sparta and one of its patron deities. Epigram C, perhaps composed later or reinscribed from an earlier original, says that Lysander crowned Lacedaemon, the "unravaged acropolis of Greece" (ἀπόρθητον Ἑλλάδος ἀκρόπολιν). Not only is "Greece" a thing, according to this epigram, but it has an acropolis, and Sparta is it.

Whether or not these epigrams were composed in the 4th century, they adopt the sort of language used by poleis other than Sparta early in the 5th century. A group of women from Corinth, for example, whose epigram we considered earlier in this book, call their own city the "Acropolis of the Greeks" in their commemoration of the Persian Wars.[32] The content and layout of the monument, which, unlike the date of the epigrams, are not really in dispute, affirm a Panhellenist message, even if Lysander and the

---

[32] = FGE Simonides XIV. See Chapter 3.

Spartans are in a position of prominence. Where the regent Pausanias had first proclaimed his own status as sole leader of the Greeks, and the one responsible for the victory at Plataea, before this inscription was replaced, Lysander's monument includes the images and names of many non-Spartans, just like the reinscribed Serpent Column did. Even without the inscribed epigrams, Lysander's Aegospotami dedication represents a new Panhellenist stance for Sparta, and represents a Spartan entry in the Panhellenist spatial politics at Delphi in which, Pausanias' original Serpent Column inscription excepted, the Spartans had not participated prior to the end of the 5th century. At Delphi in 405, Lysander might not have promoted himself more than his forebears had; but Sparta certainly claimed a position of leadership it had not seemed interested in before.

During Lysander's period in the spotlight, two Spartan monumental burials stand out as remarkable for lying provocatively in foreign territory and commemorating defeats. One of these burials is Lysander's own, erected at Panopeus in Phocis after he fell fighting at the Boeotian city of Haliartus in 395. The Spartan defeat at Haliartus, which began the Corinthian War, is one of the more inglorious episodes of Spartan history.[33] The Thebans and Spartans had been at odds for several years, their alliance in the Peloponnesian War not lasting long beyond that conflict, and with the help of Persian bribes, leading Thebans began sowing anti-Spartan sentiment in their city. Both the Spartans and Thebans used central Greek proxies to get under each other's skin. In a conflict between the Phocians and Locrians, Thebes took the latter's side, and Sparta came to the help of the former. Lysander raised a force of Phocians and others, and marched into Boeotia after he made plans with the Spartan king Pausanias to meet him at Haliartus on a prearranged day with a strong force of Lacedaemonians and others. When Lysander got to Haliartus first, he did not wait for Pausanias, but instead laid siege to the city straightaway, asking the locals, like Orchomenos, in vain to revolt from Thebes and the Boeotan federation, and embrace Spartan liberation. The Theban force that arrived to relieve the city killed many Spartans, including Lysander himself, in the shadow of the city walls. The rest of Lysander's force retreated to Mount Helicon, where from the heights they were able to kill hundreds of pursuing Thebans before the battle came to an end with no side the better for it.

---

[33] See Westlake 1985 for a discussion of this campaign and its sources, principally Xen. *Hell.* 3.5; Diod. 14.81, 89; Plut. *Lys.* 28–30; Paus. 3.5.3–6.

When Pausanias finally arrived, he decided to ask for a truce to collect Lysander's body and the other dead. For this action – which according to the traditional rules of Greek warfare formally conceded victory to the Thebans – and (as we will see) for conceding to the Athenian democrats during Athens' civil war, he faced a capital charge back at Sparta and so spent the remainder of his days as an exile in Tegea. Before he returned to the Peloponnese, however, Plutarch says that Pausanias crossed into Phocis to the west and buried Lysander near Panopeus, marking the site with a prominent monument. This memorial was still visible five centuries later, on the road between Delphi and Chaeronea, Plutarch's hometown (Plut. *Lys.* 29.3). Plutarch says Pausanias chose the site because it was in friendly territory, just over the border from Boeotia. Polly Low suggests a further reason, namely that Lysander's burial would stand as a local memorial to Spartans fighting and dying in defense of the Phocians.[34] Given how much Pausanias and Lysander disliked each other, it is astonishing that the king went through so much trouble to recover his rival's body, at great personal cost to himself.[35] The travel-writer Pausanias sticks up for the Spartan king with whom he shared a name by arguing that, if the king had tried to take Lysander's body for force of arms, Haliartus might have joined Sphacteria and Thermopylae in the annals of Spartan misfortunes (Paus. 3.5.5). (Even though I see the rhetorical point the writer Pausanias is making, it is still arresting to see Thermopylae described as a Spartan misfortune, rather than a heroic stand.) Perhaps king Pausanias would have been prosecuted at Sparta if he had simply left Lysander's body to rot in Boeotia, in which case fighting, and maybe dying, to recover his rival's corpse was his only truly Spartan option. But the care Pausanias took to get Lysander's body and memorialize it reveals a deep concern for proper commemoration even of one's political enemies.

## Commemorating Spartans at Athens

Pausanias was directly involved in an embarrassing incident at Athens that led to one of the most bizarre commemorative monuments in Greece, namely the Tomb of Lacedaemonians in the Athenian Kerameikos (which

---

[34] Low 2006: 95–96.
[35] Xen. *Hell.* 2.4.29–43 illustrates the discord between Pausanias and Lysander by recounting their opposing polices regarding Athens in 403. Lysander wanted Spartan reinforcements to help his puppet regime, the Thirty Tyrants, maintain power in Athens, whereas Pausanias did all he could do to bring an end to the civil strife in Athens in the democrats' favor in order to undercut Lysander's position.

we considered briefly in the previous chapter) (Figure 5.2; Figure 5.3). After the Thirty Tyrants and their Spartan allies were defeated at the Mounichia Hill in the Piraeus, the conflict continued to rage. The Thirty sent to Sparta asking for reinforcements, and Lysander obliged, planning to blockade the democrats by land and sea. The Spartan king, Pausanias, jealous of Lysander and fearing that the rogue leader would make Athens his private property, according to Xenophon, marched out to Athens with his own force of Spartans and allies. Pausanias positioned himself as fighting alongside Lysander for a common goal, but he secretly wanted to come to terms with the democrats to undercut Lysander's bid for more power in Athens. In a clash between Pausanias' men and the democrats, which Pausanias tried to keep to the bare minimum of intensity just so he would appear to be fighting a proper battle, things got out of hand and many people died on both sides. Though not the result he wanted, Pausanias still set up a trophy, since his side had the better of the clash. Xenophon tells us also that a tomb was constructed for the Spartan dead in the Kerameikos, an important cemetery at Athens and just outside the main gates of the city. Among the Spartan dead so honored were two

Figure 5.2 The Tomb of the Lacedaemonians in the Athenian Kerameikos (the Acropolis can be seen in the background). Author's photo.

Figure 5.3 Part of the surviving inscription on the Tomb of the Lacedaemonians,
showing the name of Thibrakos and his title of *polemarch* in retrograde lettering.
Author's photo.

*polemarchs*, high military officials named Chairon and Thibrachos, and an
Olympic victor named Lakrates (Xen. *Hell.* 2.4.33).

The Tomb of the Lacedaemonians in the Kerameikos was identified by
archaeologists long ago, and still today stands out as a major monument
lying on the wide *dromos* leading to the site that became Plato's Academy.[36]
The monument is readily identifiable by its inscription, which survives in
part and is written backwards and with Spartan letters. As we discussed in
the preceding chapter, part of the title "Lakedaimonioi" is visible, as are the
names of the two *polemarchs* listed by Xenophon, and the first letter or two
of another name. John Camp argues that this inscription would have been
on the right of the road for those entering the city, and was thus geared
more to those entering Athens than leaving it. Visitors, rather than locals,
are the target audience, according to Camp.[37] Twenty-six bodies were
buried in the tomb in two groups, with twenty-three being placed together
in one layer, and three more added later and supposedly given higher
honors. The bodies seem to have been wrapped in cloth, perhaps the cloaks
with which the Spartans adorned their honored dead. Along with the
bodies were several pieces of pottery, reflecting both Attic and Laconian

---

[36] The most thorough recent discussion of this tomb is Stroszeck 2013. For briefer overviews, see
Knigge 1991: 160–161; Camp 2001: 133–135; Scott 2018: 98–102.
[37] Camp 2001: 135.

manufacture. As Michael Scott argues, the Spartans must have had at least an oversight role for the monument's construction.[38]

There is no doubt that this tomb is a thoroughly Spartan monument meant to honor Spartans in Athenian territory. The purpose of the tomb, from Sparta's perspective, also seems at first glance fairly clear, namely to follow the custom of burying soldiers where they fell (or close to where they fell) rather than bringing them home, and to remind Athens and visitors to Athens that Spartans had won a battle in Athenian territory. We will, however, return to this question in a moment. What is more in doubt is how the Athenians would have responded to it. Julia Shear and Michael Scott both argue that, instead of representing a Spartan defeat over Athenians, in the years following the civil strife between oligarchs and democrats in Athens this monument would have represented for the Athenians the triumph of democracy over *foreign* enemies from Sparta, rather than internal enemies.[39] As Shear says, the placement of the Tomb of the Lacedaemonians near the *dēmosion sēma*, where the Athenian democrats and their allies from that conflict were buried, emphasized the military nature of the struggle, as a war between Athens and outsiders, and effaced the civil strife that had torn Athens in two.[40] If Shear and Scott are right, the Athenians managed to turn what had been intended as a reminder of Spartan triumph into a symbol of Athenian victory that also reinforced Athenian unity by undercutting the memory of civil strife between two Athenian factions.

What of the Spartan ideas behind the memorial? The Tomb of the Lacedaemonians is frequently used as one of the prime examples of Spartan battlefield burial, whereby Spartan soldiers (other than Spartan kings, who were brought back to Sparta) were buried on the spot where they fell.[41] Battlefield burial, however, is not really a fair description of what this tomb represents, since the tomb is six or seven kilometers from where the battle took place and where the soldiers died, and where Pausanias set up a trophy. The tomb lies in an Athenian burial precinct of unparalleled significance, not on a battlefield. Others have conceded that sometimes that Spartans had to remove their dead from the field to bury them in the closest friendly territory they could find. Lysander's burial might fit that bill, with the added significance of signaling to the Phocians that Lysander died in their defense, as we discussed earlier. After the Battle of Mantinea in

---

[38] Scott 2018: 99.    [39] Shear 2011: 294–301; Scott 2018: 100–101.    [40] Shear 2011: 299.
[41] The classic treatment is Pritchett 1985: 241–246, 249–251. See now Low 2006; Kucewicz 2021a. See also Chapter 1.

418, the Spartan dead were buried in the friendly territory of Tegea, just south of the battlefield, even though the Spartans won that battle and controlled the plain where their dead lay (Thuc. 5.74.2). The Tomb of the Lacedaemonians, on the other hand, is both far from the battlefield and in the heart of hostile territory.

Perhaps we can find a parallel from the late 6th century, when Sparta inserted itself into Athenian domestic affairs, that time on the side against the tyrants. Before king Cleomenes successfully expelled Hippias and his family in 510, a year or two earlier a Spartan expedition led by Anchimolios arrived in Attica by sea and fought a battle at the Athenian port of Phaleron against Hippias and his supporters, including allies of the tyrant from Thessaly. The Spartans lost that battle, and Hippias held on to power. Herodotus says that Anchimolios was buried in the *deme* of Alopeke, just to the south of the city proper and near the Temple of Herakles in Kynosarges – his tomb still visible eight decades later in Herodotus' day (Hdt. 5.63). Instead of being buried where he fell, Anchimolios was memorialized in a prominent spot near the city, along the major road between Athens and Phaleron, several kilometers from where he fell. This might appear to be a situation similar to the monument from 403, except, once Hippias was expelled from Athens within two years of Anchimolios' death, Athens would have been friendly to the dead Spartan commander who had tried to rid the city of its tyrants. After 510, Athens would not have been hostile territory for Anchimolios, whereas the experience of the Thirty made Athens paranoid about a reemergence of the kind of tyranny the Thirty represented and distinctly hostile to the Spartan actions in 404–403. As Shear and Scott argued, the Tomb of the Lacedaemonians was likely understood by the Athenians precisely as a reminder of enemies in their territory and the foreign threat the city had faced at the hands of Sparta. The monument of 403, therefore, represents a different kind of monument than the tomb of Anchimolios and other Spartan burials in foreign territory.

A famous saying reported by Plutarch in his life of Agesilaus indicates that establishing prominent burials in foreign territory was a way for Spartans to thumb their nose at and claim superiority over their enemies. An unnamed Argive tried to insult an unnamed Spartan by saying that many Spartan dead lie in Argive territory, to which the Spartan retorted that no dead Argives lie in Laconia. In other words, Argive soldiers had never managed even to get into Spartan territory (Plut. *Ages.* 31.6; see also *Mor.* 233c). Argive territory is where the first Spartan mass grave, or *polyandrion*, on or near the battlefield is attested, namely the one established after the "Battle of the Champions" between Sparta and Argos around 546. In Chapter 2, we considered the Battle of Thyrea, before which 300 picked Spartans battled 300 picked Argives. Both sides claimed victory; the Argives because two of their men survived the battle, the Spartans because, while only one of their soldiers survived, the famous Othryadas, he remained on the field while the Argives departed. Pausanias (2.38.5–6) mentions burials (*taphoi*) at the spot, along with mass graves (*polyandria*) for the Spartans and Argives as he left the battle site. While it is unclear whether these monuments are separate from each other – the *taphoi* being where the champions from each side were buried, and the *polyandria* indicating where the dead from the larger battle that followed – this seems to be good evidence for Spartan battlefield burials in, if not hostile territory, at least disputed territory.[42] As Polly Low points out, however, although it is tempting to interpret the burial seen by Pausanias as representing a Spartan claim to the territory occupied by their dead, the travel-writer saw more than one *polyandrion*, indicating that the Argives were buried here too.[43]

The Tomb of the Lacedaemonians, instead of being another example of a famed Spartan tradition, is a new type of monument, a brazen claim to superiority right in the middle of a hostile state's territory – even in the hostile state's most important site of memory. Scholars such as Shear and Scott might be right in arguing that the Athenians managed to reconceptualize the monument as a reminder of Athens standing against foreign enemies, and thus a credit to the city, but the Spartan intention behind the monument certainly was not to bolster solidarity among Athenians. Since it is with the king Pausanias that the Athenian democrats came to an agreement, and those buried in the Kerameikos died in an engagement led by Pausanias, we can assume that the Athenians and Pausanias made an arrangement regarding the tomb. Still, the monument stands as major shift in Spartan self-presentation abroad, as concerned not just about the glory and memory of its fallen, but also about asserting Spartan power over fellow Greeks in an imperial posture not unlike that of the 5th-century Athenians. The era of Lysander heralded a change in Spartan commemoration, and the larger-than-life victor of the Peloponnesian War was not the only one driving this change.

Non-Spartans also commented on a shift in Sparta's approach to war and commemoration. During the Peloponnesian War, the surrender of nearly 300 Lacedaemonians on the island of Sphacteria had upended the

---

[42] Low 2006: 93–95, 104n25; Kucewicz 2021a.     [43] Low 2006: 94–95.

Greeks' expectations of how the people who had stood their ground at Thermopylae would behave. During his glowing treatment of Brasidas the Homeric hero, Thucydides snidely remarks on the bad behavior of the Spartans who succeeded him, precious few of whom took their reputations as liberators to heart. Lysander's bolstering of a narrow and vicious oligarchy at Athens following the war was bound to elicit similar comment. The source of some of this criticism, however, might be a bit surprising: Xenophon, an Athenian with famous affinities for the Spartans.

Megistias, the seer who died willingly along with the Spartans at Thermopylae and who was honored with an epigram composed by Simonides, had a counterpart among the democratic forces against the Thirty in the Piraeus in 403. Xenophon gives a riveting account of the decisive battle in the conflict, fought on the slopes of the Mounichia hill above Athens' storied naval port (*Hell.* 2.4).[44] Xenophon himself was likely present as an eyewitness, fighting for the other side as a young member of the cavalry. As the forces of the Thirty, bolstered by the Spartan garrison at Athens stationed to support Lysander's puppet regime, filled up the road leading up the hill, from the top of the hill Thrasybulus, the democratic resistance leader, gave a rousing speech. He inspired the democrats to win back their country, their homes, their freedom, and their honor, and their wives and children, using language redolent of the battle cry shouted at Salamis in Aeschylus' *Persians*. Xenophon's readers cannot help but be reminded of that earlier conflict, in which Greeks banded together to fight for freedom against a foreign invader. Now the conflict is against the Spartans and their minions, but the terms, as Thrasybulus expressed them, are the same. Thermopylae in particular is brought to mind by the democrats' seer, left unnamed by Xenophon. Like Megistias, who foresaw his own death but fought anyway in 480, the seer in Xenophon said that the democrats would not win unless one of their number was either killed or wounded first. Then, as if driven on by fate, Xenophon says, the seer hurled himself against the battle line of the Spartans and the Thirty and so met his end.[45] The battle then broke out in earnest, with the democrats emerging victorious.

To say that Xenophon's feelings about Sparta and Athens were complicated would be a great understatement.[46] Xenophon was an aristocratic member of the cavalry, a branch of the Athenian military sympathetic to the oligarchs,

---

[44] For this battle, see Butera and Sears 2019: 35–46.
[45] For a discussion of the motif of seers predicting their own deaths, see Dillon 2017: 108–110.
[46] For a recent study of Xenophon as an Athenian and admirer of Sparta, see Humble 2021.

and seemingly on their side in battles against Thrasybulus and the democrats. After democracy was restored, Xenophon left Athens and joined the expedition of the Ten Thousand to the heart of the Persian Empire, an adventure he followed up by campaigning alongside the Spartan king Agesilaus in Asia. This latter action likely caused Xenophon's exile from Athens. In exile, Xenophon had an estate in the Peloponnese not far from Olympia, thanks to Agesilaus, and enrolled his own sons in the Spartan *agōgē*, the infamously brutal education system for Spartan warriors. Many times throughout the *Hellenica*, his history of Greece in his time, Xenophon comes across as an unabashed Spartan apologist, especially against Sparta's hated 4th-century enemy Thebes. Like Thucydides, Xenophon's historian predecessor who was also exiled from Athens, Xenophon seemed no fan of Athenian democracy, at least in its more radical manifestations. But, despite fighting for them from horseback, he seems to have hated the Thirty more, and he had no great love for Lysander. For the battles in the Piraeus, Xenophon the historian is on the side of the democratic Athenians against the Thirty and the Spartans.

Xenophon's treatment of the democratic resistance to the Thirty recalls the Persian Wars, I think deliberately, with the Spartans on the wrong side of things this time. While the democratic seer is not named like his famous predecessor, Megistias, Xenophon does point out his burial at the ford of the Kephisos River on the road between the Piraeus and the city – not quite on the very spot where he died, but not far away, either. When Xenophon wrote his *Hellenica*, some decades after the events of 403, the seer's monument was evidently well known to the Athenians, lying as it did along a much-traveled route and commemorating a famous battle. In light of the parallels between this seer and Megistias at Thermopylae, and of the stirring words of Thrasybulus before the battle in Xenophon's account, it is natural to think of this battle and its commemoration as an example of anti-Spartan remembrance, turning Sparta's most prized commemorative tropes against the Spartans. The Athenian seer becomes a new Megistias, and the Athenian democrats are the new Spartans standing for freedom at Thermopylae. Only this time, the freedom-fighters actually won a tactical victory, not merely a moral one.

## Conclusion

Neither Gylippus nor even Lysander went beyond the bounds of what the Spartans considered acceptable in terms of pursuing individual glory – even if Gylippus did allegedly steal money, for which he was condemned. Nor did they really go too far in terms of personal corruption and greed, at least not further than other Spartans had gone while still enjoying blessed memory and physical monuments at Sparta and abroad. Gylippus and Lysander followed a trail blazed by the regent Pausanias the better part of a century earlier, and further cleared by Brasidas in the first years of the Peloponnesian War. If Spartan character and power really were on the cusp of precipitous decline, which the first decades of the 4th century would bear out, it was not love of glory, even individualized glory, that brought them there.

The Tomb of the Lacedaemonians in the Athenian Kerameikos, however it was interpreted by Athenians looking to further their own interests, provides a clue, in prominently displayed inscribed stones, of a change in the Spartan approach to and commemoration of war. The Spartans now embraced the Peloponnesian War propaganda framing the city as a force for liberation around the Aegean world, and as the leaders of all Greece rather than a corner of the Peloponnese. Like the Athenians of the Age of Pericles, the Spartans were now the sorts of liberators who meddled in the affairs of others – often in the name of freedom, of course. The Tomb of the Lacedaemonians, like so many literal and figurative monuments left by the Athenian Empire all over the world, demonstrates that Sparta was now happy to remind the other Greeks that Spartans had nobly died even in the hearts of other cities.

Not greed or glory, but meddling in the affairs of others, often or perhaps usually couched in terms of Panhellenism and liberation, was the real change in how the Spartans framed war. As the disastrous 4th century would show, this new approach all but guaranteed that an endless stream of wars would flow in Sparta's direction.

# CHAPTER 6

# Agesilaus, First King of Greece

## Introduction

Lysander was the greatest man of his time, but his power was largely informal, based on his own charisma and accomplishments, and bolstered by friends and allies throughout the Aegean. The person who came closest to becoming the first king of all Greece started out as one of Lysander's protégés. Agesilaus rose to the Spartan kingship with Lysander's help and on Lysander's coattails. Once firmly in power, however, Agesilaus was determined to chart his own path and distance himself from his controversial patron.

In a book that surveyed Spartan history, Agesilaus would be a natural choice to follow Lysander as a subject, since the two initially worked together, and Agesilaus modified Lysander's imperial ambitions to strike a Panhellenic note and attack the Persian Empire in Asia. But in a book about commemoration, Agesilaus is perhaps a surprising topic, since not only did he lack the kind of ostentatious military monument Lysander had set up at Delphi, he has left us no physical monuments at all. In fact, Plutarch tells us that Agesilaus refused to allow any image of himself to be made, even on his deathbed (Plut. *Ages.* 2.2). The only famous physical monument we can connect to Agesilaus is an equestrian statue of his sister, Cynisca, erected at Olympia after she won the chariot racing competition. Her participation in that competition was Agesilaus' way of denigrating equestrian victories as due to wealth rather than personal excellence (Xen. *Ages.* 9.6).[1] The closest thing we come to even a hint in the ancient sources of a physical monument to Agesilaus is that his spear was apparently still on

---

[1] See Dillery 2019 for the intriguing suggestion that the monument to Cynisca and her "swift-footed" (ὠκύποδες) horses might have been a response to the worry that "swift-footed" (ἀρτίπους) Sparta would suffer under a "lame" (χωλός) kingship, according to a warning from the Delphic oracle. For more on the "lame kingship" and Agesilaus' rise to power, see below in this chapter.

display in Plutarch's day, half a millennium after Agesilaus died. Plutarch says that this spear looked like any other man's (Plut. *Ages.* 19.6).

Agesilaus is the favorite of the Athenian author Xenophon, who was himself enamored of Sparta and the Spartan way of life to the point that he supposedly enrolled his own sons in the Sparta education system, the *agōgē*, to be raised along with Spartan warriors. In Xenophon, Agesilaus secured a commemorator like no other, and was as concerned with his memorialization as any other famous Spartan had been. As he vastly increased the scale and length of Spartan interventions overseas, and even sponsored or at least provided cover for Spartan interference in the affairs of fellow Greeks, Agesilaus clung to personal glory and fame as a prime motivation, just as Leonidas had a century earlier. As the de facto king of Greece, Agesilaus provides an example of how some of the most decisive factors driving Spartan commemoration persisted even after Sparta had ceased to be the isolationist and timid society it was in the Archaic and early Classical eras. Agesilaus reigned while Sparta declined from leader of Greece to a second-rate backwater, beset on all sides by military conflicts of its own making. His life and times are thus an important case study of how new and old forms of commemoration among the Spartans related to Sparta's propensity to fight wars, especially wars outside of the Peloponnese.

A lot of ink has been spilled in trying to answer just why Sparta lost its power and prestige in the course of the 4th century. Agesilaus typically plays a central role in these discussions.[2] For a variety of reasons, including Sparta's inheritance laws that ensured plots of land grew smaller with each generation, the state suffered from *oliganthrōpia*, a shortage of militarily eligible men.[3] To be a full Spartiate, one had to contribute to the common messes where Spartiates dined. Without enough land, a Spartan could lose his citizenship by failing to meet this requirement. The wars of the late 5th and 4th centuries led to a further loss of men, since the Spartiates tended to take the most vulnerable, and therefore glorious, positions in the phalanx and thus died at a greater rate than other soldiers in the army. With Agesilaus at the helm, Sparta fought too many wars and lost too many Spartans in them. If the Spartan king had been more concerned with amassing traditional commemorative monuments to his glory rather than trying to make the whole world a witness to his greatness, as the Athenians tended to do, the Spartans might have held on longer as a great

---

[2] Cartledge 1987 and Hamilton 1991 are the foundational studies of this period.
[3] See Decety 2020 for a recent statistical analysis confirming Sparta's citizenship shortage.

power. Among other endemic problems, Sparta's 4th-century uniting of glory-seeking with foreign entanglements, for liberty and the cause of Greece, brought the era of Spartan supremacy to an end.

## The "Lame Kingship"

Michael Flower, followed by Sarah Ferrario, argues that Agesilaus deliberately spurned the sorts of honors pursued by Lysander in order to distance himself from his controversial predecessor and mentor.[4] Whether or not Agesilaus really was a more restrained and modest figure than Lysander, Paul Cartledge insists that all such good behavior was designed to provide cover for Agesilaus pursuing policies every bit as geared to acquiring personal power as Lysander's had been. In Cartledge's words, "personal politics and power ... should be disguised not flaunted, and the Spartan authorities assiduously flattered not flouted."[5] While Agesilaus' personal style might have differed from Lysander's, he was concerned with his own legacy and commemoration nonetheless. Where Lysander took a pragmatic approach to amassing power, including befriending and accepting huge sums of cash from a Persian prince, Agesilaus framed his own pursuit of power with appeals to Panhellenism and the liberation of the Greeks of Asia from Sparta's erstwhile allies. He ostentatiously equated himself with no less a figure than Agamemnon, mythical leader of the Greeks at Troy. And while Agesilaus supposedly rejected physical memorials, in the person of Xenophon he found a eulogizer of the highest caliber, a writer who commemorated Agesilaus with one of Greece's first biographies. Sarah Ferrario likens Xenophon to Pindar, the great 5th-century poet commissioned to memorialize athletic victors, in his treatment of the Spartan king.[6]

It is worth looking at the Delphic oracle promising doom if Sparta adopted a "lame" kingship. Agesilaus suffered a congenital defect in one leg, and only the machinations of Lysander convinced the Spartans that the "lame" kingship mentioned by the oracle referred to the ascension of an illegitimate king, namely Agesilaus' nephew, Leotychides, the heir-apparent who was suspected of being the child of the Athenian Alcibiades. Leotychides was thus disqualified, and Agesilaus made king (Plut. Ages. 3). The doom predicted by Delphi, despite Lysander's semantics, really did seem to befall Sparta during Agesilaus' reign: "Watch out, Sparta, even though you are boastful, | That a lame kingship not spring up

---

[4] Flower 1988: 131–134; Ferrario 2014: 250.   [5] Cartledge 1987: 97–98.   [6] Ferrario 2014: 250–254.

from you. | For unexpected plagues will subdue you | And the rolling waves of destructive war" (Plut. *Ages*. 3.5). Despite having won the Peloponnesian War in 404, military conflict continued to bedevil the Spartans and much of the rest of Greece besides. Aside from the drain constant warfare entails for any society, Sparta had the worst of it on the battlefield on several occasions in the 4th century, especially against the Boeotians at Leuctra in 371 and again at Mantinea in 362. The rolling waves of destructive war foretold by the oracle did indeed come to pass on Agesilaus' watch, whether one believes in such divine prophecies or not. Not only did Agesilaus invite these wars, and at times prosecute them badly, but the way he framed these wars and commemorated them as acts of liberation only exacerbated Sparta's problems, and virtually guaranteed that the Greek world was roiled with violence.

Agesilaus' Panhellenism and emulation of Agamemnon, himself associated with a war the marked the end of an era, was out of step with the traditional ways in which Sparta thought about and remembered war, even if his desire for individual glory was firmly within ancient Spartan tradition. Agesilaus transgressed against other Spartan customs too, with disastrous effect. As we will see, he overlooked the unprovoked and apparently unilateral attacks against Thebes and Athens by two different Spartans, acts of lawless aggression that should have been sanctioned according to Spartan law. He also took a lenient approach to the survivors of Leuctra, who should have been marked at Sparta as "tremblers" for living through a battle Sparta had lost and that had claimed the life of a Spartan king and, even worse, surrendering to the enemy. Whether one accepts the moralistic lessons advanced by Xenophon in his *Constitution of the Lacedaemonians*, Xenophon's claim that the Spartans came to ruin because they no longer obeyed the laws of god or the laws of Lycurgus bears the stamp of truth, at least in terms of Sparta's traditional laws and customs (Xen. *Lak. Pol.* 14). The Spartans fell from grace not simply because of the strain, corruption, and decadence the possession of an empire brought – the factors most forcefully highlighted by Xenophon and other ancient and modern commentators – but also because of how they conceived of war.

War for Agesilaus and many other Spartans of his time was advertised and commemorated as (if not genuinely believed to be) a tool of liberation and a means for the stronger to look out for the weaker. Such an attitude, though in line with how the Athenians and many other Greeks had commemorated war since at least Xerxes' invasion, was adopted at Sparta only during the Peloponnesian War, and even then only begrudgingly aside from figures such as Brasidas. Agesilaus represents the culmination of this new way of conceiving of war in Sparta, and, as his life and times reveal, this new approach to war did Sparta no favors, nor did it necessarily benefit the many thousands of other Greeks caught up in the constant conflicts of the 4th century. As if to advertise how much like the Athenians Agesilaus and Spartans sympathetic to him had become, Xenophon says that Agesilaus erected monuments to his excellence throughout the whole world (Xen. *Ages.* 11.16).[7] This sentiment is very similar to Pericles' famous words in his Thucydidean Funeral Oration: "Forcing every land and sea to be open to our daring, we [Athenians] have established eternal monuments everywhere, whether for good deeds or evil" (Thuc. 2.41.4).[8] Being remembered the world over as a conquering power or trustworthy ally is an Athenian trait, but not a particularly Spartan one, at least not in the context of Lycurgus' Sparta. We should not assume that Xenophon's expression here lines up with sentiments actually conveyed by Agesilaus; but aiming to erect monuments to one's excellence throughout the whole world is far more inviting of war than striving for a Homeric beautiful death and the accompanying material tributes, no matter how ostentatious, at Sparta or a Panhellenic sanctuary.

Lysander surrounded himself with poets to sing of his deeds, and other famous Spartans had their deeds preserved for all time in the pages of historians like Thucydides and Herodotus; but Agesilaus is among the very few who have an extant work of praise devoted solely to themselves, written by one of Greece's most famous authors.[9] Xenophon's *Agesilaus*, one of the first biographies ever written, seems more than to make up for Agesilaus' lack of physical monuments. Instead of a crumbling monumental tomb, or a now-vanished statue whose only traces are in works of literature, Agesilaus' exploits are praised in a text that has come through the manuscript tradition to appear in Penguin Classics translations to be read by undergraduates the world over (whether or not Agesilaus formally employed Xenophon for the task, which seems unlikely). Xenophon begins the treatise with unambiguous, almost embarrassing, praise of his Spartan subject: "I know that it is not easy to write the praises of Agesilaus in a way worthy of his excellence and glory, but I must make the attempt nevertheless. For it would not be appropriate that a man who became so perfectly good should not meet with praise, however insufficient, because of that

---

[7] μνημεῖα μὲν τῆς ἑαυτοῦ ἀρετῆς ἀνὰ πᾶσαν τὴν γῆν κτησάμενος . . ..

[8] ἀλλὰ πᾶσαν μὲν θάλασσαν καὶ γῆν ἐσβατὸν τῇ ἡμετέρᾳ τόλμῃ καταναγκάσαντες γενέσθαι, πανταχοῦ δὲ μνημεῖα κακῶν τε κἀγαθῶν ἀΐδια ξυγκατοικίσαντες . . ..

[9] Isocrates' *Evagoras* would also fit into this category.

very goodness" (Xen. *Ages.* 1.1).[10] This kind of treatment other Spartan warriors could only dream about, even if Xenophon should blush at penning such obvious flattery.

Nearly everyone who has read Xenophon's *Agesilaus* accuses the author of being a poor historian – a charge also levelled against his more historiographical works – and little more than a flatterer.[11] Differences in genre can partly explain why the *Agesilaus* is so apparently one-sided (his *Hellenica* includes more critical details), but that is not enough to absolve Xenophon of the charge of foisting a work of dubious utility on the scholarly community. *Nearly* everyone reads the *Agesilaus* this way, but there are exceptions. The most famous defense of Xenophon as an author and thinker in the face of texts like the *Agesilaus*, and the similarly laudatory *Constitution of the Lacedaemonians*, is an article from 1939 by the famous political philosopher Leo Strauss. Strauss reads Xenophon's flattery of Sparta and Agesilaus as deliberately ironic, overemphasizing good qualities to the point of absurdity in order to highlight their opposite. As a principle for interpreting Xenophon, Strauss suggests that "if in a given case he apparently happens to do a bad job as a writer as a thinker, he actually does it deliberately for very good reasons."[12] Strauss argues that Xenophon very much knew what he was doing, despite his modern detractors.

What was Xenophon doing, exactly, according to Strauss? He was critiquing the Lycurgan system and Agesilaus' part in it. For Xenophon, the Spartans' famous sense of shame was no more than a method of dissimulation, and the decline of Spartan virtue in the age of Agesilaus was merely a decline in that dissimulation, laying bare for all to see the Spartans' hypocrisy. In Xenophon's and Agesilaus' day, "the present Spartans were distinguished from their forefathers merely by the fact that they visibly and openly disobeyed Lycurgus' laws."[13] Xenophon, despite being a famous author of military histories and tactical treatises, preferred peace to war, and ironically critiques Sparta's military adventurism in the 4th century as a way to champion that preference.[14]

In his introduction to a translation of the *Agesilaus*, Robert C. Bartlett takes up Strauss's arguments, and concludes that Xenophon might have wished to deploy irony in order to make his philosophical mentor, Socrates, appear favorable next to a war-monger like Agesilaus,

---

[10] οἶδα μὲν ὅτι τῆς Ἀγησιλάου ἀρετῆς τε καὶ δόξης οὐ ῥάδιον ἄξιον ἔπαινον γράψαι, ὅμως δ᾽ ἐγχειρητέον. οὐ γὰρ ἂν καλῶς ἔχοι εἰ ὅτι τελέως ἀνὴρ ἀγαθὸς ἐγένετο, διὰ τοῦτο οὐδὲ μειόνων ἂν τυγχάνοι ἐπαίνων.

[11] Cawkwell 1976 is representative of the scholarship critical of Xenophon's historiographical abilities.

[12] Strauss 1939: 503.    [13] Strauss 1939: 517.    [14] Strauss 1939: 524–525.

Xenophon's other supposed mentor.[15] Bartlett detects sharp criticism, though hidden by irony and false praise, in Xenophon's treatment of Agesilaus: "If Agesilaus clearly preferred the fatherland, friends of long standing, and just and noble profits gained at some risk to 'the whole earth,' newly acquired friends, and not-so-noble, low-risk profits (1.36), he nonetheless evinced some interest also in the whole earth, newly acquired friends, and not-so-noble, low-risk profits (e.g., 1.18–19)."[16] Rather than seeing Xenophon as Agesilaus' Pindar, then, we might be better served by embracing him as a contemporary critic of the new Spartan approach to war, as most egregiously practiced by the apparently mild-mannered successor of Lysander.

## A New Agamemnon

Physical monuments or no, Agesilaus certainly wanted to be remembered the world over. What better way to achieve that than by posing as a new Agamemnon, the Mycenaean king who led the Greeks to Troy? Xenophon says that before setting sail to Asia in 396, to bring war against the territories of the Great King, Agesilaus paused to sacrifice at Aulis in Boeotia, the very spot Agamemnon had slain his daughter Iphigeneia to ensure favorable winds. The rulers of Boeotia, the Boeotarchs, upon hearing of Agesilaus' brazen deed in their own neighborhood, dispatched a force of cavalry. The Boeotian troops barged in on the Spartan king in the midst of the ceremony and hurled the sacrificial victims from the altar. Enraged and summoning the gods as witnesses to the Boeotians' treacherous deed, Agesilaus slunk away and set sail from another spot (Xen. *Hell.* 3.4.3–4). Years later, the Theban leader Pelopidas would use this incident in an attempt to gain the alliance of the Persian king, arguing that Thebes had long been Persia's friend since the Thebans had not only refused to take part in Agesilaus' expedition but had even disrupted the Spartan's sacrifice (Xen. *Hell.* 7.1.34).

Xenophon merely remarks on the fact that Aulis was where Agamemnon performed his sacrifices before the expedition to Troy, but Plutarch preserves a tradition that makes the connection between the two leaders far more explicit. In the biographer's account, Agesilaus was inspired to make the sacrifice by a dream that compared the Spartan to the Mycenaean leader as the only two men ever appointed general over all Greece. Agesilaus should therefore sacrifice at the same spot as his predecessor. In

---

[15] Bartlett 2018: 92–93.    [16] Bartlett 2018: 90.

his haste to avoid sacrificing his own daughter, as Agamemnon had done, Agesilaus ordered his own seer to perform the sacrifice of a deer, which offended the Boeotians, who had their own religious officials for such tasks in their territory (Plut. *Ages.* 6.4–6). Despite the sacrifice becoming a debacle, it is clear that Agesilaus' intention had been to broadcast his affinities with Agamemnon and follow in his footsteps by leading Greek armies as an all-powerful commander.

It is worth pausing over what message Agesilaus meant to send with his attempted stunt, since it is difficult to think of a similarly brazen self-comparison to a Homeric hero in Agesilaus' time.[17] While Thucydides treats Brasidas as if he were a Homeric hero, as Simon Hornblower and J. G. Howie argue, and while Brasidas himself happily cultivated extraordinary honors during his lifetime and received even grander honors after his death, there is no indication that he openly compared himself to a mythical warrior such as Achilles.[18] Agesilaus, on the other hand, could not have made his own self-comparison with the most powerful man in the Trojan War more explicit. Was it enough for Agesilaus that Agamemnon was a figure of immense renown who also led a military expedition from mainland Greece to Asia? Or were there more points of comparison between the Trojan War and the campaign of 396 to which Agesilaus wanted to draw attention through his act of self-commemoration?

Comparisons between Brasidas and Achilles make sense only insofar as Brasidas, like his Homeric predecessor, fought bravely and died young. The reasons, at least the stated reasons, for Brasidas' campaigns in Thrace could not have been more different from Achilles' reasons for fighting (and not fighting, which drives the plot of the *Iliad*) at Troy. Brasidas was in the north to liberate Athens' subjects. Achilles was at Troy for Achilles, and when his personal fame and glory were compromised by Agamemnon, he withdrew from battle and prayed for the deaths of his countrymen. There is some suggestion that the authorities in Sparta resented Brasidas' successes and denied their champion sufficient support and resources, but Brasidas did not take that slight as a reason to campaign against his fellow Spartans in order to avenge his own stolen glory. As we have seen, Brasidas represented a new type of Spartan in this regard. Previous generations of Spartans were much more in line with Achilles' selfish reasons for fighting. Thus, although Thucydides portrays Brasidas as a Homeric hero, and

---

[17] For Agesilaus presenting himself as Agamemnon, and the importance of Agamemnon for Spartan propaganda, see Meidani 2013.
[18] Brasidas is, however, likened to Achilles in Plato's *Symposium* (221c).

Plato's *Symposium* compares him directly to Achilles, it is only the manner of fighting that is operative in the comparison.

Ancient Greek concepts of manhood and heroism are often quite different from our own, but even so, it is difficult to imagine that many Classical Greeks wanted to exhibit the Homeric Agamemnon's personality.[19] His main impressive feature in the *Iliad* (his brief *aristeia* in Book 11 excepted) is the sheer number of soldiers he commands, both those who sailed in his contingent from Mycenae, and those in the other Greek contingents that were all bound by obligations to Agamemnon as the *wanax*, the Mycenaean commander-in-chief. Rather than fighting like Agamemnon, therefore, Agesilaus wanted to emphasize the parallels in the nature of their respective commands. Both leaders, the Homeric *wanax* and the Spartan king, were bringing coalitions from mainland Greece against a non-Greek enemy in western Asia Minor.[20] In his *Agesilaus*, Xenophon says that Agesilaus was particularly enthusiastic about his campaign against Persian territories since the struggle would not be for Greece, but for Asia (Xen. *Ages.* 1.8). Previous encounters with the Persians, especially during Xerxes' invasion of 480–479, had seen the sovereignty of mainland Greece hang in the balance. Not this time, Agesilaus seems to emphasize. He never forgave the Boeotians for spoiling his Trojan War commemoration party, which laid bare that the Spartan king did not command the kind of respect throughout mainland Greece that Agamemnon had. The experience must have been humiliating for Agesilaus, and he vented his rage against the Thebans at Coronea two years later, in 394, to which we will return momentarily.

Before we consider Coronea, it is instructive to look at the circumstances leading to the battle, in particular the forces Agesilaus led to Asia and his reaction to having to bring those same forces back to Greece. As in the case of Brasidas and Gylippus, the Spartan authorities did not provide Agesilaus with the best resources available, despite the ostensibly important and noble nature of the mission. Xenophon says that from the Spartans Agesilaus asked for and received a mere thirty full Spartiates, 2,000 *neodamōdeis* (that is, freed helots), and 6,000 allied soldiers (Xen. *Hell.*

---

[19] For a concise treatment of manhood and heroism in Homer, see Clarke 2004.

[20] As Meidani 2013: 122 points out, the Spartans also tried to claim Agamemnon as their own progenitor, a Dorian hero and son of Pelops rather than an Achaean from the house of Atreus, despite what most traditions about Agamemnon assert. In Herodotus, the Spartans reject the Syracusan tyrant Gelon's offer to help the Greeks against the Persians, since the Syracusan demanded to be made commander of the Greek forces. The Spartan rationale for this rejection of this alliance is that Agamemnon, the son of Pelops, would lament Sparta losing its traditional command of the Greeks (Hdt. 7.159.1).

3.4.2). To compare this ragtag army to the ships bristling with heroes that Agamemnon took to Troy strikes me as patently absurd. Nevertheless, Brasidas, Agesilaus' real predecessor, gained unprecedented fame and glory with his motley force, and Agesilaus had every reason to expect the same.

Perhaps the lower quality of soldiers – at least in terms of formal status – Agesilaus led would bring its own type of glory. Brasidas could brag that he achieved what he did despite having few real Spartiates. His helot veterans formed their own specially named crack force, the Brasideans, in years following their mission to Thrace. Cleon, Brasidas' Athenian opponent in the Battle of Amphipolis, had made a name for himself as a commander by leading the capture of the Spartans trapped at Pylos on Sphacteria in 425. Cleon had boasted to the Athenians that he would pull off this feat by using only allied troops, including light-armed skirmishers and other soldiers typically disdained by the hoplite classes (Thuc. 4.28.4). With this force of allies and mercenary peltasts and archers, Cleon dealt Sparta its most humiliating defeat in centuries. Of this humiliation the Athenian allies were well aware, as evidenced by the mockery one of those allied troops directed at a Spartan survivor, which we considered earlier (Thuc. 4.40.2).[21] As Cleon's contempt for the Spartans had only increased his fame, so Agesilaus might have looked forward to special commemoration for his contempt of the Persians.

The Spartans recalled Agesilaus to the Greek mainland upon the out-break of the Corinthian War, a conflict between a coalition of poleis and the Spartans engineered by the Persians to take the heat off Persian lands. Xenophon provides two different versions of how Agesilaus reacted to the sudden cessation of his campaign against the Persians.[22] In the *Agesilaus*, the Spartan king gives hardly a thought to his prospects for personal glory, but immediately obeys the summons from home and goes to the aid of his fatherland. Xenophon says that in this situation Agesilaus behaved just as if he were one of the ephors, those officials the Spartans send out with the kings on campaign to check the kings' ambitions and behavior. Xenophon gushes that Agesilaus "would not take the whole world in exchange for his fatherland" and that he would opt for "right and just" things, even if dangerous, over "secure but ignoble things" (Xen. *Ages*. 1.36).[23] In the *Hellenica*, on the other hand, Xenophon's account is subtly different. While Agesilaus does in the end heed his country's call, he first takes the

---

[21] See Chapter 4.      [22] As noted by Ferrario 2014: 253.
[23] μάλα ἔνδηλον ποιῶν ὡς οὔτε ἂν πᾶσαν τὴν γῆν δέξαιτο ἀντὶ τῆς πατρίδος . . . οὔτε αἰσχρὰ καὶ ἀκίνδυνα κέρδη μᾶλλον ἢ μετὰ κινδύνων τὰ καλὰ καὶ δίκαια. Similar praise of Agesilaus' sense of patriotic duty is also present in Plutarch's account (Plut. *Ages*. 15.4–5).

news poorly, lamenting the personal ambitions that he must abandon (Xen. *Hell.* 4.2.3).[24]

Plutarch and Xenophon, at least in the latter's *Agesilaus,* clearly mean to contrast the Spartan king with Lysander, the ultimate selfish Spartan. Would Lysander have listened to his government rather than continue to pursue his own advancement? Perhaps not. The sources commemorate Agesilaus lavishly for his obedience in this instance. Plutarch even compares him favorably to Hannibal and Alexander, the two most famous generals in ancient Mediterranean history, since Hannibal returned to Carthage only when he was in dire straits in Italy, and Alexander cared not a bit about an uprising back home in Greece, since he was focused on continuing his conquests in Asia (Plut. *Ages.* 15.4). Agesilaus' actions here, and the motivations behind them, subtly different as they are in Xenophon's two accounts, encapsulate the central theme of this book.

What is more important to the Spartans in war, or, at least, what is more prevalent in Spartan commemoration: selfless sacrifice for a higher cause, or glory and fame? The two concerns, of course, need not be mutually exclusive. The literary record commemorates Agesilaus in a fulsome way precisely because of his selfless devotion to Sparta and willingness to give up his personal ambitions, in contrast to Lysander whom the sources generally revile. The main question I hope this study answers is the extent to which commemorative practices encourage or discourage future wars. The evidence suggests that Sparta engaged in more wars – and longer and more destructive wars – the more Spartans embraced the sort of supposedly altruistic and Panhellenic reasons for war long advertised by other Greek poleis, especially Athens. Leonidas' actions at Thermopylae, and the paltry Spartan presence there in general, were according to many analyses militarily ridiculous, utterly unpragmatic, and designed to bring glory to Spartans alone at the expense of all other Greeks. But those actions made Leonidas the most famous Spartan who ever lived, a colossus in the commemorative sphere still today. Most relevant for us, Thermopylae is the ideal example of the Spartan aversion to military adventure outside of the Peloponnese. Even when the Spartans sent their full resources to Plataea, likely as much out of a desire for self-preservation as to help Athens and the other Greeks, they did not commemorate that battle as in any way related to the freedom of the Greeks or the defense of the

---

[24] ὁ δὲ Ἀγησίλαος ἐπεὶ ἤκουσε, χαλεπῶς μὲν ἤνεγκεν, ἐνθυμούμενος καὶ οἴων τιμῶν καὶ οἴων ἐλπίδων ἀπεστερεῖτο.

vulnerable. Soon after Plataea, the Spartans reverted to their isolationist focus on their home turf and left Panhellenic enterprises to the Athenians.

Agesilaus' case is perplexing in its confusion of the categories guiding this study. If Agesilaus had remained in Persian territory and continued to prioritize his own glory, he would have been doing no more than following the same self-aggrandizing drive that propelled Leonidas and many other famous Spartans. Yet this self-serving mission abroad was also couched in Panhellenic terms, of leading a Greek crusade against the Persians and freeing the Greeks of Asia. By following the directives of the Spartan authorities, apparently selflessly, he entered into a war of Greek against Greek, and played a key role in a conflict that ended with the Persians gaining a great deal of power in mainland Greece through the King's Peace of 387.[25]

Diodorus, using the now-lost work of the 4th-century historian Ephorus (a younger contemporary of Xenophon) as his main source, is notoriously of two minds regarding the virtues and vices of Agesilaus. In one passage, Diodorus condemns the Spartan king as being eager for dominance over the Greeks because of his energetic nature and love of war. Diodorus contrasts Agesilaus with his fellow king, Agesipolis, who is more inclined to avoid "enslaving" the other Greeks since he is a peaceful and just man (Diod. 15.19.4).[26] A few chapters later, Diodorus is effusive in his praise of Agesilaus' bravery and intelligence in the art of generalship, saying that he would have overrun all Asia had the Spartans not recalled him (Diod. 15.31.3–4).[27] The two sides of Agesilaus' coin, at least for Diodorus and his sources, seem to relate to whether Agesilaus was smashing the Persians (a good thing) or oppressing the Greeks (a bad thing).[28] I suggest, on the other hand, that dividing Agesilaus' actions between those aimed at enslaving Greeks and those designed to free them (or at least attack the Greeks' oppressors) embraces the freedom–slavery dichotomy rejected by traditional Spartan commemorative practices. I agree with Diodorus that

---

[25] See Lendon 1989 for the idea, based on surviving passages of the Oxyrhynchus Historian, that the accession and ascendancy of Agesilaus had a great deal to do with the outbreak, not just the conduct, of the Corinthian War, since his brand of interventionism greatly worried the other Greeks, especially Thebes.

[26] Ἀγησίπολις μὲν γάρ, εἰρηνικὸς ὢν καὶ δίκαιος, ἔτι δὲ καὶ συνέσει διαφέρων, ἔφη δεῖν ἐμμένειν τοῖς ὅρκοις καὶ παρὰ τὰς κοινὰς συνθήκας μὴ καταδουλοῦσθαι τοὺς ˝Ελληνας .... ὁ δ᾽ Ἀγησίλαος, ὢν φύσει δραστικός, φιλοπόλεμος ἦν καὶ τῆς τῶν Ἑλλήνων δυναστείας ἀντείχετο.

[27] περιβόητος δ᾽ ἦν ἐπ᾽ ἀνδρείᾳ καὶ στρατηγικῇ συνέσει ....

[28] Westlake 1986 chalks the difference up to Diodorus clumsily splicing together two source traditions in his treatment of Agesilaus, while Stylianou 1998: 119–120 thinks it is entirely consistent to be of two minds concerning Agesilaus.

Agesilaus was "fond of war," and therein lies the problem. When a warrior like Agesilaus fights for a whole host of reasons, even ones the Greeks and many of us would consider admirable, instead of just for glory and fame, contradictions will inevitably arise, as reflected in Diodorus' account. And not merely contradictions, but also more wars.

Charles Hamilton points out the irony of Agesilaus returning to Greece by retracing the steps of Xerxes, as indeed stated explicitly by the Xenophon (Xen. *Hell.* 4.2.8). This time, a Greek king was abandoning a war against Persians in order to prosecute a war against fellow Greeks.[29] Just as this was one of the actions for which Agesilaus is most praised by Xenophon (and perhaps blamed by Diodorus?), the Spartan king continued to prioritize his personal ambitions and fame even after he abandoned his Panhellenic enterprise. Perhaps the only way to frame Agesilaus in the context of the present study is as a figure who "threw Spartan commemorative practices into disarray," with severe consequences for both Spartan glory and Spartan stability.

## "They Pushed, They Fought, They Killed, They Died"

The mainland Greeks fought two great pitched battles against each other in the first months of the Corinthian War. In 394, along the banks of the Nemea River and in the shadow of Corinth's imposing acropolis, a coalition of Greek poleis took on the Spartan phalanx and lost. The Spartan hoplites once again demonstrated their superiority, given the right battle conditions, and the coalition was humiliated. During the battle, the Spartans displayed especial skill and discipline by allowing their enemies, who had been victorious on their own right wing, to march past unmolested on their way back to Corinth. The Spartans then suddenly wheeled about and slammed into the side of the enemy formation, rolling it up and killing many.[30] Plutarch records the anecdote that Agesilaus, on his way back from Asia, was far from pleased by the news of this Spartan victory. Instead, he lamented the loss of so many Greeks at the hands of other Greeks, especially since as a united force all the Greeks should instead be attacking Persians (Plut. *Ages.* 16.4). An admirable Panhellenist sentiment, perhaps, but one that had absolutely no effect on the Spartan king's desire to slaughter Thebans – his fellow Greeks – a short while later.

---

[29] Hamilton 1979: 219.
[30] For the ancient accounts of the Battle of the Nemea River, see Xen. *Hell.* 4.2–3; Diod. 14.83; Plut. *Ages.* 16. For a study of the battle, see Butera and Sears 2019: 349–359.

Xenophon writes that the Battle of Coronea of 394 was unlike any other fought in his lifetime (Xen. *Hell.* 4.3.16). On this matter, he is an authority, since he most likely took part in the battle himself.[31] Xenophon's account is certainly vivid, one of the most striking battle narratives from Greek antiquity.[32] What begins as a straightforward clash of hoplite armies, Agesilaus and his army on one side, Thebes and its allies on the other, morphs into a needlessly deadly duel between Agesilaus and the Thebans. In the battle's first phase, both right wings were victorious, as these things usually go, but instead of allowing the Thebans to pass by his own forces in an attempt to rejoin their allies who had fled to the slopes of Mount Helicon, Agesilaus slams his phalanx directly into them, face-to-face. By doing so, he adopted tactics the converse of those used by the victorious Spartan army at the Nemea River, which had decided to attack their enemy's temporarily victorious right wing from the flank and rear, to great effect. Xenophon points out that this also would have been the sensible tactic at Coronea, but Agesilaus opted for the "brave" over the "safe" (Xen. *Hell.* 4.3.19).[33]

As the two phalanxes clashed, Xenophon says only that "they pushed, they fought, they killed, they died" (Xen. *Hell.* 4.3.14; *Ages.* 2.12).[34] Agesilaus was seriously wounded in the battle, but he did not neglect the proper commemorations. He made an ostentatious display of his piety by allowing Theban soldiers who had taken refuge in a temple leave to depart unharmed. He also had his men wear garlands in honor of Apollo and the flute-players play as he had a trophy erected at the point of his victory. When the Thebans asked for a truce to recover their dead, a formal admission of defeat, Agesilaus accepted his victory and then immediately proceeded to Delphi to offer the god a tithe of his spoils from his campaigns. His dedication in the sanctuary amounted to more than 100 talents, an extraordinary sum bespeaking an even more extraordinary haul from the Persians and his other enemies.

Plutarch is critical of Agesilaus' actions at Coronea, saying that the Spartan rejected a victory without danger in favor of a bloodbath that ended in a virtual stalemate (rather than the clear victory found in

---

[31] For a discussion of the Battle of Coronea and its scholarship, see Butera and Sears 2019: 125–137.

[32] Xenophon's account in the *Agesilaus*, while mirroring that of the *Hellenica* in the essentials, is even more vivid (2.9–16). See also the accounts of the battle given in Diod. 14.84 and Plut. *Ages.* 18–19, the latter of which somewhat contradicts Xenophon's account by focusing on Theban valor – unsurprisingly, given Plutarch's Boeotian origins.

[33] ἐνταῦθα δὴ Ἀγησίλαον ἀνδρεῖον μὲν ἔξεστιν εἰπεῖν ἀναμφισβητήτως· οὐ μέντοι εἵλετό γε τὰ ἀσφαλέστατα.

[34] καὶ συμβαλόντες τὰς ἀσπίδας ἐωθοῦντο, ἐμάχοντο, ἀπέκτεινον, ἀπέθνῃσκον.

Xenophon's account), driven on as he was by "passion" and a "love of strife" (Plut. *Ages.* 18.2).[35] Even Xenophon's treatment of the battle is not without at least a suggestion of criticism, especially given the overt comparison to the much less bloody (from the Spartan side, that is) battle at the Nemea River. Robert Bartlett even goes so far as to say that upon a close reading of Xenophon, one concludes that, "courage so understood, the kind Agesilaus indisputably possessed, is a sort of senselessness, not to say madness."[36] Edith Foster has recently argued that in his *Hellenica* Xenophon emphasizes the pointlessness of many Spartan deaths, and the minor nature of the engagements in which many of these Spartans die (though this of course does not apply to Coronea, a major battle). By so doing, the historian critiques the Spartans' continuing adherence, especially in the time of Agesilaus, to ideals of the "beautiful death" as doing not much good for Sparta itself.[37]

The courage Agesilaus displayed at Coronea, however, especially because it was unsafe and bound to bring more personal glory than strategic or tactical gain, is exactly the type of courage traditionally commemorated at Sparta. The pragmatic and the practical – indeed, the "safe" – were the sorts of things Lysander pursued, the very things Agesilaus turned his back on when deciding to return home to Greece to answer his country's call rather than continue on in Asia. I submit that Agesilaus' action at Coronea was the most traditionally Spartan thing he ever did.[38] Later in his career, he deviated from the old Spartan ways when he chose the safe and sensible course, a sign of Sparta's decline, more than anything else.

In 371, after two more decades of nearly continuous military conflict, Sparta fought at Leuctra a battle as symbolic of Sparta's fall as Thermopylae had been for its ascendancy. The Thebans, led by the brilliant commander Epaminondas and anchored by the elite Sacred Band of 300 warriors, at long last crushed the Spartan phalanx decisively. Hundreds of the dwindling number of full Spartiates lay dead on the field, including Cleombrotus, Agesilaus' fellow king (Agesilaus was not present at the battle himself). The victory for the Thebans was not merely tactical.

---

[35] ἐνταῦθα τῆς νίκης ἀκινδύνου παρούσης ... ὑπὸ θυμοῦ καὶ φιλονεικίας ἐναντίος ἐχώρει τοῖς ἀνδράσιν, ὤσασθαι κατὰ κράτος βουλόμενος.

[36] Bartlett 2018: 92–93.    [37] Foster 2019.

[38] See Howie 1996: 212–213, who argues that Xenophon's accounts of Coronea include at least several elements of a Homeric *aristeia*, or extended demonstration of a hero's excellence. Given the similarities between traditional Spartan attitudes towards war and those of the Homeric heroes, Howie's comparison is certainly worth considering.

Epaminondas followed up his success at Leuctra by invading the Peloponnese, even Laconia itself, and was prevented from taking Sparta only by the Eurotas River swollen by floods. The Thebans wrested the helots from Spartan control by founding the fortified city of Messene deep in the traditionally Spartan-controlled Peloponnese, and added a reinvigorated Mantinea and a new Arcadian capital Megalopolis. Epaminondas and his Thebans had defeated the Spartans in a pitched battle, and drove the point home by stripping Sparta of its power base in the Peloponnese. Sparta was at an end as a great power.

The reception at Sparta of the news of the defeat at Leuctra is one of the canonical episodes in the history of Spartan commemoration. Xenophon says that the ephors ordered the families of the dead to bear their loss silently, but there seems to have been no need for the ephors to intervene. Those whose family members died in the battle went around the city with joyful faces in full view of everyone, while those whose husbands and sons had survived hid themselves away and appeared sad and dejected (Xen. *Hell.* 6.4.16). Despite the disaster so many dead men portended for the city, the Spartans still saw it as far better to die on the field than survive a defeat, even to fight another day. Plutarch confirms Xenophon's account but adds an important detail concerning Agesilaus' reaction. Commenting on the social death of the *tresantes*, or the "tremblers," which we discussed in Chapter 1 of this book, Plutarch says that Agesilaus relaxed the laws, to preserve needed manpower and prevent any sort of uprising from disgruntled and disgraced survivors. Agesilaus said that it was necessary "to let the laws sleep for the day."[39] In addition to preserving the laws saving the survivors of Leuctra from disgrace, as Plutarch says, Agesilaus immediately led an expedition into Arcadia and took a small town in the territory of Mantinea, all while carefully avoiding open battle in a most un-Spartan way lest the Spartans suffer another defeat (Plut. *Ages.* 29–30).

Paul Cartledge, who traces Agesilaus' role in the decline of Sparta, criticizes the Spartan king at this juncture. Instead of such a temporary measure, Cartledge argues, Agesilaus should have reevaluated the Spartan laws in general. "Devotion to the laws of Lycurgus numbed the Spartan mind – and no mind more than that of Agesilaus," Cartledge writes.[40] Almost certainly, Agesilaus was too late to halt Sparta's decline, and he was just one man. A Spartan king did not have nearly the level of authority that the term "king" indicates to us. But I do not share Cartledge's view that Agesilaus failed in this instance because he introduced a mere half measure.

---

[39] φήσας ὅτι τοὺς νόμους δεῖ σήμερον ἐᾶν καθεύδειν.    [40] Cartledge 1987: 179.

Instead, it was the sort of pragmatism represented by Agesilaus' lulling the laws to sleep that brought Sparta to such a dangerous pass. If he had allowed the *tresantes* to endure their properly Spartan lot, Sparta might have declined anyway, perhaps even more rapidly than it did in the end. But if the principles behind the laws applying to *tresantes*, as distasteful as they might be to us today, had remained in effect in the years before Leuctra, the Spartan army might not have been in Boeotia in the first place. Glory seems to have been a safer path for Sparta than hegemony.

Two other instances of Agesilaus bending or breaking Spartan laws in the interests of expediency are worth mentioning here, especially since they, too, had disastrous consequences for Sparta's position vis-à-vis the other Greeks. In 382, the Spartan general Phoebidas, *en route* to the north, took the initiative to seize the Cadmea, the acropolis of Thebes, despite Thebes and Sparta technically being at peace with each other. There is some discrepancy in the sources concerning the extent to which this action was directed by the Spartan authorities. Diodorus sees it as part of a nefarious master plan (Diod. 15.20). But Xenophon and Plutarch agree that Phoebidas ran into trouble back home for such a reckless overreach of his authority and was saved only by the intervention of Agesilaus. Stepping forward to stem the anger against Phoebidas, Agesilaus instructed the Spartans to consider only whether Phoebidas' actions had been to the good of Sparta (Xen. *Hell.* 5.2.32; Plut. *Ages.* 23.4).[41] The seizure of the Cadmea set Sparta and Thebes inexorably on the road to Leuctra.

Similarly, in 379, Sphodrias, commander of the Spartan garrison at Thespiae, attempted a surprise assault on the Athenian port of the Piraeus, but miscalculated his march and found himself and his forces exposed at daylight, still far off from the Piraeus. This action infuriated the Athenians, who turned decisively against Sparta and moved closer to Thebes, also a major blow to Spartan power. In the accounts of both Xenophon and Plutarch, Agesilaus supported the acquittal of Sphodrias, though by rights he deserved death at the hands of the Spartan laws, because Sparta was in need of men like Sphodrias (Xen. *Hell.* 5.4.20–33; Plut. *Ages.* 24–25). Xenophon, in an attempt to show that Agesilaus had been proven right, says that Sphodrias not only lived honorably after that affair but was the first to fall at Leuctra after being struck down three times as he defended the king (Xen. *Hell.* 5.4.33). Whether this later justification satisfied Xenophon's readers is an open question. Diodorus does not

---

[41] See a similar criterion applied by the Spartans to the captives from Plataea in 427 in Chapter 4.

equivocate, saying that Sphodrias got off contrary to justice because he had the kings as allies (Diod. 15.29.6).

Sparta needed men, and no doubt the likes of Phoebidas and Sphodrias were good men on the field of battle. It is difficult to believe, however, that Agesilaus' allegedly pragmatic actions in sparing their lives contrary to the law outweighed the damage done to Sparta by his overall approach to foreign intervention, which led to battles such as Leuctra, in which Sphodrias heroically died. Spartan heroism of old was especially valuable in how infrequently it had to be displayed.

Turning their backs on pragmatism and the practical benefits – not to mention the claims to do-gooderism – of war, especially war abroad, served the Spartans well for a long time. Fighting for glory and for fame, duly reflected in who and what were commemorated and what forms that commemoration took, kept Sparta out of a lot of wars, which led to Sparta's establishment as a unique power in the Greek world. Agesilaus was driven by some of these traditional Spartan impulses, even if the source tradition is less kind to him in some of those cases. For example, the reckless courage he displayed at Coronea, with which Xenophon and Plutarch have some trouble, was far less ruinous to Spartan interests, in the long term, than his championing of the cause of the Greeks of Asia and the Panhellenist sentiments undergirding his invasion of Persian territory – even though it is the latter that earns him the most effusive praise and literary commemoration, particularly in Xenophon's *Agesilaus*. By letting the laws sleep, Agesilaus signaled that the old ways of Spartan commemoration were dead. Spartan supremacy was dead along with them.

## The Warning of Thespiae

Before concluding these meditations on Agesilaus and the decline of Sparta, let us take a few moments to think about the fate of the Thespians, citizens of a Greek polis who, despite their outstanding valor, failed to become household names. The Thespians stayed with the Spartans for the last stand at Thermopylae. Where the Spartans lost almost all the famous Three Hundred, the Thespians lost 700, likely the whole of their hoplite military force. The Thespians played an outsized role, and suffered outsized casualties, in at least two other important Classical battles, Delium in 424 and the Nemea River in 394. Despite their battlefield heroics, Thespians were expelled from their city, which was razed, by the Thebans around 370. Though they later rebuilt, this was a momentous humiliation for any Greek polis to suffer at the hands of fellow Greeks.

Frank Miller and Zack Snyder did the Thespians the singular dishonor of not mentioning them at all in the film *300*, and at the site of Thermopylae itself, a modern monument to the Thespians was only erected in 1995, four decades after the much more grandiose monument was built for the Spartans. Sparta, even as a superpower, all but collapsed, largely because of its attitudes to war and commemoration. The Thespians demonstrate what can happen to those who adopt a Spartan-style attitude towards war and commemoration but lack the might and other advantages of a superpower.

Seven hundred Thespians died with the 300 Spartans at Thermopylae. We had occasion in Chapter 3 to consider the epigram attributed to their memorial at the site: "These men once dwelled on the brows of Helicon; broad Thespiae exults in their courage."[42] When we first encountered this epigram, we considered that it was only preserved by the 6th-century CE compilation of Stephanus of Byzantium, and that Page considers it a later literary exercise rather than a genuine 5th-century inscription. Strabo, though, mentions that there were five *stelai* at Thermopylae, including one that mentioned the Locrians (9.4.2). Some scholars have suggested that one of the *stelai* was for the Thespians, and this epigram was inscribed on it.[43]

For the Thespians, who lost the greatest number of soldiers in the battle, all the more extraordinary when factoring in their per capita casualties, not to be honored with an epigram, when the Spartans, Peloponnesians, and even the Sparta seer were given ones, would be remarkable. Herodotus does not mention an epigram, but makes sure to single out the Thespians for praise by listing as their bravest warrior one Dithyrambus, son of Haratides, right after he lists the three most valiant Spartans (Hdt. 7.227). We will never know whether the epigram quoted by Stephanus was inscribed soon after 480, or whether other lines honored the Thespians, but the text we have is remarkable in how much it resembles the Spartan monuments' emphasis on glory and neglect of concepts like "Greece" or "freedom."

The next battle in which we know the Thespians played an outsized role was Delium in 424. Thucydides says that the whole victorious Boeotian force lost nearly 500 men in the battle, in contrast to the defeated Athenians, who lost nearly 1,000 (Thuc. 4.101.2). The Thespians adorned

---

[42] = Philiadas I *FGE*: ἄνδρες θ᾽ οἵ ποτ᾽ ἔναιον ὑπὸ κροτάφοις Ἑλικῶνος, | λήματι τῶν αὐχεῖ Θεσπιὰς εὐρύχορος.

[43] For references, see Page 1981: 78.

their polis with a grandiose monument to their dead from that battle. A colossal marble lion was perched above nine *stelai* on which were recorded the names of the dead, some 202 of them in total.[44] Little Thespiae, then, contributed nearly half of all the casualties from the Boeotian army, a combined force representing more than seven poleis and the surrounding populations, one of which was the large city of Thebes. To put these numbers in perspective, the Athenians lost only 192 dead in the Battle of Marathon. In the same battle of Delium, the Boeotian state of Tanagra lost 63, according to the list of names inscribed on a monument now in the Schimitari Museum (no. 271). Even while participating in a victorious action, the men of Thespiae were clobbered.

The lion monument with which the Thespians memorialized the demographic disaster they suffered at Delium became a standard symbol to honor the courageous dead. The most famous lion in mainland Greece is that erected over the soldiers of the Theban Sacred Band after they were wiped out by the Macedonians at Chaeronea in 338. Another lion stood above a prominent tomb at Amphipolis in the north Aegean. The courtyard of the Archaeological Museum of Thebes is covered with marble lion monuments, ranging from modest in size to enormous (Figure 6.1). Several of these lions come from Thespiae, which seems to have been among the pioneers in funerary lions; the collection of Boeotian lions at the Thebes museum dwarfs others. The Thespians were not the first to embrace the form of the lion monument, however. Herodotus saw a lion monument erected in honor of Leonidas at Thermopylae, indicating that the Spartans pioneered the symbol early in the 5th century (Hdt. 7.225). In the garden of the Archaeological Museum of Sparta, two ghostly lions, originally tomb monuments, stand guard under the shade of a pine tree (Figure 6.2). We cannot go so far as to say that Spartan and Thespian uses of lion monuments influenced each other's practices, but the two states clearly shared some commemorative affinities.

The Thespians had a rough time of it at the Battle of the Nemea River in 394, too. In that battle, they were fighting along with the Thebans and whole host of other states against the Spartans and their Peloponnesian allies in one of the largest battles of the Classical period. Xenophon says that on the Spartan left wing, all the allies of the Lacedaemonians were overcome by their enemies, except the soldiers from Pellene. These hoplites fought stoutly against the Thespians with the result that many on both

---

[44] For the monument and its inscription, part of which is on display at the Archaeological Museum of Thebes (nos. 2016–2023), see Schilardi 1977; Roesch 2009: 3–5.

Figure 6.1 Lion funerary monument at the Archaeological Museum of Thebes. Author's photo. Permission courtesy of the Ephorate of Antiquities of Boeotia. © Hellenic Ministry of Culture and Sports / Hellenic Organization of Cultural Resources Development (H.O.C.RE.D.).

sides died where they stood (Xen. *Hell.* 4.2.20). Dying on the spot against stiff resistance was a very Spartan thing to do, and given their frequently high casualties, the Thespians seemed to do so quite regularly.

A mid–late 4th-century inscription (possibly a copy of an earlier original) from Thespiae is perhaps unique among commemorative monuments. The inscription simply lists five members of the same family and the battles in which they died: Phegeas at Oenophyta (457), Laukles at Oropos (that is, Delium, 424), Philolaios also at Oropus, and Philolaios at Coronea (394). The list starts with another Philolaios, but his battle is missing from the stone. Paul Roesch suggests Thermopylae or Plataea.[45] Stalwart Thespiae showed its devotion to battlefield heroics not only in the horrendous casualties its people suffered in combat, out of proportion to the war dead accumulated by its neighbors, but also in encouraging a singular tribute to the beautiful dead across several generations. Any Spartan family would be proud of such a legacy.

---

[45] Roesch 2009: 8–9; *SEG* 19.363: Φιλολάιος *vac.* ? | Φηγήας ἐν Οἰνοφύτοις | Λαυκλες ἐν Ὠρωποῖ | Φιλολάιος ἐν Ὠρωποῖ | Φιλολάιος ἐν Κορωνείη.

Figure 6.2  Lion funerary monuments at the Archaeological Museum of Sparta.
Author's photo. © Hellenic Ministry of Culture and Sports / Hellenic Organization
of Cultural Resources Development.

These losses in battles surely represented a demographic disaster for the
Thespians. Consider what the loss of around 400 Spartiates at Leuctra in
371 and the capture of 120 at Pylos in 425 had meant for mighty Sparta.
Thermopylae likely wiped out an entire generation of Thespian soldiers,
just as the First World War did for the major European powers in the early
20th century. After the painful and slow years of rebuilding its fighting
population, hundreds more Thespians fell at Delium, taking on far more
than their fair share of the fighting. Instead of lamenting these disasters, the
Thespians celebrated them with lion monuments, inscriptions advertising
the mettle of individual families, and perhaps also in an epigram adorning
the pass at Thermopylae. The Thespians' reward for their proud martial
valor, however, was having their walls torn down by the wary Thebans in
423, a mere year after giving so much as allies to those same Thebans at
Delium (Thuc. 4.133.1). In 373, Thebes ravaged the city (Diod. 46.6), and
at some point after Leuctra in 371, Thespiae was razed utterly and its people
expelled (Dem. 16.4). The Thebans had reasons to suspect Thespiae.
Agesilaus, for instance, fortified Thespiae in 378 to bolster Spartan efforts
against Thebes (Xen. *Hell.* 5.4.41), and the Thespians had otherwise been

hostile to Thebes on several occasions, tending to take Athens' side in things.[46]

Though Thebes was a much more powerful city than Thespiae, the grim losses suffered by the latter in a series of battles throughout the 5th century and into the 4th must have made it far more vulnerable to Thebes' bad moods. In the case of 423, Thucydides says explicitly that the Thebans took advantage of the fact that the "flower" of the Thespians had fallen against the Athenians at Delium the preceding year.[47] The Thespians left many impressive monuments to their war dead; but after amassing a peerless record of standing their ground, the Thespians lost their city – perhaps in large part because of the deadly process of amassing their record.

I should also note that in addition to being a victim of their own stubborn courage, the Thespians suffered at the hands of Agesilaus and Spartan efforts to bring "freedom" to the Greeks and interfere in the affairs of Boeotia. The Spartans' self-serving insistence that the Boeotians be independent led to the Battle of Leuctra and the collapse of Spartan power. It also doomed Thespiae, which had served as Sparta's ally and base of operations against Thebes.

Aside from being a fascinating study in commemoration in its own right, the case of Thespiae should alert us to the dangers inherent in the Spartan-style pursuit of glory and fame. One could be forgiven for getting the impression throughout this book that militarism is fine, so long as it is not tied to dressed-up campaigns abroad and the nearly continuous warfare such campaigns so often entail. In the context of Sparta, militarism *without* interventionism seems to have been preferable to militarism *with* interventionism, at least if the goal is to avoid war. Thespiae reveals the weaknesses in this line of thinking. Sparta was able to be militaristic and isolationist at the same time only because it was quite literally isolated in the southern Peloponnese from the wider world. Even Philip and Alexander did not bother with trying to add Sparta to their new Greco-Macedonian nation-state at the end of the 4th century, since they could allow the Spartans to while away their days safely cut off from what the rest of the world was doing.[48] Once the Spartans had deployed their militarism to amass power

---

[46] For a summary of these episodes, see Stylianou 1998: 367.

[47] Thuc. 4.133.1: παρεσχηκὸς δὲ ῥᾷον ἐπειδὴ καὶ ἐν τῇ πρὸς Ἀθηναίους μάχῃ ὅτι ἦν αὐτῶν ἄνθος ἀπωλώλει. For this passage, see Hornblower 1991–2008: vol. 2, 306, 411.

[48] Cartledge's treatment of Hellenistic Sparta in Cartledge and Spawforth 2002: 2–84 is a good overview of Sparta during the period of Macedonian rule. Sparta tried to reassert its power and independence on a few occasions, such as during the revolt of Agis III in 331, and the reign of Nabis in the late 3rd and early 2nd centuries, but these revivals were short-lived and failed to reestablish

in the Peloponnese through a succession of wars with their immediate neighbors, they could rest on their laurels with enough power and security to be both famous and safe. Without the preconditions of geographic security and a surrounding buffer of subjugated peoples, Spartan militarism might well have gotten the Spartans into far more trouble far earlier than it did. With a small population and a location right next to mighty and hostile Thebes, the Thespian drive to win glory killed too many Thespians, even without having to frame things as fighting for Greece or setting others free.

## Conclusion

In the 1970s and 1980s, it was all the rage to treat Agesilaus as a cipher to decode Sparta's decline. Eminent scholars such as George Cawkwell, Paul Cartledge, and Charles Hamilton explore the failure of Sparta's rigid system to conform to the new world of 4th-century Greece, and Agesilaus in particular did not rise to the perhaps insuperable challenge of envisioning or implementing a new way.[49] In some fundamental ways, I agree with my forebears and their analyses. The Spartan system was indeed ill suited to empire and foreign adventures, and Agesilaus did far too little to address social problems such as the dwindling size of Spartan estates and the consequently dwindling number of full Spartiates. As monstrously inhumane as the Spartan system of helotage was, it was also a strategic weak spot deftly exploited by Epaminondas and the Thebans after Leuctra. Agesilaus might not be to blame directly for the Battle of Leuctra, but he certainly bears a share of responsibility for the cracks in Sparta's armor that Leuctra broke open (Figure 6.3).

Yet, as I hope this exploration of Spartan commemoration makes clear, Agesilaus' traditionalism was among the least problematic aspects of his reign. The Spartan king's showdown with the Theban hoplites at Coronea,

---

Sparta as a major power. The checkered career of the Spartan king Cleomenes III presents us with an intriguing glimpse of post-Classical Sparta and how traditional military values worked in later periods. In Plutarch's biography, Cleomenes makes some statements that seem to contradict Spartan beliefs, while they are also self-contradictory. At one point, Cleomenes states his preference for fame (*doxa*) over practical advantage (*lusitelēs*, Plut. *Cleom.* 24.4), while at another, after he had fled from a disastrous battle against the Macedonians in which almost all the Spartans were killed, he speaks against a pointless death in battle (Plut. *Cleom.* 31.4–6). For Spartan values and the Battle of Sellasia in 222, which Cleomenes fled and after which he went into exile, see Trundle 2018. For the role of seeking after glory in Plutarch's *Lives* of these later Spartan rulers, see Roskam 2011.

[49] For Agesilaus' culpability in Sparta's decline, see Cawkwell 1976; Cartledge 1987; Hamilton 1979, 1991.

Figure 6.3 The Boeotian victory monument at Leuctra. Photo by C. Jacob Butera.

which earned him fame while nearly costing his life, should be less troubling than the fact he was in Boeotia fighting against Thebes at all. Fighting on in the face of good tactical sense is what the greatest Spartans had always done, but perennially interfering in the affairs of Boeotia was a relatively new development. That the Corinthian War happened at all is due in large part to Agesilaus' Panhellenist crusade in Asia, to liberate those Greeks his predecessor Lysander had sold out to the Persians. Whether this mission of liberation was the "right" thing to do, or whether Sparta could have done a better job stepping into Athens' shoes, are questions very much beside the point. The Spartans framing themselves as liberators as the Athenians had long done, and behaving like the Athenians, albeit clumsily, stretched and finally broke the Spartan system. Whether or not the framing of war as an act of liberation in service of a Panhellenist ideal of Greece directly caused Sparta to fight in more wars, this new form of commemoration and a greater number of wars certainly went hand-in-hand.

It is unlikely that any polis could have handled the burden Spartan had taken on. The Athenian Empire of the 5th century was brought down by the Peloponnesian War, and the Theban Hegemony of the 4th century lasted barely a decade. Ethnic federations such as the Thessalians under Jason of Pherai, and, ultimately, the Macedonians under Philip II, were to be the future of political and military organization in mainland Greece. Indeed, Philip justified his intervention in the affairs of Greece, and eventual conquest of Greece, by claiming to be the protector of Delphi and the unifier of Greece against the Persian Empire. Unlike Sparta, Philip had the financial and human resources to back up his rhetoric and support lengthy campaigns far from home. After the Battle of Chaeronea in 338, in which Philip decisively defeated a coalition of Greek poleis, and the foundation of a Greek league at Corinth under Philip's leadership the following year, Sparta largely withdrew from activities beyond its borders.

Philip virtually ignored the Spartans. His son, Alexander III (much better known as "the Great"), levelled against the Spartans what he must have considered a great insult. After the Battle of the Granicus River in 334, his first great victory against the Persians, Alexander sent 300 suits of Persian armor to the Athenian Acropolis as a dedication to Athena. The dedication was accompanied by the following inscription: "Alexander, son of Philip, and the Greeks except the Lacedaemonians dedicate these spoils from the barbarians who live in Asia."[50]

---

[50] Arr. *An.* 1.16.7; Plut. *Alex.* 16.8: Ἀλέξανδρος Φιλίππου καὶ οἱ Ἕλληνες πλὴν Λακεδαιμονίων ἀπὸ τῶν βαρβάρων τῶν τὴν Ἀσίαν κατοικούντων. For the meaning of this dedication, see Monti 2009, who argues that Alexander wanted to frame his campaign as a crusade against the Persians, and Alexander's official historian, Callisthenes, sought to treat this battle like the famous Battle of Marathon, as a victory of Greeks, without the help of Sparta, over Persians.

CHAPTER 7

# *From Thermopylae to* 300

## Introduction

We have traced how key tenets of Spartan commemoration were operative well before Thermopylae. Nevertheless, the Spartan myth and mirage, as later generations received them, were largely born at that battle. As Barry Strauss says, "Thermopylae is the prototype of many a last stand, from Roncesvalles to the Alamo to Isandlhwana to Bastogne."[1] In North America and Europe today the image of the Spartan warrior and the specter of Spartan militarism loom as large as they ever did. Political theorists have long recognized that Sparta's constitution, or at least Xenophon's outsider view of it and Plutarch's much later portrait, have informed the ideas of many modern political thinkers, especially Jean-Jacques Rousseau, one of the intellectual founders of the French Revolution. Today, Sparta's unique "mixed" constitution gains few admirers; rather, its fearsome warriors, standing firm for their convictions even in the face of certain death and defeat, are the real draw. Many admirers have fully bought in to Sparta's ancient propaganda, as encapsulated in and proliferated by war memorials and commemorative rituals. Ironically, this admiration is often based on an understanding of Sparta's role at Thermopylae – as a liberator selflessly standing against tyranny and fighting for civilization against barbarism – that the Spartans did not initially claim for themselves, as we have seen. When Sparta wedded its militaristic pursuit of glory to pretensions to liberation so popular today, wars grew in number and frequency, to Sparta's detriment (not to mention the detriment of many other Greeks).

The most recent surge in interest in militaristic Sparta can likely be traced to the release in 2006 of Zack Snyder's feature film *300*, based on the 1998 graphic novel by Frank Miller and Lynn Varley, which was itself largely based on the 1962 film *The 300 Spartans*. Since the release of

[1] Strauss 2004a.

197

Snyder's film, "Sparta" and "Spartan" have been applied in all sorts of marketing campaigns, from self-help books to fitness programs. More perniciously, Spartan imagery, including the lambda shield, standing for Lacedaemon, and the slogan ΜΟΛΩΝ ΛΑΒΕ, or *molōn labe*, "come and get them," supposedly uttered by Leonidas in response to the Persian demand that the Spartans lay down their weapons, have been adopted by various far-right groups. What better way to stand against the immigration of non-"Western" Muslims into Western Europe than by adopting the attitude of the Spartans standing against the invasion of Xerxes and his Persian Empire? And how better to defend the right to own any and all firearms than by defiantly echoing a Spartan king emblematic of the defense of freedom against despotism?

In this chapter, we will consider the modern reception of Sparta and Spartan militarism, and especially the afterlife of Thermopylae, that emblem of Spartan heroism and sacrifice. From 18th-century French *philosophes* and the framers of the United States Constitution, to commemorations of the Confederate dead in the American Civil War, and from theories of racial superiority that undergirded Prussian militarism and German Nazism, to Cold War monuments to Leonidas and the success of *300*, Spartan militarism continues to cast a long shadow. If we want to avoid the horrors of Spartan militarism, including its extreme violence and oppression of the marginalized, and understand the ways ancient Greek history can be used and abused in modern discourse, we should take a careful look at the modern reception of Sparta and its warriors. We must also reckon with how that reception has misunderstood Spartan ideals and their contexts.[2]

## Sparta in 18th-Century Political Theory

Elizabeth Rawson, in her seminal book *The Spartan Tradition in European Thought*, speaks of Jean-Jacques Rousseau as the "arch-priest of laconism."[3] Though Rousseau points to many historic states as exemplars for Early Modern revolutionaries to follow, he evoked Sparta most forcefully.[4] To be sure, Rousseau's ideas were far from universally shared in the 18th century. In the great debate between Athens and Sparta as models for the modern

---

[2] Carey 2019: 163–201 also surveys the modern reception of Thermopylae, with a greater focus on the Western poetic tradition. Cole 2021 is an admirable attempt to break Sparta's spell by showing that the Spartans were by no means invincible. According to Cole, Spartan militarism was not as effective as it was cracked up to be.

[3] Rawson 1969: 231–241.    [4] Mason 2012: 91.

world, Athens often came out on top. While many complained about
Periclean imperialism, and Hume pointed out that Athenian democracy
excluded more than it included, Voltaire, for one, strongly preferred
Athens to Sparta, and Fenelon viewed the Spartans as cruel, idle, and
excessively warlike, hardly the types to be copied in the modern age.[5]
Nevertheless, many of the most influential minds of the period recoiled
from Athenian direct democracy – the American founder James Madison,
for example, called democracy "the most vile form of government" – and
its supposed preference for arts and culture over action and austerity. The
most powerful of these anti-Athenian voices, and the champion of Sparta,
was Rousseau.

In 1750, Rousseau submitted an essay in response to a contest in which
participants were to answer the following question: "Has the restoration of
the sciences and arts contributed to the purification of morals?" Rousseau's
piece, now called his *First Discourse*, won the prize and stands as one of his
most important and formative writings. It is worth quoting from the *First
Discourse* at some length. Praising Sparta's virtuous ignorance, he states:

> Could I forget that it was the very heart of Greece that saw the emergence of
> that city as famous for its happy ignorance as for the wisdom of its laws,
> whose virtues seemed so much greater than those of men that it was
> a Republic of demi-gods rather than of men? O Sparta! How you eternally
> shame a vain doctrine! While the vices led along by the fine arts were
> introduced together with them in Athens, while a tyrant there collected
> with so much care the works of the prince of poets, you were chasing the
> arts, artists, the sciences, and learned men from your walls.[6]

Favorably comparing the noble actions carried out by Sparta with the
proverbial idle luxury of Sybaris, he says: "Thus one Sybarite would have
been worth at least thirty Lacedaemonians. Would someone therefore
hazard a guess which of these two republics, Sparta or Sybaris, was
overthrown by a handful of peasants and which one made Asia tremble?"

These two passages represent the heart of Rousseau's argument that the
arts and sciences introduce into a society many vices, chiefly among them
an unwarlike indolence. Sybaris, the Greek colony in Italy that was famous
for its decadent way of life, achieved nothing of note on the world stage,
especially in terms of warfare, and was ignominiously crushed. Sparta, on
the other hand, "made Asia tremble." Sparta, along with the ignorance of
its population, enjoyed remarkably wise laws, while Athens, resplendent in

---

[5] For the 18th-century "debate over Athens and Sparta," see Roberts 1994: 156–174.
[6] Translations of Rousseau are by Ian Johnston.

the trappings of high culture, was subservient to the whims of the tyrant Pisistratus. Beyond a discussion of mere virtue and vice, Rousseau is clear that the austere society of Sparta was the cause of military greatness, while luxury leads to military insignificance and even destruction by external enemies. Sparta, without luxury and with the ignorance of its citizens, humbled the mighty Persian Empire (what Rousseau means by "Asia"), the greatest empire the world had yet seen. The choice seems clear: ignoble luxury without noble military deeds, or noble austerity with military glory.

Of course, Rousseau overstates his case and misleads his readers concerning what kind of state yields the most effective soldiers. The real Sparta was remarkably fond of poetry, which was central to many festivals and rituals, including martial ones. The "Asia" that Sparta made tremble was humbled at least as much by the military might of luxurious Athens as by austere Sparta. In fact, in Herodotus' estimation (7.139), Athens, not Sparta, was the most responsible for the Greek victory in the Persian Wars. While in a pitched hoplite battle, the Spartans, who trained continuously for war, were nearly impossible to beat, in general the Spartans avoided war and used every excuse to avoid marching its army out of the Peloponnese. This isolationist tendency might in fact be a positive thing for thinkers like Rousseau, since imperialism is what funded much of Athens' luxury, but Spartan isolationism and its refusal to undertake long-term military expeditions abroad rendered Sparta far less militarily effective than its popular image would suggest, despite Rousseau's bold claim that Sparta "made Asia tremble." Isolationism, or not caring too much about "Greece" outside of its own territory, kept Spartan violence in check precisely when "Asia" was threatening the Greek mainland.

Rousseau's admiration for Sparta, however, went well beyond its supposed disdain for arts, culture, and luxury of any kind. Given that Sparta played such a formative role in Rousseau's political philosophy, we can reasonably assume that some of his most important political concepts were also inspired by Sparta, primary among them the idea of the General Will. Spelled out most clearly in his 1762 treatise, *The Social Contract*, the General Will is the common assent given by all members of a community to subsume their individual desires to the community as a whole. This collectivist spirit is something for which the Spartans themselves were indeed famous, and which supposedly inspired renowned military actions like the last stand at Thermopylae. Paul Rahe explicitly compares the Spartan solidarity that brooks no dissent, which the Greeks called *homonoia* (literally, "same-mindedness" or "unanimity"), with

Rousseau's General Will.[7] The Spartan take on freedom and subordination of the individual will to the will of the state is what even many ancients believed made the stand at Thermopylae as effective as it was, and possible in the first place. Yet, as I have argued, a desire for glory and remembrance should not be discounted as a powerful motivator in 480, likely more so than feelings of patriotism or communitarianism.[8]

Rousseau's idea of the General Will, along with his broader discussions on the nature of freedom, are very complex topics often yielding seemingly contradictory conclusions.[9] Primary among Rousseau's apparent contradictions is his idea of forced freedom, that sometimes it is necessary to *force* an individual to be free by bending their will to be in accordance with the General Will. As Cohen puts it:

> Those of us who are attracted to the ideal of a free community of equals need to take seriously the fact that one of its great exponents combined it with an (unattractively) anti-political communitarianism, with a large emphasis of solidarities built on national distinctiveness, and the fear that disagreement is the canary in the coal mine, rather than a normal condition of the only kind of political life worth hoping for.[10]

This forced consensus and forced freedom can be seen in action in an ancient Spartan context during the general Brasidas' mission to Thrace in 424, which we considered in Chapter 4. After approaching the city of Acanthus, a subject city of Athens that Brasidas wished to dislodge to the Spartan side in the war, Brasidas was taken aback by being shut out of the city. Framing himself as the liberator of Acanthus, as Thucydides portrays him at least, Brasidas extols to the people of Acanthus the genuine freedom the Spartan military will bring them. He then adds a warning, however, by saying that he and his soldiers will ravage Acanthus' ripening crops should the city be unwilling to come over to him. In effect, he forces Acanthus to be free by threat of military violence. As I have argued at greater length elsewhere, we need not dismiss Brasidas' rhetoric as mere hypocrisy. Instead, Brasidas' threat of forced freedom was very much in line with Sparta's idea of freedom existing in the subordination of the individual to the state and its laws, and in tune with Rousseau's ideas.[11]

---

[7] Rahe 2016: 35. For the Spartan constitution's unique ability to foster this *homonoia*/General Will, see Rahe's discussion in 36–63.

[8] For Spartan fear of and obedience to the laws, see Chapter 3.

[9] For more on this topic, see Cullen 1993; Cartledge 1999; Simpson 2006; Cohen 2010; MacDonald and Hoffmann 2012.

[10] Cohen 2010: 5.     [11] Sears 2015.

Insofar as it was successful, Spartan society and its military depended upon each individual Spartan prioritizing the state over his own will and desires. The Spartan phalanx could brook no dissent, or even free thought, in its ranks. The centrality of this communitarianism, or *homonoia*, or the General Will, to Spartan society is what made one Spartan's actions at the Battle of Plataea, when he refused to withdraw on the orders of his commander, so outrageous and nearly disastrous. Herodotus' story of this Spartan's disobedience, however, is rather fishy, given that the Spartan chained himself to a rock and refused to move, claiming that the rock represented his vote to stay put (Hdt. 9.52–55). It was the Athenians, not the Spartans, who voted with pebbles.[12] In any case, this ethic of communitarianism was certainly felt in Sparta by the time of the Peloponnesian War; Brasidas merely extended this principle to Sparta's allies or would-be allies. The entire Spartan war effort would be jeopardized if Athenian subjects refused to welcome the Spartans as liberators and fight on their side, which would result in the Greeks remaining unfree under the Athenian yoke. Rousseau, the "archpriest of laconism," felt the same way about the society he conceived of in *The Social Contract*. Just as the Spartan rejection of luxury made the Spartans better men and better soldiers, so, too, did their militaristic adherence to the General Will. Rousseau would not have been surprised that the luxurious and relatively individualistic Athenians never made a stand as famous as the Spartan one at Thermopylae. The Athenian empire, though, born from the spirit of "liberation," made the Athenians rather prone to violence abroad in the 5th century, much more so than the Spartans were before the Peloponnesian War.

During and after the French Revolution, Jacques-Louis David emerged as one of the most important Neoclassical painters. David favored revolutionary themes, as can be seen, for example, in his 1784 *Oath of the Horiatii*, which depicts the famous Roman brothers swearing their patriotic allegiance before venturing out to fight the Curiatii, a story told by the historian Livy. This sort of sacrificial patriotism would be revered during the Revolution that broke out five years after the painting was completed. David also explored revolutionary themes through depictions of the Spartans in his masterpiece *Leonidas at Thermopylae*, begun in 1799 during the Revolutionary period but not finished until 1814, when Napoleon ruled France and Waterloo was on the horizon (Figure 7.1). David's take on

---

[12] Flower and Marincola 2002: 205. Herodotus did declare this Spartan, Amompharetus, to be the fourth bravest man in the Spartan army during the battle (9.71).

Figure 7.1 Jacques-Louis David, *Leonidas at Thermopylae* (1814). Paris, Louvre 3690.
© RMN-Grand Palais / Art Resource, NY.

Leonidas and the Three Hundred remains one of the most famous images of Spartan warriors, and indeed of any ancient Greek subject.

Emma Clough provides an interesting overview of David's painting, its context, and David's own fortunes during the Revolutionary and Napoleonic eras.[13] As Clough notes, on the surface the painting evokes a clear parallel between the selfless patriotism of the Spartans and their leader with the French revolutionaries, fighting for freedom at home and keeping foreign despots at bay. On the other hand, Napoleon had mixed feelings about the work. When he first saw its progress, early in his reign, he scorned an image of military defeat, preferring instead portrayals of victorious generals and armies. Yet, nearing the end of his rule, when the painting was finally completed, Napoleon saw that his best outcome might be as another Leonidas, defeated on the battlefield but morally victorious. In the end, David's work shows both that the Spartans, and Leonidas and the Three Hundred in particular, could be read in various ways, and that

---

[13] Clough 2004.

Sparta and the military valor of the Three Hundred were popular and widely recognizable motifs in Revolutionary and Napoleonic France, as they had been for Rousseau a generation earlier.[14] Few things could inspire patriotic self-sacrifice in the violent revolutionary struggles at home in the name of freedom, and on the pitch of a foreign battlefield in the service of an emperor, like Leonidas and his men. Not included in this understanding of the Spartans is the fact that Leonidas and his men did not advertise that they were fighting for freedom, nor that they interested in self-sacrifice beyond the glory it would bring them.

## Sparta in 19th-Century America

On August 2, 1813, during the War of 1812, Major George Croghan was significantly outnumbered by his foes, the combined forces of the British under Major-General Henry Procter and Indigenous soldiers led by Tecumseh. Nevertheless, Croghan successfully defended Fort Stephenson in Ohio. This victory exposed the incompetence of Procter, forcing him to withdraw to Canada, and led to several more American victories in the coming months. The 160 American soldiers in the fort inflicted 96 casualties (killed, wounded, or missing) on the 1,400 soldiers of the enemy, while suffering only 8 casualties themselves, including 1 dead and 7 wounded. In the annals of warfare, the Battle of Fort Stephenson was a relatively minor affair, but decades later it was commemorated with great pomp and circumstance.

The Soldiers' Monument on the Site of Fort Stephenson was unveiled at Fremont, Ohio, in 1885. General R. R. Buckland gave an address to dedicate the monument, a Corinthian column topped by an infantry soldier. In his effusive praise of those who defended Fort Stephenson, General Buckland said: "The heroic and patriotic devotion of Major Croghan and his brave men, in their determination to hold and defend Fort Stephenson to the last man, has never been surpassed in the annals of warfare, not even by the world-renowned Spartan band at Thermopylae." To compare the successful defense of the fort, at the cost of only seven casualties, to the desperate and unsuccessful last stand at Thermopylae, in which so many defenders were killed, shows just how broadly the Battle of Thermopylae could be applied to modern military conflict. It also

---

[14] Clough also discusses Richard Glover's sweeping 1737 epic *Leonidas*, which entailed manifold interpretations in an England beset by conflicts between those loyal to King George II and those hoping for a better and more rightly patriotic king in the figure of his son, Frederick, Prince of Wales. See also Macgregor Morris 2000 for a discussion of Glover and his legacy.

demonstrates that in the late 19th century, Thermopylae was the paradigm of military heroism. Just as the Spartans had a long tradition of soldierly valor, so, too, did the residents of Sandusky County, where the fort stood. General Buckland continues in his address to praise the uncommon heroism and patriotism of the men of Sandusky County, who had "shed their blood on more than a hundred battlefields." The monument was therefore dedicated to these men, including the ones who fought at the initial engagement at the fort in 1813, but also those who fought in the Mexican War and the Civil War.

The Fort Stephenson memorial is in a Northern state, and those residents of Sandusky County so praised by General Buckland who fought in the Civil War did so on the Union side. But it was in the South, in the context of remembering those who died for the Confederacy, that the model of Thermopylae was especially powerful, the ultimate sacrifice in service of a noble but lost cause. Particularly powerful and representative are the words of Robert Stiles delivered at the dedication of the Monument to the Confederate Dead at the University of Virginia in 1893. He argues that the defeated often die for the nobler cause and display greater valor:

> It is much to know that the victor does not always wear the laurel, nor the vanquished the chain. It is more to feel that the chain may be more glorious than the laurel . . . .. By the verdict of history the Persian monarch who carried the Pass of Thermopylae has fallen before Leonidas and his Spartans, who fell in defence of it. Who now ranks Scipio above Hannibal, or Wellington above Napoleon? How many of you can so much as name the general who drove the great Corsican out of Russia?

Stiles compares the glory of the Confederate dead to the glory of the Spartans and other great warriors throughout history, even those who lost. He also embarks on a lengthy defense of the Confederate cause, arguing that it was far more just than the Union *casus belli*: "There is a naked simplicity and sincerity of right in the man who defends his hearth-stone, which does not belong to him who invades it." Here the comparison with Thermopylae is again apt. Leonidas and his Three Hundred were, after all, defending their homes and the homes of other Greeks from an aggressor invading from the north, were they not? At least in the tradition that came down to Stiles, they were. (There is another obvious parallel, too, in that both the Spartan and Southern way of life depended on enslave-ment and forced labor, regardless of appeals to liberty.) Like Buckland in the case of Sandusky Country, Ohio, Stiles emphasizes the martial charac-ter of the students at the University of Virginia, who could boast a far higher rate of enlistment, and death, in the service of the Confederacy than Harvard University could boast for the Union.

Stiles carries on the Spartan tradition of venerating great generals as heroes, even in the religious sense in which the Greeks understood the term "hero." Where Leonidas had a tomb and Brasidas a cenotaph at Sparta, in addition to the monuments and honors they received elsewhere, Stiles likens the Confederate generals Robert E. Lee and Stonewall Jackson to "demigods." As he praised the spirit of sacrifice and patriotism that animated the Confederate dead honored by the memorial for which he was speaking, he also delivered a lengthy hagiography of Lee and Jackson, remarking on their physical appearance and comportment, as well as their strategic and tactical genius. As Leonidas and the Three Hundred set the example for all future Spartans to follow, so, too, did Lee, Jackson, and those Confederate soldiers who boldly rushed into the fray to defend hearth and home, and the dubious principles on which those hearths and homes were based.

The Battle of Shiloh, fought in southwestern Tennessee in 1862, was one of the bloodiest of the Civil War, and was a defeat for the Confederacy. A monument to the 2nd Tennessee Infantry, a unit that suffered a 65 percent casualty rate in the battle, was erected near Shiloh in 1903, consisting of a common soldier standing atop a granite base. The monument itself might be less than spectacular, but its inscriptions are loaded with classicizing bombast. On one side, the stone exhorts the visitor: "Go stranger, and tell Tennessee | that here we died for her." These lines clearly mirror those attributed to Simonides inscribed for Lacedaemonians at Thermopylae. More classical allusion is found on another side of the monument's base, which says, *dignum et justum est* | *pro patria mori*, or, "it is worthy and just to die for one's country." This inscription is a slight rewording of the Roman poet Horace's famous lines, *dulce et decorum est* | *pro patria mori*, or, "it is sweet and fitting to die for one's country," a sentiment that echoes very closely the much older words of the Spartan poet Tyrtaeus, which we have considered earlier. The sacrifice of the Three Hundred was employed to inspire future generations of Spartans, and the words of Tyrtaeus were geared to recruiting more soldiers into the Spartan war machine. The monument at Shiloh likewise serves to set an example to future Tennesseans to live up to the brave example of their forebears, who bled so much in defense of their home state in 1862.

Evocation of the stand of the Three Hundred at Thermopylae in 19th-century America was not limited to occasions of military commemoration. The poet Emily Dickinson referred several times to Thermopylae, both in her poetry and in her private correspondence. Dickinson used Thermopylae as a way to express self-sacrifice in the service of one's country, and also an individual's resoluteness and principled love for the law. As James R. Guthrie puts it, "the battle of Thermopylae... provided the poet with a metatrope that evolved over the course of her adulthood from a conventional recognition of a military sacrifice made for the sake of the state to an intensely personal symbol of selflessness and emotional steadfastness."[15] While Dickinson explicitly mentions Thermopylae more than once, she also alludes to it quite strongly in several places, including in correspondence written during the Civil War, when ideas of martial virtue, but also the importance of the rule of law, were an important part of the discourse.

That Thermopylae could be used to convey such a range of ideas, and that it was readily to hand for someone as far from conventional military service as Emily Dickinson, bespeaks the widespread fame of the battle, at least among the well educated, in 19th-century America. But it should also counsel caution. The evocation of Thermopylae was never a neutral or pedantic reference to history. Rather, it was always meant to inspire a certain kind of military valor, an emulation of fallen warriors to the point of the ultimate self-sacrifice, and often in the service of an odious cause, such as the Confederacy. One did not recall Leonidas and the Three Hundred in the service of resolving things peacefully, or thinking critically of one's forebears.

## Sparta in 19th- and 20th-Century Germany

In a fascinating article, Gonda Van Steen considers the use of a famous line from Aeschylus' *Persians*, "now the struggle is for all!," in Greece during the early 1940s. This line and other Persian War tropes were initially used to foster unity among the Greeks in order to resist the Italian and German invaders of 1941, despite the divisive and repressive nature of the Greek government of Ioannis Metaxas. But by the war's end, such classical allusions were adopted by the right as a way to galvanize opposition to the left, even those leftists who had played a key role in the resistance to German occupation. Van Steen explores how different sides in Greece could make use of the same material, and how right and left influenced one another's rhetoric and propaganda.[16]

---

[15] Guthrie 2015: 174.    [16] Van Steen 2010.

In the next three sections, I want to go beyond the use of the Persian War among the Greeks to explore how Germany, Great Britain, and the United States, and to a lesser extent Greece itself, drew especially on the Thermopylae legend to promote their own respective causes, both during the war and afterward. As we will see, unlike in Greece, riven by factional strife and civil war, among the great powers there was no right versus left in the use of Thermopylae. Rather, there was only right, or at least anti-communist and anti-Soviet, use. In their fierce opposition to communism, and Soviet communism in particular, the Third Reich and United States made use of remarkably similar rhetoric, in which Thermopylae formed a centerpiece.

On January 30, 1943, just three days before the surrender of the German Sixth Army at Stalingrad – one of the decisive moments of the Second World War (or the Great Patriotic War for the Soviets) – Hermann Göring gave a speech to a delegation representing the entire Wehrmacht, the German armed forces.[17] On the tenth anniversary of Hitler's rise to power as chancellor, Göring, supreme commander of the Luftwaffe and one of Hitler's closest lieutenants, chose to focus on Germany's increasingly desperate situation on the Eastern Front. He claimed that only Germany stood between the barbarities of Russian Bolshevism and the European way of life. Where Stalin had enslaved subjects in the millions to hurl against the Germans, Germany had soldiers and a people willing to die freely for their homeland, to stem the tide of the Eastern onslaught and preserve not only Germany, but also all of Europe and the "West."

Göring's Germans look a lot like the patriotic Greeks in Aeschylus and Herodotus, and his Russians look like Greek literature's Persians, hordes driven forward by the whips of Xerxes' commanders. To make the comparison explicit, Göring quoted Simonides' famous epigram. The Germans, too, would die in honor of and to preserve their own laws: "In days to come it will be said thus: when you come home to Germany, tell them that you have seen us lying at Stalingrad, as the rule of honour and the conduct of war have ordained that we must do, for Germany's sake." Hitler himself evoked Thermopylae when he promoted General Friedrich Paulus, the ranking officer at Stalingrad, to field marshal mere days before the German surrender. Since no German field marshal had ever surrendered, Hitler reckoned that Paulus would fight to the death, just like Leonidas. Much to Hitler's chagrin, Paulus surrendered and became

---

[17] For a summary of Göring's speech, see the *Bulletin of International News* 20. 3 (Feb. 6, 1943), 100–104.

a Russian prisoner, evoking rather the captive Spartans of Pylos. There is no mistaking the importance of the Spartans, and especially Leonidas and the Three Hundred, as exemplars for Nazi Germany.

Perhaps surprisingly, in the early years of the Greek and Roman Classics as an academic discipline in Western Europe, Sparta was not initially as popular among German-speakers as it was in France and Britain. In the 18th century, Germans tended to prefer Athens to Sparta, and some German scholars actually criticized the Spartans' mission to Thermopylae and the last stand of Leonidas and the Three Hundred as a strategic and tactical failure. But during the 19th century, as Helen Roche argues, particularly among the elite ranks of the Royal Prussian Cadet Corps, Sparta became an important educational example for aspiring soldiers.[18] In his review of Roche's book in the *Journal of Hellenic Studies*, Roel Konijnendijk points out that the German military historians, such as Johannes Kromayer and Georg Veith, who popularized Thermopylae and undertook detailed studies of that battle site and others throughout Greece were products of these Prussian schools.[19] In the latter half of the century, during the period of the German Empire, or *Kaiserreich*, beginning in 1871, Sparta grew in popularity amongst an ever broader section of society, and Leonidas and the Three Hundred were generally lauded as paragons of selfless patriotism.[20] This view of the Spartans shaped how many Germans conceived of the duty of soldiers fighting in the First World War, and was instrumental in how the Germans valorized their war dead.

Before Stalingrad, Germany's Thermopylae was Langemarck, a site near Ypres in Belgium where thousands of German soldiers, particularly youth volunteers, were slaughtered in the early months of the First World War in 1914 (as part of the so-called "First Battle of Ypres").[21] Today, Langemarck is home to one of the largest First World War cemeteries for the German war dead. There, among the understated and somber grave monuments, the following inscription can be seen: "wanderer kommst du nach Deutschland, verkündige dorten du habest | Uns hier liegen gesehen, wie das Gesetz es befahl" ("traveler, come to Germany, tell there that you have

---

[18] Roche 2013, especially 33–156.
[19] Konijnendijk 2015. Kromayer and Veith's multivolume *Antike Schlachtfelder* (*Ancient Battlefields*), with its detailed topographical maps and collection of the ancient sources for pitched battles, set the standard for battlefield studies, and remains an indispensable resource for ancient military historians.
[20] For an overview of Sparta in German thought from the 18th to the 20th centuries, see Rebenich 2006. See also Losemann 2012 for the period 1870–1945.
[21] Losemann 2012: 269 cites Reinbach's remark that Prussian cadets "experienced their Thermopylae with the battle of Langemarck in 1914."

seen us lying here, as bidden by the law"). This translation and paraphrase of Simonides' lines, via the German translation of Friedrich Schiller, marks a poignant reference to Thermopylae.[22] Although it was a total military failure, Langemarck, like Thermopylae, came to be seen as a moral victory and to embody the German spirit of patriotism. In the interwar period especially, Langemarck was an important rallying cry, giving birth to the powerful myth of the "Youth of Langemarck." While the Entente powers celebrated Armistice Day on November 11, many Germans, led by influential student and youth movements, celebrated "Langemarck Day" on the very same date. November 11 was also an important day in the battle near Langemarck.[23] As Bernd Hüppauf says, "through constant repetition in literature, the media, the school curriculum and public celebrations, [Langemarck] had become synonymous with the programme of rejuvenation of the German nation developed by 'political romanticism' during the Weimar Republic."[24]

The Nazis also embraced the Langemarck myth, especially before 1933. In *Mein Kampf*, Hitler made sure to mention that he had been at Langemarck. The Nazi youth groups eventually absorbed the other German youth movements (usually by force) and co-opted Langemarck for their own political purposes. After 1933, when Hitler and the Nazis were firmly in power, they no longer needed to employ the popular Langemarck motif to such a great extent. The Battle of Verdun came to replace Langemarck in the Nazis' developing ideology of the "new man."[25] Nevertheless, Langemarck and other images of Sparta remained vitally important for the Nazis, and formed a central part of Nazi propaganda and education.

Beyond the self-sacrifice of Thermopylae, and the subservience of the Spartan individual to the state that Thermopylae exemplified, the Nazis emphasized the supposed racial characteristics of the Spartans. The pleasure-seeking and individualistic Ionians (especially the Athenians) were contrasted with the austere Dorian Spartans. The Dorians, unlike other Greeks, were thought to have invaded Greece and the Peloponnese from the north, even northern Europe, and were thus Nordic kin to the

---

[22] See the short story by Heinrich Böll entitled *Wanderer, kommst du nach Spa*, first published in 1950, that calls into question the use of Simonides' lines as propaganda prior to and during the Second World War. See Watt 1985 for a discussion of the short story and its context.

[23] For the importance of Langemarck and the "Youth of Langemarck" in interwar Germany, see Ketelsen 1985; Hüppauf 1988; and Losemann 2012: 269. See also Roche 2013 for the importance of Sparta for Prussian and Nazi-German education, from the early 19th to the mid 20th century.

[24] Hüppauf 1988: 78.    [25] Hüppauf 1988, especially 82–86.

Germans, in fact fellow Aryans. The Spartans, too, were thought to have maintained a racially pure society that dominated and exploited the lesser races in their territory, just as the Nazis hoped to do. One of the foremost scholars of the ancient world in Germany, Helmut Berve, provided the intellectual underpinnings of Nazism by stressing the appropriateness of Spartan society – its encouragement of manliness and the subordination of the individual will to the state – as a model for a German *Reich*.[26] Making it seem as if the *Indiana Jones* films contain a measure of truth, in the 1930s the arch propagandists of the Nazis, Josef Goebbels and Albert Speer, visited Greece to study "the relics of the Dorian world."[27] The alleged cultural and racial links between Sparta and Germany were an integral part of Nazi propaganda, revealed especially in Nazi education programs.

A selective understanding of the Spartans went beyond the realm of politics to drive the Nazi aesthetic. Julia Hell, in her essential book on the Third Reich's reception of classical antiquity, traces many aspects of Nazi appropriation of Spartan imagery. In one revealing section, she demonstrates how the intellectual and poet Gottfried Benn was fixated on the image of the Spartan warrior, based on bodies "perfected in the gymnasium and on the battlefield." Benn drew upon the Spartan as the masculine model for Nazi art and the Nazi state. Like the Spartans, the Nazis were to be motivated by honor instead of baser things like profit. An aesthetic based on the Spartan ideal would reinforce such notions.[28]

In an important chapter, Helen Roche details how important Sparta was in the elite Adolf Hitler Schools run by the SS from 1937 to 1945 to train the next generation of fanatical Nazi leaders. A textbook for these schools, *Der Lebenskampf einer nordischen Herrenschicht* (*The Life-Struggle of a Nordic Male Society*), written by Otto-Wilhelm von Vacano, focuses on Sparta and is laden with Nazi tropes. Waxing at length about Sparta's militarism, community-centeredness, and propensity for self-sacrifice, the book also featured a chapter on Spartan education, and how its principles could be applied in Germany.[29] Not only was Sparta popular in late 19th and early 20th-century Germany among a wide cross-section of society, for the Nazis it formed a central plank in the education of their most promising young recruits in the most elite programs. As the famous Jewish classicist Arnaldo Momigliano said, the Nazis integrated Thermopylae and Sparta into a religion that "had its major sanctuaries at Dachau and Auschwitz."[30]

---

[26] Rebenich 2006: 204.     [27] Losemann 2012: 277.     [28] Hell 2019: 353–361.
[29] Roche 2012. Roche goes into far more detail about the importance of Sparta for 19th-century Prussian and Nazi-German education in her 2013 book, *Sparta's German Children*.
[30] Momigliano 1966: 707–708, as quoted in Rebenich 2018: 698.

Another important study that demonstrates the striking similarities between the Third Reich and ancient Sparta is that of Thomas Kühne on the concept of comradeship in the Wehrmacht. Kühne focused on the regular soldiers of the Wehrmacht, as opposed to the fanatical Nazis of the SS, on the Eastern Front. He argues that it was the ideal of comradeship that allowed the Wehrmacht soldiers to participate in and provide support for Nazi atrocities, and to stick together to the bitter end, even when the defeat of Germany was imminent and obvious. In the Third Reich, comradeship encompassed many ideas and practices that would have been familiar to ancient Spartans. For example, the separation of so many German men from "civilian society" facilitated the subordination of the will of the individual soldier to the will of the state:

> For it was the army that kept the bulk of German men, 17 million in total, under control and had, by separating them physically and emotionally over years from their families and friends – from the foundations of their civilian identities – more effective means at hand to brainwash, or "re-educate," Germans than the Nazi rulers could ever have acquired at home.[31]

Bringing to mind the social death faced by the *tresantes*, or "tremblers," in Sparta, those Germans who were not subservient to the collective faced a similar fate: "Whoever was not willing to sacrifice the I on the altar of the We was threatened with an 'unbearable existence'."[32] The self-sacrificing nature of comradeship applied to women in Germany, too, just as in Sparta. On this point, Kühne quotes Hitler himself, who said, "In the Third Reich, the woman has her own battlefield. With every child she brings into the world, she fights her battle for the nation."[33] Because of the use to which comradeship had been put in the Third Reich – a use that was eerily similar to the constant camp life of the Spartan soldier and the total military orientation of Spartan society – in today's largely pacifist Germany, praising the bonds that form between fellow soldiers is viewed with deep suspicion. This suspicion is a very different reaction to soldierly bonds than is still generally seen in the US, a country that is now markedly more militaristic than Germany.[34]

Whereas some German scholars such as Berve never recanted their pro-Nazi work on Sparta, another German historian, Victor Ehrenberg, a decorated veteran of the First World War who had also idealized Sparta, came to change his views. As a Jew, Ehrenberg fled Prague for England on the eve of the Second World War, and, in light of the Nazi

---

[31] Kühne 2017: 9.    [32] Kühne 2017: 81.    [33] Kühne 2017: 86.    [34] Kühne 2017: 291.

horrors of the 1930s and 1940s, came to see Sparta as a dangerous precursor to totalitarian states.[35] The Nazi German use of Sparta warns us against the myth of neutrality when writing about and teaching historical topics, even ancient historical topics. Without commenting on the scholarly accuracy of the work of Berve and others – some of them were indeed fine philologists – those who are students and scholars of the ancient world must be on guard against their work being co-opted by odious ideologues. If ancient Greek history is to continue to be an important part of the educational curriculum (and I think that it should be), ancient Greek historians must be aware of the ways in which their subject matter has been interpreted and put to work, both in the past and the present.

## The Allies and Thermopylae

In response to the Greeks' dogged resistance to the Italian invasion through Albania in 1940–1941, Winston Churchill famously said, "Hence, we will not say that Greeks fight like heroes, but that heroes fight like Greeks." Throughout the war, the resistance of Greece, its subsequent occupation by the Germans, and its liberation by the British, would serve as a powerful symbol of the struggle for freedom against Germany and National Socialism. Greece's ancient past, especially the stand of Leonidas and the Three Hundred, would be evoked many times during the war, both in relation to Greece itself and further afield. In many ways, this use of Greece's ancient past to rally a modern war effort is similar to the use of Hellenism to attract support for Greece's war of independence against the Ottomans in the early 19th century.[36] In this section, let us consider some of the mentions of Thermopylae between 1939 and 1945 in major public outlets like *The Times* of London and the *New York Times*. On September 19, 1939, in an article called "The Price of Freedom," *The Times* compared the heroic resistance of the Poles against insuperable odds to Leonidas and the Three Hundred: "[The Polish Army] has held the pass for civilization with a valour no less heroic than that of Leonidas and the three hundred of Thermopylae. In spite of the desperate odds which it confronted, its resistance was not broken until, like the Spartans, it was struck down by treachery from the rear." Germany had invaded on September 1, and the Soviets on September 17, just two days before this

---

[35] Rebenich 2006: 203.

[36] Macgregor Morris 2000 is an important discussion of the role of Hellenism, and the imagery of Leonidas and Thermopylae in particular, in garnering support for Greek liberation in the 19th century.

article was published. It was this Soviet invasion that was likened to Ephialtes' treachery at Thermopylae, as if Poland could otherwise have held out against the might of the Third Reich. The article goes on to assure the Poles that "they have the sympathy, and indeed the reverence, not only of their allies in Western Europe, but of all civilized peoples throughout the globe who still hold the values of the spirit, and who recognize a great nation in the few who fight and die for liberty rather than in the multitudes who are mobilized for their destruction."[37]

On February 2, 1940, *The Times* reported on an address from the Anglican Primate of Finland and the Bishop of Tempere, as read by the Archbishop of Canterbury in St. Paul's Cathedral in London. The Finnish clergy insisted that in the fight against Stalin they were "defending the precious inheritance of our common Christian civilization" from "forces of heathen barbarism that have to be destroyed if law and liberty are to survive anywhere in Europe." The Archbishop of Canterbury then compared the struggle of the Finns to the Maccabean Revolt, and warned that, "magnificent as has been the resistance of this northern Thermopylae, the conditions that have given to free valour and intelligence their advantage over the dull weight of vast servile hordes will not last the winter."[38] Tellingly, the motifs of slavish, barbaric hordes, and the many against the few, is used by the British press in relation to the Soviet communists in the early months of the war, just as they would be used by Göring in 1943.

At the end of October 1940, Italy invaded Greece, followed by a German invasion in April 1941 after the Italian forces broke against Greek resistance and counterattacks. On March 18, 1941, as reported by *The Times*, the Greek king commended Greece's soldiers for "writing in blood a glorious epic of the newer Greece on the snow-covered mountains of Epirus and Albania." He chalked up the successes of the Greek soldiers to the fact that "the blood of the fighters of Marathon and Thermopylae flows in [their] veins."[39] On April 23, less than three weeks after the Germans invaded Greece, taking over from the Italians, *The Times* reported on the tributes pouring in for the New Zealand troops who fought bravely against the German advance near Mt. Olympus. The Germans themselves praised the New Zealanders, and the New Zealand prime minister said that "the fighters who stood at Marathon and Thermopylae had worthy successors in those who fought on the slopes of Mount Olympus," echoing the words of the Greek king

---

[37] *The Times*, Sept. 19, 1939, p. 7.    [38] *The Times*, Feb. 2, 1940, p. 9.
[39] *The Times*, March 19, 1941, p. 4.

in praise of his own army.[40] On April 29, as the resistance of the British, Anzac, and Greek forces was nearing its breaking point after fierce fighting, including at the pass of Thermopylae itself, *The Times* correspondent remarked that, "history records no more gallant stand than that which the few made against the many among the snow-clad mountains of Greece."[41] The evocation of well-worn Thermopylae tropes is plain in this tribute to the hopeless fight against the German onslaught.

Once Greece fell, with the capture of Athens at the end of April and the fall of Crete by the beginning of June, the hope for eventual freedom for the Greeks remained alive, and Greece continued to be a symbol in the Allied press of the stakes of the struggle against the Axis. On June 7, *The Times* printed the words of the Greek prime minister, who proclaimed that "Together with Thermopylae and the Gate of Romanos [a reference to the 1453 fall of Constantinople], the martyrdom of Crete will inspire for centuries the ideals of our race; and out of the fire of the battles in Albania, Thrace, and Crete, the phoenix of Greek freedom will rise once again."[42] In its October 31 edition, *The Times* reported on celebrations at Westminster of the first anniversary of the Greeks taking up arms against the Italian invasion force. The Greek prime minister said that "when the land of Greece was liberated in the certain day of victory, the Greeks would raise up a mound of holy earth as their ancestors did at Thermopylae centuries ago to cover the mortal remains of these heroes, and render immortal the valour and sacrifice of British and Greek comrades-in-arms."[43]

When Athens was finally liberated by British forces in October 1944, celebrations were held across Allied nations. As reported in the *New York Times* on October 15, Newbold Morris, president of the city council of New York, told a gathering of Greeks and Americans that "the courage which made it possible to turn back the Persians at Thermopylae, which won freedom for modern Greece from the Turks, which all but drove the Fascists back to the sea, has kept twenty German divisions pinned down in the Aegean throughout the war." He was joined by John D. Kalgeris, Greek consul general in New York, who said that the liberation of the Greek capital "is a victory for the ideas that Athens has represented through 2,000 years."[44] To those gathered in such celebrations, Greece's – and the world's – freedom seemed assured.

---

[40] *The Times*, April 23, 1941, p. 3.   [41] *The Times*, April 29, 1941, p. 4.
[42] *The Times*, June 7, 1941, p. 3.   [43] *The Times*, Oct. 31, 1941, p. 2.
[44] *The New York Times*, Oct. 15, 1944, p. 27.

## Sparta in the Cold War

The theme of brave Western soldiers standing against barbarous Bolshevik hordes from the East did not die with the Third Reich. Instead, the United States and its NATO allies took up the mantle of defenders of "Western Civilization" against the relentless tide of communism during the Cold War. The image of Thermopylae, along with the site itself in Greece, took on new life, as a symbol of West versus East and freedom versus tyranny, among those Western societies that had helped to destroy Nazism and now stood against their former ally in that struggle, the Soviet Union. How NATO framed its new struggle was remarkably similar to how Göring had in 1943.

Greece was far from out of the woods after its liberation in late 1944. Even before the war was over, in support of a reinstalled right-wing government in Athens British forces ruthlessly crushed leftist factions, many of whom had played leading roles in the resistance to the Nazis. Following the Second World War, Greece became a focal point for the developing Cold War as it endured several years of civil war between the Hellenic Army, supported by Britain and the United States, and the communist Democratic Army of Greece, supported by various Eastern European powers (but not, directly, by the Soviet Union). The anti-communist forces were eventually victorious in 1949, but the war left Greece devastated and riven by factional strife. Greece joined NATO in 1952, an official ally against the Soviet Union and the Eastern Bloc, though at times only military coercion kept Greece on that side, as demonstrated by the Greek military's seizure of power from 1967 to 1974. Despite, or rather because of, the internal tension in Greece, Western powers used sites in Greece itself, along with themes from Greece's past, to bolster a pro-Western, anti-communist agenda.

Dean Acheson, the American undersecretary of state after the war, summed up his view of the post-war situation in Greece in his 1987 memoirs:

> The year 1946 was for the most part a year of learning that minds in the Kremlin worked very much as George F. Kennan had predicted they would. ... The Russians themselves greatly helped our education. In picking the [Dardanelles] straits and Iran as points of pressure, they followed the route of invasion by barbarians against classical Greece and Rome and later of the czars to warm water. From Thermopylae to the Crimea the responses to pressure at these points had been traditional. If some Americans found their history rusty, neither the British nor the President did.[45]

[45] Acheson 1987.

The American response to the apparent Soviet threat to Greece, and by extension much of the "free world," was outlined by President Truman in a famous speech given to a joint session of Congress on March 12, 1947. This speech came to be known as the "Truman Doctrine," the idea that the United States was actively to protect "free peoples" the world over (Figure 7.2). Asking for Congress to approve $400 million in aid to Greece and Turkey, Truman said that without American aid, Greece's government forces could not hold out against communist insurrectionists supported by foreign powers (he did not mention the Soviet Union directly, but the point was clear). As Truman said,

> The seeds of totalitarian regimes are nurtured by misery and want. They spread and grow in the evil soil of poverty and strife. They reach their full

Figure 7.2 Statue of US President Harry Truman in Athens (splashed with red paint after an apparent act of recent anti-American protest). Photo by Lee Brice.

growth when the hope of a people for a better life has died. We must keep that hope alive.[46]

Greece would be the test case for whether America could stand against the supposed plan of the Soviet Union to achieve world domination, and financial aid (along with large groups of advisors and perhaps even military personnel) would be the way to do it.

While not everyone agreed with Truman, in general the response to the "Truman Doctrine" speech was positive. Thomas E. Dewey, the Republican governor of New York who would narrowly lose to Truman in the 1948 presidential election, declared March 25 "Greek War Relief Day" in his state. In support of Truman's plan to send aid to Greece, Dewey upped the rhetorical ante, as reported in the *New York Times* on March 23, 1947:

> The civilized world owes a lasting debt to Truman's gallant and uncon-querable people of Greece. Down through the centuries Greece has bequeathed to all of us an incalculably rich heritage. It is a heritage that lies at the foundation of Western culture . . .. During the recent war, the endurance and bravery of the Greek people, in the face of overwhelming totalitarian forces, again aroused the admiration of the civilized world just as their forebears evoked the admiration of the ancient world at Thermopylae and Salamis . . ..
>     Once again the Greek people are standing as a brave bulwark against the tides of oppression which would engulf the world.[47]

For their part, the Soviets denounced Truman's speech as naked American imperialism. On March 15, the *New York Times* provided a transcript of an editorial on the speech printed in the Soviet newspaper *Izvestia*, and broadcast in London via Radio Moscow. Mocking the simplistic equivalence claimed for ancient and modern Greeks, the *Izvestia* editors said,

> But the matter not only, and not so much, lies in the venal Greek monarch-ists and their allies, who have been pleasantly presented to the American Congressmen as direct descendants of the defender of Thermopylae, the legendary King Leonidas. It is well known that the real rulers of Greece up until now have been and are still the British military authorities.

The editorial further criticized Truman's stance by comparing it to the justifications advanced by the Nazis for expanding the Reich: "Dilations to

---

[46] For a transcript of Truman's speech, see: www.ourdocuments.gov/doc.php?flash=false%26do c=81%23.

[47] *The New York Times*, March 23, 1947, p. 3.

the effect that the United States 'is called upon to save' Greece and Turkey from expansion on the part of the so-called 'totalitarian states' are not new. Hitler also referred to the Bolsheviks when he wanted to open the road to conquests for himself."[48] The Soviet response, and some domestic opposition to the foreign entanglements the Truman Doctrine would entail, did nothing to stop the Congressional acceptance of Truman's request and the delivery of aid and personnel to Greece, which helped the Greek government forces overcome the communist insurrection by 1949.

The Truman Doctrine was the basis for the famous Marshall Plan, outlined by Sectary of State George C. Marshall in a speech at Harvard University on June 5, 1947.[49] Marshall, proposing massive economic aid to a recovering Europe, for which he would later win a Nobel Peace Prize, said that US policy "is directed not against any country or doctrine but against hunger, poverty, desperation and chaos." However, he did warn that "Any government which maneuvers to block the recovery of other countries cannot expect help from us. Furthermore, governments, political parties, or groups which seek to perpetuate human misery in order to profit therefrom politically or otherwise will encounter the opposition of the United States." While the bulk of funds from the Marshall Plan were directed to major industrial powers like Germany, Truman's aid to Greece had set the stage, and Greece remained a central preoccupation for American policymakers. As Ann O'Hare McCormick put it in an editorial for the *New York Times* on December 29, 1948, "Greece is a test of staying power" for the United States, newly risen to become the West's dominant power.[50]

Rhetoric linking ancient Greece, including Thermopylae, to modern Greece and the American opposition to Soviet Union soared in 1951. A lengthy opinion piece published on February 4, 1951, and written by former *Economist* editor Barbara Ward, is instructive. Accompanied by a striking illustration, the article is entitled "Despair Is Both Dangerous and Stupid," and aimed at rousing American spirits in light of setbacks in Korea. It is worth looking at a few passages from this piece in detail. First, Ward claims that fighting for freedom is an enduring Western value:

> The struggle to maintain and expand freedom is not new. It is the essential effort that runs like a thread through all the phases of Western civilization,

---

[48] *The New York Times*, March 15, 1947, p. 4.
[49] For a transcript of this speech, see: www.oecd.org/general/themarshallplanspeechatharvarduniversi ty5june1947.htm
[50] O'Hare McCormick 1948.

and the men who fought at Thermopylae or died with Charles Martel, who
withstood the siege of Vienna or broke the Turkish fleets at Lepanto, or
who, in our own day, covered the road from Mons and held the outpost at
Bastogne might feel a certain astonishment to see the free world rocking
simply because its defendants are once more experiencing a temporary
retreat.[51]

All of the historic battles she mentions, including Thermopylae, are
stereotypical clashes of West versus East. The recent struggles at Mons
and Bastogne represent the fight against Imperial Germany and the Third
Reich, to which the Cold War is heir – though the great West–East clash
begun at Thermopylae often seems more apropos. Ward argues that the
Soviet Union stands in a long line of would-be Eastern oppressors: "Soviet
imperialism uses techniques so old and outworn that the Greeks were
fighting against them five thousand [sic] years ago." Her error regarding
the date of the war between the Greeks and the Persian Empire, which she
places a full 2,500 years too early, is indicative of how ingrained Persian
War themes had become in the Western imagination. One could know
these themes without knowing anything about the actual events themselves, let alone the sources and scholarly arguments. As opposed to the
Soviets, Ward insists that the United States through the Marshall Plan has
shared wealth with less developed areas "without any blowing of trumpets
or thumping on the propaganda machine," a claim that volumes of
speeches, articles, and other media flatly contradict.

Let one other speech from 1951 suffice to demonstrate how prevalent
Thermopylae was in many quarters of the West. In response to a speech
delivered by President Truman to the foreign ministers of the American
republics, the foreign minister of Brazil said the following, according to the
*New York Times* of March 27:

> There exists an ostensive philosophy which, if it came to pass, would
> consecrate as a hero, Ephialtes, the Spartan traitor convicted of crime against
> his mother country, having delivered to the Persians the very lives of those
> who stood in defense of the Thermopylae Pass. The nations of our hemi-
> sphere must not fail in this assembly to demonstrate their attachment to the
> love of nation, as well as to the idea of freedom for the human person, and
> respect for spiritual liberties and the Christian way of life.[52]

Despite the fact that the Brazilian minister gets a key detail wrong –
Ephialtes was not in fact Spartan – Thermopylae once again appears in
an appeal for patriotism in the face of the Soviet threat. The traitors the

---

[51] Ward 1951.    [52] *The New York Times*, March 27, 1951, p. 10.

minster refers to are those within Western countries who sympathize with communism, a barbarous creed that threatens freedom and the "Christian way of life."

Two incidents, also from 1951 and both reported in the *New York Times*, are representative of the way the site of Thermopylae could serve as a powerful symbol in a Cold War context. On April 3, the third anniversary of the Marshall Plan and the launching of the United States Information Service's so-called "Campaign of Truth" were celebrated with great pomp at Thermopylae itself. As the *New York Times* says in the April 4, 1951, edition, Thermopylae was "where some 2,500 years ago 300 Spartans died in defense of the then Western World civilization against Asian invaders."[53] Dignitaries including the US ambassador spoke, a tree was planted, and messages of appreciation were sent to Generals George C. Marshall, Douglas MacArthur, and Dwight D. Eisenhower. A message was also sent to the Greek force serving in Korea, on the front lines in the fight against communism. The link between the iconic modern defenders of the "West" and the Three Hundred could not be clearer.

On August 8 of the same year, the *New York Times* reported that "the one-thousandth displaced person to arrive in the United States under the auspices of the American Hellenic Education Progressive Association," Maria Geroulis, arrived in the US with three pounds of soil "from the graves of King Leonidas of Sparta and the 300 Spartan heroes who sacrificed their lives at the Battle of Thermopylae in 480 B.C." The soil, contained in an Archaic Greek vase, was to be placed on the Tomb of the Unknown Soldier in Arlington National Cemetery. Upon learning that the soil would have to be sterilized to avoid contamination, Geroulis replied that, "the soil of Thermopylae has been sterilized by the heroes of the ages and such sterilization is eternal."[54] Once again, American military members are treated as the heirs of the Spartan Three Hundred, linking the causes of the Second World War and the Cold War with the Spartans' stand against a despotic Eastern invader.

In 1955, the monument now the main attraction at Thermopylae was constructed by funds raised by Greeks living in the US (Figure 7.3). This monument, which the Greek Ministry of Culture calls a *heroön*, a hero-shrine, features a colossal bronze statue of Leonidas, apparently based on the "Smiling Hoplite" found at Sparta and popularly identified as Leonidas. Behind Leonidas stands a low wall decorated with relief sculptures and flanked by figures representing the Taygetus mountain range and

---

[53] *The New York Times*, April 4, 1951, p. 12.     [54] *The New York Times*, Aug. 18, 1951, p. 13.

Figure 7.3 Modern Leonidas monument at Thermopylae, with the inscription
"*molōn labe.*" Author's photo.

the Eurotas River, symbols of Sparta's homeland. It is impossible to ignore
the Cold War context of this monument, which builds on the
Thermopylae symbolism used earlier in the 1950s.[55] Only in 1995 was
a monument to the 700 Thespians who died in the last stand at
Thermopylae added, slightly to the west of the main Spartan monument.
Across the old highway is the low hillock on which the last stand supposedly took place, and where many arrowheads were excavated in apparent confirmation of that fact. Today, the hillock boasts a plaque bearing
Simonides' famous epigram. Visitors to the site are also able to visit a flashy
historical center, complete with models of the battlefield and cartoonish
images of Spartan warriors that evoke the film *300* – and even Spartan-
warrior-themed T-shirts for children. The site of Thermopylae remains

---

[55] See the Hellenic Ministry of Culture's official website for the monument: https://culture.lamia.gr
/en/blog/thermopylae-monument-leonidas.

a popular tourist stop, but it was during the Cold War that it was first developed into a major public monument.

Perhaps the best-known Cold War-era celebration of the Spartans and Thermopylae is the 1962 film *The 300 Spartans*, shot on location in Greece (but further south, near Perachora and Lake Vouliagmeni, not at Thermopylae) and made with the cooperation of the Greek government. The film asserts both the truth and the importance of its subject matter. As Tae Yang Kwak point outs, after the action is finished, the film ends by noting that the sacrifice of the Three Hundred represents "'a stirring example for free people throughout the world of what a few brave men can accomplish once they refuse to submit to tyranny' followed by acknowledgements thanking the Greek King and Queen, and the Greek government and army for making the film possible."[56] Though it met with scant critical success, *The 300 Spartans* had a profound impact on the young Frank Miller, who later wrote the comic series *300*, made into a blockbuster film of the same name, which we will discuss in the next section.[57] In a *New York Times* article on the later film, Alex Beam notes the influence of *The 300 Spartans*, and how it was interpreted as a commentary on the Cold War. Beam notes that William Golding, author of *Lord of the Flies*, remarked upon seeing *The 300 Spartans* that "a little of Leonidas lies in the fact that I can go where I like and write what I like. He contributed to set us free."[58] No matter that Leonidas himself did not claim to fight for freedom and that "freedom" was not part of the initial Spartan commemorations of the battle and the Persian Wars.

## Sparta Today

In many ways, it has never been a better time to be a fan of Sparta. From Zack Snyder's 2006 film *300*, which grossed nearly half a billion dollars worldwide, to the ubiquity of Spartan-themed fitness events, such as the famed "Spartan Race," Sparta is all over modern pop culture.[59] Given Sparta's troubling history of militarism, slavery, and xenophobia, however,

---

[56] Kwak 2007: 196.

[57] The *New York Times* (Sept. 20, 1962) review of the film is representative: "A viewer now can see by what means the Persians and the Greeks annihilated each other, but beyond that it is shallow stuff no more memorable than a weather report, dated 480 B. C."

[58] Alex Beam, "Meanwhile: Hot Times at the Hot Gates," *New York Times*, March 8, 2007. Golding's comment is more than a little reminiscent of John Stuart Mill's line that "the Battle of Marathon, even as an event in English history, is more important than the Battle of Hastings."

[59] *300*'s box office performance: www.imdb.com/title/tt0416449/; the Spartan Race: www.spartan.com/en.

and the ways that Spartan imagery is often put to use today, our continued fascination with Sparta is not necessarily a good thing, as writers such as Sarah Bond and Myke Cole caution.[60] Let us first turn to the phenomenon of *300* before considering how Sparta is deployed to bolster some of today's most pernicious far-right movements.

Zack Snyder's cinematic hit was based on the 1998 comic book series *300*, written by Frank Miller and inked by Lynn Varley. Miller, one of the most famous and influential figures in the world of comics, was inspired by the 1962 film *The 300 Spartans*.[61] The geopolitical context of Miller's work is obviously quite different from that of the film that inspired it, and it is also far removed from the post-9/11 world of Snyder's 2006 film. Like the film adaptation, Miller emphasizes the brutality and violence of the Spartan way of life, but also the Spartan love of freedom in standing up to a numberless and alien enemy. While the extreme violence of Spartan society is well suited to the graphic novel medium, there is more than a hint that Miller means to portray Sparta as a society in which few of us would want to live. As Lynn Fotheringham argues, Miller might even mean to elicit sympathy for the arch-traitor Ephialtes – the Greek (a local to the Thermopylae region in Herodotus, a Spartan in Miller's telling) who showed the Persians the way to outflank Leonidas and the Three Hundred – and thereby critique the harshness and even injustice of the militaristic and eugenic Spartan system.[62] In the end, though, there is little mistaking that the Spartans are the "good guys" in Miller's series, and numberless Asian hordes an enemy to be resisted.[63]

Also from 1998 is the historical novel *Gates of Fire: An Epic Novel of the Battle of Thermopylae*, by Steven Pressfield. Not only did Pressfield's book achieve commercial success, it also came to be taught as required reading at major US service academies, such as West Point.[64] Nathaniel Fick, an officer in the US Marines and a combat veteran of Afghanistan and Iraq, wrote in the *Washington Post* that in *Gates of Fire* he could recognize the

---

[60] See Sarah Bond's 2018 article for the online Classics journal *Eidolon*: https://eidolon.pub/this-is-not-sparta-392a9ccddf26; and Myke Cole's 2019 *New Republic* piece: https://newrepublic.com/article/154563/sparta-myth-rise-fascism-trumpism. See also Cole's 2021 book, in which he tries to undercut right-wing fascination with Sparta by arguing against Sparta's seeming invincibility.
[61] See the profile of Miller and the making of the movie *300* in the *New York Times*: www.nytimes.com/2006/11/26/movies/26ito.html?pagewanted=all&_r=0.
[62] Fotheringham 2012.
[63] A brilliant alternative to Miller's *300* is *Three*, by Ryan Kelly, Kieron Gillan, and Jordie Bellaire (2014, Portland, OR). This graphic novel, for which Stephen Hodkinson served as a historical consultant, centers on helot protagonists after Leuctra, when Sparta was in marked decline.
[64] As Pressfield boasts on his own website: https://stevenpressfield.com/books/.

men under his own command, and he gave the book to all the members of his platoon to read. As Fick summarizes the importance of Thermopylae, as fictionalized by Pressfield, "Three hundred Spartan infantrymen held off the invading Persians long enough to save Greece and perhaps all of Western civilization."[65]

Told through the perspective of a *perioikos* – a member of the free yet subordinate class in Laconia – *Gates of Fire* is a generally positive portrayal of the unique and uniquely militaristic nature of Spartan society, and the soldierly virtues of its citizens, all while gripping readers with gory scenes of combat and accounts of esprit de corps in the face of certain death. A former US Marine himself, Pressfield emphasizes the qualities of good military leaders and the soldiers they inspire, and does so in such a way that many military educators continue to find the book useful for their own purposes. While the system of helotage and the exclusivity of Spartan citizenship are treated in the book, they do little to detract from the sympathetic portrayal of the Three Hundred and the society for which they fight.[66]

Pressfield followed up the success of *Gates of Fire* by publishing more novels featuring the virtues of military leadership, including two books about Alexander the Great, 2004's *The Virtues of War: A Novel of Alexander the Great*, and 2006's *The Afghan Campaign*. Both novels, like *Gates of Fire*, feature vivid portrayals of ancient combat and studies of leadership and human nature in war. Now a renowned fiction and nonfiction writer of war, it was *Gates of Fire* and its Spartan subject that put Pressfield on this path. Prior to *Gates of Fire*, his breakout hit was 1995's *The Legend of Bagger Vance: A Novel of Golf and the Game of Life*, made into a 2000 film starring Will Smith, which has nothing to do with war (at least on the surface). Pressfield's study of – and success with – the Spartans ensured that war would become his preferred vehicle for analyzing the human condition.

Zack Snyder's *300* lacks the deep character studies of Pressfield's work, and, though it is based on Miller's comic series, lacks even the nuance and ambiguity of Miller's take on the subject. Especially because of its post-9/11 context, while the US "War on Terror" raged in Afghanistan and Iraq, *300*

---

[65] www.washingtonpost.com/archive/entertainment/books/2005/07/17/a-former-marine-captain-in-afghanistan-and-iraq-tells-of-the-books-that-helped-him-most-nathaniel-fick/b40467b9-9f7e-4e e1-8c22-d940b5dddaco/.

[66] For more on Pressfield's novel, its themes, and its impact, see Bridges 2007, who argues that Pressfield doesn't shy away from war's brutality or its negative impact on the human character, including in the case of the Spartans; and Fotheringham 2012, who claims that Pressfield's depiction remains overwhelmingly positive, despite engaging with some of the more vile aspects of the Spartan way of life.

proved much more controversial than its predecessors. While the original source material – Herodotus and, perhaps, Aeschylus – might ultimately be to blame for the Orientalist portrayal of Xerxes and the Persians as decadent, outlandish, despotic, and numberless, Snyder certainly ran with the material, making sure to portray Xerxes' soldiers as stereotypically "Middle-Eastern" against an all-white cast of Spartans.[67] He also ensures that viewers come away with a clear impression of selfless patriots fighting for freedom against a foreign tyrant and his enslaved subjects. There is no hint that Leonidas, played by Gerard Butler, is anything other than a virtuous king fighting for a virtuous society, even if some members of that society, such as the grotesquely portrayed ephors, fail to live up to the society's values.

I here offer an anecdote that I think is reasonably representative of the type of audience to which *300* pandered. While I attended a screening of the movie with my fellow Cornell Classics graduate students (likely on opening night, since all Classicists are unduly excited whenever an ancient film arrives, no matter its quality), during the scene in which Xerxes places his hands on Leonidas' shoulders, someone from the overwhelmingly white and male audience shouted out, "ew, gay!," to the raucous laughter of most in the theater. Of course, not only boorish homophobes enjoyed the film, and I myself have frequently suggested that, as inaccurate and offensive as the film is, it does a rather good job of portraying how the Greeks themselves seemed to view the Persians and their invasion – not that we should emulate the chauvinistic attitudes of the Greeks.

But something sinister, and I think dangerous, lies beneath the cartoon-ish stereotype directed by Snyder. As Tae Yang Kwak argues, race, culture, and history are so misunderstood in today's America that most American viewers of the film identify with the wrong side. In 2006, which party best represented the foreign invader seeking to crush its enemy with over-whelming military might? One does not have to sympathize with the Taliban to understand the US military as hardly an outnumbered band

---

[67] Victor Davis Hanson, a leading proponent of a simplistic "West" versus "East" view of history, claims in his *City Journal* review of *300*, "If the Spartans seem too cocky and self-assured in their belief that they are the more effective warriors of a superior culture, blame Herodotus, not Zack Snyder." www.city-journal.org/html/your-shield-or-it-9420.html. Edith Hall 1989: 99 calls Aeschylus' *Persians*, in featuring the Battle of Salamis the only surviving tragedy to depict a historical event, "the first unmistakable file in the archive of Orientalism, the discourse by which the European imagination has dominated Asia ever since by conceptualizing its inhabitants as defeated, luxurious, emotional, cruel, and always as dangerous." On Orientalism in general, see the groundbreaking work of Said 1978, which must inform our readings of "East versus West" or "clash of civilizations" tropes.

of plucky freedom fighters standing in the face of impossible odds and almost certain death. As Kwak puts it, "Why do both fans and detractors [of *300*] in America readily and unselfconsciously identify almost exclusively with the film's Spartans? The answer is a complex confluence of racism, Orientalism, and American exceptionalism, coexisting within the cognitive dissonance of contemporary American identity as both anti-imperialistic and pro-hegemonic."[68] Given that *300* ends with the Greeks charging to final victory at Plataea, inspired by the retelling of the story of Thermopylae, it is hard to miss the message that lovers of freedom everywhere should do as the Spartans did. No matter that the geopolitical realities of the 21st century are hopelessly different from those of 480 BCE, or that the Spartans' portrayal in many ancient sources is little more than propaganda that misses how even the Spartans themselves conceived of the battle at the time.

The current migrant crisis facing Europe, in which many thousands of migrants and refugees have fled to Europe from North Africa and the Middle East in the wake of the Arab Spring and Syrian Civil War, has led to an increase in white European identitarian movements. These movements claim to oppose the "Islamization" of Europe and to defend "Western Civilization," and as such look to the Spartans and the Spartan stand at Thermopylae as an example of free "Westerners" stemming the tide of slavish "Easterners."[69] A warning to readers: the groups referred to here, through their websites and other materials, trade in odious and dangerous white supremacist and otherwise bigoted and xenophobic tropes. There is some nasty stuff out there with the stamp of Sparta on it.

One of the more prominent of these identitarian groups is Generation Identity, which uses the iconic Spartan lambda shield as its logo.[70] The logo carries an unmistakable message: Just as the Spartans stood against Xerxes' hordes in the defense of "freedom" and the "West," so, too, do the members of Generation Identity defend the "West" and "Western values" from encroaching migrants from predominantly Muslim countries. This and other groups peddle in conspiracy theories including "white replacement," which claims that "white" people are being intentionally and

---

[68] Kwak 2007: 194.

[69] In addition to Thermopylae, other anti-Islamic tropes are also used, such as the "Gates of Vienna," referring to the siege in 1683 that prevented the Ottomans from expanding further into Europe (see, for example: https://gatesofvienna.net/), and the Battle of Tours/Poitiers in 732, when Charles Martel prevented Islamic expansion from Spain into France. For more on the appropriation of Sparta by new far-right movements, see Muller 2022.

[70] www.generation-identity.org.uk/.

systematically replaced by non-white populations, especially Muslim ones. Such rhetoric harks back to that deployed in the Third Reich to justify the violent expansion of Aryan *Lebensraum* and the consequent extermination of non-Aryans. The members of Generation Identity do not merely talk the talk. For example, in 2018 Generation Identity spearheaded the "Defend Europe" mission in the Alps, during which passes through the mountains frequented by migrants and refugees were guarded by white identitarians to prevent Muslims and others from penetrating further into Western Europe. Many of these anti-immigrant "guards" eventually received jail sentences for their attempt as vigilantes to intimidate migrants.[71]

The identitarian movement is also prominent in the United States, especially since the 2016 election of Donald Trump to the presidency.[72] These American hate groups, like their European counterparts, make frequent use of classical imagery, including Spartan imagery, but also the Roman SPQR, and even stylized images of Roman *fasces*, the bundle of rods and axes meant to symbolize power in the Roman Republic, and the literal root of the word "fascism."[73] Aside from the lambda shield, the Corinthian helmet, most typically identified with Spartan hoplites, also makes frequent appearances among right-wing groups, as does Leonidas' pithy saying to the Persian demand that the Spartans lay down their weapons at Thermopylae: "*molōn labe*," or "come and get them." *Molōn Labe* is in fact the Modern Greek title for the film *300*, and appears on modern monuments to Leonidas, including the one at Thermopylae itself, but also on the Leonidas that stands in front of the public athletic facility in the modern town of Sparta. In the US, "*molōn labe*" frequently appears along with a stylized Corinthian helmet in the promotional materials of gun-rights advocates, including members of the National Rifle Association.[74] Dangerous American antigovernment movements have appropriated Sparta too. During the infamous storming of the US capitol

---

[71] www.france24.com/en/20190829-france-far-right-activists-generation-identity-prison-sentence-alps-anti-migrant-operation.

[72] See, for example, Identity Evropa, which trades on many Classical symbols in executing its white supremacist mission: www.splcenter.org/fighting-hate/extremist-files/group/identity-evropaamerican-identity-movement.

[73] The Southern Poverty Law Center's collection of images used by the white supremacist groups at the "Unite the Right" rally in Charlottesville, VA, in 2017, is instructive: www.splcenter.org/hatewatch/2017/08/12/flags-and-other-symbols-used-far-right-groups-charlottesville.

[74] A subject I have addressed in the *Washington Post*: www.washingtonpost.com/news/made-by-history/wp/2018/02/21/what-the-ancient-greeks-can-teach-us-about-gun-control/?utm_term=.f41a19d6d819.

on January 6, 2021, by supporters of Donald Trump's failed re-election bid for the presidency, Spartan imagery was abundant among the insurrectionists.[75]

The Spartans can today be symbols of rather innocuous principles, such as physical fitness and endurance, and also of more complex ideas such as the nature of patriotism, self-sacrifice, and effective leadership.[76] But, more alarmingly, the Spartans can be used to give historical heft and legitimacy to extremist movements against migrants and refugees, and against any perceived threat to "Western Civilization" and the "white race" – no matter how nebulous or artificial such concepts are. I do not think Zack Snyder, let alone Frank Miller or Steven Pressfield, intended their work to be interpreted in such ways. But the celebratory treatment of Sparta in modern literature and pop culture should give us pause. Those of us who study ancient history need to be more diligent in illuminating the less savory elements of ancient Sparta, such as extreme violence, brutal exploitation of others, and xenophobia that were not only bad in and of themselves but also damaging to Sparta's long-term stability, especially when paired with open-ended campaigns of "liberation" abroad.

## A Walk through Modern Sparta: Ancient Ghosts and Modern Monsters

We have spent a lot of time in this book thinking about ancient Spartan monuments to wars and the war dead, and what those monuments tell us about Spartan society and especially Spartan militarism and Sparta's militaristic self-presentation to the wider ancient world. In this chapter, we have considered some of the ways that Sparta's ancient fame translated into modern fame, inspiring a host of ideas and movements, many of them pernicious. But there is no denying, that for good or ill, Sparta is famous, as much today as ever, and the modern town of Sparta makes the most of this fame. Let us finish this chapter with a new spin on the tour of Sparta we conducted in Chapter 1. Here, we will take a trip to today's Sparta and ponder the ways Sparta's past as the most famously warlike state in Greece informs its present. (See Map 2)

---

[75] For the January 6 insurrectionists' (and those of others with similar views and aims) appropriations of Sparta, see the important chapter by Hodkinson 2022.

[76] Even the seemingly innocuous principles, however, can have a dark side. We saw earlier how the Nazis idealized Spartan fitness and athleticism. See also Gidney 2015, who investigates how fitness regimes in early 20th-century Canada were aimed at instilling a narrow form of patriotism.

Most visitors to Greece, following along in guided tours of the Athenian Acropolis, or the Sanctuary of Apollo at Delphi, or the Palace of Minos at Knossos on Crete, would be taken aback by a trip to Sparta. One really has to look for the ancient remnants of the city, and when one finds them, they are not impressive by the standards of the Parthenon, and even the most substantial structures that remain tend to be from the Roman period, long after Sparta's Classical heyday. Even though it is off the beaten tourist path, a visit to Sparta is well worthwhile, not least because of its stunning natural setting, but also because it is a genuine Greek town, humming with daily life unencumbered by the tourist extravaganza of Athens' historic Plaka area (Figure 7.4).

Like the ancient Spartan in Chapter 1, the first thing the modern traveler notices is the Taygetus mountain range separating Laconia from Messenia to the west. Capped with snow for much of the year, these mountains dazzle with the interplay of light and shadow on their peaks and slopes, and are also home to Mistras, the remarkably preserved Byzantine city that early visitors from Western Europe to the area mistook for ancient Sparta itself. There is something fitting in the way the tourist town of Mistras idolizes Constantine XI Palaiologos, the last

Figure 7.4 The Roman theatre of Sparta beneath the acropolis, with the modern town in the middle distance and Mount Taygetus in the background. Author's photo.

Byzantine emperor, who died at the fall of Constantinople in 1453. He is still embraced in much of the Orthodox world as a symbol of the "West's" stand against the "East." The other side of Laconia is defined by mountains, too, the less imposing but still substantial Parnon range. The area around Sparta is remarkably green and fertile compared to much of central and southern mainland Greece, thanks to the waters of the Eurotas River, which, along with the mountains, also served as a protective barrier in antiquity. The topographical layout of Sparta and Laconia can be seen well from the vantage point of the Menelaion, identified as the ancient shrine to Menelaus and Helen (and site of an important Bronze Age complex long predating the later shrine) located on a ridge a few kilometers to the southeast of the town. The archaeological site of ancient Sparta, on a low rise at the northern limit of the town, also offers spectacular views of Taygetus. The archaeological site's most impressive remains are a Christian basilica and a Roman-period theater, but some hints of Sparta's Classical might are still present, including the "Round Building," the sanctuary of Athena Chalkioikos, and the Persian Stoa, all discussed earlier.[77]

The clearest indicators of Sparta's pride in its ancient warriors are scattered throughout the bustling modern town. In the main square, or *plateia*, a modern statue of a dying soldier kneels at one end, with paraphrased verses from Tyrtaeus inscribed on his plinth (Figure 7.5).[78] A few blocks away is another square, named after Leonidas since the remains of what has long been thought to be Leonidas' tomb are at its center, right across from the "History Café" and the "Leonidas" grill shop (complete with a Corinthian helmet logo). In front of the public athletic facility, at the end of the main boulevard named after Constantine XI Palaiologos, is a modern statue of Leonidas, decked out in full armor and wearing a sword. Along with an inscription mentioning the piece's 1968 dedication, is the ubiquitous *molōn labe* slogan, mirroring the one beneath the slightly earlier Leonidas at Thermopylae itself. On the side of Leonidas' plinth are lines from the 19th-century Greek poet Dionysios Solomos exhorting the Three Hundred to rise again in order to see how much their children still resemble them. This monument claims unambiguously that today's Spartans are the true descendants of those who fought Xerxes. In order to drive home further the continuity between ancient and modern Sparta, just up the street from the Leonidas monument is a marble *stele* on which is inscribed a list of Laconian Olympic victors from 720 BCE until the present day, at least 2004 (Figure 7.6). Modern Sparta might not look like much, just as Thucydides

---

[77] See Chapter 1.     [78] For more on Tyrtaeus' verses, see Chapter 2.

Figure 7.5 Modern monument in the central square of Sparta, with a paraphrase
from Tyrtaeus inscribed on it. Author's photo.

predicted, but it does its best to remind visitors – and, perhaps more importantly, its own residents – of its ancient virtues.

Modern Sparta exists today, however, not as a remnant of the ancient city, with continuous ties stretching back millennia, but because it is a powerful symbol. Modern Sparta is entirely a modern creation, or refoundation in 1834, seeking to cash in on ancient glories at a time when Greek nationalism was resurgent. As Paraskevas Matalas argues, and as we considered earlier, Sparta is inhabited today because early travelers to the site from Western Europe imbued it with significance based on romantic readings of its ancient remains, such as the Tomb of Leonidas, which most scholars now doubt actually belonged to the hero of Thermopylae. Even the scientific archaeological excavations of the area had as their primary goal the identification of finds with famous historical figures.[79] For Matalas, Sparta's ghosts were what drove the living in the Early Modern period. In many ways, these ghosts continue to do so.

[79] Matalas 2017: 51.

Figure 7.6 Monument in Sparta to Laconian Olympic victors from 776 BCE to the present day. Author's photo.

I will have more to say in the Epilogue about the worrying militarism inherent in such modern monuments and many modern interpretations of ancient material.[80] For now, it is worth noting that Sparta's ancient ghosts can also inspire modern monsters. Today, Laconia is one of the centers of support for Greece's Golden Dawn party (*Chrysi Avgi* in Greek), a xenophobic and neo-Fascist organization whose logo is the famous Greek "meander" pattern stylized to resemble a swastika. The regional headquarters of Golden Dawn is on Sparta's Lycurgus Street, almost in view of the prominent modern statue of Lycurgus, the legendary ancient lawgiver. One of Golden Dawn's primary platforms, in line with similar parties in Europe, is to prevent immigration from primarily Muslim or "non-Western" countries, thus preserving "Western Civilization" from "barbarous" "invasions." Sparta, therefore, is a powerful symbol for Golden Dawn and their sympathizers.

[80] See the Epilogue.

Aside from recent migrants fleeing war and instability, Golden Dawn also targets the Roma, historically derided as "Gypsies," a sizable population of whom lives on the outskirts of Sparta, on the banks of the Eurotas River, near the ancient sanctuary of Artemis Orthia. In recent years, a Laconian village has asked Golden Dawn for strong-arm help against "Gypsies," and Golden Dawn thugs have clashed with Roma in Kalamata, capital of the neighboring region of Messenia.[81] Golden Dawn and the Greek "Gypsy" problem are the subject of a discussion forum on the prominent neo-Nazi website Stormfront.[82] The case of Golden Dawn and Sparta's own Roma population shines a light on the dark irony of a town with so many monuments to those who supposedly fought for "freedom" against "tyranny" having its own marginalized population and those who seek to perpetrate violence against it. The same inconsistency lurks behind ancient portrayals of Sparta fighting for freedom against slavery, all while brutally subjugating their fellow Greeks the helots and others. Those Greeks, such as the Athenians, who really did frame the war against the Persians as a struggle for a free Greece, also depended on slavery and could use their freedom fighting as cover for or blatant justification of their oppression of others. Fortunately, based on the results of the elections held in 2020, support for Golden Dawn might be on the wane, and in the most recent elections of 2023, the party was barred from fielding candidates.[83] It is nevertheless instructive that Sparta would stand out as a natural home for such a group, cautioning us to be careful to avoid valorizing Spartan warriors and their society as things we should emulate today.

## Conclusion

As Shakespeare quipped in *The Merchant of Venice*, "the Devil can quote scripture for his purpose." That 18th-century *philosophes*, Third Reich propagandists, American Cold Warriors, and graphic novelists can all bend the Spartans to their own – often seemingly diametrically opposed –

---

[81] Village enlists Golden Dawn help: http://hellasfrappe.blogspot.com/2013/04/greek-village-near-sparti-calls-golden.html; Golden Dawn violence in Kalamata: https://greece.greekreporter.com/2013/04/09/roma-golden-dawn-conflict-at-kalamata-hospital/.

[82] www.stormfront.org/forum/t958971/. Once again, these groups are truly odious, and I do not recommend spending much time on their websites. They do, however, provide a service in demonstrating just how thin the veneer of "respectable politics" really is, and that we must be ever vigilant in combatting racism and xenophobia, since the horrors of the 20th century are not necessarily relegated to the past.

[83] Waning support for Golden Dawn: www.theguardian.com/news/2020/mar/03/golden-dawn-the-rise-and-fall-of-greece-neo-nazi-trial. The party barred from participating in the 2023 election: www.aljazeera.com/features/2023/5/3/barred-from-polls-a-greek-neo-nazi-seeks-way-back-to-politics.

purposes demonstrates the fertility of Spartan soil. The case of Sparta, perhaps more than any other topic from classical antiquity, reveals how important it is to be honest and accurate in evaluating the ancient evidence and its reception, and to be vigilant against the misuse of antiquity to promote hateful agendas in the modern world. Even those agendas that are not as blatantly hateful can still push a society towards violence and militarism, encouraging an unthinking patriotism and self-sacrifice in the service of wars that might or might not be just.

As I hope the rest of this book has shown, even an honest and accurate understanding of the ancient Spartans should give us pause. Aside from the obviously revolting aspects of Spartan society, foremost among them slavery and helotage, a society built largely around warfare and military virtues, and the commemoration of those virtues in its past heroes, is more likely than not to opt for violence and war in the future, and to see these as good things. When military virtues are justified by appeals to "liberation" abroad or the defense of "civilization" against "barbarism," of good Greeks against bad Persians, all restraints on violence and war melt away. The Spartans fought more wars, not fewer, when they embraced the propaganda of liberation, and fighting for Greece against "barbarians." Spartans were less prone to warfare when they simply pursued glory and fame – though that Spartan reality was quickly forgotten by the time of the Peloponnesian War, and has made barely a dent in the modern reception of Spartan history, society, and culture.

# Epilogue
## Dulce et Decorum Est

The Latin poet Horace, writing during the reign of Augustus, penned the now famous line: *Dulce et decorum est pro patria mori* ("sweet and fitting it is to die for one's country") (*Odes* 3.2.13). The rest of the stanza runs as follows:

> *mors et fugacem persequitur virum*
> *nec parcit inbellis iuventae*
> *poplitibus timidoque tergo.*
> For death overtakes even a fleeing man
> Nor does it spare the unwarlike knees
> Or frightened back of youth.

In battle, the cowardly and courageous are apt to die in equal measure, so one might as well die courageously and be comforted by the good deed of noble patriotism.[1] Recall that the Spartan poet Tyrtaeus expressed almost exactly the same thing (F 10.1–2): "It is a fine thing to die, falling in the front ranks | A good man battling for his country."[2] Horace's poem reaffirms that in the ancient Mediterranean world, for both Greeks and Romans, dying courageously in battle for the interests of one's country was universally acknowledged to be a good thing – even, as hard as it might be to imagine, a sweet thing for the one dying. Ancient literature provides no shortage of such calls to arms.

After the horrors of the First World War, Horace's words were sometimes met with disdain. Most famously, Wilfred Owen, in his own poem called "Dulce et Decorum Est," published shortly after the war, presents Horace's exhortation as nothing more than a murderous and contemptible lie. Consider Owen's last few lines:

> If you could hear, at every jolt, the blood
> Come gargling from the froth-corrupted lungs,

---

[1] See Harrison 1993, who argues that Horace really did think that the person dying for his country could feel a sense of pleasure.
[2] τεθνάμεναι γὰρ καλὸν ἐνὶ προμάχοισι πεσόντα | ἄνδρ' ἀγαθὸν περὶ ᾗ πατρίδι μαρνάμενον.

> Obscene as cancer, bitter as the cud
> Of vile, incurable sores on innocent tongues,—
> My friend, you would not tell with such high zest
> To children ardent for some desperate glory,
> The old Lie: *Dulce et decorum est*
> *Pro patria mori.*[3]

How could anyone who had witnessed the industrial slaughter of 1914–1918, including the utterly novel horrors of poison gas attacks, have found anything sweet in dying for one's country, or in war at all? Surely, the "War to End All Wars" exposed the dangers of the type of militaristic patriotism espoused by Horace and Tyrtaeus. In the age of the machine gun and mustard gas, the Spartans, seemingly eager for proving themselves on the battlefield, must be relegated to a mere curiosity, or, at best, relics from an obsolete age and an obsolete battlefield. Of course, the "War to End All Wars" did no such thing, and the 20th century descended into even greater horrors in the decades to come. But even though peoples and nations kept on fighting wars, and sadly seem poised to keep on doing so indefinitely, wars must now be seen as an evil, perhaps sometimes a necessary one, but with nothing "sweet" about them.

And yet, many contemporary commemorative practices assume and perpetuate a certain degree of militaristic patriotism, even if it is not recognized as such by most of those who observe such practices. One of the most beloved poems to come out of the First World War is 1915's "In Flanders Fields" by John McCrae. Not only is this poem regularly recited at Canadian and British Remembrance Day ceremonies every November 11, it is also recited in elementary schools, including the ones my own children attended. The poem is worth considering in full:

> In Flanders fields the poppies blow
> Between the crosses, row on row,
> That mark our place; and in the sky
> The larks, still bravely singing, fly
> Scarce heard amid the guns below.
>
> We are the Dead. Short days ago
> We lived, felt dawn, saw sunset glow,
> Loved and were loved, and now we lie,
> In Flanders fields.
>
> Take up our quarrel with the foe:
> To you from failing hands we throw

---

[3] Owen 1920: 15.

The torch; be yours to hold it high.
If ye break faith with us who die
We shall not sleep, though poppies grow
In Flanders fields.[4]

The first two stanzas of McCrae's poem provide a stirring lament for those who died in the slaughterhouse of the Ypres salient. McCrae himself was a victim of Flanders. He died of pneumonia in early 1918, just over two years after his poem was first published, while in charge of a Canadian field hospital in Boulogne, only a few kilometers from the Belgian border and the poppies of Flanders.

The third stanza, however, sounds a much different note. Instead of lamenting the waste and loss of war, McCrae exhorts his readers to take up the torch passed by the dead and continue the quarrel lest those who have already died find no rest because they died in vain. McCrae's final lines are a call to arms, not a call for peace. In the world of the poem, there is room for an eternal relay race of soldiers, generation after generation, rushing onto the field of battle to wage wars that never end.

McCrae's imagery of passing the torch finds a central place in the Canadian National War Memorial at Vimy Ridge in France, Canada's overseas monument to those who fell in the First World War, and one of the most grandiose and memorable of all war memorials [Figure E.1].[5] The Vimy Memorial was designed and built by Walter Allward over the course of many years, with every detail worked out precisely, including the luminous stone quarried in Croatia. The monument was unveiled only in 1936 in a lavish ceremony presided over by King Edward VIII (in one of his few public roles before abdicating) and attended by thousands of Canadian veterans who made the overseas pilgrimage. The monument is dominated by two large pillars, which Allward said were meant to symbolize the cooperation between the English and French peoples in the war. In front of the pillars stands a hooded woman, looking solemnly down at the Tomb of the Unknown Soldier. This woman is known as Canada Bereft and symbolizes the abstract idea of Canadian nationhood for which those who died had fought. She bears a striking similarity to the Mourning Athena found on the Athenian Acropolis, who likewise represents her country as she gazes pensively at what is most likely a casualty list of those Athenians who died fighting overseas. Behind Canada Bereft are several other figures, including the "Spirit of Sacrifice," who takes

---

[4] McCrae 1919: 3.
[5] For more on this monument, including its ties to and resonances with classical imagery, see Sears 2018a.

Figure E.1 The Canadian National Vimy Memorial in France, showing figures
representing Canada Bereft, the Spirit of Sacrifice, and the Passing of the Torch.
Author's photo.

on a cruciform posture, and the "Passing of the Torch," a man reaching
upward to pass the torch to those who would take the place of the dead.
McCrae's poem almost certainly influenced Allward's stirring imagery.

Unlike McCrae, however, Allward did not conceive of his monument as
a call to arms, and he must have had something different from continued
military conflict in mind when he employed the passing-of-the-torch
imagery. Allward wanted his monument to convey the futility of war, its
utter pointlessness and waste. He claimed that he conceived of the monument's general design after being visited by a nightmare in which thousands of muddied and bloodied Canadians were being cut down by
machine-gun fire, only to have the shades of the dead come alongside
them to give aid. While Allward detested war and its violence, he wanted to
honor the dead by showing us all how much we owe to them, how much
the dead continue to render us their aid. Allward sought a way to commemorate the dead without spurring future generations on to similar fields
of slaughter. As if to drive home his pacific point, at one stage of the design
process Allward had placed a German Pickelhaube, the telltale spiked
helmet, under the feet of one of his figures. Allward in the end abandoned

this particular image, since it struck him as too militaristic and jingoistic. Instead, Allward opted to show a group of figures breaking a sword, and another group providing succor to those in need.

In addition to offering a meditation on the horrors of war and the need for peace, Allward was trying to make sense out of a senseless war, or at least provide some meaning for the death and maiming of thousands of Canadians in the fields of France and Belgium. One way he did this was through the figure of Canada Bereft, a figural embodiment of Canada that was unique to the Vimy Memorial. The United States has Uncle Sam, and France has Marianne, but before the Vimy Memorial, Canada had no equivalent. I have suggested elsewhere that Canada Bereft shares not only a visual resemblance to the famous Mourning Athena from the Athenian Acropolis – both are female figures serving as abstractions of their respective peoples in the guise of mourning, or at least contemplation of the death of their soldiers – but both figures served to focus the remembrance of the war dead onto the object for which the dead gave their lives. As Canada, like Athens as it expanded its power during the early to mid-5th century BCE, struggled to comprehend the deaths of so many of its people in a conflict far overseas, Allward's Canada Bereft helped the nation to conceive of itself as a real entity, and one perhaps worth the deaths of so many.

Despite Allward's intentions for his monument, the use that the Canadian government and various heritage organizations have made of it in recent years aligns it much more closely to the sentiments of "In Flanders Fields." The Vimy Memorial as a way to glorify a sanitized version of Canada's military history, and as a contemporary call to arms, is an instructive case in how monuments and commemorative practices are used today to perpetuate militaristic patriotism, and justify current policies and military actions abroad. In the mid-2000s, the Canadian government undertook a multimillion-dollar restoration project for the various battlefield memorials in France and Belgium. While this project was initiated in early 2001, the majority of the work was undertaken while Canadian soldiers were deployed in Afghanistan, and it would be reasonable to think that the government promoted the project as part of its effort to maintain public support for an overseas military campaign that proved a hard sell. The last restoration to be completed was that of the Vimy Memorial, and it was reopened to the public in 2007 with great fanfare. Vimy fever in Canada was only beginning. In 2012, the Bank of Canada issued a new twenty-dollar banknote featuring an image of the Vimy Memorial, along with poppies and other symbols of remembrance and

Canada's past military glory. The celebration of this banknote by The Vimy Foundation, an advocacy group dedicated to promoting the import-ance of Vimy Ridge for Canada's past and present, is telling:

> Thanks to the Bank of Canada, the victory of Vimy Ridge will be depicted on the new bill, allowing Canadians to carry a piece of history in their wallets. Just as Canadian innovation was successfully demonstrated on the battlefield of Vimy and with the architectural design of the memorial some years later, the new series of Canadian notes are at the frontier of bank note technology and will set a benchmark worldwide.[6]

By 2012, it was impossible for Canadians to escape Vimy imagery, and this only intensified as the battle's centenary approached in 2017. The principal line used by those promoting the celebration of the Battle of Vimy Ridge was that "Canada was born at Vimy." Not only was this victory painted as a major accomplishment and even a turning point in the war but it was the first battle in which all divisions of the Canadian Expeditionary Force fought together, supposedly helping to solidify Canada's sense of nationhood. The confederation of Canada, after all, had only been a half-century earlier, in 1867, and most of those who initially signed up to fight in the First World War had actually been born in Britain. By 2017, hardly anyone in Canada was unaware of the Battle of Vimy Ridge, including the dubious notions that Canada fought much harder and better than the British and French before them, and that Canada was forged in that epic struggle. There was even a one-minute television public service announcement created by Historica Canada, the group responsible for Heritage Minutes – one-minute sanitized celebra-tions of milestones in Canadian history that were ubiquitous on Canadian televisions throughout the 1990s.[7] Walter Allward's "sermon on the futility of war," and the costly battle it commemorated, were brought into the service of Canadian patriotism, and to the promotion of the idea that Canada only fights good fights, including the one it was currently fighting in Afghanistan. Far from futile, Vimyism had taught Canadians that war can be glorious, and can be an instrument in creating great nations and solidifying great peoples. As Ian McKay and Jamie Swift warn in their book *The Vimy Trap, or How We Learned to Stop Worrying and Love the Great War*, the meaning and legacy of the First World War were hotly debated at

---

[6] The Vimy Foundation website offers a treasure trove of modern commemorative practices and ideas: www.vimyfoundation.ca/.
[7] See Historica Canada's website for more information on its mission and scope: www.historicacanada.ca/.

the time. The idea that Canada was born in the trenches of Vimy is a startlingly recent notion, one that sanitizes the battle's cost and the historical questions surrounding it.[8]

War as the forge in which new nations are wrought is a very old and very common idea. The United States became an independent republic through the Revolutionary War against King George III, and the martial heritage of the American nation is reflected through many of its civic rituals, including in "The Star Spangled Banner," the national anthem. Delacroix's famous 1830 painting "Liberty Leading the People" remains today an indelible image of the violent struggle against the *Ancien Régime* to create the French Republic. The ancient Greeks, too, though infamously quarrelsome and disunited, began to think of themselves as a common nation or ethnicity after fighting the foreign power of the Persian Empire. As is not uncommon, peoples often define themselves by what they are not, as against an identifiable "Other." As Edith Hall pointed out in her seminal *Inventing the Barbarian: Greek Self-Definition through Tragedy*, the Persian Wars led to the emergence of Greek Orientalism, that is of viewing the eastern power of Persia as a decadent barbarian power against which Greekness could be understood. As Hall notes, Aeschylus' tragedy *The Persians* – performed just a few years after the Persians were driven out of Greece, and performed in front of an audience that included veterans of that war and who had seen their city of Athens sacked and burned twice – is perhaps the world's first work of orientalist literature, representing the Persians as decidedly not Greek, and the Greeks as decidedly not Persian.[9] The war against the Persian invaders had given the Greeks all that they needed to begin to understand themselves as a distinct people.

Aeschylus had also provided the Greeks with positive attributes by which they could identify themselves as Greeks. As the Greek fleet prepared to sail out against the Persians at Salamis, Aeschylus put these words in the mouths of the Greek sailors: "O sons of the Greeks, go forth! Set free your fatherland, your children, | your wives, the shines of your paternal gods, and the tombs of your | ancestors! Now the contest is for all!" (Aesch. *Pers.* 400–405). Herodotus, also writing about the Persian Wars, puts similar sentiments in the mouths of the Athenians when they refuse to come to terms with the Persians:

> There are many compelling reasons preventing us [from betraying our fellow Greeks], even if we wanted to. Greatest among these are the burned

[8] McKay and Swift 2016.    [9] Hall 1989: 99.

and destroyed images of our gods, for whom were are compelled to punish utterly those who committed such acts, rather than come to an agreement with them. Second is the Greek thing (*to hellēnikon*), with common blood, a common tongue, common temples and sacrifices of the gods, and a shared way of life. It would not go well for the Athenians to be the betrayers of these things. (8.144.2)[10]

Common shrines, common gods, common "blood," common language, and common customs are what make the Greeks Greek, and the Persians not Greek. The war against the Persian Empire and Xerxes' invasion force of 480–479 firmly established the criteria by which the Greeks defined Greekness.

The Spartans thought that their unique constitution and way of life resulted from a series of semi-mythical wars fought against the Messenians, the context for Tyrtaeus' poems. Not only did the Messenian Wars provide the Spartans with abundant land and enslaved populations to work it, allowing the Spartans to train fulltime as hoplites, they also necessitated the Spartans' constant war footing, in case the Messenians should revolt. For their part, the Messenians looked back to the long-lost era of the Messenian Wars to understand – or, more precisely, to construct – their own ethnic identity after their liberation at the hands of Epaminondas. As Spartan and Messenian identity became more disentangled and contrasted during and after Epaminondas' foundation of Messene in 369 BCE, the Spartans, too, thought anew about the origins and nature of their state through the Messenian Wars.[11]

In this line of thinking, wars not only give birth to nations, but they also show a nation's citizens how they are supposed to act. We have already discussed at length how the Spartan poet Tyrtaeus used the backdrop of the Messenian Wars to encourage the Spartans to be better and braver soldiers, from which they would gain glory and avoid the shame of having to wander the earth as beggars driven from their land. In Athens, it became a well-worn cliché that new generations of Athenians were duty bound to live up to the example set by their ancestors who had fought the Persians. Orators and pamphleteers such as Pericles, Lysias, and Isocrates urged the

---

[10] πολλά τε γὰρ καὶ μεγάλα ἐστὶ τὰ διακωλύοντα ταῦτα μὴ ποιέειν μηδ᾽ ἢν ἐθέλωμεν, πρῶτα μὲν καὶ μέγιστα τῶν θεῶν τὰ ἀγάλματα καὶ τὰ οἰκήματα ἐμπεπρησμένα τε καὶ συγκεχωσμένα, τοῖσι ἡμέας ἀναγκαίως ἔχει τιμωρέειν ἐς τὰ μέγιστα μᾶλλον ἤ περ ὁμολογέειν τῷ ταῦτα ἐργασαμένῳ, αὖτις δὲ τὸ Ἑλληνικὸν ἐὸν ὅμαιμόν τε καὶ ὁμόγλωσσον καὶ θεῶν ἱδρύματά τε κοινὰ καὶ θυσίαι ἤθεά τε ὁμότροπα, τῶν προδότας γενέσθαι Ἀθηναίους οὐκ ἂν εὖ ἔχοι.
[11] Luraghi 2008, especially 209–248; Thomas 2019: 59. Davis and Stocker 2021: 1–14 argue that the foundations of Messenian identity were in the Late Bronze Age, and there was a stronger Messenian identity than Luraghi and others allow, even prior to liberation from the Spartans.

Athenians not to leave the country worse than they had inherited it. The generation of Athenians that had fought at Marathon and Salamis were remembered as the Greeks' "Greatest Generation," a shining model for all future Athenians. The Battle of Vimy Ridge, therefore, is promoted by lobby groups and governments not only to provide Canadians with a fuller understanding of Canadian history but also in order to inspire new generations of Canadians to act as those who fought at Vimy did. Boosters of the battle hope Canadians today at the very least support those who are following in the footsteps of Vimy's soldiers, such as those who were until recently deployed in Afghanistan. The heroes of Vimy have passed the torch. It is up to today's Canadians "to hold it high."

Where the First World War holds a central place in modern Canada's self-identity, or at least the identity successive federal governments wish to promote, the Second World War looms much larger in the American psyche. It has now become commonplace to refer to the generation of Americans who grew up during the Great Depression and then fought against the forces of fascism as "the Greatest Generation." Tom Brokaw popularized this term as the title of his 1998 book, which he was inspired to write after visiting Normandy for the 40th anniversary of the D-Day invasion.[12] Talking to veterans of those epochal events, Brokaw became convinced that this was "the greatest generation any society has ever produced." The nobility of the sacrifices this generation made during wartime, as shown by, among other things, horrendous casualty numbers, is increased by the notion that these people fought not for fame or glory but because "it was the right thing to do." Brokaw's and others' concept of the Greatest Generation might be of a people kinder and more virtuous than the ancient Greeks, who unabashedly fought for fame and personal glory. The upshot, however, of the Greatest Generation's example remains clear: Today's Americans (and citizens of other countries who fought the good fight in the Second World War) should emulate the Greatest Generation in sacrificing all, even their lives, for their country and its ideals. What better arena exists for such a sacrifice than a righteous military action against the world's forces of evil?

The American monuments to the Second World War range from somber and reflective, such as the thousands of crosses arranged in rows at Omaha Beach in Normandy and the fountains and open spaces of the World War II Memorial on the Washington Mall, to patriotic and triumphalist, such as the flag-raising image of the iconic Iwo Jima

[12] Brokaw 1998.

Memorial for the US Marine Corps. All of these monuments, like virtually all war monuments, emphasize the sacrifices made by soldiers fighting overseas. For example, inscribed on the small chapel in the American cemetery at Omaha Beach are the following words: "Their graves are the permanent and visible symbol of their heroic devotion and their sacrifice in the common cause of humanity." Whereas we increasingly view the First World War as an exercise in abject folly in the service of an obsolete imperialism, with no side being entirely in the right, our understanding of the Second World War tends to be less ambiguous. The evils of Hitler and Nazism needed to be stopped, and large-scale military action was likely the only option, even if we can still debate the ethics and effectiveness of the military response.

Nevertheless, the way that conflict is memorialized in the United States and in other countries allows for the encouragement of today's generation to live up to the example of the Greatest Generation. Today's citizens ought to take up arms nobly for their country, no matter if the conflicts in which those arms are used might be decidedly less clear-cut than the fight against Nazism. What can the "Greatest Generation" and their "heroic devotion" possibly imply other that today's Americans fall short? If an enemy like Hitler fails to materialize, do today's leaders need to frame much messier and morally questionable conflicts in such a way as to evoke a similarly patriotic response in the citizenry? To what extent are the monuments to the Second World War and other conflicts, along with various commemorative rituals such as Veterans' Day and Memorial Day, useful as modern calls to arms? By emphasizing the heroism and nobility of those who fought and died, even the most somber war memorials might imply "*dulce et decorum est* . . . ."

One casualty of nearly every war memorial is historical context and nuance, which is ironic given that even the most controversial memorials are defended as being vital to preserving "history." What is missing from the Vimy Memorial, and its two columns representing the cooperation between the French and English peoples, is that shortly after the Battle of Vimy Ridge Canada very nearly erupted into civil war as French Canadians in Québec vehemently protested the use of conscription. Even though much of the war was fought in France, French Canadians were never enthusiastic about taking part in what they saw as a British imperial exercise. American memorials gloss over the facts that the United States took two years to enter the Second World War, years in which Britain endured a horrific bombing campaign at the hands of the Luftwaffe, and that many Americans actually supported Hitler in the 1930s. The US even accepted some Nazis as immigrants after the war because they promised to be useful anti-communists while the Cold War took shape. In recent decades, institutions such as the Holocaust Memorial Museum in Washington DC have shone a light on the non-military victims of fascism and war. Institutions are beginning to acknowledge the atrocities committed by the Allies, such as the internment of Japanese Americans and the firebombing of Dresden. Germany, with its own Holocaust memorials and the opening up of former concentration camps as museums, provides an important example to the world of presenting the darkest parts of its history and its role in the Second World War in an honest way. Most other countries, however, fall short in preserving "history," at least in their war memorials.

In recent years, the focal point for the debate over the place and purpose of war memorials in the United States has been the statues of Confederate generals placed in prominent locations in many southern cities and towns, and even some northern ones. The infamous Unite the Right rally in Charlottesville, Virginia, in 2017, which led to the murder of Heather Heyer by a white supremacist, was ostensibly a protest against the proposed removal of an equestrian statue of Confederate general Robert E. Lee. Aside from the overt messages of white supremacy and racism, more "moderate" voices stood against the statue's removal on the grounds that Robert E. Lee was a part of history, and thus his image should remain to prevent the erasure of history. Similar debates continue to rage about a number of Confederate monuments. Aside from the fact that such monuments do a poor job of representing "history" – including its context, nuances, and ambiguities – those defending these monuments rarely acknowledge the context of their commissioning.

Most of these monuments were not erected immediately after the Civil War, to commemorate courageous leadership even in the service of a lost cause (similar to the mythology surrounding Leonidas and the 300 Spartans at Thermopylae, as we have seen). A majority of the Confederate monuments in question were set up in the 20th century, during periods in which Black Americans were fighting for and winning more civil rights. Instead of merely commemorating the bravery and skill of General Lee, and encouraging other Southerners to exhibit similar virtues, these monuments were clearly meant to assert the superiority of whites and stand against the struggle of Black Americans to obtain their due as American citizens.[13] There are many ways to respond to these

---

[13] For an overview of these Confederate monuments, and the debates surrounding them, see Cox 2021.

Confederate monuments other than simple removal, although, in some cases, removal might be the best option. To preserve "history," the best course might be to surround the monuments with interpretive displays that outline both the context of the Civil War, and the context of the monuments' commissioning. At the very least, these controversial and frequently offensive monuments should no longer enjoy places of prominence in town squares and public parks, since such positioning can only imply the virtues of the figures represented and call upon those viewing them to behave likewise. In other words, we ought to turn these monuments into something more like museums.

To compare the function of war memorials to museums in preserving and educating about "history," let us consider Canada's Vimy Memorial and the United States' World War II Memorial in relation to the Canadian War Museum in Ottawa and the National WWII Museum in New Orleans. The size and grandeur of the Vimy Memorial, along with imagery such as the Passing of the Torch, allows easily for the monument to be interpreted as a tribute to the bravery and noble sacrifices of the Canadian war dead, regardless of Allward's original intentions for the monument. Indeed, that is how the monument and the Battle of Vimy Ridge are typically represented in today's Canada. The Canadian War Museum, on the other hand, while it does reinforce the now-standard line about Vimy Ridge, has the space to present some of war's more difficult ethical questions and ambiguities. In the exhibit on strategic bombing in the Second World War, for instance, the interpretive panel states that the morality and effectiveness of the bombing of civilian populations are still in question – which drew the ire of Canadian veterans groups, who seemed to think the museum should exist only to commemorate and celebrate rather than educate.

The American World War II Memorial features the "Freedom Wall," on which 4,048 gold stars are placed, each representing 100 Americans who died in the war, along with the inscription, "here we mark the price of freedom." As is perhaps fitting for a memorial, which might not be the place to explore war's nuances, there is no suggestion that those who died did so in anything other than a righteous struggle for the freedom of the United States itself. The National WWII Museum, by contrast, has an extensive exhibit on the racist caricatures employed in American wartime recruitment posters and propaganda, especially in regard to the Japanese against whom the Americans were fighting in the Pacific. Far from celebrating such imagery, the museum forces visitors to confront the bad things done by their own side. After visiting this museum, those who confronted and wrestled with the American use of racist stereotypes are likely to be more thoughtful when considering the imagery used to represent those against whom America now fights.

Museums are by no means perfect or without agendas of their own. But if their exhibits are done carefully and thoughtfully, museums offer the interpretive space needed for providing a genuine education about history, including military history, and are as such much more valuable for the preservation of history than most war memorials are. War memorials are, in fact, part of history, in that they both reflect and help to shape how a society views itself, its soldiers, and its military past and present. Just as was the case in ancient Sparta, the commemoration of the war dead does far more than merely preserve memory. Rather, it provides examples of what a society thinks are good actions for its members to take, and good attitudes from them to have. Military commemoration typically encourages society's members to emulate the dead, but only in those actions and attitudes that a society deems salutary and fit to be represented by a memorial.

More often than not, modern memorials, like ancient ones, stress concepts like duty, honor, courage, and sacrifice, and that fighting and dying for one's country is not only good, but even sweet and fitting, *dulce et decorum*. In short, we must appraise memorials and commemoration carefully and critically; we must consider the context of their establishment; and we must consider, to the extent we are able, the context of the events that memorials and commemorative rituals claim to preserve for the next generation. I hope that, like Walter Allward, we come to grasp the futility and waste of war, and come to conceive of memorials and commemorative rituals as ways to turn us away from war and towards peaceful alternatives, as much as is within our power. We must find ways to interpret the violence and destruction of previous wars as warnings against future ones, rather than as calls to arms to live up to the supposedly uncomplicated examples set by our forebears. As wars continue to rage around the world, including Ukraine, where Russia's destructive invasion has lasted for a year and a half as I write these words, the task of avoiding and ending war is as urgent as ever.

Sparta's unyielding adherence to and representation of its militaristic way of life caused the Spartans to live in a state of paranoid fear of those they oppressed to make that way of life possible. Once Sparta combined these militaristic sentiments, including the desire for glory and fame, with missions of "liberation" and interventionist campaigns abroad, Sparta's relationship to war hastened the state's demographic and military collapse under the weight of its own obsolete system. Fighting for freedom meant that the glory-seeking Spartans fought wars more often, for longer periods, and further away. Sparta could not handle the strain. It is beyond the scope of this book to consider how much of our own blood and treasure, and those of the places where we now fight wars, has been wasted in the name of "freedom" and similarly noble aspirations. We might not fight openly for glory and fame anymore (even if we still sometimes do), but we certainly fight to set others free and help those who supposedly cannot help themselves. Let us prevent our own attitudes towards war and the war dead, and our own commemorative rituals and monuments, from doing to our societies what militarism tied to interventionism did to Sparta and other ancient powers. We can do more than jettison romantic ideas of glory and memory. With the Spartans as a cautionary example, we can look anew at the ethics and practical effects of choosing war as the means to help others. *Dulcius et decorius est pro patria vivere*, 'tis more sweet and more fitting to live for one's country.

# References

Acheson, D. 1987. *Present at the Creation: My Years in the State Department.* New York.

Allgaier, B. 2022. *Embedded Inscriptions in Herodotus and Thucydides.* Wiesbaden.

Adkins, A. W. H. 1977. "Callinus 1 and Tyrtaeus 10 as Poetry." *HSPh* 81: 59–97.

Allison, J. W. 1984. "Sthenelaidas' Speech. Thucydides 1.86." *Hermes* 112: 9–16.

Aloni, A. 2001. "The Proem of Simonides' Plataea Elegy and the Circumstances of Its Performance." In D. Boedeker and D. Sider (eds.), *New Simonides: Contexts of Praise and Desire.* Oxford. 86–105.

Alonso-Núñez, J. M. 2002. *The Idea of Universal History in Greece.* Leiden.

Anderson, B. 2016 (1983). *Imagined Communities: Reflections on the Origin and Spread of Nationalism.* Revised edition. London.

Anderson, C. A. 2008. "Archilochus, His Lost Shield, and the Heroic Ideal." *Phoenix* 62: 255–260.

Andrewes, A. 1971. "Two Notes on Lysander." *Phoenix* 25: 206–226.

1978. "Spartan Imperialism?" In C. R. Whittaker and P. Garnsey (eds.), *Imperialism in the Ancient World: The Cambridge University Research Seminar in Ancient History.* Cambridge. 91–102.

Arrington, N. T. 2015. *Ashes, Images, and Memories: The Presence of the War Dead in Fifth-Century Athens.* Oxford.

Assmann, J. 2011. *Cultural Memory and Early Civilization: Writing, Remembrance, and Political Imagination.* Cambridge.

Azoulay, V. 2017. *The Tyrant-Slayers of Ancient Athens: A Tale of Two Statues.* Trans. J. Lloyd. Oxford.

Badian, E. 1999. "The Road to Acanthus." In R. Mellor and R. Trittle (eds.), *Text and Tradition: Studies in Greek History and Historiography in Honor of Mortimer Chambers.* Claremont, CA. 3–35.

Balot, R. K. 2014. *Courage in the Democratic Polis: Ideology and Critique in Classical Athens.* Oxford.

Bartlett, R. C. 2018. "An Introduction to the Agesilaus." In G. A. McBrayer (ed.), *Xenophon: The Shorter Writings.* Ithaca, NY. 79–106.

Baumbach, M., A. Petrović, and I. Petrović (eds.). 2010. *Archaic and Classical Greek Epigram.* Cambridge.

Beam, A. 2007. "Meanwhile: Hot Times at the Hot Gates." *The New York Times*, March 8, 2007. www.nytimes.com/2007/03/08/opinion/08iht-edbeam .4844292.html.

Bearzot, C. 2005. "Philotimia, tradizione e innovazione: Lisandro e Agesilao a confronto in Plutarco." In A. Pérez Jiménez and F. B. Tichener (eds.), *Historical and Biographical Values of Plutarch's Works: Studies Devoted to Professor Philip A. Stadter by the International Plutarch Society*. Logan, UT. 31–49.

Bérard, R.-M. 2020. "La politique du cadavre: traitements funéraires et usages civiques des morts à la guerre en Grèce archaïque et classique." *Annales (HSS)* 75: 3–38.

Bershadsky, N. 2012. "The Border of War and Peace: Myth and Ritual in Argive-Spartan Dispute over Thyreatis." In J. Wilker (ed.), *Maintaining Peace and Interstate Stability in Archaic and Classical Greece*. Mainz. 49–77.

Berve, H. 1967. *Die Tyrannis bei den Griechen*. 2 volumes. Munich.

Bilis, T. and M. Magnisali. 2011–12. "Issues Concerning the Architectural Reconstruction of the Monuments of the Sanctuary of Apollo Amyklaios." *Mouseio Benaki* 11–12: 125–135.

Bloedow, E. F. 1987. "Sthenelaidas the Persuasive Spartan." *Hermes* 115: 60–66.

Boedeker, D. 2001. "Heroic Historiography: Simonides and Herodotus on Plataea." In D. Boedeker and D. Sider (eds.), *New Simonides: Contexts of Praise and Desire*. Oxford. 120–134.

2015. "Two Tales of Spartan Envoys." In C. A. Clark, E. Foster, and J. P. Hallett (eds.), *Kinesis: The Ancient Depiction of Gesture, Motion, and Emotion – Essays for Donald Lateiner*. Ann Arbor, MI. 103–115.

Boedeker, D. and D. Sider (eds.). 2001. *New Simonides: Contexts of Praise and Desire*. Oxford.

Boëldieu-Trevet, J. 1997. "Brasidas: la naissance de l'art du commandement." In P. Brulé and J. Oulhen (eds.), *Esclavage, guerre, économie en Grèce ancienne*. Paris. 147–158.

Bommelaer, J.-F. 1981. *Lysandre de Sparte: histoire et traditions*. Athens.

Bond, S. E. 2018. "This Is Not Sparta: Why the Modern Romance with Sparta Is a Bad One." *Eidolon*, May 7, 2018 (online publication): https://eidolon.pub /this-is-not-sparta-392a9ccddf26.

Bosworth, A. B. 1993. "The Humanitarian Aspect of the Melian Dialogue." *JHS* 113: 30–44.

2009. "Thucydides and the Unheroic Dead." In O. Palagia (ed.), *Art in Athens during the Peloponnesian War*. Cambridge. 168–187.

Bouyia, P. 2010. "Herakleia in Trachis." *NAC* 39: 79–100.

Bridges, E. 2007. "The Guts and the Glory: Pressfield's Spartans at the Gates of Fire." In E. Bridges, E. Hall, and P. J. Rhodes (eds.), *Cultural Responses to the Persian Wars: Antiquity to the Third Millennium*. Oxford. 405–421.

Brockliss, W. 2019. *Homeric Imagery and the Natural Environment*. Washington, DC.

Brokaw, T. 1998. *The Greatest Generation*. New York.

Bruni, G. B. 1979. "Mothakes, neodamodeis, Brasideioi." In M. Capozza (ed.), *Schiavitù, manomissione e classi dipendenti nel mondo antico*. Rome. 21–31.

Budin, S. L. 2008. "Simonides' Corinthian Epigram." *CPh* 103: 335–353.

Burns, T. 2011. "The Virtue of Thucydides' Brasidas." *J Polit* 73: 508–523.

Butera, C. J. and M. A. Sears. 2019. *Battles and Battlefields of Ancient Greece: A Guide to Their History, Topography and Archaeology*. Barnsley.

Cairns, D. F. 1993. *Aidōs: The Psychology and Ethics of Honour and Shame in Ancient Greek Literature*. Oxford.

Calame, C. 2018. "Pre-Classical Sparta As Song Culture." In A. Powell (ed.), *A Companion to Sparta*. Hoboken, NJ. 177–201.

Camp, J. M. 2001. *The Archaeology of Athens*. New Haven, CT.

Carey, C. 2019. *Thermopylae: Great Battles*. Oxford.

Cartledge, P. 1982. "Sparta and Samos: A Special Relationship?" *CQ* 32: 243–265.

1987. *Agesilaos and the Crisis of Sparta*. Baltimore.

1999. "The Socratics' Sparta and Rousseau's." In S. Hodkinson and A. Powell (eds.), *Sparta: New Perspectives*. London. 311–337.

2002. *The Greeks: A Portrait of Self and Others*. Second edition. Oxford.

2007. *Thermopylae: The Battle That Changed the World*. New York.

2013. *After Thermopylae: The Oath of Plataea and the End of the Graeco-Persian Wars*. Oxford.

2022. "Lichas: A Mini-Biography." In N. Marinatos and R. K. Pitt (eds.), *Thucydides the Athenian*. Athens. 201–216.

Cartledge, P. and P. Debnar. 2006. "Sparta and the Spartans in Thucydides." In A. Rengakos and A. Tsakmakis (eds.), *Brill's Companion to Thucydides*. Leiden. 559–587.

Cartledge, P. and A. Spawforth. 2002. *Hellenistic and Roman Sparta: A Tale of Two Cities*. Second edition. London.

Cavanagh, W. 2018. "An Archaeology of Ancient Sparta with Reference to Laconia and Messenia." In A. Powell (ed.), *A Companion to Sparta*. Hoboken, NJ. 61–92.

Cawkwell, G. L. 1976. "Agesilaus and Sparta." *CQ* 26: 62–84.

Christesen, P. 2010. "Kings Playing Politics: The Heroization of Chionis of Sparta." *Historia* 59: 26–73.

2014. "Sport and Society in Sparta." In P. Christesen and D. G. Kyle (eds.), *A Companion to Sport and Spectacle in Greek and Roman Antiquity*. Malden, MA. 146–158.

2018. "The Typology and Topography of Spartan Burials from the Protogeometric to the Hellenistic Period: Rethinking Spartan Exceptionalism and the Ostensible Cessation of Adult Intramural Burials in the Greek World." *ABSA* 113: 307–363.

2019. *A New Reading of the Damonon Stele. Histos* Supplement 10. Newcastle upon Tyne.

Christien, J. 2018. "Roads and Quarries in Laconia." In A. Powell (ed.), *A Companion to Sparta*. Hoboken, NJ. 615–642.

Clarimont, C. W. 1983. *Patrios Nomos: Public Burial in Athens during the Fifth and Fourth Centuries* B.C. (2 vols.). Oxford.

Clarke, M. 2002. "Spartan ἄτη at Thermopylae: Semantics and Ideology at Herodotus, *Histories* 7, 234." In A. Powell and S. Hodkinson (eds.), *Sparta: Beyond the Mirage*. London. 63–84.

2004. "Manhood and Heroism." In R. L. Fowler (ed.), *The Cambridge Companion to Homer*. Cambridge. 74–90.

Clough, E. 2004. "Loyalty and Liberty: Thermopylae in the Western Imagination." In T. Figueira (ed.), *Spartan Society*. Swansea. 363–384.

Cohen, J. 2010. *Rousseau: A Free Community of Equals*. Oxford.

Cole, M. 2019. "The Sparta Fetish Is a Cultural Cancer: The Myth of the Mighty Warrior-State Has Enchanted Societies for Thousands of Years. Now It Fuels a Global Fascist Movement." *The New Republic*, August 1, 2019 (online publication): https://newrepublic.com/article/154563/sparta-myth-rise-fascism-trumpism.

2021. *The Bronze Lie: Shattering the Myth of Spartan Warrior Supremacy*. Oxford.

Connor, W. R. 1984. *Thucydides*. Princeton.

Cox, K. L. 2021. *No Common Ground: Confederate Monuments and the Ongoing Fight for Racial Justice*. Chapel Hill, NC.

Crane, G. 1998. *Thucydides and the Ancient Simplicity: The Limits of Political Realism*. Berkeley.

Cullen, D. E. 1993. *Freedom in Rousseau's Political Philosophy*. DeKalb, IL.

Currie, B. 2002. "Euthymos of Locri: A Case Study in Heroization in the Classical Period." *JHS* 122: 24–44.

2005. *Pindar and the Cult of Heroes*. Oxford.

Daverio Rocchi, G. 1985. "Brasida nella tradizione storiografica. Aspetti del rapporto tra ritratto letterario e figura storica." *Acme* 38: 63–81.

Davis, J. L. and S. R. Stocker. 2021. *A Greek State in Formation: The Origins of Civilization in Mycenaean Pylos*. Berkeley.

Decety, N. 2020. "Attrition-Based 'Oliganthrōpia' Revisited." *Klio* 102: 474–508.

De Jong, I. J. F. (ed.). 2012. *Homer* Iliad *Book XXII*. Cambridge.

Diller, H. 1962. "Freiheit bei Thukydides als Schlagwort und als Wirklichkeit." *Gymnasium* 69: 189–204.

Dillery, J. 1996. "Reconfiguring the Past: Thyrea, Thermopylae and Narrative Patterns in Herodotus." *AJPh* 117: 217–254.

2019. "Cynisca's Swift-Footed Horses: CEG 820 (IG V.1 1564a, IvO 160) and The Lame Kingship of Agesilaus." *ZPE* 210: 17–19.

Dillon, M. 2007. "Were Spartan Women Who Died in Childbirth Honoured with Grave Inscriptions?" *Hermes* 135: 149–165.

2017. *Omens and Oracles: Divination in Ancient Greece*. London.

Dmitriev, S. 2011. *The Greek Slogan of Freedom and Early Roman Politics in Greece*. Oxford.

Ducat, J. 2006a. *Spartan Education: Youth and Society in the Classical Period*. Trans. E. J. Stafford. Swansea.

2006b. "The Spartan 'Tremblers.'" Trans. P. J. Shaw. In S. Hodkinson and A. Powell (eds.), *Sparta and War*. Swansea. 1–56.

2018. "The 'Perioikoi'." In A. Powell (ed.), *A Companion to Sparta*. Hoboken, NJ. 596–614.

Duffy, X. S. 2016. Monuments, Memory, and Place: Commemorations of the Persian Wars. PhD diss., University of Birmingham. Birmingham.

Ellis, J. R. 1994. "Thucydidean Method in the Kylon, Pausanias and Themistokles Logoi." *Arethusa* 27: 165–191.

Evans, F. 2019. *Public Art and the Fragility of Democracy: An Essay in Political Aesthetics*. New York.

Evans, J. A. S. 1988. "The Medism of Pausanias. Two Versions." *Antichthon*. 22: 1–11.

Ferrario, S. B. 2014. *Historical Agency and the "Great Man" in Classical Greece*. Cambridge.

Figueira, T. 2016. "Politeia and Lakonika in Spartan Historiography." In T. Figueira (ed.), *Myth, Text, and History at Sparta*. Piscataway, NJ. 7–104.

2018. "Helotage and the Spartan Economy." In A. Powell (ed.), *A Companion to Sparta*. Hoboken, NJ. 565–595.

Fisher, N. R. E. 1994. "Sparta Re(de)valued: Some Athenian Public Attitudes to Sparta between Leuctra and the Lamian War." In A. Powell and S. Hodkinson (eds.), *The Shadow of Sparta*. London. 347–400.

Flower, M. A. 1988. "Agesilaus of Sparta and the Origins of the Ruler Cult." *CQ* 38: 123–134.

1998. "Simonides, Ephorus, and Herodotus on the Battle of Thermopylae." *CQ* 48: 365–379.

2009. "Spartan 'Religion' and Greek 'Religion'." In S. Hodkinson (ed.), *Sparta: Comparative Approaches*. Oxford. 193–229.

2018. "Spartan Religion." In A. Powell (ed.), *A Companion to Sparta*. Hoboken, NJ. 425–451.

Flower, M. A. and J. Marincola (eds.). 2002. *Herodotus* Histories *Book IX*. Cambridge.

Foster, E. 2019. "Minor Infantry Defeats and Spartan Deaths in Xenophon's *Hellenica*." In A. Kapellos (ed.), *Xenophon on Violence*. Berlin. 83–101.

Fotheringham, L. S. 2012. "The Positive Portrayal of Sparta in Late-Twentieth-Century Fiction." In S. Hodkinson and I. Macgregor Morris (eds.), *Sparta in Modern Thought: Politics, History and Culture*. Swansea. 393–428.

Fragkopoulou, F. 2012. "Lakonia and Samos during the Early Iron Age: A Revised Look at the Messenian War Dates." In N. C. Stampolides and A. Kanta (eds.), *Athanasia: The Earthly, the Celestial and the Underworld in the Mediterranean from the Late Bronze Age and the Early Iron Age*. Heraklion. 101–111.

Fragoulaki, M. 2021. "The Mytho-Political Map of Spartan Colonisation in Thucydides: The 'Spartan Colonical Triangle' vs. the 'Spartan Mediterranean'." In A. Powell and P. Debnar (eds.), *Thucydides and Sparta*. Swansea. 183–219.

Franchi, E. 2018. "Commemorating the War Dead in Ancient Sparta: The Gymnopaidiai and the Battle of Hysiai." In V. Brouma and K. Heydon (eds.), *Conflict in the Peloponnese: Social, Military and Intellectual*. Nottingham. 24–39.

2019. "Memories of Winners and Losers: Historical Remarks on Why Societies Remember and Commemorate Wars." In M. Giangiulio, E. Franchi, and G. Proietti (eds.), *Commemorating War and War Dead: Ancient and Modern*. Stuttgart. 35–69.

Giangiulio, M. 2019. "Do Societies Remember? The Notion of 'Collective Memory': Paradigms and Problems (from Maurice Halbwachs on)." In M. Giangiulio, E. Franchi, and G. Proietti (eds.), *Commemorating War and War Dead: Ancient and Modern*. Stuttgart. 17–33.

Giangiulio, M., E. Franchi, and G. Proietti (eds.). 2019. *Commemorating War and War Dead: Ancient and Modern*. Stuttgart.

Gidney, C. 2015. *Tending the Student Body: Youth, Health, and the Modern University*. Toronto.

Gomme, A. W., A. Andrewes, and K. J. Dover. 1945–1981. *A Historical Commentary on Thucydides* (5 vols.). Oxford.

Graziosi, B. and J. Haubold. 2003. "Homeric Masculinity: ἠνορέη and ἀγηνορίη." *JHS* 123: 60–76.

Green, P. 2006. *Diodorus Siculus, Books 11–12.37.1: Greek History, 480–431 BC, the Alternative Version*. Austin.

2010. *Diodorus Siculus, the Persian Wars to the Fall of Athens: Books 11–14.34 (480–401 BCE)*. Austin.

Greenhalgh, P. A. L. 1972. "Patriotism in the Homeric World." *Historia* 21: 528–537.

Grote, G. 1851. *The History of Greece*. 12 volumes. Boston.

Guthrie, J. R. 2015. *A Kiss from Thermopylae: Emily Dickinson and Law*. Amherst, MA.

Habicht, C. 1970. *Gottmenschentum und griechische Städte*. Second edition. Munich.

Hägg, R. (ed.). 1999. *Ancient Greek Hero Cult: Proceedings of the Fifth International Seminar on Ancient Greek Cult, Organized by the Department of Classical Archaeology and Ancient History, Göteborg University, 21–23 April 1995*. Stockholm.

Halbwachs, M. 1992. *On Collective Memory*. Chicago.

Hall, E. 1989. *Inventing the Barbarian: Greek Self-Definition through Tragedy*. Oxford.

Hamilton, C. D. 1979. *Sparta's Bitter Victories: Politics and Diplomacy in the Corinthian War*. Ithaca, NY.

1991. *Agesilaus and the Failure of Spartan Hegemony*. Ithaca, NY.

Hansen, P. A. (ed.). 1983. *Carmina Epigraphica Graeca Saeculorum VIII–V a. Chr.* Berlin.

Hanson, V. D. 2007. "With Your Shield or On It: Zack Snyder's *300*: A Spirited Take on a Clash of Civilizations." *City Journal*, March 7, 2007 (online publication): www.city-journal.org/html/your-shield-or-it-9420.html.

Harley, T. R. 1941. "A Greater than Leonidas." *G&R* 11: 68–83.

Harrison, S. J. 1993. "Dulce et Decorum: Horace *Odes* 3.2.13." *RhM* 136: 91–93.

Hartog, F. 1988. *The Mirror of Herodotus: The Representation of the Other in the Writing of History*. Berkeley.

Harvey, D. 2004. "The Clandestine Massacre of the Helots (Thucydides 4.80)." In T. Figueira (ed.), *Spartan Society*. Swansea. 199–218.

Hell, J. 2019. *The Conquest of Ruins: The Third Reich and the Fall of Rome*. Chicago.

Henriksén, C. (ed.). 2019. *A Companion to Ancient Epigram*. Newark, NJ.

Herodotus. 2003. *The Histories*. Trans. A. de Sélincourt. Introduction and notes by J. Marincola. New York.

Hibler, D. 1993. "The Hero-Reliefs of Lakonia: Changes in Form and Function." In O. Palagia and W. D. E. Coulson (eds.), *Sculpture from Arcadia and Laconia: Proceedings of an International Conference Held at the American School of Classical Studies at Athens, April 10–14, 1992*. Oxford. 199–204.

Hobsbawm, E. 2012. "Mass-Producing Traditions: Europe, 1870–1914." In E. Hobsbawm and T. Ranger (eds.), *The Invention of Tradition*. Cambridge. 263–308.

Hodkinson, S. 2006. "Was Classical Sparta a Military Society?" In S. Hodkinson and A. Powell (eds.), *Sparta and War*. Swansea. 111–162.

——— 2020. "Professionalism, Specialization, and Skill in the Classical Spartan Army?" In D. Lews, E. Stewart, and E. Harris (eds.), *Skilled Labour and Professionalism in Ancient Greece and Rome*. Cambridge. 335–361.

——— 2022. "Spartans on the Capitol: Recent Far Right Appropriations of Spartan Militarism in the USA and Their Historical Roots." In K. Beerden and T. Epping (eds.), *Classical Controversies: Graeco-Roman Antiquity in the Twenty-First Century*. Leiden. 59–84.

——— 2023. "Plutarch and Sparta's Military Characteristics in the Parallel Lives." In P. Davies and J. Mossman (eds.), *Sparta in Plutarch's Lives*. Swansea. 23-52.

Hoffmann, G. 2000. "Brasidas ou le fait d'armes comme source d'héroïsation dans la Grèce classique." In V. Pirenne-Delforge and E. Suárez de la Torre (eds.), *Héros et héroïnes dans les mythes et les cultes grecs*. Liège. 365–375.

Hornblower, S. 1991–2008. *A Commentary on Thucydides* (3 vols.). Oxford.

——— 2006. *Thucydides and Pindar: Historical Narrative and the World of Epinikian Poetry*. Oxford.

How, W. W. and J. Wells. 1912. *A Commentary on Herodotus*. Oxford.

Howie, J. G. 1996. "The Major Aristeia in Homer and Xenophon." In F. Cairns (ed.), *Papers of the Leeds International Latin Seminar 9*. Leeds. 197–217.

Howie, J. G. 2005. "The Aristeia of Brasidas: Thucydides' Presentation of Events at Pylos and Amphipolis." In F. Cairns (ed.), *Papers of the Langford Latin Seminar 12*. Oxford. 207–284.

Humble, N. 2021. *Xenophon of Athens: A Socratic on Sparta*. Cambridge.

2022. "Sparta: Separating Reality from Mirage." In A. Glazebrook and C. Vester (eds.), *Themes in Greek Society and Culture: An Introduction to Ancient Greece*. Second edition. Oxford. 194–216.

Hüppauf, B. 1988. "Langemarck, Verdun and the Myth of a New Man in Germany after the First World War." *War & Society* 6: 70–103.

Irwin, E. 2005. *Solon and Early Greek Poetry: The Politics of Exhortation*. Cambridge.

Jacoby, F. 1945. "Some Athenian Epigrams from the Persian Wars." *Hesperia* 14: 157–211.

Jaffe, S. N. 2017. *Thucydides on the Outbreak of War: Character and Contest*. Oxford.

Jones, C. P. 2010. *New Heroes in Antiquity: From Achilles to Antinoos*. Cambridge, MA.

Jordan, B. 1990. "The Ceremony of the Helots in Thucydides IV, 80." *AC* 59: 37–69.

Jung, M. 2006. *Marathon und Plataiai. Zwei Perserschlachten als 'lieux de mémoire' im antiken Griechenland*. Göttingen.

Keesling, C. M. 2010. "The Callimachus monument on the Athenian Acropolis (CEG 256) and Athenian commemoration of the Persian Wars." In M. Baumbach, A. Petrović, and I. Petrović (eds.), *Archaic and Classical Greek Epigram*. Cambridge. 100–130.

2012. "The Marathon Casualty List from Eua-Loukou and the Plinthedon Style in Attic Inscriptions." *ZPE* 180: 139–148.

2017. *Early Greek Portraiture: Monuments and Histories*. Cambridge.

Kennell, N. M. 1995. *The Gymnasium of Virtue: Education and Culture in Ancient Sparta*. Chapel Hill.

2018. "Spartan Cultural Memory in the Roman Period." In A. Powell (ed.), *A Companion to Sparta*. Hoboken, NJ. 643–662.

Kern, P. B. 1989. "The Turning Point in the Sicilian Expedition." *CB* 65: 77–82.

Ketelsen, U.-K. 1985. "'Die Jugend von Langemarck.' Ein poetisch-politisches Motiv der Zwischenkriegszeit." In R. P. Janz and F. Trommler (eds.), *"Mit uns zieht die neue Zeit." Der Mythos der Jugend*. Frankfurt. 68–96.

Kienlin, A. von. 2003. "Zu den Staatsgräbern im Kerameikos." *Architectura* 33: 113–122.

Kinnee, L. 2018. *The Greek and Roman Trophy: From Battlefield Marker to Icon of Power*. London.

Knigge, U. 1991. *The Athenian Kerameikos: History, Monuments, Excavations*. Athens.

Konijnendijk, R. 2015. "Review of *Sparta's German Children* by H. Roche." *JHS* 135: 302–303.

2019. "Commemoration through Fear: The Spartan Reputation as a Weapon of War." In M. Giangiulio, E. Franchi, and G. Proietti (eds.), *Commemorating War and War Dead: Ancient and Modern*. Stuttgart. 257–269.

Koukouli-Chrysanthaki, C. 2002. "Excavating Classical Amphipolis." In M. Stamatopoulou and M. Yeroulanou (eds.), *Excavating Classical Culture: Recent Archaeological Discoveries in Greece*. Oxford. 57–73.

Kourinou, E. 2000. *Σπάρτη. Συμβολή στη Μνημειακή Τοπογραφία της*. Athens.

Kowerski, L. M. 2005. *Simonides on the Persian Wars: A Study of the Elegiac Verses of the "New Simonides."* London.

Krentz, P. 2011. *The Battle of Marathon*. New Haven.

Kucewicz, C. 2021a. "The War Dead in Archaic Sparta." In R. Konijnendijk, C. Kucewicz, and M. Lloyd (eds.), *Brill's Companion to Greek Land Warfare beyond the Phalanx*. Leiden. 83–121.

2021b. *The Treatment of the War Dead in Archaic Athens: An Ancestral Custom*. London.

Kühne, T. 2017. *The Rise and Fall of Comradeship: Hitler's Soldiers, Male Bonding and Mass Violence in the Twentieth Century*. Cambridge.

Kwak, T. Y. 2007. "The Clash of Civilizations: Obfuscating Race, History, and Culture in *300*." In K. McDonald (ed.), *Americanization of History: Conflation of Time and Culture in Film and Television*. Newcastle upon Tyne. 192–211.

Laforse, B. M. 1998. "Xenophon, Callicratidas and Panhellenism." *AHB* 12: 55–67.

Laqueur, T. 2016. *The Work of the Dead: A Cultural History of Mortal Remains*. Princeton.

Latacz, J. 1977. *Kampfparänese, Kampfdarstellung und Kampfwirklichkeit in der Ilias, bei Kallinos und Tyrtaios*. Munich.

Lazenby, J. F. 1985. *The Spartan Army*. Warminster.

1993. *The Defence of Greece, 490–479 B.C.* Warminster.

2004. *The Peloponnesian War: A Military Study*. London.

Lendon, J. E. 1989. "The Oxyrhynchus Historian and the Origins of the Corinthian War." *Historia* 38: 300–313.

2010. *Song of Wrath: The Peloponnesian War Begins*. New York.

Levene, D. S. 2010. *Livy on the Hannibalic War*. Oxford.

Lévy, E. 2005. "La Sparta de Platon." *Ktema* 30: 217–236.

Lewis, D. M. 1977. *Sparta and Persia*. Leiden.

2018. *Greek Slave Systems in Their Eastern Mediterranean Context, c. 800–146 BC*. Oxford.

Lissarrague, F. 1990. *L'autre guerrier: archers, peltastes, cavaliers dans l'imagerie attique*. Paris.

Loraux, N. 1977. "La 'belle mort' spartiate." *Ktema* 2: 105–120.

2006. *The Invention of Athens: The Funeral Oration and the Classical City*. New York.

2018. "The 'Beautiful Death' from Homer to Democratic Athens." Trans. D. Pritchard. *Arethusa* 51: 73–89.

Losemann, V. 2012. "The Spartan Tradition in Germany, 1870–1945." In S. Hodkinson and I. Macgregor Morris (eds.), *Sparta in Modern Thought: Politics, History, and Culture*. Swansea. 253–314.

Low, P. 2003. "Remembering War in Fifth-Century Greece: Ideologies, Societies, and Commemoration beyond Democratic Athens." *World Archaeology* 35: 98–111.

2006. "Commemorating the Spartan War Dead." In A. Powell and S. Hodkinson (eds.), *Sparta and War*. Swansea. 85–109.

(ed.). 2008. *The Athenian Empire*. Edinburgh.

2010. "Commemoration of the War Dead in Classical Athens: Remembering Defeat and Victory." In D. M. Pritchard (ed.), *War, Democracy, and Culture in Classical Athens*. Cambridge. 341–358.

2011. "The Power of the Dead in Classical Sparta: The Case of Thermopylae." In M. Carroll and J. Rempel (eds.), *Living through the Dead: Burial and Commemoration in the Classical World*. Oxford. 1–20.

Low, P., G. Oliver, and P. J. Rhodes (eds.). 2012. *Cultures of Commemoration: War Memorials Ancient and Modern*. Oxford.

Lucchesi, M. A. 2016. "Gylippus in Plutarch's 'Parallel Lives': Intratextuality and Readers." *Ploutarchos* 13: 3–31.

Luginbill, R. D. 2002. "Tyrtaeus 12 West: Come Join the Spartan Army." *CQ* 52: 405–414.

2014. "The Battle of Oinoe, the Painting in the Stoa Poikile, and Thucydides' Silence." *Historia* 63: 278–292.

Luraghi, N. 2008. *The Ancient Messenians: Constructions of Ethnicity and Memory*. Cambridge.

Luraghi, N. and S. E. Alcock (eds.). 2003. *Helots and Their Masters in Laconia and Messenia: Histories, Ideologies, Structures*. Washington, DC.

Macgregor Morris, I, 2000. "'To Make a New Thermopylae': Hellenism, Greek Liberation, and the Battle of Thermopylae." *G&R*. 47: 211–230.

2009. "Liars, Eccentrics and Visionaries: Early Travellers to Sparta and the Birth of Laconian Archaeology." In W. G. Cavanagh, C. Gallou, and M. Georgiadis (eds.), *Sparta and Laconia: From Prehistory to Pre-Modern*. London. 387–395.

Mackowiak, K. 2018. "Hagnon et Brasidas à Amphipolis: chronique d'une 'fin de culte' annoncée?" *RHR* 235: 311–328.

MacLeod, C. W. 1977. "Thucydides' Plataean Debate." *GRBS* 18: 227–246.

Malkin, I. 1987. *Religion and Colonization in Ancient Greece*. Leiden.

1994. *Myth and Territory in the Spartan Mediterranean*. Cambridge.

Mari, M. 2010. "Atene, l'impero e le « apoikiai »: riflessioni sulla breve vita di Anfipoli ' ateniese'." *ASAA* 10: 391–413.

2012. "Amphipolis between Athens and Sparta: A Philological and Historical Commentary on Thuc. V 11, 1." *MediterrAnt* 15: 327–353.

Marincola, J. 2016. "The Historian as Hero: Herodotus and the 300 at Thermopylae." *TAPhA* 146: 219–236.

Mariggio, V. A. 2007. "Le voyage en Asie des Spartiates Sperthias et Boulis." *LEC* 75: 193–205.

Mason, H. 2012. "Sparta and the French Enlightenment." In S. Hodkinson and I. Macgregor Morris (eds.), *Sparta in Modern Thought: Politics, History and Culture*. Swansea. 71–104.

Matalas, P. 2017. "Travellers and Ruins in the Spartan Landscape: A Ghost Story." In S. Voutsaki and P. Cartledge (eds.), *Ancient Monuments and Modern Identities: A Critical History of Archaeology in 19th and 20th Century Greece*. London. 41–61.

Matthaiou, A. P. 1988. "Νέος λίθος τοῦ μνημείου με τα ἐπιγράμματα για τους Περσικούς πολέμους." *Horos* 6: 118–122.

    2003. "Ἀθηναίοισι τεταγμένοισι ἐν τεμένεϊ Ἡρακλέος (Hdt. 6. 108. 1)." In P. Derow and R. Parker (eds.), *Herodotus and His World: Essays from a Conference in Memory of George Forrest*. Oxford. 190–202.

McCauley, B. A. 1993. Hero Cults and Politics in Fifth Century Greece. PhD diss., University of Iowa. Iowa City.

McKay, I. and J. Swift. 2016. *The Vimy Trap, or How We Learned to Stop Worrying and Love the Great War*. Toronto.

McCrae, J. 1919. *In Flanders Fields and Other Poems*. New York.

McDonald, C. and S. Hoffman. 2012. *Rousseau and Freedom*. Cambridge.

Meidani, K. 2013. "Agesilaos as Agamemnon at Aulis: A 4th Century Invention or the Continuation of a Long Tradition?" In P. Cartledge, A. Gartziou-Tatti, and N. Birgalias (eds.), *Πόλεμος, ειρήνη και πανελλήνιοι αγώνες: στη μνήμη Pierre Garlier*. Athens. 107–129.

Meier, M. 1998. *Aristokraten und Damoden: Untersuchungen zur inneren Entwicklung Spartas im 7. Jahrhundert v. Chr. und zur politischen Funktion der Dichtung des Tyrtaios*. Stuttgart.

Meiggs, R. and D. Lewis (eds.). 1988. *A Selection of Greek Historical Inscriptions: To the End of the Fifth Century* B.C. Revised edition. Oxford.

Metcalf, R. D. 2009. "Socrates and Achilles." In P. L. Fagan and J. Edward Russon (eds.), *Reexamining Socrates in the "Apology."* Evanston, IL. 62–84.

Millender, E. G. 2002. "Νόμος Δεσπότης: Spartan Obedience and Athenian Lawfulness in Fifth- Century Thought." In V. B. Gorman and E. W. Robinson (eds.), *Oikistes: Studies in Constitutions, Colonies, and Military Power in the Ancient World. Offered in Honor of A. J. Graham*. Leiden. 33–60.

    2006. "The Politics of Mercenary Service." In S. Hodkinson and A. Powell (eds.), *Sparta and War*. Swansea. 235–266.

    2018. "Spartan Women." In A. Powell (ed.), *A Companion to Sparta*. Hoboken, NJ. 500–524.

Miller, M. C. 1997. *Athens and Persia in the Fifth Century* B.C.: *A Study in Cultural Receptivity*. Cambridge.

Moles, J. L. 1994. "Xenophon and Callicratidas." *JHS* 114: 70–84.

Momigliano, A. 1966. *Terzo contributo alla storia degli studi classici e del mondo antico*. Rome.

Monti, G. 2009. "Alessandro, Sparta e la guerra di vendetta contro i Persiani." *AncSoc* 39: 35–53.

Muller, J. 2022. "Pop Culture against Modernity: New Right-Wing Movements and the Reception of Sparta." In K. Beerden and T. Epping (eds.), *Classical Controveries: Reception of Graeco-Roman Antiquity in the Twenty-First Century*. Leiden. 103–122.

Musti, D. and M. Torelli. 1991. *Pausania, Guida della Grecia: Libro III: La Laconia*. Milan.

Nafissi, M. 1991. *La nascita del kosmos: studi sulla storia e la società di Sparta*. Naples.

Nenci, N. 2018. "The Votive of Aiglatas, Spartan Runner: Old Evidence, New Knowledge." *ABSA* 113: 251–278.

Nichols, M. P. 2014. *Thucydides and the Pursuit of Freedom*. Ithaca, NY.

Nobili, C. 2011. "Threnodic Elegy in Sparta." *GRBS* 51: 26–48.

Nora, P. (ed.). 1997. *Les lieux de mémoire* (3 vols.). Third edition. Paris.

Ober, J. 2005. *Athenian Legacies: Essays on the Politics of Going on Together*. Princeton.

O'Hare McCormick, A. 1948. "Greece Is a Test of Staying Power." *The New York Times*, December 29, 1948, p. 20.

Ollier, F. 1933–1943. *Le mirage spartiate* (2 vols.). Paris.

Oswald, S. 2014. Trends in Early Epigram. PhD diss., Princeton University. Princeton.

Owen, W. 1920. *Poems*. London.

Page, D. L. (ed.). 1962. *Poetae Melici Graeci*. Oxford.

(ed.). 1981. *Further Greek Epigrams*. Cambridge.

Papastamati, S. 2017. "The Poetic of 'Kalos Thanatos' in Euripides' 'Hecuba': Masculine and Feminine Motifs in Polyxena's Death." *Mnemosyne* 70: 361–385.

Papazarkadas, N. 2014. *The Epigraphy and History of Boeotia: New Finds, New Prospects*. Leiden.

Paradiso, A. 2004. "The Logic of Terror: Thucydides, Spartan Duplicity and an Improbable Massacre." In T. Figueira (ed.), *Spartan Society*. Swansea. 179–198.

Paradiso, A. and J. Roy. 2008. "Lepreon and Phyrkos in 421–420." *Klio* 90: 27–35.

Parker, R. 1989. "Spartan Religion." In A. Powell (ed.), *Classical Sparta: Techniques behind Her Success*. London. 142–172.

Pavlides, N. 2010. "Worshipping Heroes: Civic Identity and the Veneration of the Communal Dead in Archaic Sparta." In H. Cavanagh, W. Cavanagh, and J. Roy (eds.), *Honouring the Dead in the Peloponnese: Proceedings of the Conference Held at Sparta 23–25 April 2009*. Nottingham. 551–576.

2011. Hero-Cult in Archaic and Classical Sparta: A Study of Local Religion. PhD diss., University of Edinburgh. Edinburgh.

2020. "Non-Spartans in the Lakedaimonian Army: The Evidence from Laconia." *Historia* 69: 154–184.

Pearson, L. 1986. "The Speeches in Timaeus' History." *AJPh* 107: 350–368.

Pelling, C. 1991. "Thucydides' Archidamus and Herodotus' Artabanus." In M. A. Flower and M. Toher (eds.), *Georgica: Greek Studies in Honour of George Cawkwell*. London. 120–142.

Pesely, George E. 1985. "The Speech of Endius in Diodorus Siculus xiii, 52, 3–8." *CPh* 80: 320–321.

Petrovic, A. 2007. *Kommentar zu den simonideischen Versinschriften.* Leiden.

  2016. "Archaic Funerary Epigram and Hector's Imagined Epitymbia." In A. Efstathiou and I. Karamanou (eds.), *Homeric Receptions across Generic and Cultural Contexts.* Berlin. 45–58.

Pettersson, M. 1992. *Cults of Apollo at Sparta: The Hyakinthia, the Gymnopaidiai and the Karneia.* Stockholm.

Pipili, M. 2018. "Laconian Pottery." In A. Powell (ed.), *A Companion to Sparta.* Hoboken, NJ. 124–153.

Pomeroy, S. B. 2002. *Spartan Women.* Oxford.

Powell, A. 2004. "The Women of Sparta – and of Other Greek Cities – at War." In T. J. Figueira and P. Brulé (eds.), *Spartan Society.* Swansea. 137–150.

Pritchard, D. M. 2022. "Honouring the War Dead in Democratic Athens." In E. M. Economou, N. C. Kyriazis, and A. Platias (eds.), *Democracy and Salamis: 2500 Years after the Battle that Saved Greece and the Western World.* 285–305.

Pritchett, W. K. 1974. *The Greek State at War, Part II.* Berkeley.

  1985. *The Greek State at War, Part IV.* Berkeley.

Proietti, G. 2011. "Osservazioni sul monumento degli 'epigrammi di Maratona' (IG I³ 503–4): Il problema del lapis B." *ZPE* 179: 41–47.

  2013. "The Marathon Epitaph from Eua-Loukou: Some Notes about Its Text and Historical Context." *ZPE* 185: 24–30.

  2015. "I Greci e la memoria della vittoria: alcune considerazioni sui trofei delle Guerre Persiane." *Hormos* 7: 148–175.

  2019. "La stele dei Maratonomachi (o 'stele di Loukou')." *Axon* 4: 31–50.

  2021. Prima di Erodoto: Aspetti della memoria delle Guerre persiane. Berlin.

Prost, F. 2018. "Laconian Art." In A. Powell (ed.), *A Companion to Sparta.* Hoboken NJ. 154-176.

Raaflaub, K. A. 2004. *The Discovery of Freedom in Ancient Greece.* Chicago.

Rahe, P. A. 2015. *The Grand Strategy of Classical Sparta: The Persian Challenge.* New Haven.

  2016. *The Spartan Regime: Its Character, Origins, and Grand Strategy.* New Haven.

  2019. *Sparta's First Attic War: The Grand Strategy of Classical Sparta, 478–446 B. C.* New Haven.

  2020. *Sparta's Second Attic War: The Grand Strategy of Classical Sparta, 446–418 B.C.* New Haven.

Rawlings, H. R. III. 1981. *The Structure of Thucydides' History.* Princeton.

  2016. "KTEMA TE ES AIEI . . . AKOUEIN." *CPh* 111: 107–116.

Rawson, E. 1969. *The Spartan Tradition in European Thought.* Oxford.

Rebenich, S. 2006. *Leonidas und die Thermopylen: Zum Sparta-Bild in der deutschen Altertumswissenschaft.* Stuttgart.

  2018. "Reception of Sparta in Germany and German-Speaking Europe." In A. Powell (ed.), *A Companion to Sparta.* Hoboken, NJ. 685–703.

Roberts, J. T. 1994. *Athens on Trial: The Antidemocratic Tradition in Western Thought*. Princeton.

Roesch, P. 2009. *Les inscriptions de Thespies (IThesp)*. *9: IThesp 484–682 (Épitaphes: polyandria, épitaphes archaïques)*. Lyon.

Richer, N. 2010. "Elements of the Spartan Bestiary in the Archaic and Classical Periods." In A. Powell, S. Hodkinson, and P. Christesen (eds.), *Sparta: The Body Politic*. Swansea. 1–84.

2012. *La religion des Spartiates: croyances et cultes dans l'Antiquité*. Paris.

Roche, H. 2012. "Spartanische Pimpfe: The Importance of Sparta in the Educational Ideology of the Adolf Hitler Schools." In S. Hodkinson and I. Macgregor Morris (eds.), *Sparta in Modern Thought: Politics, History and Culture*. Swansea. 315–242.

2013. *Sparta's German Children: The Ideal of Ancient Sparta in the Royal Prussian Cadet-Corps, 1818–1920, and in National-Socialist Elite Schools (the Napolas), 1933–1945*. Swansea.

Roisman, J. 1987a. "Alkidas in Thucydides." *Historia* 36: 385–421.

1987b. "Kallikratidas, a Greek Patriot?" *CJ* 83: 21–33.

Romilly, J. de. 1966. "Thucydides and the Cities of the Athenian Empire." *BICS* 13: 1–12.

2012. *The Mind of Thucydides*. Trans. E. T. Rawlings. Ithaca, NY.

Romney, J. M. 2014. "Cowering Gumnētes: A Note on Tyrtaeus Fr. 11.35–8 W." *CQ* 64: 828–832.

2018. "Let Us Obey: The Rhetoric of Spartan Identity in Tyrtaeus 2 W." *Mnemosyne* 71: 555–573.

2020. *Lyric Poetry and Social Identity in Archaic Greece*. Ann Arbor.

Rood, T. 1998. *Thucydides: Narrative and Explanation*. Oxford.

Rookhuijzen, J. Z. Van. 2018. *Herodotus and the Topography of Xerxes' Invasion: Place and Memory in Greece and Anatolia*. Berlin.

Roskam, G. 2011. "Ambition and Love of Fame in Plutarch's Lives of Agis, Cleomenes, and the Gracchi." *CPh* 106: 208–225.

Rutherford, I. 2001. "The New Simonides: Toward a Commentary." In D. Boedeker and D. Sider (eds.), *New Simonides: Contexts of Praise and Desire*. Oxford. 33–54.

Said, E. 1978. *Orientalism*. New York.

Sainte Croix, G. E. M. de. 1954. "The Character of the Athenian Empire." *Historia* 3: 1–41.

Sanders, G. D. R. 2009. "Platanistas, the Course and Carneus: Their Places in the Topography of Sparta." In W. G. Cavanagh, C. Gallou, and M. Georgiadis (eds.), *Sparta and Laconia: From Prehistory to Pre-Modern*. London. 195–203.

Schilardi, D. U. 1977. *The Thespian Polyandrion (424 B.C.): The Excavations and Finds from a Thespian State Burial*. Princeton.

Scott, A. G. 2015. "The Spartan Heroic Death in Plutarch's 'Laconian Apophthegms'." *Hermes* 143: 72–82.

2017. "Spartan Courage and the Social Function of Plutarch's Laconian Apophthegms." *MH* 74: 34–53.

*References*

Scott, M. 2010. *Delphi and Olympia: The Spatial Politics of Panhellenism in the Archaic and Classical Periods.* Cambridge.

    2018. "Viewing Sparta through Athenian Engagement with Art and Architecture." In P. Cartledge and A. Powell (eds.), *The Greek Superpower: Sparta in the Self-Definitions of Athenians.* Swansea. 87–114.

Sears, M. A. 2010. "Warrior Ants: Elite Troops in the *Iliad.*" *CW* 103: 139–155.

    2015. "Thucydides, Rousseau, and Forced Freedom: Brasidas' Speech at Acanthus." *Phoenix* 69: 242–267.

    2018a. "Mother Canada and Mourning Athena: From Classical Athens to Vimy Ridge." *Arion* 25: 43–66.

    2018b. "What the Ancient Greeks Can Teach Us about Gun Control." *The Washington Post*, February 21, 2018 (online publication): www.washington post.com/news/made-by-history/wp/2018/02/21/what-the-ancient-greeks-can-teach-us-about-gun-control/?utm_term=.f41a19d6d819.

    2019a. "The Tyrant as Liberator: The Treasury of Brasidas and the Acanthians at Delphi." *CPh* 114: 265–278.

    2019b. *Understanding Greek Warfare.* London.

    2020. "Brasidas and the Un-Spartan Spartan." *CJ* 116: 173–198.

    2022. "Ordering the Polis: Government and Public Adminstration." In A. Glazebrook and C. Vester (eds.), *Themes in Greek Society and Culture: An Introduction to Ancient Greece.* Second edition. Oxford. 60–81.

Shear, J. L. 2011. *Polis and Revolution: Responding to Oligarchy in Classical Athens.* Cambridge.

Sheppard, A. 2016. The Development of Epigram in Classical Greece. PhD diss., Stanford University. Stanford.

Sider, D. 2001. "Fragments 1–22 W²: Text, Apparatus Criticus, and Translation." In D. Boedeker and D. Sider (eds.), *New Simonides: Contexts of Praise and Desire.* Oxford. 13–32.

    2007. "Sylloge Simonidea." In P. Bing and J. S. Bruss (eds.), *Brill's Companion to Hellenistic Epigram: Down to Philip.* Leiden. 113–129.

    2020. *Simonides: Epigrams and Elegies.* Oxford.

Simonton, M. 2018. "The Burial of Brasidas and the Politics of Commemoration in the Classical Period." *AJPh* 139: 1–30.

Simpson, M. 2006. *Rousseau's Theory of Freedom.* London.

Snell, B. 1969. *Tyrtaios und die Sprache des Epos.* Göttingen.Sears

Stewart, A. 2008a. "The Persian and Carthaginian Invasions of 480 B.C.E. and the Beginning of the Classical Style: Part 1, The Stratigraphy, Chronology, and Significance of the Acropolis Deposits." *AJA* 112: 377–412.

    2008b. "The Persian and Carthaginian Invasions of 480 B.C.E. and the Beginning of the Classical Style: Part 2, The Finds from Other Sites in Athens, Attica, Elsewhere in Greece, and on Sicily; Part 3, The Severe Style: Motivations and Meaning." *AJA* 112: 581–615.

Stehle, E. 2001. "A Bard of the Iron Age and His Auxiliary Muse." In D. Boedeker and D. Sider (eds.), *New Simonides: Contexts of Praise and Desire.* Oxford. 106–119.

Steiner, D. T. 1999. "To Praise, Not to Bury: Simonides fr. 531P." *CQ* 49: 383–395.

Steinhauer, G. 2004–2009. "Στήλη πεσόντων της Ερεχθηίδος." *Horos* 17–21: 679–692.

Stibbe, C. M. 1998. "Lakonische Keramik aus dem Heraion von Samos: ein Nachtrag zu AM 112, 1997, 25–142." *MDAI(A)* 113: 103–110.

Stichel, R. H. W. 1998. "Zum 'Staatsgrab' am 3. Kerameikos-Horos vor dem Dipylon in Athen." *MDAI(A)* 113: 133–164.

Strauss, B. 2004a. "Go Tell the Spartans." *MHQ* 17: 16–25.

2004b. *The Battle of Salamis.* New York.

Strauss, L. 1939. "The Spirit of Sparta or the Taste of Xenophon." *Social Research* 6: 502–536.

Stroszeck, J. 2013. "Το μνημείο των Λακεδαιμονίων στον Κεραμεικό: ένα ταφικό μνημείο στο προσκήνιο του αθηναϊκού εμφυλίου πολέμου του 403 π. Χ." In P. Cartledge, A Gartziou- Tatti, and N. Birgalias (eds.), *Πόλεμος, ειρήνη και πανελλήνιοι αγώνες: στη μνήμη Pierre Garlier.* Athens. 381–402.

Stylianou, P. J. 1998. *A Historical Commentary on Diodorus Siculus Book 15.* Oxford.

Tentori Montalto, M. 2017. *Essere primi per il valore : gli epigrammi funerari greci su pietra per i caduti in guerra (VII-V sec. a.C.).* Pisa.

Thiel, R. 2011. "Ein Staatsfeind als Held?: Simonides' Plataiai-Elegie im politischen Kontext des griechischen Sieges über das Perserreich." *APF* 57: 381–391.

Thomas, R. 2019. *Polis Histories: Collective Memories and the Greek World.* Cambridge.

Titchener, F. B. 1988. A Historical Commentary on Plutarch's *"Life of Nicias."* PhD diss., University of Texas at Austin. Austin, TX.

Tiverios, M. A. 2007. "Panathenaic Amphoras." In O. Palagia and A. Choremi-Spetsieri (eds.), *The Panathenaic Games: Proceedings of an International Conference Held at the University of Athens, May 11–12, 2004.* Oxford. 1–19.

Tomlinson, R. A. 1992. "The Menelaion and Spartan Architecture." In J. M. Sanders (ed.), *PHILOLAKON: Lakonian Studies in Honour of Hector Catling.* London. 247–255.

Trevett, J. 1990. "History in [Demosthenes] 59." *CQ* 40: 407–420.

Trundle, M. 2018. "Spartan Responses to Defeat: From A Mythical Hysiae to a Very Real Sellasia." In J. H. Clark and B. Turner (eds.), *Brill's Companion to Military Defeat in Ancient Mediterranean Society.* Leiden. 144–161.

Vaillancourt, A. and A. G. Scott. 2018. "Othryadas: The Development of a Historical and Literary Exemplum." In L. Frantantuono (ed.), *Pushing the Boundaries of Historia: Essays on Greek and Roman History and Culture in Honor of Blaise Nagy.* London. 147–165.

Valavanis, P. D. 1999. "'Das stolze runde Denkmal': Bemerkungen zum Grabmonument am dritten Horos." *MDAI(A)* 114: 185–205.

Van Steen, G. 2010. "'Now the Struggle Is for All' (Aeschylus's *Persians* 405): What a Difference a Few Years Make When Interpreting a Classic." *Comparative Drama* 44: 495–508, 552.

van Wees, H. 1996. "Heroes, Knights and Nutters: Warrior Mentality in Homer." In A. B. Lloyd (ed.), *Battle in Antiquity*. Newburyport, MA. 1–86.

    2018. "Thermopylae: Herodotus vs. the Legend." In L. W. van Gils, I. J. F. de Jong, and C. H. M. Kroon (eds.), *Textual Strategies in Ancient War Narrative: Thermopylae, Cannae and Beyond*. Leiden. 19–53.

Vernant, J.-P. 1991. "A 'Beautiful Death' and the Disfigured Corpse in Homeric Epic." In F. I. Zeitlin (ed.), *Jean-Pierre Vernant, Mortals and Immortals: Collected Essays*. Princeton. 50–74.

Ward, B. 1951. "Despair Is Both Dangerous and Stupid." New York Times, February 4, p. 146.

Watt, R. H. 1985. "'Wanderer, kommst du nach Sparta': History through Propaganda into Literary Commonplace." *Modern Language Review* 80: 871–883.

Waywell, G. 1999–2000. "Sparta and its Topography." *BICS* 43: 1–26.

Wellington, J. 2017. *Exhibiting War: The Great War, Museums, and Memory in Britain, Canada, and Australia*. Cambridge.

Welwei, K.-W. 2004. "Orestes at Sparta: The Political Significance of the Grave of the Hero." In T. J. Figueira and P. Brulé (eds.), *Spartan Society*. Swansea. 219–230.

West, M. L. (ed.). 1992. *Iambi et elegi Graeci ante Alexandrum cantati: II, Callinus, Mimnermus. Semonides, Solon, Tyrtaeus, Minora adespota*. Oxford.

Westlake, H. D. 1968. *Individuals in Thucydides*. Cambridge.

    1980. "Thucydides, Brasidas, and Clearidas." *GRBS* 21: 333–339.

    1985. "The Sources for the Spartan Debacle at Haliartus." *Phoenix* 39: 119–133.

    1986. "Agesilaus in Diodorus." *GRBS* 27: 263–277.

Whitley, J. 2011. "Hybris and Nike: Agency, Victory and Commemoration in Panhellenic Sanctuaries." In S. D. Lambert (ed.), *Sociable Man: Essays on Ancient Greek Social Behaviour in Honour of Nick Fisher*. Swansea. 161–191.

Willemsen, F. 1977. "Zu den Lakedämoniergräbern im Kerameikos." *MDAI(A)* 92: 117–157.

Winter, J. 2017. *War beyond Words: Languages of Remembrance from the Great War to the Present*. Cambridge.

Woodward, A. M. and M. B. Hobling. 1924–1925. "Excavations at Sparta, 1924–1925." *ABSA* 26: 116–310.

Wylie, G. 1992. "Brasidas – Great Commander or Whiz-Kid?" *QUCC* 41: 77–95.

Zavvou, E. and A. Themos. 2009. "Sparta from Prehistoric to Early Christian Times: Observations from the Excavations of 1994–2005." *ABSA* 16: 105–122.

Ziogas, I. 2014. "Sparse Spartan Verse: Filling Gaps in the Thermopylae Epigram." *Ramus* 43: 1–19.

# Index

*300*, 189, 197, 223, 224, 225–227
300 Spartans, The, 197, 223

Academy, of Plato, 164
Acanthus, xv, 125, 133, 201
Achilles, xv, xvi, 35–38, 43, 47, 80, 82, 109,
  151, 178
  as an example for Brasidas, 118
  as an example for Socrates, 111
acropolis, of Athens, 85, 97, 230, 238
acropolis, of Corinth, 88
acropolis, of Sparta, 25, 31, 77, 135–137, 153, 158,
  160, 231
acropolis, of Thebes, 187
Actium, battle of, 116, 119
Adeimantos, Corinthian general, 88
Admirals' Monument, at Delphi, 158, 160, 171
Aegina, 97
Aegospotami, battle of, 27, 93, 157, 158
Aeschylus, 86, 168, 207, 226
Agamemnon, 35–36, 173
  and Agesilaus, 177–179
Agesilaus
  and Agamemnon, 177–179
  and freedom, 173, 175, 182, 193
  and Lysander, 171, 173, 181, 185
  and Panhellenism, 157, 173, 182, 183, 188
  and Spartan laws, 187–188
  and Sparta's decline, 172–173
  and the decline of Sparta, 194
  and Thespiae, 192
  and Xenophon, 172
  at Coronea, 184–185
  friendship with Xenophon, 13
  his campaign in Asia, 180, 182
  his devotion to Sparta, 180–181
  his fondness for war, 183, 185
  his lack of commemorative monuments,
    171–172, 175
  his response to Leuctra, 186–187
Agesipolis, 182

*agōgē*, 169, 172
*agōn*, 146, *See* athletes, athletic commemoration
agora, of Sparta, 30, 135
*aidōs*, 37, 108, *See* shame
*aischron*, 44, 45, 110, 113, *See* shame
*aischunē*, 108, *See* shame
Alcibiades, 144, 155, 173
Alcidas, 121
Alcman, 13
Alexander the Great, 5, 181, 196
Allward, Walter, 238
Alopeke, 166
Amphictyonic Council, 79, 117
Amphipolis, xiv–xv, 20, 30, 100, 122, 128, 190
  and Brasidas, 125–127, 133
Amyklai, 27
Anchimolios, 166
Andromache, 36
Antiochus the Great, 117
Aphaia, Temple of, on Aegina, 29
Aphrodite, 88
Apollo, 27, 92, 160, 184
Apology. *See* Plato
Arab Spring, 227
Arakos, 160
Arcadia, Arcadians, 49, 158, 186
Archias, 52
Archidamus, 106, 109, 110, 123, 147
  his invasions of Attica, 148
Archilochus, 40–41, 46
*aretē*, xvi, 46, 82, 109, 139
Arginusae, battle of, 156
Argos, Argives, 49, 56–58, 59, 94, 166
Aristagoras of Miletus, 95
*aristeia*, 139, 179
Armistice Day, 210, 237
Arrhabaeus, 124
Artemis Orthia, shrine of, 31, 61, 234
Asia, 97, 171, 179–180
Astyanax, 36
Athena, 160

Athena Chalkioikos, shrine of, xviii, 21, 30, 77, 135, 137, 231
Athenaeus, 77
Athens, Athenians, 91
    and Brasidas, 119, 130
    and civil strife, 136, 165, 166
    and Melos, 109–110
    and naval warfare, 121, 153, 155
    and the battle of Arginusae, 157
    and the First Peloponnesian War, 148
    and the Ionian Revolt, 95
    and the Sicilian Expedition, 144, 145, 149, 151
    at Artemisium, 69
    at Delium, 189
    at Plataea, 76
    campaigns against Brasidas, 127–129
    commemorative practices of, 1–2, 11, 16–17, 19, 82–87, 91, 93, 97, 165, 175, 242, 243
    conflict with Sparta, 96, 187,
        *See* Peloponnesian War
    in 18th-century thought, 199, 209
    its defeat by Sparta, 153, 157
    its empire, xiv–xv, 27, 64, 78, 96, 97, 105, 122, 125–127, 195, 202
    sources for, 12
athletes, athletic commemoration, 23, 31, 71, 83, 118, 130, 136, 146, 171, 173, 231
Augustus, 116, 119

beautiful death, the, 19, 23, 28, 39, 45, 53, 59, 68, 175, 185
Beaverbrook, Lord, 6–7
Belgium, 209
Black Sea, 77
Boeotarchs. *See* Boeotia, Boeotians
Boeotia, Boeotians, 66, 91, 109, 123, 161, 177–178, 189, 190
Boulis, 102–103
Brasidas
    and freedom, 101, 107, 123, 125, 126, 175, 201
    and the helots, 48, 122, 129, 137–138, 180
    and the Spartan authorities, 122, 178, 180
    as a Homeric hero, 138–139, 178
    as a source for his own commemoration, 139–140
    at Acanthus, 125
    at Amphipolis, 125–127, 128
    at Megara, 123–124
    burial honors of, xiv–xvi, 17, 20, 30, 130–133
    his career, 101, 121
    his commemoration at Sparta, 135–137
    his death, 128
    his mission to Thrace, 121–122
    his treasury at Delphi, 133, 142, 159
    in Macedonia, 124, 125, 127

    in the Chalcidice, 127
    on shame, 109
Brasideioi, 129, 137–138
Briseis, 35
burials. *See* tombstones
    in foreign territory, 142, 161–162, 167
    in the city, 19, 22, 29, 46, 50, 130–133, 135, 150
    on the battlefield, 22, 50, 76, 107, 165, 167, 169, 209
Byzantine Empire, 230

Cadmea. *See* Acropolis, of Thebes
Callicratidas, 146, 154–158
Callimachus, Athenian polemarch, 83–84
Callinus, 41–42, 43–44, 47
Canada, 5, 6–7, 204, 237, 238–242, 244, 245
Canadian War Museum, 247
Carneia, 62
Carthage, Carthaginians, 92
cavalry, 168
cemeteries, 19
cenotaphs, xvi, 5, 17, 84, 129, 135, 136, 137, 153, 206
Chaeronea, battle of, 190, 196
Chalcidice, 122, 127
Chalcis, 91
Champions, battle of the, 56–58, 59–60, 167
Chersonese, 132
Christianity, 214, 221
Churchill, Winston, 213
city founders, 132
Civil War, American, 205–206, 246
Civil War, Syrian, 227
Cleandridas, 147–148
Clearidas, 128
Cleombrotus, 185
Cleomenes I, 101, 103, 166
Cleon, xv, 122, 128, 180
Cnemus, 120
Cold War, 216–223
colonization. *See* Herakleia Trachinia
Confederacy, Confederate monuments, xviii, 2, 205–206, 246
Constantine, 77
Constantine XI Palaiologos, 230, 231
Constantinople, 231
Corcyra, 103, 119, 121
Corinth, Corinthians, 52, 81, 87–88, 94, 123, 160, 183
    and the Sicilian Expedition, 144
    conflict with Athens, 96, 97, 103–105, 106–107
Corinthian War, 161, 180, 183
Coronea, battle of, 179, 184–185, 188, 191
Coronea, battle of, 447 BCE, 96
Crete, 215, 230
Croesus, 57

Cynisca, 171
Cyprus, 97
Cypselus, 133
Cyrus, 155

Damonon, Damonon stele, 31
*damos*, Spartan, 50
daring, 119, 120
Darius, 65, 83, 102
David, Jacques-Louis, 202–204
Delium, battle of, 109, 189
Delphi, xvii, 14, 23, 30, 70, 73, 77, 80, 91, 107, 116,
    133, 171, 173, 184, 230
  its commemorative topography, 158–160, 161
democracy, democrats, 9–10, 11, 36, 103, 112, 121,
    136, 157, 162, 165, 168
dēmosion sēma, 165
Demosthenes, Athenian general, 138, 145, 146, 152
Demosthenes, Athenian orator, 79, 130
Dickinson, Emily, 206
Diodorus Siculus
  on Agesilaus, 182
  on Callicratidas, 156
  on Gylippus, 149–152
  on Plataea, 77
  on Sparta, 96
  on the Sicilian Expedition, 145
  on Thermopylae, 67, 70
Dioscuri, 160
Doris, Dorians, 116–118, 210

Egypt, 96
Eion, 126
Epaminondas, 185, 186, 194, 243
Ephialtes, 214, 220, 224
ephors, 3, 22, 106, 180, 186
Ephorus of Cyme, 68, 182
Epidamnus, 98
epigrams, 65, 84, 86, 87, 93, 94, 154, 160, 168, 189
  as a source for the Persian Wars, 71
epigraphy, 12, 19, 65, 71, 86, 87, 91, 143, 191
Erechtheis, Athenian tribe, 86
Eretria, Eretrians, 83, 95
Euboea, 69
Eumnastos, the Spartiate, 54
Euripides, 151
Eurotas river, 25, 27, 61, 186, 222, 231
Euxine. *See* Black Sea
excellence, 46, 47, 76, 78, 82, 85, 151, *See aretē*

fascism, 228, 233
First Peloponnesian War, 48, 96, 118, 147, 148
First World War, 7, 192, 236, 244
Fort Stephenson, battle of, 204
France, 9, 202, 204, 209, *See* French Revolution

freedom, 23, 38, 63, 64, 65, 69, 71, 76, 78, 82, 85,
    89, 90, 91, 92, 154, 158, 169, 197, 223, 227, 234
  and Agesilaus, 173, 174
  and the General Will, 201
  and the liklihood of war, 93, 99, 181, 193,
    229, 248
  as debated at Sparta, 106
  in the Peloponnesian War, 100, 103–105,
    106–108, 123, 126, 134, 160, 168, 202
  in the Second World War, 213, 214
  of Sparta, 110
French Revolution, 197, 202, 242
Funeral Oration, xiv, 1, 16, 109, 175

Gallipoli Peninsula. *See* Chersonese
Gates of Fire, 224
Gelon, 91–92
General Will, the, 200–202
*geras*, 35, 151
Germany
  during the First World War, 209–210
  during the Third Reich, 207–209, 210–213,
    214, 218, 228
  in the 19th century, 209
Gerousia, 96
Girls. *See* women
glory, 181, 188, 193
Goebbels, Josef, 211
Golden Dawn, 233
Göring, Hermann, 208
Great Britain, 208, 209, 213, 215, 216, 237, 245
Greatest Generation, 244
Greece, Modern, 207, 213, 214–215, 216–220, 223,
    230, 232
Grote, George, 156
Gylippus
  and Cleandridas, 147
  and the Sicilian Expedition, 144–145
  as a successor to Brasidas, 144
  his alleged corruption, 146
  his background, 146
  his lack of commemorative monuments,
    143, 152
  his treatment by Thucydides, 144–146
  his treatment in Diodorus, 149–152
  his treatment in Plutarch, 149
Gymnopaidiai, 31, 34, 50, 58–62, 135
Gytheion, 26

Hagnon, 132
Halbwachs, Maurice, 8
Haliartus, 161
Hannibal, 181
harmosts, 128
Hector, 36–38, 47, 82, 109

Hecuba, 37, 151
Helen, 26, 27
Helicon, mount, 161, 184
Hellespont, 65
helots, 4, 32, 34, 71, 122, 129, 137–138, 144, 234, *See*
     Messenia, Messenians
  and Brasidas, 180
  revolt of, 96
  their liberation, 186
Hera, Heraion, xviii, 34, 53, 153
Heracles, 78
Herakleia Trachinia, 116–118
Herakles, 117
Hermocrates, 145, 151
Herodes Atticus, 86
Herodotus
  as a source for epigrams, 72–73
  his historical method, 145
  on Athens, 64, 65, 100, 200, 242
  on Corinth, 87
  on memory, xvi, 7
  on Persia, 226
  on Sparta, 13, 18, 39, 52, 102–103
  on Thermopylae, 67, 68, 70, 80
  on Thyrea, 60
heroes, hero cult, xiv, 9, 20, 35–38, 118, 130–133,
     179, 206, 221
Himera, battle of, 92
Hipparchus. *See* Pisistratus, Pisistratids
Hippias, 83, 95, 166, *See* Pisistratus, Pisistratids
Hitler, Adolf, 208, 210, 212, 245
Hobsbawm, Eric, 9
Holocaust Memorial Museum, Washington
     DC, 246
Homer, xiv, xvi, 9, 28, 33, 35–38, 44–45, 58, 81,
     94, 102
  and Brasidas, 120, 138–139
  on shame, 109
*homoioi*, 3, 49, 50, *See* Spartiates, Spartiates
*homonoia*, 200, *See* General Will, the
Horace, 206, 236
Hume, David, 199
Hyacinthia, 27
Hydarnes, 102

identitarianism, 227–229
*Iliad*, xv, 35–38, 44–45, 58, 81, 102, 178
Illyria, Illyrians, 127
imperialism, Spartan, 116, 123, 128
inscriptions. *See* epigraphy, epigraphy
Ionia, Ionians, 95, 143, 155, 210
Ionian Revolt, 95, 97
Islamophobia, 228, 233
isolationism, 96, 152, 182, 200
Istanbul, 77

Isthmus of Corinth, 88
Italy, Modern, 207, 214
Ithome, mount, 49

Jackson, Stonewall, 206
Jason of Pherai, 117
justice, 106

Kephisos river, 169
Kerameikos, 17, 19, 136–137, 164, 167
King's Peace, 182
kings, Spartan, 3, 17, 19, 51, 118, 165, 180, 186,
     *See* monarchy, monarchs
*kleos*, 35, 37, 38, 46, 80, 81
Korean War, 219, 221
kudos, 35
Kynosarges, 166

Lakrates, 136, 164
Langemarck, battle of, 209–210
Lee, Robert E., 206, 246
Leonidas, xvi, 17, 181, 190, 203
  his later reception, 205, 209, 213, 221, 226, 228
  his modern monument at Sparta, 231
  his plans at Thermopylae, 69–71, 80
  in Persian War epigrams, 72–73, 74–76
  tomb of, 30, 135, 231, 232
Leotychides, 173
Leuctra, battle of, 4, 22, 32, 48, 117, 174, 185–186,
     188, 192, 194
liberation, liberators. *See* freedom
liberty, liberation. *See* freedom
lions, lion monuments, 75, 118, 189–190
Livy, 202
Locris, Locrians, 73, 161, 189
Long Walls, 153
Loukou, 86
Lycopas, 52
Lycurgus, Athenian orator, 84
Lycurgus, Spartan lawgiver, 13, 19, 101, 174,
     176, 186
Lysander
  and Agesilaus, 171, 173, 181, 185
  and Callicratidas, 155
  and Panhellenism, 161
  and the Persians, 155
  and the Thirty Tyrants, 163
  his burial in Phocis, 142, 161–162, 165
  his career, 153
  his commemoration at Delphi, 159
  his commemorative monuments, 153–154
  his death, 161
  his divine honors, 142, 153
  his victory over Athens, 157
Lysandreia, 153

Macedonia, Macedonians, 27, 38, 124, 127,
190, 195
Madison, James, 199
Mantinea, 186
Mantinea, battle of, 362 BCE, 174
Mantinea, battle of, 418 BCE, 165
Marathon, battle of, 11, 17, 18, 21, 190
its commemoration, 83–85
its commemoration at Delphi, 158
its later reception, 214
Spartan absence at, 95
Mardonius, 29, 66
Marshall Plan, 219, 220, 221
Marshall, George C., 219
McCrae, John, 237
Medes, Medizing, 73, 79, 90, 102, *See* Persia,
Persians
Megalopolis, 186
Megara, Megarians, 81, 89, 123–124
Megistias, 72–73, 169
Melian Dialogue, 109–110
Memorial Day, 245
memory, collective, 7–8
memory, cultural, 8–9
Mende, 127
Menelaion, 27, 231
Menelaus, 26, 27
mercenaries, 122, 180
Messene, 186
Messenia, Messenians, 3, 25, 27, 32, 33, 47–52, 55,
94, 230, 243, *See* helots
and Pylos, 114
Messenian Wars, 243, *See* Second Messenian War
Methone, 119, 129
Mexican War, 205
Miller, Frank, 189, 197, 223, 224
Miltiades, 83, 132, 158
Mistras, 24, 230
*molōn labe*, 198, 228, 231
monarchy, monarchs, 3, 9
mōthax, 146
Mounichia, battle of, 163, 168
Mourning Athena, 238
Mycenae, 179
Myrmidons, 58
Mytilene, 149

Nafplio, 24
Napoleon, 203
National Rifle Association, xix, 228
National WWII Museum, New Orleans, 247
nationalism, 10
NATO, 216
Naupaktos, 115
Navarino, bay of. *See* Pylos, battle of

Naxos, Naxians, 88
Nazis, Nazism. *See* Germany, during the Third
Reich
Nemea River, battle of the, 183, 190
neodamōdeis, 138, 179
New Zealand, 214
Nicias, 146, 148, 152
Nike of Paionios, 114
Nikopolis, 116
Nora, Pierre, 11
Notium, battle of, 155
Nymphis, 77

Octavian. *See* Augustus
Odysseus, 47, 139
Oenophyta, 191
Oinoe, 148
oliganthrōpia, 172
oligarchy, oligarchs, 3, 121, 136, 168, *See* Thirty
Tyrants
Olympia, 14, 23, 114, 133, 154, 169, 171, 231
Olympus, mount, 26, 66, 214
Orchomenos, 161
Orientalism, 87, 226, 242
Oropus. *See* Delium, battle of
Othryadas, 57, 60, 167
Ottoman Empire, 1, 119, 213
Owen, Wilfred, 236

Painted Stoa, 21, 29
Palace of Nestor, 49
Palatine Anthology, 59, 75, 76, 89
Panathenaic amphorae, 137
Panhellenism, 74, 76, 79, 83, 84, 86, 89, 90, 107,
155, 157, 160, 173, 181, 183, 188
Panopeus, 161, 162
Paris, Trojan prince, 26
Parnon, mount, 231
Parthenon, 230
*patrios nomos*, Athenian, 17, *See* Athens,
commemorative practices of
patriotism, 102
Patroclus, 35, 37, 47
Pausanias, ancient travel-writer, xvii, 13, 14, 25
on Delphi, 158
on Lysander's burial, 162
on Messenia, 48
on Spartan topography, 135, 136
on Thermopylae, 68
Pausanias, Spartan king, 161, 162–164, 165, 167
Pausanias, Spartan regent, 18, 30, 71, 80, 101
his commemoration in epigrams, 77–79
tomb of, 135
Peace of Nicias, 129
Pelopidas, 177

*Index*

Peloponnesian League, 108, 120
Peloponnesian War, 161
  and leadership, 127
  and the Sicilian Expedition, 145
  compared to the Persian Wars, 100
  its end, 153
  its origins, 96, 97, 100, 103–105, 106–107, 119
Perdiccas, 124, 127
Pericles, xiv, 1, 109, 119, 147, 175
*perioikoi*, 4, 19, 71, 113, 225
Persia, Persians, xvii, 5, 21, 28, 95, 153, 155, 177,
  179, 226
  and the Corinthian War, 180
  conflict with Athens, 97, 103
Persian Empire, 171, 200, 242
Persian Stoa, xvii, 21, 22, 29, 231
Persian Wars, 11, 21, 29, 33, 38, 45, 51, 61, 82, 84,
  220, 242
  compared to the Peloponnesian War, 100
  sources for, 72, 98, *See* epigrams
  Spartan leadership in, 95
  the importance of Thermopylae, 65–67
  their commemoration, 65, 93, 101, 107–108,
  157, 169
Phaleron, 166
Philiadas of Megara, 74
Philip II of Macedonia, 195
Philistus, 145, 149, 152
Phocis, Phocians, 161–162
Phoebidas, 187, 188
Phormio, 120
Pindar, 92, 173, 177
Piraeus, 168, 187
Pisistratus, Pisistratids, 83, 103, 134, 166, 200
Plataea, battle of, 11, 18, 61, 64, 66, 71, 89, 90, 181,
  191, 202
  its commemoration, 76, 77, 78, 79–82
Plataea, Plataeans, 18, 83, 107–108
Plato, 108, 110–111, 164, 179
Pleistoanax, 147, 148
Plutarch
  on Agesilaus, 172, 181, 184
  on Callicratidas, 156
  on Corinth, 87–88
  on Gylippus, 148–149
  on Sparta, 3, 13, 19, 39, 146, 147
  on Thermopylae, 68
polyandrion, polyandria, 18, 50, 76, 166
Polycrates, 52–53, 55, 94
Polydeuces, 160, *See* Dioscuri
Polyxena, 151
Poseidon, 77
Potidaea, 98, 103, 128
Pressfield, Steven, 224
Priam, 37, 151

Priene, 143
promachoi, 37
Pylos, 48
Pylos, battle of, xv, 34, 112–115, 121, 130, 138, 149,
  167, 180, 192, 209

religion. *See* heroes, hero cult
  Spartan, 22, 32, 34, 50, 62, 71
Remembrance Day, 5, *See* Armistice Day
Revolutionary War, American, 242
Roma, 234
Rome, Romans, 5, 12, 38, 117, 202, 228
Round Building, 135–137, 231
Rousseau, Jean-Jacques, xix, 197, 198–202
Russia, 2, 208, 248, *See* Soviet Union

Sacred Band, 185, 190
Salamis, battle of, 64, 84, 86, 87–89, 168, 242
Samos, xviii, 15, 34, 52–56, 94, 153
Sardis, 83, 97
Saronic Gulf, 97
Scione, 127, 130
Second Messenian War, 47, 49, 94, *See* Messenia,
  Messenians
Second World War, 208–209, 213–215, 221,
  244, 246
Sepeia, battle of, 95
Serpent Column, 73, 77, 78, 108, 159
shame, 37, 44, 45, 46, 108–115, 176
Shiloh, battle of, 206
Sicilian Expedition, 144–145, 148–149
Sicily, Sicilians, 91–92, 103, 144–145, 154
similars. *See* Spartiates
Simonides, 72–73, 75, 90, 168, 222
  his later reception, 206, 208, 210
  on Thyrea, 59–60
  the New Simonides, 58, 61, 79–82
slavery, 37, 38, 81, 85, 86, 91, 97, 98, 182, 205, 234,
  *See* helots
Smiling Hoplite, 17, 25, 29, 135
Snyder, Zack, 189, 197, 223, 225
*Social Contract, The. See* Rousseau, Jean-Jacques
Socrates, 109–110, 176
Solomos, Dionysios, 231
Soros, 84
Sosibius, 57
Sounion, 83
Soviet Union, 213, 216, 218, 219
Spartan Mirage, 2, 12–16, 197
Spartiates, 3, 34, 49, 54, 102, 113, 144, 179, 194,
  *See homoioi*
Speer, Albert, 211
Spercheios river, 73
Sperthias, 102–103
Sphacteria. *See* Pylos, battle of, Pylos, battle of

Sphodrias, 187, 188
Stagiros, 125
Stalingrad, battle of, 208
Stephanus of Byzantium, 74
Sthenelaidas, 106
Strabo, 73
Strauss, Leo, 176
Strymon River, 122
surrender, consequences of, 114
Syracuse, Syracusans, 104, 144, 150, 151, *See* Siciliy, Sicilians

Talthybius, 28, 102
Tanagra, 190
Tanagra, battle of, 91, 96, 118, 148
*taphoi. See* burials
Taygetus, mount, xvii, 3, 25, 26, 221, 230
Tecumseh, 204
Tegea, Tegeans, 89–90, 94, 147, 166
Tempe, vale of, 66
Thasos, 40
theater, of Sparta, 135
Thebes, Thebans, 48, 90–91, 107, 169, 177, 187
   alliance with the Persians, 66, 68
   and the Corinthian War, 161
   and Thespiae, 192, 194
   at Coronea, 179, 184–185
   at Delium, 192
   at Leuctra, 185–186
   conflict with Athens, 96
   its hegemony, 195
Themistocles, 102
Theopompus, Spartan king, 51
Thermopylae, battle of, 23, 34, 39, 59, 181, 191
   and Spartan colonization, 115–118
   and the role of shame, 112
   as a fight for freedom, 64
   historical overview, 65–71
   in epigrams, 72–76
   its later reception, 197, 202–204, 205, 206–207, 209, 210, 219, 221, 227
   its modern monument, 221
   the Thespians at, 189
Theseus, 134
Thespiae, Thespians, 70, 74, 187, 188–194, 222
Thessaly, Thessalians, 27, 117, 124, 154, 166
Thetis, 36
Thirty Tyrants, 136, 163, 166, 168
Thrace, Thracians, 48, 121–122, 178
Thrasybulus, 168
Three Hundred Spartans, The, 224
Three Hundred, the, xvi, 12, 18, 30, 67, 188, 203
   and Pylos, 113
   reasons for their deployment, 69–70
   their later reception, 205, 223

their monument at Sparta, 135
Thucydides
   and Amphipolis, 126
   and speeches, 152
   his historical method, 145
   his possible views on Lysander, 154
   on Athens, 16, 23, 34, 104
   on Brasidas, xiv, xvi, 119–120, 121, 126, 138–139, 154, 178
   on Gylippus, 144–146, 151
   on Hermocrates, 145
   on Pausanias, 77, 78
   on Pylos, 113
   on shame, 109–110
   on Sparta, 13, 23, 34, 48, 78, 96, 104
   on the Sicilian Expedition, 144
Thurii, 147
Thyrea, battle of, 56–58, 59–60, 167
Timaeus, 145, 149
*timē*, 35
Titus Flamininus, 38
*tolmē*, 120 *See daring*
Tomb of the Lacedaemonians, in Athens, 136–137, 163–167
Tomb of the Unknown Soldier, at Vimy Ridge, 238
Tomb of the Unkown Soldier, Arlington, 221
tombs. *See* burials
tombstones
   *en polemoi*, 19, 21, 22, 28
Trachis. *See* Herakleia Trachinia
tragedy, Attic, 37
tragic warner, 106
tremblers, 20, 32, 174, 186–187, 212
*tresantes. See* tremblers
Trojan War, 27, 29, 80, 151, 178
trophies, 57, 130, 151, 163, 165
Troy, Trojans, 35, 36–38
Truman, Harry S., 217–219, 220
Trump, Donald, 228
tyranny, tyrants, xv, 11, 95, 100, 133, 134, 159, 223
   Spartan opposition to, 103, 106–107, 166
Tyrtaeus, 13, 22, 33, 39–47, 48, 49–50, 69, 94, 206, 231, 236, 243

Ukraine, Russian invasion of, 2, 248
United States of America, 5, 9, 204, 206, 216, 217–221, 225, 226, 242, 244, 245
   during the Cold War, 208

Varley, Lynn, 224
Venetians, 119
Verdun, battle of, 210
Veterans' Day, 245
Vietnam War, 10

Vimy Ridge, 238–242, 244, 247
Vitruvius, 21
Voltaire, 199

*wanax*, 179
War of 1812, 204
War on Terror, 225
Waterloo, battle of, 202
women
    Corinthian, 88
    their status in Sparta, 3–4, 22, 39, 40
World War I. *See* First World War, the
World War II. *See* Second World War, the
World War II Memorial, Washington
    DC, 244

Xenophon
    and Agesilaus, 13, 172, 173, 174–177, 180, 187
    and Athens, 169
    and Panhellenism, 155
    on Callicratidas, 156, 157
    on Coronea, 184
    on Sparta, 13, 15, 20, 22, 168–169
Xerxes, xvii, 5, 12, 29, 34, 38, 64, 102, 179, 183,
    226, 243
    at Thermopylae, 65–67, 70

Ypres, 209, 238

Zeus, 36
Zeus Eleutherios, 90

·